The Poverty
of Communism

The Poverty
of Communism

Nick Eberstadt

Transaction Books
New Brunswick (USA) and Oxford (UK)

Library of Congress Catalog Number: 87-19097
ISBN 0-88738-188-X
Printed in the United States of America

Library of Congress Cataloging-in-Publication Data

Eberstadt, Nick, 1955–
    The poverty of communism.

    Bibliography: p.
    Includes index.
    1. Poor—Communist countries. 2. Communist
countries—Economic conditions. 3. Communist countries—
Social conditions. I. Title.
HC710.P6E24   1987   362.5'09171'7   87-19097
ISBN 0-88738-188-X

To my parents
Frederick and Isabel Nash Eberstadt

Contents

Acknowledgements

Most of the essays in this book were written on the premises of the Harvard University Center for Population Studies. Over the years that I have been associated with it, the Center has been a warm and welcoming home. It has been a generous home as well. For all my debts to the Center, I would be seriously remiss if I did not mention two in particular: to the Director of the Center, Professor David E. Bell, whose encouragement, interest, and support has done so much to make my work possible; and to Miss Ellen Hopkins, the Center's Administrative Assistant, whose assistance to me—as she and I both know—has been above and beyond the call of duty, year in and year out.

Several of the essays in this book were written on the premises of the American Enterprise Institute for Public Policy Research, which has provided me with a friendly and obliging base from which to conduct research in Washington. Michael Novak, Director of AEI's Social Policy Program, and Douglas J. Besharov, Director of its Project on Individual and Social Responsibility, have not only seen to it that AEI's considerable institutional amenities and support be available to me, but have vigilantly, even jealously, checked to make sure that my time would always be my own. A scholar cannot ask for greater luxury.

The Esther A. and Joseph Klingenstein Fund provided the grant which made possible the preparation of this book. For its timely and generous support, I owe the Klingenstein Fund a special thanks.

Kerstin Rios typed and processed the manuscript for this book. Unlike gems, her work is nearly flawless.

Chapter 5—"Understanding, And Misunderstanding, Soviet Power"—is much the better thanks to Mary Tedeschi. So is my entire life.

Chapter 8—"The Cost of Pax Sovietica"—was co-authored by Mr. Thomas E. Ricks, now of the *Wall Street Journal*. He has kindly permitted

ix

me to reprint our work on this volume. For so dear and trusted a friend, this formal mention of his contribution, while surely necessary, is also far from sufficient.

The final acknowledgement is due another dear friend, John Podhoretz, who suggested the title for this book.

Introduction

Poverty has always been a matter of concern; today, however, it is also a matter of state. To a degree never before witnessed, contemporary regimes are held to be accountable for the material circumstances of, and prospects for, their subjects and citizens. In the international arena, the issue of poverty has come to be ever more central a feature in the ideological conflict between states. Today, in fact, a government's record in dealing with poverty is widely understood to reflect upon its very legitimacy: its right, in other words, to be a government at all.

What accounts for the remarkable rise of "poverty" within the hierarchy of political considerations? In both corridors of government and international fora, there is today increasing talk about "human rights." Yet to ascribe the growing attention toward poverty to a presumed triumph of humanitarian sentiment on the part of modern man would seem ill-advised, if not perverse. In recent memory—and at this writing—pestilential programs have been methodically inflicted upon hapless populations in various corners of the world by the established authorities presiding over them. These same authorities, more often than not, have fashioned themselves to be the most "modern" of states, and have proclaimed most vocally their commitment to the cause of "human rights."

For all the benefits which enlightened rule may today in many places confer, we should not assume that the masters of men in earlier and less "scientific" times were always ignorant of, or insensate to, the suffering of the poor. In the days when religious belief played a greater role in personal life and affairs of state than it seems at present to do, uncharitable behavior was widely understood to expose mortals to the perils of eternal judgment. Political power may typically have been unaccountable in earlier times, but the rulers wielding it were not infrequently God-fearing men, and the God-fearing man knows an ultimate accountability in the contemplation of the fate of his own soul.

1

Heightened political attention to poverty owes less to improvements in moral fiber to perfection of governmental institutions than to major changes in the factors which affect state power. Many factors might be mentioned: among them, the advent of "total war" and its attendant requirements of mobilization, must surely figure prominently. But perhaps no factor has been so important as the birth of the Marxist-Leninist state. For the Marxist-Leninist state was a fundamentally new form of government, and it presumed a fundamentally new correspondence between the power of its apparatus and the poverty of populations. To an extent that may not be fully understood, the emergence of poverty as an issue in international politics, and the dimensions this issue has assumed, may be traced to the stimulus of the Marxist-Leninist state.

At once messianic and materialistic, the Marxist-Leninist state claimed to possess the understanding necessary for the creation of an earthly paradise, and demanded the total authority over its subjects that was said to be needed for the monumental transformations envisioned. The elimination of exploitation and material deprivation was integral to the Communist vision which the Marxist-Leninist state sought to incarnate. Far-reaching exertions and sacrifices—including the total sacrifice of liberty—were required of every population under Marxist-Leninist authority, and were justified by the material achievements the new order was producing, or would produce. All-embracing state machines were erected, and ambitious social experiments involving hundreds of millions of human beings were pressed forward, in the name of progress against poverty. Marxist-Leninist states claimed special successes against poverty, and challenged the moral authority of any and all political orders that were said to be less beneficial than their own to the poor and the vulnerable in other places.

Seventy years have passed since the October Revolution, sixty-five since the establishment of the Soviet state over Russian soil. In the interim, Marxist-Leninist states modeled closely upon the Soviet original have been established over a widening expanse of territory. In the mid-1980s, perhaps a third of the population of the earth lived under regimes adhering by their own profession to the precepts of Marxism-Leninism. It is not premature to inquire about the fate of the poor in these places. This book is an attempt to help answer such inquiries.

The essays in this book, all written in the early and mid-1980s, examine state power and human poverty under Marxist-Leninist rule. Not all of the Communist experiments currently underway are discussed in the following pages. Fledgling communist states, such as those presently consolidating themselves in Afghanistan, Nicaragua, and sub-Saharan Africa, and under Vietnamese authority in Southeast Asia, are by and large omitted from this assessment: they have yet to establish total control over the economies and societies they mean to transform; their tenure in power is in some cases too brief to provide adequate indications of results; and their ability to gather (much less willingness to divulge) accurate and comprehensive information about the material circumstances of their subjects is at best questionable. Nor is Yugoslavia included; what was once a fully Sovietized satellite seems today to be a peculiar hybrid, reminiscent in certain regards of an earlier Balkan despotism. Albania, for better or worse, is given short shrift, and North Korea only briefly mentioned. The studies in this volume focus on the principal states of established Communist power: the Soviet Union, China, the Soviet satellites in Eastern Europe and Mongolia, Cuba, and Vietnam.

Many of the essays in this book discuss the availability and reliability of statistics pertaining to poverty under Communist authority. Under the best of circumstances, there are usually serious difficulties in measuring poverty. By its very nature, poverty resists quantification. Under Communism, the reliability of data on poverty is further affected by the political influences to which numbers gathering is subjected in such regimes. These influences differ by place and time, but they move by a distinct set of rules. As these essays indicate, central authorities in Communist countries are not above falsifying data that are held to be especially significant. Under some Communist regimes, certain statistics pertaining to poverty have been accorded this privileged treatment.

For the most part, however, deliberate falsification of data by central authorities does not seem to be a prime factor obscuring the picture of poverty under Communism. It may be more pertinent to ask whether the central authorities under Communist rule are able to obtain an accurate depiction of the society under their command *for themselves*. Needless to say, ambitious and far-reaching social experiments conceived and conducted against a backdrop of misinformation are not likely to stand the vulnerable groups within a population in good stead.

Most essays in this book focus upon material poverty, as reflected in statistics about health, nutrition, and education. There is virtue in examining such basic, and predominantly physical, measures. Statistics on longevity, for example, may be compared over time or across political systems in a way that data on purchasing power simply cannot. In assessing health, nutrition, and education through basic physical indicators, moreover, we are examining areas in which Communist regimes have claimed some of their most important results—and in ways which might be expected to highlight those results most dramatically.

Some people will object that such measures provide only a critically incomplete glimpse at the poverty of populations. I understand these objections. In fact, I concur with them. The assessment of material poverty is necessary to any comprehensive examination of poverty in its entirety, but by no means describes exhaustively the varieties of deprivation from which a person or a population may suffer. The statistically-oriented essays in this book make no systematic attempt, for example, to assess *spiritual* poverty under Communism, even though this may afflict individuals no less sorely than material want. Judgments about such matters are inescapably personal, and may best be rendered by the reader for himself. The essays on administration and power in the U.S.S.R. (Chapters 4 and 5), however, may help to convey some things about life under Soviet-style systems that cannot be captured by numbers alone.

All of the essays collected in this book have been printed elsewhere. The version of the manuscript used for Chapter 5 is longer than the one that first appeared in print, while Chapter 11 has been shortened to avoid overlap and repetition. Otherwise, apart from a few stylistic and typographical changes, these essays read as they originally appeared. Students of Communist regimes are often tempted to rework arguments or amend conclusions with the benefit of hindsight. It is a natural response—possibly all the more understandable when information on the countries in question is so regulated and politically controlled, and when events in these places are (seemingly) so unpredictable. For better or worse, I have tried to resist the impulse to correct myself. If these essays are to be of use, they should be able to withstand the first tests of time.

It may be useful to provide an update on two of the topics touched upon in this book: the argument that the health of the Soviet population has deteriorated in recent decades, and the discussion of the possibility that Cuban authorities may in recent years have been falsifying their country's statistics on infant mortality.

When "The Health Crisis in the Soviet Union" (Chapter 1) first appeared in early 1981, it provoked considerable comment and some furious reactions. Some American academics held that my examination of Soviet health problems was not only shallow and mendacious, but that it posed a threat to world peace. One critique along these lines was offered by a sociologist from Oregon ("On the Uses of Disinformation to Legitimize the Revival of the Cold War: Health in the USSR."[1]) A less restrained response appeared in *The Daily World* under the byline of Herbert Aptheker, the prolific American Communist. The column likened me not only to Hitler's propaganda minister, Joseph Goebbels, but also to Julius Streicher, the Jew-baiting editor of the Nazi tabloid *Der Stuermer*. The most interesting aspect of the column was its repeated misspelling of the name of Murray Feshbach (perhaps the leading American student of Soviet population trends, whose research had prompted my essay). "Feshbach" had somehow become "Fishback." While such an error might not have immediately suggested itself to a reader of my original essay, the mistake would be quite in keeping with an effort to transliterate the name back into Roman letters from Cyrillic.

Critique also came from more respectable quarters. Two and a half years after the essay first appeared, two analysts from intelligence agencies in Washington made the case in America's foremost demographic journal that the increase in infant mortality rates reported by Soviet authorities in the early 1970s was only a statistical artifact, and that in reality health conditions in the U.S.S.R. had probably been improving. Chapter 2, "A Second Look at the Health Crisis in the Soviet Union," is my reply to these arguments.

In the intervening years the debate about health in the U.S.S.R. has continued. Various possible explanations for a pronounced long-term decline in health levels within an industrial country have been proposed; some writers have wondered whether in fact there had been any decline at all. These discussions have been conducted in an increasingly rarified atmosphere. What have been missing from this atmosphere are hard data on the Soviet public health situation. Starting in 1974, Soviet statistical yearbooks, communiques, and scholarly journals began to omit previously routine data on population, mortality, and health. Soviet authorities conducted their third postwar census in 1979, but as of 1985 not even the preliminary age-sex breakdown from that count had been officially released. (Such numbers would have been useful to outside observers for divining trends in fertility and mortality for the 1970s). It was not simply demographic esoterica which disappeared from public view. By its 1979 edition, the COMECON statistical yearbook was omitting the Soviet Union from its table on infant mortality in member states; by 1984 the U.S.S.R. was no longer listed in its table on members states' life expectancy. By early 1985 it had become difficult to obtain even so pedestrian a figure as the U.S.S.R.'s crude death rate.

March 1985 saw the accession to power in the Soviet Union of Mikhail S. Gorbachev. Almost immediately thereafter, there was much discussion in the Western media of the new "openness" of his Soviet regime. No such "openness" was evident on the part of Soviet health authorities. Data on mortality, longevity, and popular health continued to be withheld from public sources. The health situation in the U.S.S.R. remained enshrouded in an officially fashioned secrecy, as if the health of the Soviet population were deemed a matter of national security.

In late 1986, the official attitude towards health data evidenced a change. Basic data pertaining to mortality and health began to reappear in some Soviet publications. While Soviet authorities have yet to sanction the level of "openness" on information regarding public health in the U.S.S.R. that was experienced in, say, Brezhnev's first decade of supreme power, the new numbers do provide some basis for assessing recent trends.

According to the newly released numbers, the infant mortality rate in the U.S.S.R. was lower in 1985 than it had been in 1980. (At this writing, data are still unavailable for the late 1970s.) On the other hand, these data provide a number for the infant mortality rate in 1985 that is 5 percent higher than the one reported earlier for 1970, and more than 11 percent higher than the one previously reported for 1971. If accurate, and comparable with data from before the statistical blackout, the new numbers would place Soviet infant mortality rates in 1985 at about the same level they had been in 1967. By these official figures, it would appear that virtually no progress was made in infant health in the U.S.S.R. in a period extending almost twenty years—and that Soviet infant mortality in the mid-1980s was higher than it had been a decade and a half earlier.

Soviet authorities have also released some data relating to life expectancy. These numbers place the combined life expectancy at birth of men and women in the U.S.S.R. at 70 years for 1971–72. For 1978–79, they show a figure of 68. For 1983–84 and 1984–85, the figure remains at 68. The final figure presented is for the second half of 1985 and the first half of 1986: for that period, combined life expectancy is put at 69.[2]

If these figures are accurate, they indicate that life expectancy in the U.S.S.R. in the mid-1980s was lower than it had been a decade and a half earlier. The presentation of these numbers, however, raises questions as well as answering them. The round figures of "68" for 1978–79, for example, contrasts with information from an official briefing for Western journalists in June 1981 held by Alexander Smirnov, then identified as deputy director of the demographic section of the State Planning Committee, who reportedly stated that "life expectancy . . . is now just over 69."[3] Such seeming inconsistencies await explanation. Questions also arise over the most recent figure in the new series on life expectancy. Soviet statistical authorities are not in the habit of calculating life expectancy for the second half of one year and the first part of another. This unconventional computation lends itself to an easy political interpretation: namely, that health conditions in the U.S.S.R. improved almost immediately after Mikhail Gorbachev's ascent to power. It is easy to see why the Gorbachev regime would wish such numbers in circulation; the accuracy and meaningfulness of such numbers, however, is another matter altogether. Ward Kingkade of the U.S. Bureau of the Census has noted, for example, that recently released mortality rates for the elderly population in the U.S.S.R. look as if they are being smoothed on the basis of a simplifying formula, rather than being drawn from direct results.[4] Such a change in statistical procedures could have a significant impact on computed life expectancy, for the mortality of older age groups directly affects estimates of life expectancy at birth. To date, the method by which the new figures on life expectancy were calculated had not been officially explained. At this writing, it is impossible to tell whether the rise in life expectancy reported by Soviet statistical authorities represents actual reductions in mortality, or reflects instead the consequences of changes in actuarial technique.

At 69 years, the U.S.S.R.'s life expectancy would be lower than the most recent numbers the International Bank for Reconstruction and Development (also known as the World Bank) has ascribed to such places as Chile, Guyana, Panama, and Uruguay; it would be about the same as the World Bank's current figure for Grenada.[5]

As for infant mortality, Soviet figures for 1985 would appear to be in the same general range as the World Bank's latest numbers for Panama and Tonga. In the days when they still explained the methods by which infant mortality data were gathered, Soviet statistical authorities excluded certain categories of high-risk newborns from the tally. Standardizing the Soviet classification system with that approved by the World Health Organization would have increased its measured infant mortality in the early 1970s by 14 percent, according to one Western estimate,[6] or by 22 to 25 percent according to another.[7] If such adjustments were still required for international comparability, Soviet infant mortality rates in the mid-1980s would have been higher than those the World Bank ascribes to such places as Barbados, Fiji, Jamaica, and the Seychelles.[8]

If my essays about health problems in the U.S.S.R. drew a vigorous response, my proposal that Cuba's stated achievements in reducing infant mortality be examined for inconsistencies, and possible falsifications, evinced an almost equally heated reaction from some students of the Cuban scene. My analysis of Cuban health statistics (Chapter 9, and part of Chapters 10 and 11) does not prove conclusively that Cuban authorities have deliberately falsified their country's infant health statistics. It suggests instead that *the simplest explanation* for the inconsistencies identified would be systematic falsification, beginning in the early 1970s and extending into at least the mid-1980s.

In the period since these essays were completed, additional information bearing on the reliability of Cuba's infant mortality statistics has become available. The most important piece of this information is surely Cuba's 1981 census. The first volumes of that census were received by the Library of Congress in April 1986, and were catalogued later in the year. The data in these volumes will permit efforts to compare previously published survival rates for children during the 1970s with the numbers of boys and girls of different ages identified to be alive in 1981. These census results assume additional significance because Cuban statistical authorities have to date, in contrast to conventional practice, been reluctant to release any preliminary results from which the age and sex structure of the Cuban population in 1981 might be divined. Estimating child survival rates on the basis of the 1981 census will not be a straightforward task. The exercise is complicated by the fact that sizeable numbers of Cubans left legally and escaped illegally from the island in the intercensal period (that is, between 1970 and 1981), including tens of thousands of children. For these reasons, analysis of the 1981 census will be a major undertaking. We must await the results of these efforts.

In the meantime, it may be useful to take note of some revelations that are easier to interpret. Cuba's 1985 statistical yearbook has recently become available in the United States. Some of the paradoxes noted in Chapters 9 and 10 of this book not only continue, but seem even more acute in Cuba's latest data of public health. Those chapters mention, for example, the contrast between Cuba's officially reported trend in infant mortality, which has been in rapid decline, and its trends in notifiable (typically infectious) diseases typically associated with poverty and poor infant health—many of which have reportedly been rising. Between 1975 and 1985, the infant mortality rate in Cuba is reported to have dropped by 40 percent. Over the same period, the reported incidence per 100,000 population of acute diahrrea rose 52 percent; food poisoning, 63 percent; acute respiratory infection, 146 percent; German measles, 220 percent; and chicken pox, 406 percent.[9] How infant mortality could be so rapidly declining in an environment in which morbidity from such illnesses had, apparently, undergone consequential increase, is a question that awaits an answer.

The integrity of the system by which public health data are tabulated is pertinent to assessing the possibilities that deliberate or systematic tampering with statistics might take place. It is therefore of interest to learn that a "mid-level official of the health ministry" who left Cuba in 1981 has subsequently claimed that his ministry has been known to falsify health data. According to this former official, a public health physician, "medical records were falsified to make it appear" that the dengue fever epidemic that swept Cuban in 1981 "had been brought under control."[10]

Of course this is only one self-identified witness of officially sanctioned falsification of health data, and his testimony refers to only one episode. In the mirror of his assertions, however, Cuba's recent and confusing treatment of information on its AIDS problem seems to come into focus.

In 1985, as the AIDS epidemic was attracting worldwide attention, Cuba's newspaper and radio stations, following the Soviet practice, began routinely to allege that the AIDS virus was of U.S. origin, created in military or CIA laboratories for the purposes of biological warfare. Cuba's media repeatedly denied the existence of AIDS in Cuba. As late as January 22, 1986 Cuba's national radio network was broadcasting statements by the Ministry of Public Health to the effect that not even a single Cuban was infected with AIDS. Three months later, on April 26, 1986 the Cuban government announced the death of what was said to be the first Cuban to succumb to AIDS. The victim was described as a male scenographer who had visited New York in 1982. This original report, as it happened, came into conflict with subsequent accounts; at this point at least three "first deaths" from AIDS have been described in the Cuban media.

On April 17, 1987, *Granma,* the official organ of the Communist Party of Cuba, announced that some carriers of AIDS had been identified through testing, but that they totalled only "108." Nine days earlier, however, *Journal do Brasil* had published an article reporting a statement by Fidel Castro, in a meeting with Brazilian officials, noting that there were "three hundred" cases of AIDS in Cuba. In late April 1987 the Cuban government was officially acknowledging only three deaths from AIDS. That same month a Cuban refugee who had just escaped to the United States was quoted as saying that the AIDS situation in Cuba had become "explosive."[11] The same refugee referred to a "secret hospital" where identified carriers of AIDS "are all sent." On the basis of other refugee accounts, it appears now that this hospital may actually be a detention center, manned by armed guards and administered by Cuba's Ministry of the Interior, a branch of the state's security apparatus. These same accounts claim that the Ministry of the Interior, not the Ministry of Public Health, has ultimate authority over information on AIDS.[12]

For Cuba, AIDS may today be a topic of special political sensitivity. The disease is believed to be prevalent at the moment in many areas of tropical Africa. As many as 300,000 to 400,000 Cubans are believed to have rotated through sub-Saharan Africa as soldiers and technicians between 1975 and 1985 alone; in the mid-1980s, the number of Cuban personnel in sub-Saharan Africa at any given point in time was said to be approximately 70,000. For reasons of state, the Castro regime might well wish to downplay AIDS' source of contagion, and its impact on the *internacionalistas* sent overseas. The discrepancies in Cuba's official statements about its AIDS situation, and the discrepancies between these statements and the accounts of refugees and escapees, have yet to be resolved. Should it eventually be proven that the Cuban government knowingly suppressed or distorted information of the prevalence or severity of its AIDS problem, moreover, this would not in itself prove that data in infant mortality had been systematically falsified. It would, however, indicate that Cuban authorities were willing in principle to alter data on the health of the population to serve what was designated as higher political purposes—purposes presumably deemed to be more important than the health of the people themselves.

It is precisely the distinction between purposes of state and the well-being of the individual which is central to an understanding of poverty under Communism. Poverty is, irreducibly, a phenomenon experienced by and represented in individual human beings. Communist philosophy, while enshrining the notion of "people's rights," does not recognize as legitimate the proposition that these rights may be divided into individual units. The performance of Communist states in providing for the poor within their boundaries is shaped, and ultimately limited, by this irresolvable tension.

Among intellectual circles in the West, it is today fashionable to argue that whereas Communist rule deprives its subject populations of freedom, it nevertheless provides them with bread. That peoples living under Communism lack liberty is disputed by no one—least of all by orthodox Marxist-Leninists, to whom the "bourgeois" notion of liberty is philosophical anathema. Readers of this book may judge for themselves the success of Communist regimes in supplying daily bread.

Notes

1. *Science And Society,* Winter 1981–82.
2. *Vestnik Statistiki,* December 1986.
3. *London Times,* June 12, 1981.
4. W. Ward Kingkade, personal communications, May 8, 1987.
5. *World Bank Atlas,* 1986.
6. Christopher Davis and Murray Feshbach, *Rising Infant Mortality in the USSR In The 1970s,* (Washington, D.C.: U.S. Bureau of the Census, Series P-95, #74, September 1980).
7. Barbara A. Anderson and Brian D. Silver, "Infant Mortality in the Soviet Union: Regional Differences and Measurement Issues," *Population And Development Review,* December 1986.
8. It should be emphasized that the World Bank's figures for such things as life expectancy and infant mortality are typically provisional projections rather than hard estimates based directly upon census, survey, or vital registration system data.
9. *Anuario Edistadistica de Cuba 1985* (Havana: Comite Estatal de Estadisticas, n.d.)
10. Transcript of interview with subject No. 229, courtesy of Sergio Roca, Research Project on the Efficiency of the Cuban Economy, Adelphi University; cited in Sergio Diaz-Briquets, "How to Figure Out Cuba: Development, Ideology, And Mortality," *Caribbean Review,* Spring 1986.
11. *Washington Times,* April 16, 1987.
12. Radio Marti, April 22, 1987.

Part I

The Soviet Union

1

The Health Crisis in the Soviet Union

If we could judge it solely by advances in health, the twentieth century would be a fabulous success. Few of us who take food and doctors for granted realize or appreciate this. In 1900 life expectancy for the whole of the human race was about thirty years.[1] Today it is twice as long: at least sixty-one years, possibly sixty-three or more.[2] Since the human lifespan was probably never much less than twenty years for any length of time—to drop much below that level is to court eventual extinction[3]—this means that about three-fourths of the improvement in longevity in the history of our species has occurred in the last eighty years.[4]

Over much of this century the nation in the vanguard of the revolution in health was the Soviet Union. In 1897, Imperial Russia offered its people a life expectancy of perhaps thirty years. In European Russia, from what we can make out, infant mortality (that is, death in the first year) claimed about one child in four,[5] and in Russia's Asian hinterlands the toll was probably closer to one in three. Yet by the late 1950s the average Soviet citizen could expect to live 68.7 years;[6] longer than his American counterpart, who had begun the century with a seventeen-year lead. By 1960 the Soviet infant mortality rate, higher than any in Europe as late as the 1920s, was lower than that of Italy, Austria, or East Germany, and seemed sure to undercut such nations as Belgium and West Germany any year.

Results like this could not have been achieved without a total transformation of living conditions for the U.S.S.R.'s sizable Asian and Muslim minority. This indeed has taken place.[7] By 1960 Moscow could demonstrate that its Central Asians were living fifteen years longer than the Iranians, twenty years longer than the peoples of Pakistan, and nearly twice as long as the Afghans. In the face of these and other equally impressive material accomplishments, Soviet claims about the superiority of their "socialist" system, its relevance to the poor countries, and the inevitability of its triumph over the capitalist order were not easily refuted.

Things look very different today. The 1960's and the 1970's have proved devastating to Soviet society. To observant travelers and analysts this is apparent in a hundred different ways; none, however, is so dramatic as the turn in health of the Soviet peoples. As Christopher Davis and Murray Feshbach's startling report[8] argues in convincing detail, health conditions in the U.S.S.R. have worsened steadily since the mid-1960s, and the deterioration shows no signs of stopping.

Although its findings are sensational, *Rising Infant Mortality in the USSR* is a very careful piece of work. The credentials of its authors are unimpeachable: Davis is now England's leading authority on Soviet health care, Feshbach the foremost American expert on Soviet population trends. Their study is based on data not from spy satellites, intelligence agencies, or "think tanks," but rather from reports released by the Soviets themselves.

As the title suggests, Davis and Feshbach pay closest attention to infant mortality. According to Moscow's Central Statistical Bureau (TsSU), infant mortality increased by more than a third between 1970 and 1975. Since 1975 TsSU has not reported the U.S.S.R.'s infant mortality rate, but Feshbach's estimate, based on the fragmentary evidence of local reports and adjusted for the approximately 14 percent of all infant deaths that authorities do not include in their mortality totals,[9] is that it could be as high as forty per thousand today (1981).[10] Infant mortality rates in both Western Europe and the United States are currently (1981) under thirteen per thousand.

Epidemic infant mortality, however, is only part of the picture. Except for teenagers, who are virtually indestructible so long as they do not kill themselves or each other, nearly every age group in the Soviet Union had higher death rates in 1975, the last year in which such figures were published, than in 1960. For men and women over thirty trends were particularly harsh. Death rates jumped almost 20 percent for people in their fifties, and by more than 30 percent for those in their forties. Men fared much worse than women: since 1965 their life expectancy may have declined as much as four years, to something like sixty-two today. Women, however, have not been spared: their life expectancy was around seventy-three years in the early 1970s, and may have dropped since then. This means that the average Soviet life span could be less than sixty-eight years today—lower, in other words, than it was in the late 1950s.

Measured by the health of its people, the Soviet Union is no longer a developed nation. Caloric intake, educational attainment, and the ratio of doctors to people all seem to be higher in the U.S.S.R. than in Western Europe, and yet in the U.S.S.R. life expectancy is six years lower, and its infant mortality rate three times as high. There is not a single country in all of Europe, in fact, in which lives are so short, or babies' death rates so high—not even impoverished, half-civilized Albania.[11] In the realm of health, the Soviet Union's peers are to be found in Latin America and Asia. If Feshbach's estimates are right, life expectancy in the U.S.S.R. is about the same as the average for Costa Rica, Jamaica, Malaysia, Mexico, and Sri Lanka. By the same token, the Soviet infant mortality rates could be replicated in a nation composed in equal parts of Chile, the Dominican Republic, Panama, Taiwan, and Trinidad. These countries, however, are moving up, while the Soviet Union is moving down. If current trends persist, most of Latin America and East Asia will surpass the Soviet Union in a matter of years.

There can be no mistaking it: the Soviet Union is in the grip of a devastating health crisis. We can only understand the full severity of this situation when we remember how difficult it is to push life expectancy down these days. The amenities of modern life—cheap food, clean water, mass education, rapid communication, easy travel, competent doctors, wonder drugs, and the like—make it extremely hard to stay sick or die young. The health-promoting force of these innovations is so powerful that it cannot be overcome even by modern warfare: World War I did not succeed in lowering France's life expectancy, or World War II Japan's.* The only country in modern times to have suffered a more serious setback in life expectancy was the Democratic Republic of Kampuchea, Pol Pot's Cambodia.** Clearly, something in Russia is going very, very wrong.[12]

What is it that ails the Soviet Union? We cannot be sure. The only people in a position to know are the Soviet authorities, and they have been reluctant to advertise their nation's health crisis, or to highlight the flaws in their system responsible for it. As a consequence, Westerners are left with a puzzle in which most pieces are missing. Some of the blank spaces can be filled in reasonably well through detective work, and Davis and Feshbach turn out to be very good detectives. However, theirs is primarily a study of infant mortality, and every age group has its own set of vulnerabilities. The declining quality of baby food and nursing formula, the rising (though, by Western standards, hardly scandalous) rate of illegitimacy, and the uterine damage caused by the six to eight abortions the average Soviet woman undergoes during the childbearing years[13]—all of which Davis and Feshbach document—may partly explain the increase in infant mortality, but it will not account for the rising death rates of

* Although life expectancy in Japan did drop during the year before surrender.
** This essay was written before data on the mortality toll exacted by China's Great Leap Forward had become available. See Chapters 6 and 7 on this matter.

metalworkers in Kharkov, elderly men in Georgia, or the middle-aged women who work on the U.S.S.R.'s collective farms.

We are not left wholly in the dark, however. The biggest problems affect everyone. One of these is alcoholism. Americans consider themselves a nation of problem drinkers, and not without reason, but the thirst for alcohol in the Soviet Union is a problem of an entirely different dimension. In the early 1970s, according to a study by Duke University's V. G. Treml, the Soviet Union's per capita intake of hard liquor was more than twice as high as America's or Sweden's.[14] Another report by Treml suggests that drinking is even heavier today, thanks in part to the increase in purchasing power Soviet citizens enjoyed during the years of détente. Urban families in the Soviet Union devote nearly the same proportion of their weekly budget to alcohol that American families devote to food,[15] and things have gotten to the point where factory foremen mark their workers sober and fit for duty if they can stand.[16]

Mortality breakdowns by cause of death are hard to come by for the Soviet Union, but John Dutton, a researcher now at North Carolina State University, has made a strong case for the complicity of heart disease in pushing up men's death rates,[17] and this is something alcoholism can exacerbate or even cause. Vodka and *samogon* (Russian moonshine) seem to take their toll on women and children as well. Davis and Feshbach note that Soviet doctors now rate alcoholism the third most frequent cause of illness for women, and that a report from Lithuania connects excessive drinking on the part of mothers and of mothers-to-be with half or more of the infant deaths in that Republic.[18]

Then there is pollution. Again, we think of this as a Western affliction, which indeed it is. The condition, however, seems to take on new meaning in the U.S.S.R. Its most obvious manifestation is air pollution. Western visitors have compared the air quality in some Soviet cities unfavorably with Japan's.[19] Davis and Feshbach show that the nation's rising incidence of respiratory disease is rather unfavorably linked with what Soviet doctors call "changes in the environment associated with urbanization." But those forms of pollution which can be seen are probably the least dangerous. Misuse and overuse of pesticides and fertilizers, the careless release of industrial waste and heavy metals into the waters, and radiation emitted from poorly constructed or only partially safeguarded nuclear facilities present far more deadly perils.

A *samizdat* book cited in *Rising Infant Mortality*[20] suggests the sort of price the Soviet people may be paying for their government's indifference to these hazards. Purportedly based on suppressed official data, this study by "Boris Komarov" claims that birth defects in the U.S.S.R. are rising by 5 to 6 percent a year, and that the number of "defective" children whose care must be left to the state is increasing by more than 200,000 annually. The work of "Komarov" is as yet uncorroborated, but if pollution is in fact wreaking this sort of havoc on the newborn it must be killing off adults as well.[21]

Soviet reports often refer to death by "trauma"; this category seems to include suicide, murder, and fatal accidents. Suicide in the U.S.S.R. may be on the rise, but there is really no way of telling—for official purposes, it does not exist. Conceivably, a spate of suicides could affect a nation's death rate, but suicide accounts for such a small fraction of all deaths— less than 1 percent even in Scandinavia—that this in unlikely. The same holds true for murder: a few populations suffering from pathologically high homicide rates do in fact experience a slight shortening of life span, but there is no evidence that any of the Soviet peoples are among these.

Accidents are another story. Heavy machinery and electrical equipment are dangerous under the best of circumstances, and become no safer when produced on shoddy assembly lines and placed in the hands of drunken workers. The Soviet Union may have only a tenth as many motor vehicles as the United States, but it has just as many traffic fatalities.[22] The carnage in the factory and in the field, under the tractor or the blades of the harvester, is even greater. Davis and Feshbach have estimated elsewhere that as much as a fifth of the rise in death rates for men in their late thirties may be attributed to the increasing frequency of accidents.[23]

Could a progressive decline in the health of an entire country, affecting people of nearly every ethnic background[24] and nearly every age group, take place without a breakdown in the medical system? In theory, the answer is yes, but given the specifics of the Soviet situation—a monotonous but clearly ample diet, a slow but steady improvement in housing, a well-educated and relatively skilled populace—some sort of failure in medical care would seem almost a foregone conclusion. Davis and Feshbach, always conservative in their appraisals, feel they lack sufficient evidence to *prove* the Soviet health care system is in decline; the picture they paint, however, hardly inspires confidence.

Influenza, which has been reduced to a nuisance in the rest of the industrial world, is not yet under control in the Soviet Union, and kills tens of thousands of babies each year. The proportion of children dying from "pneumonia," in fact, is said to be on the increase. Many of the young victims, it seems, start out ridden with rickets, which weakens them to the point where flu can finish them off. Rickets is unknown in the rest of the rich world, and in much of the poor world as well, because it is so easy to cure: it comes from a want of vitamin D, and is remedied by either a change in diet, food fortification, or cheap and convenient vitamin supplements. If Soviet medicine is unable to deal with these simple problems, it is unlikely to be effective against the more complicated challenges of cancer, renal disorder, or ischemic heart disease.

Why might the quality of medical care in the Soviet Union be declining? There are at least three reasons. First, the Soviet health strategy seems decidedly misguided. When extra funds are to be had, they are spent expanding facilities rather than upgrading them. Medicine is not a prestigious profession in the U.S.S.R. It is considered women's work, which means its practitioners can expect to be underpaid and poorly provided for.[25] Like the Red Army of an earlier era, Soviet physicians assault the adversary in huge numbers, but without sufficient ammunition. The U.S.S.R. has more than twice as many health personnel as the United States, but they must work in hospitals which frequently lack necessary drugs and anesthetics, in which such items as disposable bedding and needles are unknown, and in which even obtaining sterilized instruments can be a demanding ordeal.[26] Their morale is probably not improved by the Ministry of Health's obvious insensitivity to the needs of the infirm. (What other nation can boast a cardiology clinic on the top floor of a five-story walk-up in its capital city, as Moscow reportedly does?) For these and other reasons, doctor and patient alike do their best to avoid the hospital. According to Davis and Feshbach, obstetricians, gynecologists, and pediatricians now only work a twenty-eight hour week, and the number of patients treated per bed fell 20 percent from 1958 to 1974.

Corruption may also be playing its part. For obvious reasons, figures on the Soviet Union's "second economy" are unavailable, but it is known to be enormous, and to touch nearly everything.[27] Among the goods for sale in the shadow markets are medical services, and patients who want to be sure of quick or competent treatment must be ready to pay their state-provided doctors a handsome "tip." Similarly, the invalid in search of nominally free but perennially scarce medication must be willing to pay cash and forgo questions. By pulling medical resources out of circulation, the "second economy" works precisely against those people who need help most: the poor and the people scattered in the country. Corruption is said to be on the rise in every part of the U.S.S.R.'s enormous "socialist" bureaucracy.[28] If this is true it could help to account for a growing health problem on the part of the U.S.S.R.'s most vulnerable groups.

Finally, there is evidence that the Kremlin has decided to economize on medical care for its people. As medical techniques become more sophisticated, complex, and ambitious, they necessarily become more expensive, since diagnosing and treating disease must remain a human task in an increasingly automated economy. Yet over the past generation the Soviet Union has devoted an ever smaller fraction of its GNP to combatting illness. According to one plausible set of estimates, the share was 9.8

percent in 1955, but only 7.5 percent in 1977.[29] We may quibble with these specific numbers, but the trend is clear, and the Soviets themselves acknowledge it. According to one official source quoted in *Rising Infant Mortality,* health expenditures as a share of the national budget fell from 6.6 percent around 1965 to 5.2 percent in 1978. The Soviet Union may be the only advanced society to allocate progressively more modest proportions of its output to maintaining the health of its people.[30] (See Chapter 10)

It is one thing for a nation's leadership to embark upon a foolhardy policy or to find its plans undercut by the honesty of subordinates; it is quite another to pursue a course which will surely mean unnecessary hardship for most of its people. How can we account for what is apparently a high-level decision on the part of a "socialist" government to neglect health care? Inexplicable though this may seem to us, there could be good reasons for it if we take account of Soviet politics. In fact, from the perspective of the Politburo, this cruel choice might seem not only logical, but even reasonable.

From the financial standpoint, the towering problem of the post-Stalin era has been the inefficiency of the economy. A vigorous and dynamic economy is a *sine qua non* for successful long-term competition with the West. Unfortunately, the Soviet economy has always been an unpredictable machine, and in recent years it has become increasingly temperamental and stubborn. To force it on, its attendants must stoke it with ever greater quantities of capital. The U.S.S.R.'s rate of economic growth has dropped sharply since the mid-1960s, slipping below that of its OECD (Organization for Economic Cooperation and Development) rivals in the 1970s, and yet investment has been eating up an ever larger share of total output. From 1965 to 1977 (the last year for which there are detailed estimates) capital requirements for the economy rose from something like one ruble in four to very nearly one in three.[31] But investment had to be propped up at all costs; this necessarily meant trimming back elsewhere.

But what is expendable? The United States and its NATO allies were financing their rising allocations to social services at the expense of the military,[32] but for Soviet leaders this course was and remains unthinkable.[33] (More than global ambitions are at stake here: a reduction in the role of the military in Soviet society could have very unsettling effects at home.) The masters of the planned economy were left with only one option: they had to reduce the proportion of goods and services for consumers.

In theory, this would be a simple operation; after all, their command over both society and economy is supposed to be total. In reality, it would prove a tricky business. It was no longer possible to force the populace to tighten its belt indefinitely in the name of a distant socialist utopia. When

Stalin died, standards of living by many measures were lower than they had been under Nicholas II.[34] As his successors disassembled his apparatus of terror, they discovered beneath it a phenomenon they associated with bourgeois nations, but understood only poorly: consumer expectations. These could be a powerful force, and had to be taken very seriously, as Nikita Khrushchev's unhappy career was to attest, for in the final analysis he was expelled from office in disgrace at least partly because he couldn't fill the larder.[35]

This lesson was not lost on Brezhnev and Kosygin. If they were put in a position where they had to enforce sacrifices on the consuming public, they would do so quietly and very carefully. Tampering with the diet had become dangerous: peasants, workers, and bureaucrats alike now judged a regime by what it put on their plates. The availability and quality of food would have to be improved, even if it meant buying tens of million of tons of grain from adversaries.[36] Nor would it be feasible to save money by cutting back on the production of such things as brassieres or refrigerators: even a schoolboy would know that nothing in a public economy is so jealously coveted as private property. But who would notice or complain if the government skimped a bit on public, and therefore essentially intangible, services like health care? Denying a sick man an operation, after all, is not nearly so difficult as taking away a healthy man's shoes.

There is more to keeping people healthy, however, than checkups and digitalis. Medicine's role in lengthening lives is conspicuous because it is basically curative; of even greater importance are those quiet facets of our daily routine which prevent illness from breaking out in the first place. Decent meals, we all know, are a vital ingredient to a healthy life; less celebrated but perhaps no less essential is the web of personal relationships which can support us against adversity. A mother's care for her baby, a family's attention to its elderly or troubled members, and the will to live which such things inculcate, in an often unnoticed way, do for the health of an affluent nation what a ministry of health could never hope to duplicate.

Davis and Feshbach do not pass judgment on the state of mental and social health in the U.S.S.R. They are wise not to: their study is careful, fully documented, and grounded in statistics. By contrast, the evaluation of a nation's mood can only be impressionistic, ambiguous, and highly subjective. Nevertheless, the human element of any social problem is important, and remains impossible to ignore. If we treat the bits of information supplied by *Rising Infant Mortality* and the accounts of refugees and Western tourists as possibly misleading but important clues which we must put together into a plausible and consistent whole, we will have a better chance of understanding the role of human relations in the health crisis in the U.S.S.R.

Let us look at the evidence we have on hand. Death rates for men and women, babies and adults, for city and country, and so far as we can tell, for every ethnic group, are on the rise. Alcoholism, as I have pointed out, is apparently pandemic. (It is so much a part of daily life, in fact, that the state provides drying-out stations in the cities and alcoholic wards for most of the large factories.) Although we cannot tell about murder or suicide, death rates for accidents seem to be unusually high, and increasing.

Rising Infant Mortality points out that Soviet experts have linked the illness of many babies with contaminated infant formula; it seems that even though this prooblem has been recognized for several years, it has gone uncorrected. The morbidity rate for children in state-run day care centers, Davis and Feshbach note, is twice as high as for those whose families look after them. Despite the evidently appalling conditions that must be endured in these institutions,[37] some 40 percent of the Soviet Union's parents send their children to them. Abortion serves as the nation's primary form of contraception, and in any given year on the order of ten to sixteen million babies are aborted. The number of live births, by contrast, hovers between four and five million.

Moreover, refugees tell of dying patients denied treatment because their ambulance driver was out shopping,[38] or turned up too drunk to get behind the wheel. Visitors who can read Russian often remark on the incessant complaints about absenteeism in the local papers, and the frequency with which party leaders insist that economic targets could be met, even exceeded, if only more workers showed up at their jobs.

What do these things say about alienation and depression, the desire of people to look after their health and to keep others alive? How can we fit these bits of information together to suggest that some virulent strain of anomie is *not* running rampant or that the Soviet social order is *not* in the midst of a deadly decay?

The spectacle of an industrial country embarking on a path toward preindustrial standards of health is deeply disturbing. A mortality crisis of the sort the U.S.S.R. is now suffering is alien to everything we understand about modern life. In the world as we know it, in fact, that Soviet health crisis should be impossible. How then do we account for it?

Perhaps we might begin by acknowledging what our surprise and confusion with this "inexplicable" turn of events already make amply clear: that those of us in the West are remarkably ignorant about the Soviet Union. We should consider why this is so. Some might blame secretive *apparatchiki* or restrictive Intourist itineraries, and of course such things contribute to the problem, but they are not really at its heart. By comparison with other communist regimes—Mao's China, for example, or contemporary Bulgaria, to say nothing of North Korea or Albania—Brezhnev's Soviet Union seems almost relaxed in its attitude toward "foreign spies" and "state secrets." And while our access to Soviet information is deliberately rationed and manipulated, much more is available than is sometimes claimed: as Robert Byrnes has noted, the day has finally come when Sovietologists often have more material at their disposal than they can assimilate.[39]

We are indeed unfamiliar with the U.S.S.R., but this is not so much for a want of information as a lack of understanding. For understanding the Soviet Union, in the words of the French scholar Alain Besançon, requires us to "remain mentally in a universe whose coordinates bear no relationship to our own."

I do not propose to chart out this universe here. The health crisis in the Soviet Union, however, cannot be comprehended without considering several often misunderstood points about Soviet government and Russian society. No serious discussion of the mortality crisis can ignore the Soviet regime's seeming inability to prevent a deterioration in the nation's health, and no account of that can be satisfactory if it ignores the contradiction in Soviet political concerns as they are enunciated on the one hand by the rhetoric of Kremlin leaders and on the other by the operational structure of the state.

To oversimplify only slightly, the men in Moscow are forever addressing themselves to questions of the future, while the apparatus under them is fighting against what we in the West would consider problems of the past. In an era of nationalism and decolonization the U.S.S.R. stands out as an imperial remnant of the nineteenth century (Soviet rhetoric notwithstanding): a "Union" in which Ukranians, Finns, Kazakhs, Jews, Uzbeks—in all more than 100 peoples—find themselves thoroughly "guided" by a Russian minority.[40] In a century characterized by, and largely reconciled to, secularization and the waning of faith, the Soviet state not only professes a creed which explains the past and affirms the providence of the future, but bows to the cults of personality.[41] While this seemingly anachronistic tendency can be explained in part by accidents of geography and history, it can also be traced to conditions reflecting realities laid down by the Russian people, who comprise the largest national group within the U.S.S.R. and whose officers both dominate the government and give Soviet rule its distinctive flavor.

Of all the European peoples, the Russians were the least "Europeanized" before the Revolution. One must wonder whether they do not remain so to this day.[42] Anyone familiar with Russian literature will know that the

Russian universe is not easily described. It is complex and contradictory—and no less so for occasionally appearing amorphous. But this should not prevent us from identifying some of the more obvious elements within it. Foreign visitors from the Marquis de Custine to Hedrick Smith have noted that central to the Russian view of the world is a tremendous patriotism and love of the land. This makes itself felt with an intensity unknown in the West, and it is expressed in everything from folk sayings ("One's own sorrow is dearer than a foreign joy") to the official name for World War II, which the Soviet Union, alone among all contestants, refers to as "The Great Patriotic War."

In highlighting the differences between the Russian and the Western point of view, certain incidents seem especially instructive. When asked which of his many punishments at the hands of the Soviet government had been hardest to bear, Alexander Solzhenitsyn unhesitatingly replied "exile." He had suffered the unspeakable horror and injustice of the Gulag, and endured the better part of two decades of KGB harassment, but to Solzhenitsyn nothing could be worse than to be torn from his people and forced to live apart. While this speaks to a deep and even extraordinary sense of patriotism, it does not speak to this alone.

Implicit in Solzhenitsyn's response is a special attitude toward authority and suffering which is in keeping with at least one important strand of Russian history. We may remember the words of the people of Novgorod, who in the days before Kievan Rus' entreated the Vikings to "come and reign and rule over us" because "our land is great and fruitful, but there is no order in it." We may remember as well that the first two saints canonized by the Russian Orthodox Church, Princes Boris and Gleb, died not as martyrs of faith but as victims of their brother's plot, accepting their fate without resisting. The advice of the monk Sylvester, confessor to Ivan the Terrible, was "Beat your son and he will comfort you in old age"; It is not at all odd to find folk sayings such as these: "Whom I love I beat"; "Happiness without suffering is incomplete"; "Don't argue with misfortune, suffer." And what do we make of this casual observation in the Collection of National Juridical Customs (1900): "If the father leads an inordinate life which brings economic ruin, the children either leave or submit to their fate, but seldom complain against their father"?

Dostoevsky once wrote that the "fundamental spiritual need of the Russian people is . . . for suffering, perpetual and insatiable, everywhere and in everything." It might be unwise to dismiss these words. For hundreds of years Western visitors have remarked that in the Russian view of the world suffering is not something to fear, or even to face with equanimity, but rather more like a collective reserve of strength, to be added to and drawn on.

Perhaps this attitude can help to explain the current health crisis in the U.S.S.R. By this I do not mean, of course, that Russian mothers are indifferent to their children's illnesses, or that Russian men hope for expiation in a death from alcoholism. If anything, Russian mothers seem closer to their children than mothers in the West. I would suggest instead that deep nationalism and unthinking respect for authority, in combination with a faith in the strength that is to come of suffering, lay foundations for a distinctive and necessarily troubled style of government.

Autocracy and repression were not unique to Russia, but the response to them arguably was. Imperial Russia's most revered rulers were not enlightened men like Alexander II but instead despots like Ivan the Terrible and Peter the Great, who brought frightful suffering down upon the people, but for a purpose which could be seen and understood. The constraints and opportunities such a situation presents to potential leaders should be evident.

Though hardly inevitable, Joseph Stalin's system might be said to represent a final logical extension of this particular pattern of governance. The hardships he put his country through could scarcely have been imagined under the czars,[43] if only because the technology and organizational skill which were to make them possible did not then exist. At the same time, Stalin's results were incontestable. This is a point those of us in the West often overlook. Stalin inherited a country that was the primary casualty of World War I, and bequeathed to his successors a "superpower". It is but a single measure of the success of the "Leader," and his understanding of the endurance of his nation, that between 1940 and 1953, a period marked by an immensely destructive world war costing perhaps twenty million Soviet lives and a series of purges claiming perhaps not many less,[44] the U.S.S.R. doubled its production of coal and steel,[45] tripled its output of cement and industrial goods, and *increased its pool of skilled labor by a factor of ten*. These rates of growth were geometrically higher than in the less devastated and terror-free West.

Most surprising, however, was the popular reaction. There was of course revulsion, and there were at least a few large-scale revolts.[46] But strange as it sounds, the Stalinist era seems to have been a spiritually satisfying time for a great many of those who survived it.[47] Even today, after a full generation of so-called "de-Stalinization," this man, who saw to the death of at least twenty million and perhaps as many as fifty million of his own subjects,[48] is admired and even worshiped by a stratum of discontents (evidently vastly larger in number than the dissidents[49]) who feel that life lost much of its meaning when the state fell into the hands of mere economic knitters.[50]

The seeds of today's mortality crisis, I would argue, lie in Stalinism. It is not that Stalin's own rule was a failure: in many ways it can be seen as an achievement of brilliance. Despite the continuing purges, the politically inflicted famines, and World War II, for example, Stalin managed to raise life expectancy in the Soviet Union from about forty-four when he assumed total power to about sixty-two when he died. The problem is that Stalinism has brought on an extensive failure of government in a system where the government encompassed not only political administration but the economy and society itself. To put it simply, Stalin's was an impossible act to follow. For Stalinism was a self-immunizing process, but not a self-correcting system. Thus, it was at once inconceivable for his successors to continue on the tyrant's path and impossible to stray far from it.

This was not yet clear in the 1950s. Stalin's death was followed by a period of intense elation.[51] For a time it seemed possible that Socialist Utopia might be within striking distance. It was said that a new era had dawned, that the ascetic dedication of the Revolution would be married to the contentments of consumerism to bring forth a New Soviet Man. By the early 1960s it had become clear that this would not be possible.[52] Stalin's world was dead, and with it had died both the Red Terror[53] and the possibility of absolute faith in the nation's leadership. The self-sacrificing obedience these engendered would not last long. A new world of consumerism, however, could not be born. Only "liberalization" could breathe the sort of life into the Soviet economy which consumerism would require of it.

But meaningful liberalization would threaten the political apparatus directing society, and hence the Party itself. This was unacceptable. Thus the peoples of the Soviet Union found themselves caught between two worlds. They had been stranded without faith, and at the same time deprived of an option for the "good life." Given the shape of things, moreover, there were no prospects for a future any better. At this point the U.S.S.R. experienced a quiet but monumental change: in the words of John Bushnell, the New Soviet Man turned pessimist.[54] Almost immediately thereafter things began to fray. If the problem was distinctively Russian in its construction, its results were to affect all, without regard to language or ethnicity.

Preoccupied as we Americans were by our own troubles in the 1960s and the 1970s, it is perhaps understandable that we did not immediately recognize that the Soviet Union was grappling with problems far more profound than our own. During the 1980s it may become increasingly clear that we are witnessing the wearing down of a system.[55] The pace of the planned economy, whose performance is unencumbered by business cycles, has slowed to a creep over the past fifteen years. Despite a constant infusion of new technology and a steady upgrading of the education of the workforce, there have been no improvements in overall productivity in the U.S.S.R. for more than five years; in agriculture and other important sectors of the economy, the efficiency of expenditure has been dropping for most of the past decade.

The simplest routines of management seem to have become arduous struggles, to be won only on occasion. In 1965, for example, only 1.7 percent of the state's construction and assembly projects were abandoned before completion. By 1975, according to official figures, the proportion was over 40 percent. Discipline and morale are on the wane. Since the early 1950s per capita sales of alcohol have risen by a factor of five; thanks to *samogon,* total consumption may have increased even more rapidly. Corruption and marketeering, acts of "economic sabotage" punishable by death under Stalin, account for as much as 20 percent of Soviet turnover today. The state is finding it increasingly difficult to keep track of people in its controlled society. In 1962 the difference between the Soviet adult population and the number politically "registered" was 3.4 million; by 1975 it was nearly ten million—one in sixteen. And then, not perhaps unrelated to any of these things, there was the rise in death rates for nearly every group in society.

By some measures—electrical output per capita, the availability of meat[56] and clothing, average waiting time for new apartments—the standard of living is noticeably better today than in the early 1960s. But prospects for the future are incontestably worse. For the first time since Operation Barbarossa, Soviet leaders must think seriously about combatting anarchy. Today's anarchy, of course, is far less threatening, but it is also less easily confronted. Crack divisions and Russian patriotism will not keep alienation and dissatisfaction from the gates of Moscow. To hold its country together today, the Politburo must rely on the cohesive power of its most effective instruments of government and those institutions which enjoy the deepest and most widespread support.[57] What would these be? At the risk of being arbitrary, I would suggest that four seem to stand out above all others: the army, the secret police, the restrictive and highly sophisticated system of political privilege, and the black markets.[58] There are risks in leaning on any of these pillars in the current crisis. Feeding elitism or unleashing the black market, for example, could increase morale or efficiency temporarily, but could only intensify the long-term problems the Communist Party of the Soviet Union must eventually face. In the current struggle, the CPSU (Communist Party of the Soviet Union) must rely heavily on inertia, but if the past fifteen years are any measure, inertia will not serve them at all.

The Soviet health crisis presents the Politburo with serious problems. The increase in death and disease probably cannot be stemmed soon at any acceptable cost. Cutting the liquor monopoly's output might force sobriety upon the Slavs, but this would be financially disastrous—taxes on alcohol could pay the state's full health *and* education bill[59]—and could do more than any *samizdat* tract to awaken the masses. The health budget could be increased, but only at the expense of military preparedness or economic growth. The rise in death rates, then, may well continue. But consider what this means. An increase in mortality and morbidity necessarily is a burden on the economy and a drain on resources. It is not at all clear that the country can afford this. The Soviet economy is currently stalling; according to some analysts, it may even have entered negative growth.[60]

Inefficiency is in large part to blame for this slowdown; the debilitation of the workforce, and the demoralization which underlies it, do not bode well for the cadres charged with achieving a turnaround. The impending labor shortage, assured by the fact that there are fewer fifteen-year-olds than twenty-five-year-olds in the U.S.S.R. today (1981),[61] can only be worsened by a deterioration in the health of the population, and despite its attempts at modernization the Soviet economy is still highly labor-intensive. If the economy begins to shrink, Moscow must decide which will feel the loss: the factory, the army, or the consumer.

This is not a situation which can be muddled through. If investment is cut back, the economy will presumably be even feebler in the future. A cutback in military expenditures might not only imperil the chances of successful long-term competition with the United States, with whom the Red Army has finally achieved parity,[62] but possibly security within the Soviet sphere of influence. A continuing peacetime cutback in goods and services for the consumer could intensify the health crisis, and even contribute to an erosion of the legitimacy of the Soviet government. As a backdrop to all of this, there is a continuing shift in the composition of the Soviet population. In 1950, there were five Russians for every Muslim; by the end of the century, the ratio will be down to two-to-one.[63] Thus not only the power of the Soviet economy, but the effectiveness of the state in mobilizing it, are likely to be called into question by the health crisis and related difficulties in the upcoming years.

One cannot help wondering how these problems will affect U.S. relations with Moscow. Predictions are inappropriate; we understand too little about the U.S.S.R., and unexpected events might in any case prove decisive. Still, we must bear in mind that improving the ability of the state apparatus to project itself abroad and improving people's lives are two quite different things. In Bismarck's day the fortunes of a nation rested largely on the skill and eloquence of its emissaries, the competence and reliability of its informants, the judgment of its leaders, and the strength of its armies.

Bismarck, of course, lived in a world which did not yet know of development aid, the doctrine of universal human rights, or the United Nations, but the laws governing international success may not be entirely different in his age and ours.

Soviet diplomats, trade representatives, and propagandists may or may not be more skillful than their counterparts in the West.[64] There is little doubt however that they are better financed. To give but one example: in 1978, the year of Moscow's neutron bomb scare, the Soviet Union spent $2 billion around the globe denouncing American militarism.[65] For a variety of reasons, Soviet intelligence-gathering agencies are generally regarded as more sophisticated and better financed than those of the West.[66] Despite their insularity and evident paranoia, it can also be argued that (at least at the highest echelons) Soviet leaders tend to be more experienced, shrewd, and, in important ways, perhaps even more reasonable than the men in Washington with whom they must deal.

Fortunately for us all, the differences in military strength between East and West remain untested, but impartial analysts tell us the match is fairly even. Still, we must remember two things. First, Soviet military and diplomatic doctrine is, by some accounts, geared to a greater degree than Western doctrine to the application of force in day-to-day situations;[67] second, neither the United States nor the Soviet Union is spending more than a fraction of the money on weapons that it could afford in a time of crisis.[68] A case could be made that Russian leaders, remembering 1905 and 1917, fear that conflict abroad will bring with it a great risk of instability, and even overthrow, at home. But if we take all this into account, we should see that it is at least also possible for Soviet power in the world to increase even as the domestic base upon which it is built deteriorates.

It should not be necessary to explain that short-term strength, in tandem with a prospect of long-term weakness, is not a prescription for international stability—especially when the government in question is both immensely powerful and demonstrates expansionist tendencies. Those who would discount the effects of the Soviet health crisis on international politics, or would see within that crisis only incentives for an inward turn in Moscow's attention, should also consider whether this unhappy situation might have profound consequences for the rest of the world as well.

Originally published in *The New York Review of Books,* February 19, 1981. Reprinted with permission, all rights reserved.

Notes

1. Samuel H. Preston, *Mortality Patterns in National Populations* (New York: Academic Press, 1976).

2. *World Development Report, 1980* (Washington: World Bank, 1980). The low estimate assumes a life expectancy of sixty for China; the high would be in line with the Bank's assertion that it is currently (1980) seventy. Even if life expectancy in the People's Republic were lower than this, however, the world average could quite easily exceed sixty-three, for in many regions of the world estimates lag far behind the gains the people have achieved. A recent trip to Java, for example, has convinced me that Djakarta's mortality data understate the length of life on that island of ninety million by at least five years.

3. With life expectancy at eighteen for men and twenty for women, parents must have an average of six and a half or seven children to keep the population from declining. See Ansley J. Coale and Paul Demeny, *Regional Model Life Tables and Stable Populations* (Princeton: Princeton University Press, 1966). Few societies have registered fertility rates much higher than this; when they have, it has seldom been under the harsh conditions such a low life span would imply. Archaeologists now tell us that neolithic man's lifespan was about eighteen to twenty years, and we know that his life was a battle to maintain his numbers.

4. The rich and the poor are still separated by an enormous gap in life chances: infant mortality is four or five times higher today in the poor world than the rich, and a baby from the less developed regions can expect to die nearly twenty years before one who was fortunate enough to have been born at the same time in Europe, North America, Japan, Australia, New Zealand, or Israel. But if we take these tragic differences to mean that the poor have nothing to show for their participation in the twentieth century, we will be seriously mistaken. Progress in the less developed countries has been rapid and substantial. In India, for example, the length of the average life has nearly doubled since Independence. (Those who claim that the plight of the subcontinent's poor has gone unimproved for centuries always seem to forget this.) Over the past generation poor nations have consistently outpaced rich nations in the race to a healthier life. From 1960 to 1975, no rich country managed to improve its life expectancy by as much as 10 percent; by contrast, not a single poor country raised its own standing by *less* than 10 percent. These gains were absolute as well as relative. Since 1950 the collective life expectancy of the rich nations has increased by about a decade; for the poor nations, it is up more than fifteen years. See *Health: A Sector Paper* (Washington: World Bank, February 1980) and *World Atlas of the Child* (Washington: World Bank, 1979).

5. See Ansley J. Coale, Barbara A. Anderson, and Erna Harm, *Human Fertility in Russia Since the Nineteenth Century* (Princeton: Princeton University Press, 1978) and V.O. Schmelz, *Infant and Early Childhood Mortality Among Jews of the Diaspora* (Jerusalem: Hebrew University, 1971).

6. D. Peter Mazur, "Using Regressions to Estimate Life Expectation in the USSR," *Journal of the American Statistical Association*, March 1972.

7. See Charles K. Wilber's overly glowing account of this progress: *The Soviet Model and Underdeveloped Countries* (Chapel Hill: University of North Carolina Press, 1969).

8. Christopher Davis and Murray Feshbach, *Rising Infant Mortality in the USSR in the 1970s*, United States Bureau of the Census, Series P-95, No. 74, September 1980.

9. Soviet authorities evidently consider infants of less than seven months' gestation, one kilogram in weight, and less than thirty-five centimeters in length who die within the first week of birth to be "nonbabies." For further details, see Davis and Feshbach's report.

10. *Washington Post*, June 26, 1980.
11. Where life expectancy is currently sixty-nine. See Alfred Sauvy, "La population de l'Albanie," *Population*, March-April 1980. Albania's level of development may be gleaned from the reported popularity of its annual "Festival of Electric Light."
12. At this point we should address two potential objections to Davis and Feshbach's report. The rise in Soviet mortality rates cannot be explained away by improvements in statistical coverage. The need for reliable numbers in a centrally planned economy is obviously great, and the Soviet statistical system has been a highly sophisticated operation for decades. See Vladimir G. Treml and John P. Hardt, eds., *Soviet Economic Statistics* (Durham: Duke University Press, 1972). Nor can the rise in death rates be passed off as a matter of demographic shifts, as long-living and slow-breeding Slavs are gradually replaced by Asian and Muslim comrades. The Asianization of the Soviet population, other things being equal, would indeed push death rates up, even if health conditions for each individual ethnic group went unchanged. But demographic shifts cannot account for more than about a tenth of the increase in mortality which has actually been registered. The rest must be due to a deterioration of health on the part of various Soviet nationalities.
13. Soviet medical reports quoted by Davis and Feshbach put the ratio of abortions to live births anywhere between two and a half to one and four to one. Since the U.S.S.R.'s total fertility rate is slightly over two, this works out to approximately six to eight abortions per woman. (In the United States, the average number of abortions per woman per lifetime is currently about 0.5). Six to eight, however, may be an underestimate: according to Soviet feminists, the figure is nearer ten. See the *Philadelphia Bulletin*, November 27, 1980. The Soviet Union's astounding abortion problem has not only gone unexplained, but largely unexamined in the West. One must wonder, however, whether the regime does not encourage dependence on abortion because it opens itself more easily to "policy-oriented" manipulation than do other forms of contraception.
14. Vladimir G. Treml, "Alcohol Consumption in the USSR," *Journal of Studies on Alcohol*, April 1975.
15. See Vladimir G. Treml, "Alcoholism and State Policy in the Soviet Union," in Zbigniew M. Fallenbuchl, ed., *Economic Development in the Soviet Union and Eastern Europe*, vol. 2 (New York: Praeger, 1976).
16. *Literaturnaya Gazeta*, April 5, 1978, quoted in Boris Weil, "Alcoholism in the USSR," *Free Trade Union News*, October 1979. Ludmilla Throne of Freedom House kindly brought this source to my attention.
17. John Dutton, Jr., "Changes in Soviet Mortality Patterns, 1959/1977," *Population and Development Review*, June 1979.
18. Although all Soviet peoples, including those who are Muslims, probably have their share of alcoholics, alcoholism is predominantly a problem of the Slavs. In the Republic of Georgia, for example, only 20 percent of the population is Russian, yet Russians account for 80 percent of the hospitalized alcoholics. See David E. Powell, "Alcoholism in the USSR," *Survey*, Winter 1971.
19. Others present a somewhat more optimistic picture. See Victor Mote, "The Geography of Air Pollution in the Soviet Union" in Fred Singleton, ed., *Environmental Misuse in the Soviet Union* (New York: Praeger, 1976).
20. Boris Komarov (pseud.), *The Destruction of Nature: The Intensification of the Ecological Crisis in the USSR* (Frankfurt/Main: Posev Verlag, 1978).

21. Alcoholism, of course, is a known cause of birth defects as well. It is possible that the combination of heavy pollution and heavy drinking exerts a special strain on the body's filtering systems; surprisingly, there has been little research in the West about this.
22. See Toli Welihozkiy, "Automobiles and the Soviet Consumer," in U.S. Congresss Joint Economic Committee, *Soviet Economy in a Time of Change* (Washington: Government Printing Office, October 10, 1979). Over the 1970s the number of traffic deaths has fallen in the U.S. and risen steadily in the U.S.S.R.
23. Christopher Davis and Murray Feshbach, "Life Expectancy in the Soviet Union," *Wall Street Journal,* June 20, 1978.
24. The Soviet Union does not publish mortality breakdowns by ethnic background. However, Davis and Feshbach have managed to collect infant mortality data for twenty Soviet cities for 1970 and 1974. In thirteen of the twenty, infant mortality was up. These cities represent every major region of the U.S.S.R.: the Baltic Republics, the Ukraine, the RSFSR (including Siberia), the Caucasus, and the inner Asian frontier. Although Russian ethnics tend to be disproportionately represented in cities, a rise in infant mortality presumably could not be powered by a decline in their health alone.
25. A Soviet medical certificate, in fact, can mean very little. Israelis have learned that a large fraction of the Soviet "doctors" they resettle are not qualified to practice medicine, and consequently require them to take a qualification test which many of them do not pass. As the inspection of recent issues of the *Israel Press Digest* will confirm, this has made for a bitter and protracted debate.
26. See William A. Knaus, *Inside Russian Medicine* (New York: Summit Press, 1981).
27. See Gregory Grossmann, "Notes on the Illegal Private Economy and Corruption," in *Soviet Economy in a Time of Change,* op. cit.
28. Konstantin Simis, "The Machinery of Corruption in the Soviet Union," *Survey,* Winter 1977.
29. Imogene Edwards, Margaret Hughes, and James Noren, "U.S. and U.S.S.R.: Comparisons of GNP," in *Soviet Economy in a Time of Change,* loc. cit. These are their "dollar estimates" for Soviet output; their "ruble estimates" are lower, but follow the same pattern.
30. From 1965 to 1977, for example, the fraction of the American GNP going to health care increased from about 8 percent to about 11 percent. In large part this was due to Medicare and Medicaid, which much improved the medical care available to the poor. Following the institution of this form of semi-socialized medicine, American infant mortality rates, which had dropped disturbingly little over the previous decade, fell by almost half. See Kwang-sung Lee, et al., "Neonatal Mortality: An Analysis of the Recent Improvement in the United States," *American Journal of Public Health,* January 1980. At the same time, ischemic heart disease, which had been on the rise for half a century, began to subside; its incidence in the general population is more than 25 percent lower today than fifteen years ago. See R. A. Stallones, "The Rise and Fall of Ischemic Heart Disease," *Scientific American,* November 1980, and Ira Rosenwaike, et al., "The Recent Decline of Mortality of the Extreme Aged: An Analysis of Statistical Data," *American Journal of Public Health,* October 1980.

31. See "U.S. and USSR: Comparisons of GNP," loc. cit., and *Allocation of Resources in the Soviet Union and China*, U.S. Congress Joint Economic Committee hearings, June 26–July 9, 1979 (Washington: U.S. Government Printing Office, 1980).
32. See Herbert Stein, "Federal Budget Dilemmas of 1980," *AEI Economist*, October 1979. From 1965 to 1978 the proportion of the American GNP consumed by defense dropped from 8.7 to 5.2 percent.
33. Of course, this attitude is not inconsistent with a desire for a strategic arms limitations agreement, especially if there is reason to hope that this can be hammered out to one's own particular advantage.
34. See Gertrude E. Schroeder, "Consumption in the USSR: A Survey," *Studies on the Soviet Union*, No. 4, 1970.
35. It is often argued that Khrushchev was ousted because he threatened the stability of the Party apparatus and the bureaucracy beneath it. Seweryn Bialer makes this case forcefully in his *Stalin's Successors* (New York: Cambridge University Press, 1980). There is no doubt that Khrushchev managed to alienate practically the entire top level of Soviet leaders through his erratic performance; the shortcoming of his "hare-brained schemes," however, was not only that they inconvenienced *apparatchiki*, but that they produced generally disappointing economic results.
36. In the nineteenth century Ernst Engel, a German economist, observed that households tended to spend smaller fractions of their income on food as their affluence increased. The people of the Soviet Union may be more prosperous today than they were fifteen years ago, but they seem to spend just as large a proportion of their disposable income on food. Since 1965 the purchasing power of the consumer economy (that is, GNP minus investment and defense expenditures) has increased by something like 51 percent; expenditures on food have increased by something like 52 percent. See "U.S. and U.S.S.R.: Comparisons of GNP," loc. cit. This is out of keeping with the laws of consumer economics, but such laws should not be expected to operate where prices are systematically gerryrigged and allocations of resources determined not by a market but a Politburo.
37. See for example Vera Golubeva, "The Other Side of the Coin," in the Soviet feminist magazine *Women and Society*, translated into English in the May/June 1980 issue of *Freedom Appeals*.
38. See, for example, Florence Pitts, "Hotel Cosmos: How the Biggest Soviet Hotel was Built," in *Freedom at Issue*, November/December 1980.
39. Robert F. Byrnes, "Moscow Revisited: Summer 1978," *Survey*, Autumn 1977/1978.
40. See Hélène Carrère d'Encausse's superb *Decline of an Empire* (New York: Newsweek Books, 1979).
41. Lest anyone forget, the cult of personality did not end with Stalin. Leonid Brezhnev currently (1981) promotes one of his own. The Soviet press recently has been abuzz with praise for his memoirs, and his work has already "sold" millions of copies. See *Survey* magazine's articles under the heading "The New Literary Personality" in its Autumn 1977/1978 issue, and Graeme Gill's "The Soviet Leader Cult: Reflections on the Structure of Leadership in the Soviet Union," *British Journal of Political Science*, June 1980.
42. The following discussion draws heavily on these sources: Astolphe de Custine, *Journey for Our Time* (London: Hollis and Carter, 1952); Hedrick Smith, *The*

Russians (New York: Quadrangle, 1976); Karl Baedeker, *Russia: A Handbook for Travelers* (New York: Scribner's, 1914); Georgie Ann Geyer, *Young Russians* (New York: Etc. Press, 1975); G. P. Fedotov, *The Russian Religious Mind* (Cambridge: Harvard University Press, 1960); Dinko Tomasic, *The Impact of Russian Culture on Soviet Communism* (New York: Glencoe Publishing Company, 1953); V. I. Dal, *Sayings of the Russian People* (Moscow, 1957); Geoffrey Gorer and John Rickman, *The People of Great Russia* (New York: Chanticler Press, 1950); Francesca Wilson, *Muscovy: Russia Through Foreign Eyes* (New York: Praeger, 1970); Margaret Mead, *Soviet Attitudes Towards Authority New York: Schocken, 1966*; and John S. Reshetar, Jr., "Russian Ethnic Values" in C. E. Black, ed., *The Transformation of Russian Society* (Cambridge: Harvard University Press, 1960). It is also much the better for the generous and incisive advice of Suzanne Massie, from whose considerable expertise in Russian culture I have benefitted.

43. According to Robert Conquest's *Kolyma: The Arctic Death Camps* (New York: Oxford University Press, 1978) more political prisoners died in a single Siberian camp in a single year under Stalin than in all the czars' jails in the nineteenth century, a rough indication, at least, of the sorts of differences we are talking about.

44. A recent *samizdat* manuscript by Joseph Diadkin, a dissident scientist, deals with this question of "unnatural deaths" under Stalin. A preliminary summary of his forthcoming report can be found in the July 23, 1980 edition of the *Wall Street Journal*.

45. The following discussion relies primarily on Roger Clarke, *Soviet Economic Facts* (New York: Wiley, 1972); Abram Bergson and Simon Kuznets, eds., *Economic Trends in the Soviet Union* (Cambridge: Harvard University Press, 1963); and United Nations, *Patterns of Industrial Expansion, 1938/58* (New York: United Nations, 1960).

46. For an account of these see George Fischer, *Soviet Opposition to Stalin* (Cambridge: Harvard University Press, 1952), and Alexander Solzhenitsyn's *Gulag Archipelago* (New York: Harper and Row).

47. Note Hedrick Smith's surprise at this in his *The Russians*, loc. cit. It has been reported that when a picture of Stalin flashes on screen in a Soviet theater, about half of the audience will applaud.

48. According to Joseph Diadkin, the total number of "unnatural deaths" under Stalin was between forty-three and fifty-two million. How many of these we actually attribute to the dictator is a matter of opinion. Some analysts, for example, blame the severity of the Terror in the late 1930s on "excesses" on the part of Stalin's underlings. More seriously, Stalin cannot be held directly accountable for the estimated twenty million deaths the Soviet people suffered at the hands of the Germans, although the argument can be made that if he had not executed Marshal Tukhachevsky and virtually the entire top echelon of military officers just before World War II the Red Army might have offered greater resistance to the Wehrmacht.

49. As Bialer notes, there are between eight and ten thousand active dissidents in the Soviet Union today. See *Stalin's Successors*, op. cit. Naturally, this may be just the visible edge of submerged dissent, but as Andrei Amalrik made clear in his *Will the Soviet Union Survive Until 1984?* (New York: Harper and Row, 1970), the dissidents and the neo-Stalinists have rather different class backgrounds. The former are almost all members of the intelligentsia, while those who cheer for Stalin at the movies tend to come from the working class.

50. See Harrison E. Salisbury's "Stalin Makes a Comeback," *New York Times Magazine,* December 23, 1979.
51. This feeling is reflected in Alexander Werth's *Russia Under Khrushchev* (Boston: Hill and Wang, 1962).
52. The exact date of this shift is unclear, but it very likely came in the early 1960s, with the simultaneous collapse of the last Stalinist panaceas and the frustration of various attempts at liberalization. Useful markers might be the failure of the Virgin Lands scheme in agriculture, the exposure of Lysenkoism as fraud in science, the rejection of Liberman-style reforms in economics, and, of course, the ouster of Khrushchev. For more information on the first three incidents, see Lazar Volin, *A Century of Russian Agriculture* (Cambridge: Harvard University Press, 1970), David Joravsky, *The Lysenko Affair* (Cambridge: Harvard University Press, 1970), and George R. Feiwel, *The Soviet Quest for Economic Efficiency* (New York: Praeger, 1972).
53. A measure of the relaxation was the drop in prison camp populations from something like 10.5 million under Stalin to about 1.5 million a few years later. See Alain Besançon, *The Soviet Syndrome* (New York: Harcourt Brace Jovanovich, 1978).
54. John Bushnell, "The New Soviet Man Turns Pessimist," in Stephen F. Cohen, Alexander Rabinowitch, and Robert Sherlett, eds., *The Soviet Union Under Stalin* (Bloomington: Indiana University Press, 1980).
55. The following discussion relies primarily on Robert Wesson's *The Aging of Communism* (New York: Praeger, 1980). This book is a reliable and incisive reference for those concerned with the many aspects of the political problem confronting communist states today.
56. This must be examined skeptically. It is not clear how Soviet authorities calculate their availabilities of meat: almost certainly the figures they give do not take full account of losses due to trimming, transportation, spoilage, and so forth. The Food and Agriculture Organization, which is not in the habit of questioning the statistics of its member states, automatically reduces the estimate it receives from the Soviet Union by 20 percent.
57. There is a contradiction here for, as Bialer indicates, the smooth functioning of the Soviet system depends in no small part on the promotion of apathy. See *Stalin's Successors,* loc. cit.
58. There is a fifth force which can be drawn on: this is Russian nationalism. As James Billington has remarked, among the few organizations in the Soviet Union to enjoy genuine mass support are the Russian societies for the preservation of historical monuments, which he sees as vents of sorts for patriotism and nationalism. See his "Soviet Attitudes and Values: Prospects for the Future" in the Wilson Center's *The USSR and Sources of Soviet Foreign Policy* (Washington: Smithsonian Institution, n.d.). Of course, Russian nationalism cuts both ways against an internal threat: its centripetal force could be met or exceeded by the reaction of the other peoples of the U.S.S.R. who for the first time may constitute a majority of the Soviet population.
59. "Alcohol in the USSR: A Fiscal Dilemma," op. cit.
60. *Economist,* December 29, 1979.
61. See Murray Feshbach and Stephen Rapawy, "Soviet Population Trends and Policies" in U.S. Congress Joint Economic Committee, *Soviet Economy in a New Perspective* (Washington: Government Printing Office, 1976).
62. Much has been written on this. See for example SIPRI, *World Armaments and Disarmament, 1980* (New York: Crane Russak, 1980).

63. See Eric M. Breindel and Nick Eberstadt, "Paradoxes of Population," *Commentary*, August 1980.
64. On the one hand, Soviet negotiators and representatives are often said to be cruder and more openly cynical than those they face, and Soviet policy has been marked by at least one tremendous and expensive setback—the Sino-Soviet rift. On the other hand, it can also be argued that the distribution of benefits from the Soviet-American grain deal of 1972 or the pattern of votes on the floor of the UN (in which it seems to take a brutal invasion of a Soviet neighbor to shake the assembly's confidence in the U.S.S.R.) are in no way unrepresentative of Soviet skill abroad. A useful discussion of the debate may be found in Adam Ulam's *Expansion and Coexistence: Soviet Foreign Policy, 1917–1973* (New York: Praeger, 1974).
65. Richard F. Staar, "Soviet Union," in Peter F. Duignan and Alvin Rabushka, eds., *The United States in the 1980s* (Stanford: Hoover Institute Press, 1980).
66. See in particular Sir William Hayter, *Russia and the World* (New York: Taplinger, 1970).
67. Raymond L. Garthoff, "Soviet Views of the Interrelation of Diplomacy and Military Strategy," *Political Science Quarterly*, Fall 1979.
68. During World War II, both the United States and the Soviet Union allocated more than 40 percent of their resources to their military efforts. Today the proportion in the U.S. is under 6 percent, and in the U.S.S.R., depending on whom we believe, anything from 7 percent to over 20 percent. See Arthur M. Cox, "The CIA's Tragic Error," *New York Review*, November 6, 1980, and Igor Birman, "The Way to Slow Down the Arms Race," *Washington Post*, October 27, 1980.

2

A Second Look at the Health Crisis in the Soviet Union

In their article "Infant Mortality Trends in the Soviet Union" (*Population and Development Review*, June 1983), Ellen Jones and Fred W. Grupp argue that the apparent deterioration of health levels in the U.S.S.R. during the Brezhnev years is largely illusory. They suggest that faulty Soviet data and unbalanced statistical manipulations by Western analysts are principally responsible for the impression that health conditions in the Soviet Union are in decline. This delightfully simple explanation seems to occur to most inquisitive and skeptical people when they first learn of the U.S.S.R.'s seemingly unique health problems. It is only with further research that such skepticism can be dispelled. Despite their admirable attempts at investigating the issue, Jones and Grupp have stumbled into many of the pits that observers of Soviet society and specialists in demographic analysis must learn to avoid. Greater familiarity with, and attention to, their subject matter could have led these two researchers to very different conclusions from those expressed in their article.

The argument made by Jones and Grupp can be summarized in six points:

1. Western analysts measuring increases in reported infant mortality in the U.S.S.R. use as their base a year in which reported figures were unusually low and they thereby exaggerate the extent to which the rate has risen.
2. Much of the rise in reported infant mortality has been due to improved registration of births and deaths in the U.S.S.R.'s less developed Central Asian republics and in other "Muslim" regions.
3. The rise in reported rates of infant mortality, due mainly to a tightening up of records in low-health regions, has been largely responsible for the nominal decline in Soviet life expectancy.

4. In actuality, there is good reason to believe that infant mortality has been declining in the U.S.S.R.'s "Muslim" regions, irrespective of some figures that make it appear to be rising.
5. In European Russia, infant mortality rates, and patterns of health improvement, have been similar to those in the rest of the developed world.
6. Such problems as the U.S.S.R. may have experienced with infant mortality are similar to those of other developed countries.

Let us examine the support for each of these points in turn.

First, Jones and Grupp object to measuring subsequent rises in Soviet infant mortality rates against the 1971 level, which they say was abnormally and inexplicably low. They base their charge on an assertion that the U.S.S.R.'s 7.3 percent drop in reported mortality between 1970 and 1971 was a highly unusual event. They could have done better homework here. If they had checked back, they would have learned that infant mortality has dropped by more than 7 percent in four of the last sixteen years for which the U.S.S.R. Central Statistical Administration has published figures. If they had looked further, they would have found that single-year declines of that magnitude are not uncommon even in countries where infant mortality rates are lower and, therefore, presumably more difficult to depress. Jones and Grupp present a chart comparing American and West German infant mortality rates to those reported for European Russia. In the United States, infant mortality has dropped by more than 6 percent, (1976–81) twice in the last five years.[1] In West Germany it has dropped by more than 7 percent in four of the last nine years for which we have data;[2] the average rate of decline between 1972 and 1981, in fact, was over 8 percent.

Jones and Grupp are correct in suggesting that the apparent rise in infant mortality would be cut from 22 percent to 13 percent if the 1974 figure (the last one Soviet statistical sources have as yet released) were compared with 1970 instead of 1971. But they should not take this to mean that the rise in Soviet infant mortality rates has been exaggerated. One Soviet publication has given a figure of 30.8 for infant mortality for 1975;[3] and a careful analysis of Soviet mortality data by Christopher Davis and Murray Feshbach has led them to produce an estimate of 31.1 for 1976.[4] If we measure infant mortality in 1970 against these numbers, we get increases of 22 percent and 23 percent, respectively. If we measure them against the 1971 level, we get increases of 36 percent and 37 percent. There is reason to believe, then, that the apparent rise in Soviet infant mortality in the early 1970s is more significant—and serious—than Jones and Grupp's use of figures would suggest.

On their second point, Jones and Grupp argue that birth and death registration in the U.S.S.R.'s "Muslim" areas was incomplete in the early 1970s, and hence, that a tightening up of vital registration could lead to a rise in reported rates of infant mortality even as actual health conditions were improving. Their case for underregistration in the "southern tier" rests principally on three pieces of evidence: an article by Viktor Kozlov, a leading Soviet ethnographer, suggesting that many regions in Soviet Central Asia experienced problems with their vital registration systems in the 1960s; a Soviet book that, they say, acknowledges that underregistration was still a problem in the 1970s; and calculations that Jones and Grupp made themselves and that, they state, indicate underregistration of births in some "Muslim" republics was still on the order of 7 to 9 percent in the 1970s.

Let us examine these pieces of evidence. There is widespread agreement among Soviet and Western scholars that the U.S.S.R. was underreporting both births and deaths from the "southern tier" in the 1950s and early 1960s. But this fact should not be taken to mean that the problem necessarily extended into the 1970s, nor should Kozlov's cautious statement from the 1960s be stretched to cover later years. In the summer of 1983 a team of Westerners met with Kozlov and his colleagues at the Institute of Ethnography in Moscow, and asked specifically about the quality of birth and death statistics in Soviet Central Asia. Kozlov and his colleagues reported that vital registration in these places had been "essentially complete" since the late 1960s.[5] In their view, then, fluctuations in birth and death rates in the U.S.S.R. over the 1970s reflected real trends, not artifacts. Some credence should be lent to their opinions, since members of the Institute of Ethnography were involved in the preparation of the 1979 census.

The book Jones and Grupp draw upon to substantiate their claim that birth and death registrations were incomplete in the Central Asian republics in the 1970s does not say any such thing. Indeed, it could not. *Regional Features of Population Reproduction of the USSR,* although published in 1972, is in fact a collection of pieces from a symposium from 1968. If they were to read this source, Jones and Grupp would see that the data presented reach only into the early 1960s.

As for Jones and Grupp's calculations, which purport to show serious underregistration of births in several Central Asian republics well into the 1970s: these cannot be criticized. They are simply not presented either in the body of their article or in its footnotes. The most the reader will find is a note mentioning that "the computed underregistration estimate is extremely sensitive to mortality assumptions." One can only speculate about their methodology. It is worth noting, however, that the U.S. Census

Bureau has done its own analysis of underregistration of birth in the U.S.S.R., and one in which methodology was carefully and completely described.[6] According to the Census Bureau study, discrepancies between ZAGS (registration) numbers for the 1960s and the 1970 census count indicate a 3.1 percent underregistration of births for the U.S.S.R. in the first half of the 1960s, and a 1.6 percent underregistration for the second half of the 1960s. Jones and Grupp use 3 percent underregistration as a threshhold beyond which registration is "essentially complete." By this definition, the Census Bureau's study would indicate that vital registration for the U.S.S.R. as a whole was "essentially complete" in the second half of the 1960s—a judgment which squares with that of the researchers from the Soviet Academy of Science's Institute of Ethnography.

At such low levels of underregistration as appear to have prevailed in the U.S.S.R. in the late 1960s, it would seem unlikely that improved coverage would have much effect on nominal infant mortality rates for the U.S.S.R. as a whole. Indeed, during the "tightening up" of vital registration in the 1960s, the infant mortality rate underwent steady decline.

Third, Jones and Grupp imply that once rising infant mortality is explained away, the entire conundrum of declining Soviet life expectancy disappears as well. They seem to believe that rising infant mortality has been a primary factor in the apparent drop in Soviet life expectancy. This is a fundamental mistake. In 1974—the last year for which Soviet statistical sources give an infant mortality figure for the nation as a whole—infant deaths accounted for less than 6 percent of all reported deaths in the U.S.S.R. Between 1970 and 1974 (to use the benchmarks Jones and Grupp prefer) the absolute increase in reported infant deaths accounted for less than 12 percent of the overall rise in Soviet mortality. The impact of infant mortality on overall changes in health looks even smaller if we compare death rates in 1974 with those from 1964. Reported infant mortality rates were almost the same in 1964 and 1974, but the crude death rate for the nation as a whole was 22 percent higher in 1974 than it was ten years earlier. Clearly, it is not just infants whose death rates were climbing. Between the early 1960s and 1976—the last year for which age-specific death rates for the U.S.S.R. have been released—nearly every adult age group experienced a rise in reported death rates. Table 1 in this chapter demonstrates this. For several age groups, the jump in mortality appears to have been even more pronounced than for infants: age-specific death rates for men and women in their forties, for example, were up nearly 40 percent. It is this pronounced and general rise in death rates, not an aberrant rise in infant mortality, that has been dragging down estimates of life expectancy for the Soviet Union since the 1960s. Infant mortality rates were in fact the last category to join in this overall upsurge.

Fourth, Jones and Grupp believe that "the real trend of infant mortality in the Soviet southern tier throughout the 1970s was one of continuing decline." In support of this notion, they cite a Soviet source to the effect that infant mortality in Tadjikistan fell from 90 to 63 per thousand live births between 1977 and 1979, and a report that whooping cough was cut by 56 percent, and pneumonia by 25 percent, in Kirgizia between 1973 and 1974.

It seems strange for Jones and Grupp to take a reported 30 percent drop in infant mortality over two years at face value when they find a 7 percent drop in one year so suspect. Inconsistency notwithstanding, it is curious to see such figures advanced as evidence of *secular* improvements in health. Tadjikistan's rate of improvement is anomalous: if it could be sustained, infant mortality there would be falling by over 80 percent every decade, and Tadjikistan would be a model rather than an embarrassment for Soviet health authorities. Precipitous two-year drops in mortality rarely come about as a result of social policy or economic development. Usually they reflect recovery: from a famine, an epidemic, breakdown in public order, or some other disaster. Soviet journals, however, seldom report directly on disasters: usually they cover them indirectly, by referring to the progress that has been made in responding to them. Jones and Grupp do not seem to be familiar with this practice. Had they been, they might have realized that their numbers for Kirgizia and Tadjikistan (if accurate) actually demonstrate not what they were trying to prove, but the opposite: namely, that infant mortality rates in Central Asia are high and unstable, and still shaped by epidemic.

Fifth, to prove that health levels were roughly the same in European Russia and the West in the 1960s, Jones and Grupp's chart reported infant mortality rates for the United States and West Germany against those for the "European" republics of the U.S.S.R. They do not seem to realize that those figures are not comparable. As the UN's *Population and Vital Statistics Report* has pointed out: "[Soviet] data have always excluded live-born infants of less than 28 weeks gestation, less than 1,000 gram in weight, and [less than] 35 centimeters in length who die within 7 days of birth."[7] By those rules, roughly 14 percent of the infant deaths in the United States in the 1960s would have been excluded from the infant mortality count.[8] Comparisons that do not adjust for this difference in coverage cannot help being misleading.

A more useful comparison of health levels in European Russia and the West can be made with life expectancy estimates from the U.S. Census Bureau. For 1975, life expectancy in the United States and West Germany was put at 73; for European Russian (RSFSR, the Ukraine, Moldavia, Belorussia, Estonia, Latvia, Lithuania) the unweighted average is 69.[9] The four-year difference in life expectancy is significant; more importantly, however, the trends for the West and for European Russia went in opposite directions. Life expectancy rose by more than a year in both the United States and West Germany between 1970 and 1975; by contrast, the United States Census Bureau estimates that it fell by nearly a year in the Soviet Union.[10]

Sixth, Jones and Grupp argue that Soviet difficulties in reducing infant mortality during the 1970s (such as they were) should be seen as common to all developed societies. They say that there is a natural, if not inevitable, slowdown in the speed of infant mortality reductions once health conditions are good. They say that underweight babies, who are most vulnerable to setbacks in health, are beneficiaries of advances in Soviet obstetrics,

TABLE 2.1
Reported increases in mortality for different age groups in the Soviet Union, 1961–76
(death rate per 1,000, both sexes)

Age group	Low year	Death rate	High year	Death rate	Percent increase
20–24	1967	1.5	1976	1.7	11
25–29	1964	2.0	1971	2.2	10
30–34	1964	2.5	1976	3.0	20
35–39	1961	3.0	1976	3.8	27
40–44	1961	3.7	1976	5.3	43
45–49	1965	5.0	1976	6.9	38
50–54	1961	7.5	1976	9.3	24
55–59	1964	10.7	1976	13.4	25
60–64	1961	16.7	1976	18.9	13
65–69	1964	24.1	1976	28.0	16
70+	1961	63.0	1973	75.5	20

Source: Davis and Feshbach, cited in note 3.

TABLE 2.2
Ratio of the incidence of infectious diseases per 100,000 population:
U.S.S.R. versus U.S.

Disease	1970	1979
Typhoid fever	52.9:1	29.2:1
Diphtheria	2.1:1	3.3:1
Whooping cough	7.7:1	13.5:1
Tetanus	3.9:1	3.8:1
Polio (acute: paralytic)	5.5:1	8:1
Measles	8.4:1	23.4:1

Source: Murray Feshbach, "Issues in Soviet Health Problems," cited in note 14.

and may distort infant mortality tallies by being added today, but removed tomorrow. They assert that, in the absence of hard data on infant mortality for the second half of the 1970s and the early 1980s, we may safely assume that Soviet infant mortality rates are declining because of increasing numbers of obstetricians and pediatricians, and increased supplies of infant formula.

It is a little difficult to know which of these misconceptions should be addressed first. We might as well start with the argument about slowdowns in progress against infant mortality. There is nothing in the experience of Western nations to suggest that reductions in infant mortality must decelerate once a country reaches the level attained by the U.S.S.R. in the early 1970s. In 1974 infant mortality was nearly twice as high in the U.S.S.R. as in West Germany or the United States, yet in ensuing years the pace of mortality reduction in the United States and West Germany quickened. Reductions in infant mortality accelerated largely because of social policy: through welfare measures that began in the United States under the banner of the ''Great Society,'' and in Germany under the aegis of Social Democratic government policies. That the Soviet Union's infant mortality rate appears to have been not much lower in the early 1970s than it had been in the early 1960s may tell us something about its governmental policies, but it has nothing to do with ''natural'' laws of human population.

There is no reason to expect the safeguarding of vulnerable newborns to impair progress in reducing infant mortality. In the United States, the dramatic decline of infant mortality rates after 1965 was powered primarily by the improvement in survival ratios for high-risk, low-birthweight babies.[11] As neonatal mortality fell, death rates for the second through the eleventh month of life also declined. The same has been true in other Western nations: when neonatal mortality falls, the risks in the rest of the first year do not increase. If things are different in the U.S.S.R., it would only be because the U.S.S.R. stands as an exception to rules of health care, as these are understood in the West.

There is no *prima facie* reason to expect greater numbers of graduates from Soviet medical institutions, or greater amounts of Soviet infant formula, to push infant mortality rates down. Between 1965 and 1978 the average number of visits to the doctor per person per year rose from 6.8 to 9.8—that is, by more than 40 percent.[12] Over those same years, according to U.S. Census Bureau estimates, life expectancy in the U.S.S.R. fell by about three years.[13] Whatever else the modern Soviet medical system may do, it does not seem to be able to improve the nation's health through increased diagnosis and treatment. Indeed, as Table 2 in this chapter shows, the Soviet medical system's ability to deal with basic health problems appears to have lagged further behind that of the U.S.

system over the course of the 1970s. The Soviet medical system is fundamentally different from medical systems in the West; those who are interested in learning about it might well begin with the incisive work of Christopher Davis, Murray Feshbach, and William Knaus.[14]

When it comes to Soviet infant formula, more does not necessarily mean better. Indirect criticisms of the quality of Soviet infant formula appeared in Soviet journals in the 1970s.[15] The U.S.S.R.'s agreement with the American firm Abbott Laboratories, though shrouded in silence, is taken by many observers as a sign that the U.S.S.R.'s infant formula industry needed some serious straightening out. But the health effects of Soviet infant formula depend not only on its contents, but also on the transportation and marketing systems that distribute it. There are few reasons to be sanguine about these. In Samarkand in the summer of 1983, for example, I found infant formula from 1978 still on sale. No Western country would allow this.

The U.S.S.R. is a unique society. Neither its economy nor its government operates along Western lines, and for this reason its social problems are often very different from the ones we see and understand in the West. Researchers who do not take the time to familiarize themselves with the U.S.S.R., and the important differences in rhythms of life between the U.S.S.R. and Western nations, do not always appreciate this. For better or worse, the U.S.S.R. cannot be understood by gazing into a Western mirror. Nor can its health problems be explained away by relying on models and reference points that those of us in the West understand intuitively and through our own life experiences.

This article was originally published in *Population and Development Review*, March 1984. Reprinted with permission, all rights reserved.

Notes

1. U.S. Bureau of the Census, *Statistical Abstract of the United States, 1982/83* (Washington, D.C.: Government Printing Office, 1982).
2. Statistiches Bundesamt, *Statistishes Jahrbuch 1982 fur die Bundesrepublik Deutschland* (Stuttgart and Mainz: W. Kohlhammer Verlag, 1983).
3. S. P. Burenkov et al., *Socialist Public Health: Tasks, Resources, Perspective Development* (Moscow: Meditsina, 1979) (in Russian), cited in Christopher Davis and Murray Feshbach, *Rising Infant Mortality in the USSR in the 1970s* (Washington, D.C.: Bureau of the Census, Series P-95, No. 74, September 1980).
4. Davis and Feshbach, cited in note 3.
5. Rosemarie Crisostomo et al., "Report of the Soviet Central Asian Demographic Study Group, July 27–August 25, 1983" (Cambridge: Harvard Center for Population Studies, processed).

6. Godfrey Baldwin, *Estimation and Projections of the Population of the USSR by Age and Sex: 1950 to 2000* (Washington, D.C.: Bureau of the Census, September 1973).

7. *Population and Vital Statistics Report,* Statistical Papers, Series A, Vol. XXI, No. 3, 1969, cited in Davis and Feshbach (see note 3).

8. Davis and Feshbach, cited in note 3.

9. U.S. Bureau of the Census, *World Population: 1977* (Washington, D.C.: Government Printing Office, 1977); Stephen Rapawy and Godfrey Baldwin, "Demographic Trends in the Soviet Union, 1950–2000," in U.S. Congress, Joint Economic Committee, *Soviet Economy in the 1980s: Problems and Prospects* (Washington, D.C.: Government Printing Office, 1983).

10. Kwang-Sung Lee et al., "Neo-natal mortality: An analysis of recent improvement in the United States," *American Journal of Public Health* (January 1980).

11. Rapawy and Baldwin, cited in note 9.

12. Christopher Davis, "The Economics of the Soviet Health System," in *Soviet Economy in the 1980s,* cited in note 9.

13. Rosemarie Crisostomo, "The Demographic Dilemma of the Soviet Union" (Washington, D.C.: Bureau of the Census, August 1983).

14. See, for example, Davis and Feshbach, cited in note 3, Davis, cited in note 12; Murray Feshbach, "Issues in Soviet Health Problems," in *Soviet Economy in the 1980s* (cited in note 9); and William Knaus, *Inside Soviet Medicine* (New York: Summit Press, 1981).

15. Davis and Feshbach, cited in note 3.

3

Human Factors in Soviet Economic Development

In economic performance the human factor is always prominent. It cannot be otherwise. Economies are operated by (and to an irreducible extent, for) human beings; consequently mass behavior in its diverse dimensions sets both daily constraints and less immediate limits upon economic activity.

Human aspects of the economic process are decisively shaped by the fact that labor is an animate commodity. Physiological needs determine the minimum requirements which the production system must satisfy if household routines (much less national objectives) are to be pursued. "Human resources," unlike natural resources, may be augmented in the very process of being used. No less importantly, the delicate and inescapably human quality of motivation affects not only the supply and quality of manpower, but also the efficiency with which all other "inputs" are brought into use.

More than most other national directorates, current (1982) leadership in the Soviet Union might be expected to recognize the importance of human factors in economic development. There are both practical and theoretical reasons for this. Intellectually, the Communist Party of the Soviet Union lays claim to the Marxist-Leninist tradition; it is therefore incumbent upon the CPSU to protect and to promote teachings of those two prolific writers. No good Marxist can be unaware of the broad implications of the labor theory of value, or would deny the moral necessity of organizing production to meet human needs. By the same token, an historical materialist cannot help but recognize the role of human numbers in shaping economic and political events.[1] From the practical standpoint, the current Soviet leadership's concern with human factors in development has been conditioned by events. World War II and the years of adjustment that followed

43

it saw tens of millions of Soviet citizens perish, including many of the most talented, and promising, minds of the nation. The devastation brought on by unexpected war and forced-paced recovery have been a principal consideration in the shaping of Soviet policy since the death of Stalin.

Today, the importance of the human factor is once again being impressed upon Soviet leaders, although for entirely different reasons. For the first time in postwar history, Soviet planners are facing a situation in which overall manpower is scarce. Confronted by budgetary constraints and demographic trends which are not amenable to immediate change, Soviet decision makers must now seek ways to maintain economic growth despite an abrupt deceleration in investment (down by some accounts from about 7 percent growth per year in the early 1970s to a planned 3 percent for 1981–85[2]) and an even more dramatic slowdown in the growth of the working-age population (which rose by 26 million between 1970 and 1982, but will increase by only 6 million between 1982 and 1995).

The Eleventh Five-Year Plan (1981–85) marks a decisive break with the past: improvements in productivity must now be the principal—indeed, the overwhelming—impetus behind economic growth. Between 1950 and 1980, improvements in "total factor productivity," a Western measure which estimates the net efficiency in use of all factors drawn into production, including labor—appears to have accounted for less than 40 percent of the U.S.S.R.'s increment in economic output. It is meant to provide something like 75 percent of the Soviet economy's growth in the early 1980s.[3] These plans, moreover, have been cast in a background in which total factor productivity is believed to have been *declining* for at least a decade, and perhaps at an accelerating pace.[4] To stem this adverse trend, and to meet the objectives of the Eleventh FYP, Soviet economic and political policy will have to come to terms with a variety of unavoidably human issues.

Analyzing the human dimensions of the U.S.S.R.'s recent economic performance and future prospects raises a complex continuum of questions. These might best be examined on three separate planes. The first is the plane of human numbers. The size, composition, and location of a population shapes both consumption requirements and manpower supplies. Population statistics are less likely to be affected by questions of interpretation than most other economic data, although Soviet demographic numbers are by no means free of inconsistencies.[5] Population numbers also afford an unusually reliable glimpse into some aspects of the future, since the pensioners and workers of the year 2000 have already been born, and will travel through the age pyramid in cohorts whose size can be projected with reasonable accuracy through anticipated survival ratios.

The second is the plane of issues relating to "human capital." Output and demand respond not only to changes in population numbers, but also to changes in the health, education, and skills of that population. Trends in human capital formation are generally more difficult to measure and assess than basic population trends, since most of the important variables in the former are inherently unobservable. "Capital formation" through education, for example, can only be measured through a variety of imperfect proxies: years of schooling, expenditure per pupil, or output later in life somehow discounted for all other intervening phenomena.[6] Nevertheless, certain important facets of "human capital" may be traced through statistics on health, and others may be reflected in patterns of consumption.

The third, and perhaps least satisfactory, plane of analysis concerns human motivation. Output and efficiency are affected by human considerations which do not relate directly either to a population's size or to investments in its potential for production. Discipline, morale, expectation, and incentive weave together to form a sort of social web that conditions, and at times determines, individual economic behavior and aggregate productivity. Questions of motivation involve such nonnumerical quantities as emotion and *zeitgeist*, and for this reason are perhaps better understood by the social historian or the novelist than by the economist or the demographer.[7] Nevertheless, any economic discussion of the human dimensions of Soviet economic performance which ignores this ephemeral area would be critically incomplete, and almost certainly misleading. Indications of the nature of the motivation situation in the U.S.S.R. may be seen in labor relations policy, consumption and health statistics, and may also be gleaned from less official but more evocative sources of information.

Human Numbers

Like other more industrial countries, the U.S.S.R. has witnessed a gradual aging and a continual net urbanization of its population over the past thirty years, and has seen aggregated rates of fertility and natural increase drop. In many respects, however, the postwar demographic history of the Soviet Union is unique, and promises to continue to be so. Planners and policymakers in the U.S.S.R. consequently face a number of demographic challenges that are unfamiliar to their counterparts in developed, market-oriented societies.

Economic imbalances relating to the Soviet pattern of urbanization are one set of population-driven concerns. Although the phrase "Soviet urbanization" often brings to mind the industrialization drive of the 1930s, the fact of the matter is that the growth of the cities is principally a postwar phenomenon. Between 1950 and 1980, according to Rapawy and Baldwin's estimates,[8] the fraction of the Soviet population living in urban areas rose from 39 to 63 percent. In absolute terms, this was a rise of almost 97 million people, out of total increase in the urban population of about 130 million since the start of the First Five-Year Plan in 1928.

When cities grow, the task of feeding them grows as well. Indeed, demands placed on agriculture for surplus food may increase more rapidly than the urban population, since city people the world over generally have higher incomes and greater political influence—hence greater scope for the articulation for their demands—than country people. In postwar U.S.S.R., the pace of urbanization has not been matched by improvements in agricultural productivity, despite expensive and ambitious efforts to invigorate this lagging sector.

As an array of careful studies by Western analysts and scholars have by now made clear, Soviet agriculture's disappointing performance in the recent past is less a matter of bad weather than bad policy. Policy problems can make themselves felt through a broad array of intermediaries, especially in a planned economy. While many difficulties in the Soviet food system are manifest through the transportation system and through pricing/allocation mechanisms, others make their impact through the agencies of demographics.

The U.S.S.R.'s rural population has been declining since the 1950s, and at an accelerating pace: in the 1970s alone the Soviet countryside lost about 7 million inhabitants. But the process of selective outmigration has tended to remove from the *kolkhoz* precisely those groups whose productivity in farmwork might be expected to be highest. By the late 1970s, older women were the typical *kolkhoz* workers; scarcely 20 percent of the collective farm labor force was made up of "able-bodied men" (the designation for those between 15 and 59).[9]

Developed, market-oriented societies currently face serious economic problems associated with the aging of their populations. In West Germany, where the situation is most pronounced, current projections suggest there will be only two people of working age (20–65) for every person of retirement age (over 65) by the beginning of the twenty-first century.[10] In the Soviet Union, this particular dilemma is less acute. According to Rapawy and Baldwin's projections, the ratio of those over 65 to those 20–65 will be about one to seven in the year 2000. Even if current Soviet retirement ages (60 for men, 55 for women) are not raised, the ratio of "able-bodied" to "retirement" populations promises to be on the order of three to one. In any event, the economic burden implied by these numbers might be expected to weigh lighter than it would in the West, since Soviet pensions are rather modest and a significant fraction of senior citizens (today, perhaps half of all men and a third of all women) supplement this income by continuing to work.

Prospective Soviet manpower problems are of a different nature. In part, as Goodman and Schleifer note,[11] they stem from the success of past efforts to expand the workforce. Cohort for cohort, Soviet labor force participation ratios are among the highest in the world for both men and women. With a pronounced slowdown in the growth of the "able-bodied" population already underway, and likely to last until at least the mid-1990s, substantial additions to the labor force can only be obtained from still higher participation rates. Yet there appear to be few remaining sources which might be tapped without raising other economic difficulties. Further incorporation of teenagers into the workforce, for example, would seem to raise tradeoffs between the output of youths today and the future contributions that might be offered by better trained adults, while increased female participation in the labor force might prove inconsistent with fertility levels necessary for growth in the future.[12]

The essence of this difficulty is that the U.S.S.R. has in many ways maintained a labor-intensive development strategy well past the point where economic growth could be significantly stimulated by putting idle manpower to work. Simple arithmetic would suggest that if the Soviet economy is to meet the Eleventh Five-Year Plan, it will be necessary not only to maintain a high level of labor productivity among new entrants to the workforce, but also to improve the productivity of the men and women already at work. As Goodman and Schleifer indicate, the pattern of past manpower policies is such that there is plenty of room for such improvements from even the purely technical perspective. Approximately half of the U.S.S.R.'s industrial labor force, for example, is still engaged principally in manual labor.

In a multi national entity like the U.S.S.R., demographic and economic problems can go undetected if aggregates and averages are not separated into component parts. Culturally, linguistically, educationally, and economically, there are differences in the Soviet Union between the predominant Russian national group and the more than one hundred other officially recognized ethnicities. In demographic terms, the most important distinction is the one separating the U.S.S.R.'s European populations from its nationalities of Muslim origin. This distinction seems to complicate the process of managing manpower problems and planning for economic growth.

As Feshbach[13] notes, the Soviet "Muslim" population is probably over 45 million people today; this is more than the entire populations of Egypt or Iran, and only slightly less than Turkey's. Like similar ethnic groups on the other side of the Soviet Union's southern border, the U.S.S.R.'s "Muslims" have high rates of fertility. Where Russians, Ukrainians, Estonians and other European nationalities appear to be at "sub-replacement" fertility, Tadzhiks, Uzbeks, Turkmen and other "Muslim" peoples typically seem to have five children or more. (Only 1 percent of the RSFSR's Russians live in families of seven or more; this compares with 43 percent of Uzbekistan's Uzbeks.) With the exception of the Azeris, the Tatars, and a few smaller groups, the U.S.S.R.'s people of Muslim origin appear to have broken the "law" of demographic transition. Despite demonstrable progress in health care, literacy, per capita income, and other indices of social well-being over the past two generations, they have maintained their pre-industrial regimen of births. As both Feshbach and Rapawy/Baldwin point out, birth rates in several Central Asian republics are estimated to have increased between 1950 and 1980.[14] Falling birth rates for the U.S.S.R.'s Central Asian "Muslims" are to be found only in projections about the future.

As a result of differential rates of population growth, the ratio of "Muslims" to Russians has been changing with surprising speed. In 1959, there were about five Russians for every person of Muslim heritage in the U.S.S.R.. By 1979, the ratio was down to about three to one. By the turn of the century, given the likelihood of near-zero population growth for the Slavic nationalities, a ratio of two to one seems possible. Even more striking is Feshbach's projection that the 0–9 cohort might contain almost as many children of Muslim as of Russian descent by the year 2000. For political reasons, one would anticipate that educational policies, linguistic measures, and other means of promoting "assimilation" among this growing group of peoples will assume greater importance over the coming decades.

One need not wait until the twenty-first century, however, to identify economic repercussions from the "Muslim" pattern of population growth. Of the new entrants to the Soviet labor force over the rest of this decade and through the early 1990s, approximately 90 percent will come from Central Asian republics and Kazakhstan. In the U.S.S.R. ethnic groups and national republics do not overlap perfectly; indeed, as Feshbach remarks, almost a quarter of the Soviet Union's "Muslims" live in the Russian republic. Although figures on population growth by nationality are considerably more difficult to obtain than on growth by physical location, it appears that 90 percent or possibly even more of the increment in the Soviet labor force over the next decade will be accounted for by workers of Muslim origin.

For planners intent upon boosting rates of economic output, this situation creates special challenges. Despite improvements in the quality of education in "Southern tier" republics over the past three decades, young adults of Muslim background still seem to lag in training and work skills behind their European counterparts. Moreover, they have shown little inclination to move out of their native republics and into the regions of projected manpower shortage: Western Siberia and the Soviet Far East.[15] Rather, they have demonstrated a desire to remain in their own communities, even when by official measures migration would appear to be more economically rewarding.[16]

Upon inspection, the U.S.S.R.'s postwar urbanization appears not as an homogeneous, but rather as an ethically differentiated phenomenon. While Slavs and other European peoples tended to move, peoples of Muslim origin tended to remain in the countryside. In Turkmenistan, there appears to have been no increase in the rate of urbanization over the 1970s; in Tadzhikistan, the fraction of people living in cities appears actually to have dropped. Elsewhere in Soviet Central Asia, marginal increments in urbanization rates appear to have much to do with in-migration from other republics. In many rural "Muslim" regions there are signs of apparent labor redundancy, including comparatively low and declining measure of days officially worked per year and hours officially worked per day. If the population continues to grow rapidly in rural "Muslim" areas, and if Soviet "Muslim" migration patterns remain distinctive, Soviet policymakers will have to think seriously about new directions in regional development policy. Since such a re-orientation would quite clearly mean adopting a "second-choice" strategy, with the corresponding risk of slower economic growth, Soviet authorities will have reason to pay increasing attention to the complex subject of differentiated population policy over the coming years.

"Human Capital"

"Human capital" is a complex fabric of varied construction, but in all societies and for all individuals a dominant strand in it is health. Health is not only a universally desired personal attribute, valued for its own sake, but also a productive quantity in the economic equation. Improved health increases the vitality of a population, extending potential worklives and reducing the losses that come from illness or debilitation. Good health makes it easier for children and adults alike to retain the lessons of education and pick up new skills. Poor health and sickness impose a range of economic costs upon families even when health care is provided free of charge by the state. In the national economy, health problems are associated with the loss of economic potential, and reduced growth. Severe health problems—those affecting mortality as well as morbidity rates—not only constrain labor productivity, but also limit national production by altering the growth of the labor force and the shape of the age pyramid.

In the years immediately following World War II, the U.S.S.R. registered remarkably rapid improvements in general health standards. According to Soviet data, life expectancy stood at 48 in 1939; by 1954, it was put at 62, and by the late 1950s it was estimated to be very close to 70.[17] In barely twenty years, it appeared that the U.S.S.R. had matched sixty years of American and Western European health progress. Then, a dramatic and highly unusual reversal seems to have taken place. By the mid-1960s, the Soviet lifespan was no longer increasing. By the early 1970s, it had apparently entered into decline.

Much is still unclear about this deterioration in health conditions, including its precise dimensions. Since the mid-1970s the Central Statistical Administration has grown increasingly reticent about mortality for the Soviet Union as a whole, and in individual republics in particular. However, in the early 1970s, when age-specific mortality rates were still being published annually, rising death rates were characteristic of infants, older women, and almost all male cohorts over age 20.

One attempt to update Soviet life expectancy figures on the basis of the fragmentary and incomplete evidence currently available is presented in the Rapawy/Baldwin paper. According to these U.S. Census Bureau estimates, life expectancy for men has fallen by about five years (from 67 to 62) since 1964, and has dropped by about three years (from 76 to 73) for women. If these are accurate, life expectancy in the U.S.S.R. has undergone a secular decline during the Brezhnev era, and is now almost four years lower than it was in the early 1960s. Soviet life expectancy, in fact, may be lower in the early 1980s than it had been in the late 1950s.

Little information is currently available on the ethnic differentials behind the Soviet mortality increase, but Rapawy and Baldwin's figures suggest surprising differences in life expectancy between Republics in the mid-1970s. As might be anticipated, estimates for the least developed Central Asian republic—Kirgiziya, Tadzhikistan, and Turkemenia were lowest, corresponding roughly with life expectancy for Lebanon (66).[18] But life spans appeared to be longest in Georgia and Armenia (73 and over); only there would life expectancies appear to be comparable with contemporary levels for North America and much of Western Europe. Interestingly, life expectancy in the RSFSR is estimated to be closer to Central Asian than to Caucasian levels; in fact, at 68, they would be the same as in Uzbekistan. The magnitude of the RSFSR's health difficulties in the 1970s are suggested by the fact that Census Bureau estimates for male life expectancy at birth are higher for Mexico.

Mounting health difficulties can be expected to affect labor productivity;

in the U.S.S.R., they have been sufficiently pronounced to alter labor force growth. Both Soviet and Western demographers have remarked on the surprisingly slow pace at which the U.S.S.R.'s sex ratio is being restored to its pre war level, and in recent years, as Feshbach notes,[19] population projections for the year 2000 have been revised steadily downwards. In large measure, both phenomena relate to unexpected and uneven increases in age-specific mortality. Although Western analysts have yet to quantify the impact of this new pattern of "disinvestment" on the performance of the Soviet economy, there can be no doubt that health problems have contributed consequentially to the economic slowdown of the past fifteen years.

To check and reverse a decline in health levels for broad segments of the population, Soviet decisionmakers must understand the proximate, and underlying, causes of increased age-specific mortality. The etiology of increasing mortality undoubtedly differs by age group. Feshbach mentions a recent Soviet study in which 6 percent of the seven-year-olds examined in Leningrad were found to be suffering from rickets and hypertrophy. These children were born in the 1970s, not the postwar years, and were living in one of the U.S.S.R.'s model cities. Reports such as this one (there are, unfortunately, others) make it injudicious to rule out malnutrition as a cause of increasing health difficulties for infants and children.

For adults, the principal proximate cause of mortality increase is known: it is the rise in cardiovascular disease. As Feshbach points out, death rates associated with heart and circulatory system ailments have approximately doubled since the early 1960s.

Cardiovascular disease can be caused or exacerbated by a number of lifestyle characteristics, including lack of exercise, imbalanced diet, smoking, and stress. It is also related to alcoholism. In the U.S.S.R., increasing alcohol consumption—and especially use of hard liquor—may go far in accounting for rising mortality. Purchasing power has substantially increased since the 1950s, and intoxicants have proved to be strongly superior goods. According to estimates produced by Gertrude Schroeder and Imogene Edwards, over a sixth of the average Soviet household budget goes to hard liquor (as against 1 to 6 percent in Western nations).[20] And V. G. Treml has ventured a guess, based on his research into the Soviet alcohol economy, that a quarter or more of the families in "Slavic" republics currently spend over a third of their income on spirits.[21] While no surveys are available in the West against which this speculation might be checked, Feshbach does show that official Soviet reports indicate more is spent on drink than clothing in Latvia, and that half of the U.S.S.R.'s hospital beds in 1978 were occupied by patients with alcohol-related illnesses.

Even for illnesses that are in some sense self-inflicted, mortality and morbidity can be reduced by effective health care intervention. As Christopher Davis makes clear,[22] the Soviet health system has expanded substantially since the mid-1960s. Between 1965 and 1980, health sector employment rose by 40 percent, and the fraction of health workers in the labor force increased from 5.3 to 5.6 percent. Encounters between health workers and the public also increased, with annual per capita visits jumping from 6.8 in 1965 to 9.8 in 1978. Unfortunately, these changes were not sufficient to prevent deterioration of general health conditions.

Why was the health system's response not more effective? Davis' paper provides some clues. It appears, for example, that the Soviet health strategy remained largely labor-intensive. At a time when health problems and health sector employment were increasing, the share for health in the official budget was falling (from 6.5 percent in 1965 to 5.0 percent in 1978). As a consequence, medical sector wages dropped from 82 to 75 percent of the national average, making medical workers one of the lowest paid groups on the Soviet occupational scale.

Davis hints that the U.S.S.R. may have an intellectual problem with the health sector: since it does not create tangible goods, it is relegated to the "nonproductive sphere," in planning classifications. But the performance of the health system may also be affected by more practical concerns. One of these is a tendency to compartmentalize services by status group. As Davis emphasizes, there is actually a multiplicity of health care systems in the Soviet Union. Besides the "public" system, there is one for the Ministry of Defense, the KGB, the MVD, and Ministry of Railroads, and of course the Fourth Main Administration for ranking citizens and political figures. With health services secure for occupations and individuals judged especially important to operations of state, the general and far more massive expenditures necessary to upgrade health care quality in the rest of the system may appear to be a matter of less immediate political urgency.

The tendency of government to economize on public services that augment human capital when budgets are tight is not limited to the U.S.S.R. Within the U.S.S.R., it is apparently not limited to the health care system. Gertrude Schroeder estimates that per capita expenditures on health actually fell in 1981. She also estimates growth in educational expenditures to have been significantly less rapid than the growth of overall consumption in the 1970s, although consumption growth was slowing down. Restrictions on human service allocations can be prompted by increased efficiency of expenditure or technical advances which shift returns schedules upwards. Unfortunately, there is little evidence of either in the U.S.S.R.'s public services today. It seems more likely that Soviet decisionmakers have opted for a financial convenience whose economic consequences will only be felt gradually.

The U.S.S.R. is the first industrialized nation to experience secular peacetime decline in its life expectancy. It may, however, no longer be alone. According to official figures, life expectancy in rural Poland fell by more than a year between the mid-1970s and the early 1980s.[23] In Czechoslovakia and Hungary, life expectancy for men was slightly lower in 1979 than it had been in 1964.[24] It may only be a coincidence that these four nations are all in the Soviet bloc. Eastern Europe's current health situation has not been examined in detail by Western scholars (1982); as yet little has been written on the components and causes of these apparent increases in mortality rates.* The seeming deterioration of health in Eastern Europe may yet turn out to be merely a statistical artifact. If it is not, the implications of what would be a fundamentally new trend in health patterns would seem extremely worrisome and far-reaching.

Human Motivation

In Western nations, the role of human motivation in economic performance remains a sensitive and controversial subject. Personal or national attitudes can seldom be associated with economic results precisely; consequently, generalizations about willingness to work or innate cleverness have often proved to be a breeding ground for uninformed prejudices. At the same time, informed managers have often recognized that output depends upon much more than the allocation of resources.[25] Managerial research has consistently validated this insight; variations in motivation and performance occur not only within individual shops, but also between otherwise similar firms, industries, and economies. In its study of the British auto industry, for example, the Central Policy Review Staff concluded that attitudinal factors were the principal cause of the U.K.'s poor performance; even when educational levels were equivalent and factory equipment was identical, British autoworkers produced half as much per shift as their counterparts on the continent.[26] Just as important as the recognition that motivation-related differences in performance exist, however, is the understanding that these are not immutable. Public and private sector managers in Western nations have set themselves to improving individual and collective performance through a wide variety of financial and nonpecuniary policies.

The question of motivation is no less important in Socialist than in capitalist economies. For Socialist nations, however, the answers must be

*Chapter 10, "Health Of An Empire," examines this phenomenon in greater detail.

sensitive to Marxist-Leninist theory and the politics of central planning. By definition, the ultimate objective of all Marxist-Leninist governments must be the attainment of communism. In Communist society, material reward and personal effort are not meant to correspond directly; instead, the individual's contribution is to be stimulated by commitment to a system which is guaranteeing the satisfaction of the needs of all. In the process of constructing Socialism, however, planners in a Marxist system must in theory take care to see that the structural incentives for improved productivity do not strengthen "capitalist" tendencies within society, for this would only complicate and delay the task of achieving communism.[27] Thus, the complex task of shaping incentives may be further complicated by the knowledge that certain incentives are ideologically or politically impermissible.

The Soviet Union's progress in mobilizing its population to more efficient individual performance is described in part by Goodman and Schleifer, and is the subject of Blair Ruble's paper on Soviet labor unions.[28] Important aspects of the Soviet motivation question are also highlighted by Gertrude Schroeder's review of Soviet living standards.[29]

Described on paper, Soviet labor unions might sound functionally similar to the labor unions of Japan: both bear simultaneous responsibility for protecting a wide range of workers' rights and improving labor productivity. In theory, this would seem to augur well for Soviet economic performance: in Japan, after all, the labor movement is widely believed to have been instrumental in facilitating increases in economic efficiency.[30] Yet viewed in practice, there are also enormous differences in the environments in which Japanese and Soviet labor unions operate. Whatever the origins of the modern Japanese labor ethic, the impetus for improved union productivity is reinforced by the workings of the domestic labor market. Approximately two-thirds of the Japanese non-farm work force does not belong to unions; instead, contrary to popular American belief, they typically work in small firms where pressure upon wages can be intense and employment security—including unemployment insurance—is minimal.[31] Japan's labor union performance is thus conditioned by the understanding that it is a protected sector in a dynamic and highly competitive economy.

In contrast with Japan, over 98 percent of the U.S.S.R.'s non-farm work force belongs to state-run unions. These unions operate in an economy in which improved sectoral performance is to be achieved through parallel development with—rather than direct competition against—the international market economy, and in which costs of production are seen as only one of several factors that determine the evolution of industrial structure. Union members perform in an environment in which the labor laws of the

Stalinist era have been noticeably relaxed. As Ruble notes, criminal sanctions against labor indiscipline were removed in 1956; truancy and absenteeism no longer figure in the Soviet penal code.

Positive incentives, however, do not seem to have satisfactorily filled the space left open by the repeal of penalties. The "human relations" approach to labor problems, which was of great interest to Soviet managers in the 1960s and 1970s, does not seem to have yielded the results that were desired. As Ruble points out, the consequence has been a growing perception on the part of Soviet managers that motivation and discipline are on the wane in the work force. While this perception may be partly attributed to nostalgia or unrealistic hopes from earlier periods, it does indicate that the current labor productivity situation, for whatever reasons, is becoming increasingly unsatisfactory to a large number of the officials who must implement production plans.

In fairness, there is much in the press that would seem to justify managerial discontent. According to *Literaturaya Gazeta*, for example, a spot check of Moscow department stores a few years ago revealed that over half of the sales personnel on duty were intoxicated.[32] The Soviet press, of course, must instruct as well as inform. But if stories like this one reflect widespread tendencies, the challenges facing managers are indeed increasing.

Faced with what appears to have been judged a failure of incentives, Soviet labor policy appears to be inching cautiously back toward directives. As Goodman and Schleifer point out, the Soviet government is again becoming more directly involved in the allocation of labor within the economy, and is reinstituting certain civil penalties against worker malfeasance.

The Soviet debate about incentives, control, and labor productivity is continuing. Aspects of this debate are strangely reminiscent of arguments that shaped British colonial policy almost half a century ago. In those days, many foreign observers feared that the supply curve for indigenous labor was "backward-bending": in other words, that "natives" would do less work if wage rates rose. Others argued that labor supply and productivity problems could be eased through "inducement goods." Money, they argued, was not useful to wage earners unless there were products to buy with it; thus, labor productivity would be determined not only by capital investment, but also by the quality and availability of consumer goods that might "induce" natives to work in the monetized sector.[33]

To those who emphasize the inducements of consumerism, living standards—and expectations about living standards—are an integral element in determining worker productivity. It is extraordinarily difficult for Westerners to assess living standards in Socialist economies. In the West, quality, convenience, and availability are typically reflected in the market price of merchandized goods. In the Soviet Union, a full understanding of living standards requires knowledge about shortages and queues, shadow markets and the economics of favors. When Gertrude Schroeder suggests that Soviet living standards, in material terms, are currently at about two-thirds the Italian level, it is important to realize that this does not mean that residents of provinces south of Rome might be indifferent when choosing between their baskets of goods, delivered as market economies deliver their produce, and the Soviet basket of goods delivered through the various Soviet channels of distribution. Instead, this is a statement about how much material wellbeing the Soviet economy would provide consumers if it behaved like a market economy—a rather breathtaking "if."

Intertemporal comparisons of living standards within the U.S.S.R. are less subject to ambiguity, although they are nevertheless complicated by both conceptual and statistical difficulties. There is little doubt that the Soviet consumer was considerably better off materially in the early 1980s than in the 1950s. By Schroeder's estimate, per capita "consumption" in the U.S.S.R. has nearly tripled since 1950, with the availability of food-stuffs doubling and consumer durables multiplying by a factor of fourteen. Yet despite this improvement, Schroeder argues that the consumer sector is characterized by "massive desequilibria." Moreover, annual changes in consumption, though still positive by her reckoning, have decelerated sharply since the mid-1960s. She implies that the quality of food is declining, and that "creeping inflation" not registered by official indices may be widespread.

Goodman and Schleifer go further: they refer to "widespread pessimism" among workers about prospects for raising living standards. For this to be so, workers would have to believe one or more of the following propositions: (1) that official estimates of consumption growth substantially overstate progress in the past; (2) that past progress is not a reliable guide to prospects for the future; (3) that today's food shortages and economic difficulties are not merely transient aberrations.

Over the past two years Western visitors have made much of the scarcity of preferred foods in Soviet shops and the reinstitution of food rationing in the big cities.[34] Yet such events would seem likely to prove transitory, in part because they are so very conspicuous. On the other hand, many of the economic trends of the past twenty years, though less commonly remarked upon, would seem to signal that, despite the achievements of the past generation, prospects for consumers are no longer as bright as in the heyday of "goulash Communism."[35]

As Schroeder and Edwards have written, "remarkably little progress toward a modern pattern (of consumption) has been made in recent decades" despite substantial increases in purchasing power. Engel's law seems to have been suspended; the fraction of the Soviet household's budget devoted to foodstuffs and beverages is still over 40 percent—almost exactly the same as in the early 1960s.

Concomitant to that stasis in consumption patterns has been a sudden and rapid change in saving patterns. Between 1975 and the early 1980s, according to the Defense Information Agency, household savings have been increasing by 11 percent a year.[36] As Gregory Grossman has demonstrated elsewhere,[37] financial assets of Soviet households, according to official statistics, rose by 60 percent between the end of 1976 and the end of 1981, even though nominal disposable income appears to have risen by less than 20 percent. In large part, the rapid rise in savings rates appears to be a response to shortages of consumer goods in the official markets. It may also speak to the growing importance of an unofficial economy for goods and services, and for which households need to maintain contingent cash balances.[38] That consumers are experiencing increasing difficulties with official marketing and distribution channels is substantiated further by the increasingly common tendency, mentioned by Goodman and Schleifer, to supply food to workers directly through their factories, and by a semantic change in the Soviet language which has been noted by both emigres and Soviet commentators: whereas consumers used by "buy" (kupit') goods and services, they now "acquire" (dostat') them.[39]

The enfeeblement of the consumer sector would seem to be a systemic setback for central economic planning: with the growth of an underground economy and diminishing public confidence in the utility of official currency or markets, it would be increasingly difficult to direct labor or encourage efficiency through planned prices and other officially determined economic signals. Yet at the same time, there is evidence that the consumer sector's difficulties relate not only to the implementation routine, but also to an official attitude toward consumer blandishments which is at best ambivalent.

Although an unusually low fraction of the U.S.S.R.'s output is directed into consumption, this by itself is no proof of a bias against consumers: Japan, a consumer society if ever there was one, seems to have much the same breakdown of resources between consumption and non-consumption sectors. More telling has been the official response to anticipated changes in consumer purchasing power. Despite the primacy of food and drink among consumer concerns and the longstanding Russian fondness for socializing, Soviet authorities have provided only 100,000 public dining facilities for the entire U.S.S.R.—one-quarter as many as in the United States. Despite the almost universal preference for convenience food, only a quarter of the foodstuffs sold in Soviet markets in 1977 were packaged.[40] And in a society in which Soviet women must serve not only as wage earners and goods gatherers, but also as housekeepers, the household appliance industry has been allowed to stagnate: one Soviet source estimated that only 15 percent of the housework in the U.S.S.R. was mechanized, against its estimate of 80 percent for the United States.[41] There may be an unintended symbolism in the well-known Soviet practice of producing consumer durables as side operations in plants built for and geared toward heavy industry.

It may not be premature to ask whether the Brezhnev regime has had a political problem with consumerism. Long ago Oscar Lange argued that there is no technical reason why publicly managed economies should be less successful in meeting consumer needs than market-oriented systems.[42] Nevertheless, it is possible to imagine a number of practical dilemmas which consumerism might pose to a Marxist-Leninist government. The most basic of these dilemmas concerns the role of the Communist Party. If consumer preferences were to determine the development of the economy, then the purpose, and even the legitimacy, of Party primacy could be exposed to doubt. As long as the Communist Party remains the vanguard of the struggle for Socialism and embodies the collective wisdom of the masses, economic forces which constrain it from pursuing its objectives will be regarded with suspicion by many leading officials.

Concluding Comments and Speculations

The Soviet Union's current population problems, its health difficulties and its apparent failure to meet consumer expectations are matters of interest both within the U.S.S.R. and outside it. These "human" problems are fundamentally new to the Soviet Union; they are associated with the most recent stage in Soviet life—although causal links are far from certain. Nevertheless, the historical significance of these difficulties is surely not lost on either leaders or citizens in the U.S.S.R.; they come during the first protracted period of international security and domestic tranquility that the Soviet state has ever enjoyed.

In the Marxist-Leninist ontology, the notion of "historical stages" assumes tremendous importance; analyses of a given society's stage of historical development are often seen to serve as guides for policy. It is possible to argue that the Soviet Union has entered a unique, and only poorly understood, "historical stage": having been in operation for 60 years, it has seen three generations of citizens raised under the aegis of Socialism—as the state has defined the term. Of the U.S.S.R.'s 270 million inhabitants, over 240 million have known only the Soviet system; within a generation there will be no popular memory of life before the CPSU. The "New Soviet Man" may already have been created. If so, certain responsibilities common to all entrenched, ambitious, and historic systems of governance may now be weighing on the centrally planned economy of the U.S.S.R.

The current generation of Soviet adults were raised during the time of Khrushchev. To many, Khrushchev seemed a leader with a genuine faith in the ability of the Soviet state to lead the Nation to the Communist stage of development. Indeed, in 1961 Khrushchev made a public pledge that the U.S.S.R. would achieve communism by 1980. By his estimation, the nation was in the midst of the "rapid building of communism." By 1980, Khrushchev's successors had instead adopted more cautious and business-like description of their nation: a "developed socialist society."[43] Memory often plays an active role in shaping morale, expectations, and ultimately the economic behavior of individuals; it is possible that this shift in perceptions has had tangible economic consequences.

Historical factors incumbent upon Soviet socialism might also affect the economic performance of individuals more directly. As Theodore W. Schultz has noted, economic growth occurs in the context of disequilibrium, and the productivity of individuals is directly affected by their ability to deal with disequilibrium.[44] For the environment in which Soviet workers and consumers find themselves, maximizing household welfare may depend as much upon an ability to deal with social and political disequilibria as with economic disequilibria. The macroeconomic implications of such a microeconomic tradition merit examination.

The problems of human economics presently facing Soviet leaders seem formidable. Current arrangements have not to date proved capable of resolving manpower and consumer problems, reversing the deterioration in health conditions, or stemming the decline in total factor productivity. But this should not be taken to mean that these tasks are beyond the competence of the Soviet system. Western analysts have always had difficulty predicting Soviet performance in the face of challenges. The U.S.S.R.'s record for meeting challenges—as the CPSU's leadership has identified them—is impressive. Indeed, in a fundamental sense the Soviet state appears to be a problem-oriented apparatus. It is likely that the eventual successors to the Brezhnev generation will want to respond to the "human" problems that have emerged in the years since the ouster of Khrushchev. Their efficacy in doing so will have repercussions on more than individual economic performance.

This article originally published in U.S. Congress Joint Economic Committee, *Soviet Economy In the 1980s: Problems and Prospects* (Washington: Government Printing Office, 1983). Reprinted with permission.

Notes

1. Lenin himself drew explicit connection between the global demographic balance and the triumph of socialism. See, for example, "Better Fewer, But Better," in V.I. Lenin, *Selected Works* (Moscow: Foreign Languages Publishing House, 1947), Vol. II.
2. U.S. Congress Joint Economic Committee, *Allocation of Resources in the Soviet Union and China—1981* (Washington: Government Printing Office, 1982).
3. Calculated from Stanley H. Cohn, "The Soviet Path to Economic Growth: A Comparative Analysis," *Review of Income and Wealth,* March 1976, and Abram Bergson, "Soviet Economic Slowdown And The 1981–85 Plan," *Problem of Communism,* May–June 1981.
4. Herbert S. Levine, "Possible Causes of the Deterioration of Soviet Productivity Growth in the Period 1976–80," U.S. Congress Joint Economic Committee, *Soviet Economy in the 1980s: Problems and Prospects* (Washington: Government Printing Office, 1983).
5. See, for example, Murray Feshbach, "Between the Lines of the 1979 Soviet Census," *Problems of Communism,* January–February 1982.
6. For a clear exposition of this problem, see Mark Blaug, *An Introduction to the Economics of Education* (Harmondsworth, England: Penguin Books, 1976).
7. Some students of the Soviet economy have extracted useful insights into the workings of the U.S.S.R.'s economy from Soviet literature. The master of this art was Alexander Gerschenkron. See "A Neglected Source of Economic Information on Soviet Russia" and "Reflections on Soviet Novels" in his *Economic Backwardness in Historical Perspective* (Cambridge: Harvard University Press, 1966).
8. Stephen Rapawy and Godfrey Baldwin, "Demographic Trends in the Soviet Union: 1950–2000," in *Soviet Economy in the 1980s, loc. cit.*
9. See Ann Lane, "U.S.S.R.: Private Agriculture on Center Stage," in *Soviet Economy in the 1980s, loc. cit.*
10. Calculated from Deutscher Bundestag Drucksache, *Bericht Über Bevölkerungsentwicklung Im BRD* (Bonn: Statistiches Budesamt, 1980).
11. Ann Goodman and Geoffrey Schleifer, "Soviet Labor Markets in the 1980s," in *Soviet Economy in the 1980s, loc. cit.*
12. These issues are explored in more detail in Cynthia Weber and Ann Goodman, "The Demographic Policy Debate in the USSR," *Population and Development Review,* June 1981.
13. Murray Feshbach, "Trends in the Soviet Muslim Population—Demographic Aspects," in *Soviet Economy in the 1980s, loc. cit.*
14. An increase in the birth rate, of course, does not necessarily imply increase in total fertility rates. Changes in age structure can raise the ratio of births to population even as age-specific fertility rates are declining.
15. See Murray Feshbach, "Prospects For Outmigration From Central Asia and Kazakhstan During the Next Decade," in U.S. Congress, Joint Economic Committee, *Soviet Economy in a Time of Change* (Washington: Government Printing Office, 1979).
16. There are serious difficulties in using official measures of production, consumption and income to judge actual standards of living in the U.S.S.R. These problems seem to be most pronounced in the Central Asian republics. See

Nancy Lubin, *Labor and Nationalisty in Soviet Central Asia* (London: Macmillan, 1985) for a detailed and illuminating discussion of these limitations.

17. *Vestnik Statistiki,* various issues.
18. Estimates in this paragraph are drawn from U.S. Bureau of the Census, *World Population: 1979* (Washington: Department of Commerce, 1979).
19. Murray Feshbach, "Issues in Soviet Health Problems," in *Soviet Economy in the 1980s, loc. cit.*
20. Gertrude E. Schroeder and Imogene Edwards, *Consumption in the USSR: An International Comparison* (Washington: U.S. Congress, Joint Economic Committee, 1982).
21. Vladimir G. Treml, "Alcohol in the Soviet Underground Economy," in Gregory Grossman, ed., *Studies In The Second Economy of Communist Countries* (Berkeley: University of California Press).
22. Christopher Davis, "The Economics of the Soviet Health System," in *Soviet Economy in the 1980s, loc. cit.*
23. *Christian Science Monitor,* March 11, 1982.
24. *Population Index,* Winter 1981.
25. There is rich literature on the relationship between motivation and productivity. For an introduction to this, see Mason Haire, *Psychology In Management* (New York: McGraw-Hill Co., 1956).
26. Central Policy Review Staff, *The Future of the British Motor Car Industry* (London: Her Majesty's Stationery Office, 1975).
27. This argument is made eloquently in Alain Besancon, "Anatomy of a Specter," *Survey,* Autumn 1980.
28. Blair A. Ruble, "Soviet Trade Unions and Labor Relations After 'Solidarity,' " in *Soviet Economy in the 1980s, loc. cit.*
29. Gertrude E. Schroeder, "Soviet Living Standards: Achievements and Prospects," in *Soviet Economy in the 1980s, loc. cit.*
30. Such arguments can be found in Ezra Vogel, *Japan: Learning From Number One* (Cambridge: Harvard University Press, 1979).
31. Ernest van Helvoort, *The Japanese Working Man: What Choice? What Reward?* (Vancouver: University of British Columbia Press, 1979), and *The Economist,* February 23, 1980.
32. Cited in Vladimir G. Treml, *loc. cit.*
33. See for example Colin W. Newbury, "Historical Aspects of Manpower and Migration in Africa South of the Sahara," in Peter Duignan and L. H. Gann, eds., *Colonialism In Africa, vol. 4: The Economics of Colonialism* (Cambridge: Cambridge University Press, 1974).
34. See, for example, George Feifer, "Russian Disorders," *Harper's,* February 1981, and *Washington Post,* August 23 and September 2, 1981.
35. The change of sentiment is evident, among other places, in the unofficial literature emanating from the Soviet Union. Moods and expectations may only be measured imperfectly, but the differences between the society described in Aleksandr I. Solzhenitsyn's *The First Circle* (New York: Harper and Row, 1966) and in Alexander Zinoviev's *The Yawning Heights* (New York: Vintage Books, 1980) appear sufficiently pronounced to circumvent questions of calibrated measurement.
36. *Allocation Of Resources . . ., loc. cit.*
37. Gregory Grossman, "A Note on Soviet Inflation," in *Soviet Economy in the 1980s, loc. cit.*

38. This argument is made by Gregory Grossman in "The 'Shadow Economy' in the Socialist Sector of the USSR," an unpublished paper for the NATO Economics Colloquium held in Brussels in March 1982.
39. See Ilya Zemtsov, "The Ruling Class in the USSR" in the Israeli journal *Crossroads*, Winter 1979–Spring 1979; see also N. Samokhvalov, "Zolotye krokhi," *Sovetskaia Russiia*, April 12, 1980. (The latter is cited in Treml, *loc. cit.*)
40. Schroeder and Edwards, *loc. cit.*
41. *Ibid*.
42. Oscar Lange, "On the Economic Theory of Socialism," *Review Of Economic Studies*, October 1936 and February 1937.
43. Jerome M. Gilison, *The Soviet Image of Utopia* (Baltimore: Johns Hopkins University Press, 1975).
44. Theodore W. Schultz, "The Value of the Ability to Deal With Disequilibria," *Journal of Economic Literature*, April 1975.

4

Administering Utopia

Administrative policy in a communist setting is both an enormously demanding and an extremely complex business, for it must deal with a far broader, and more obviously contradictory, array of considerations than those that face the bourgeois states of the West. From a logical standpoint, the quest for total control over economy and society brings with it the burden of total responsibility: the supervisors of the planned economy must not only follow and adjust the prices of literally millions of goods but also attend as best they can to the complete material needs of their people. Under such conditions, domestic policy necessarily extends far beyond the genteel limits of "fine-tuning." Indeed, more than one totalitarian state has found it appropriate to attempt to regulate, through far-reaching birth-rate policies, the very pace at which new entrants are absorbed into society.

From a strategic standpoint, the communist state's domestic policy is inextricably linked into, and limited by, its foreign policy. As the commanders of a directed society struggle to maximize their freedom to direct, they find that setbacks abroad contribute to the pressure for concession and compromise on the home front, whereas successes in the international arena increase the opportunities for consolidating political control and forcing forward socioeconomic change at home. Indeed, the domestic policy of the communist state may be decisively shaped by the desire to project power beyond its own borders; since the international environment is usually turbulent, this makes for discontinuities.

From an ideological standpoint, the administrators of the communist apparatus are in the unenviable position of managing a system that is meant to be "objectively" infallible. The intellectual justification for party-led central planning is not merely aesthetic; proponents of this method of governance contend that it will move society toward the materialization of utopia more rapidly and effectively than any less ambitious policy. Consequently mistakes, setbacks, and "nonincremental adjustments" take on a special importance.

Finally, communist administrators must come to terms with the brutal, but quite unavoidable, fact that time works against them. The politics of unlimited ambition cannot be happily wedded to the mundane art of everyday management. As time passes, the strains in the relationship become ever more evident. It cannot be otherwise: over time a regime necessarily develops a track record, and for a system wishing a moral claim upon material perfection, a track record can only be extremely inconvenient. Indeed, in the final analysis history is the enemy of the totalitarian state. For memory is generated passively and spontaneously, and it serves as a relentless force of resistance against an all-encompassing government. Memory strikes at the ability of the totalitarian government to execute neat and effective tactical reversals in domestic policy; in a deeper sense, it frustrates the state's efforts to mobilize the people. (The cost of memory is surely apparent, for example, to the Kremlin today [1983]: how much easier it would be to manage that controlled society if the vast majority of the Soviet Union's adult population did not remember that Khrushchev had promised "Communism"—earthly paradise—by 1980).

As a result of these limits and contradictions, communist administrative policy demonstrates paradoxical qualities. For one thing, the tactical and the strategic aspects of domestic decisions are quite likely to be in conflict with each other. For another, the well-placed *apparatchik* is likely to have at once both more power at his disposal and less freedom to maneuver than his presumed counterpart in the West.

Western scholars often find it difficult to imagine, much less understand, the so-called decisionmaking environment of the communist policymaker, which means that studies of administrative action in communist nations are frequently disappointing. Westerners typically fall into one of two analytical traps. The first is to allow themselves to be taken in by the parlor tricks of "quantitative methodology." Unfortunately, in data analysis, as with other detective work, the evidence is no more reliable than the witness. State-provided numbers will not change their story, even under mechanical duress.

The second great danger is that one may be lost in a wilderness of "mirror imagery." It is natural to seek the familiar in an alien setting, and political organizations of all sorts look much more alike when they are reduced to paper than when they are observed in the wild. There *are* important similarities in decisionmaking and administration between communist governments and those we understand better. But to emphasize them, while ignoring the context in which decisions are made and the results that are expected, is to be deceived.

Two recent studies of the Soviet Union illustrate the difficulties scholars continue to encounter in bringing themselves to understand totalitarian administration. Jan Ake Dellenbrant assumes that modern methods of data analysis can extract special meaning from opaque Soviet statistics.[1] As a result of this misplaced faith, he largely divorces himself from reality even as he manipulates "real world" numbers. By contrast, Gordon B. Smith's collection on what he calls "public policy" in the U.S.S.R. pays special attention to organizational structure and the delegation of authority.[2] Unfortunately, the glare of mirror imagery impairs Smith's vision, and hence many of the insights that might be gleaned from his approach are either obscured or lost altogether.

Dellenbrant, to his credit, recognizes that policy cannot be judged in isolation from results. To evaluate the efficacy of the Soviet effort to mobilize politically and develop economically its fifteen republics, his *Soviet Regional Policy* assembles from regional Soviet statistical handbooks a "data set" of more than 6,500 "observations"—on such things as Komsomol membership, tractor-to-farmer ratios, and per capita housespace in the cities—for the years 1956 to 1973, and then applies regression analysis, factor analysis, and hierarchical cluster analysis to them. He concludes that both political mobilization and economic development have proceeded in the republics but that substantial differences remain.

This conclusion is unlikely to be challenged: it is a commonplace. On the other hand, Dellenbrant's use of numbers and models will draw criticism from those who have been initiated into the mysteries of statistics and will do more to mislead than enlighten the fledgling student of Soviet regional development. Dellenbrant presents nonsense-results (i.e., that hierarchical clustering schemes show Komsomol recruiting patterns to be similar in Uzbekistan and the Ukraine) with the solemnity customarily reserved for findings having significance. He places far too much trust in questionable Soviet numbers. Anyone who works with social statistics from the U.S.S.R. should know that these are often subject to *systematic* bias; systematic bias confounds the tools of applied probability. The per capita income numbers provided by Soviet handbooks, for example, simply do not provide, in and of themselves, a satisfactory standard for appraising differences either in productive capacity or in standards of living among the republics. Unless these are reworked, they are unsuitable for cardinal or ordinal analytical techniques. Nancy Lubin's excellent Oxford dissertation (published as *Labor and Nationality in Soviet Central Asia* by Macmillan in 1985) makes this point with some force and comes as a welcome corrective to blithe computer runs.

Perhaps most important, Dellenbrant appears to stumble on the interpretation of his printouts. He takes it for granted, for example, that a rise in a republic's level of Komsomol or Communist party membership means that political mobilization is proceeding apace. Yet surely this is not the only perspective available. Communist parties, after all are meant to be elite—not mass—organizations. Unless one is familiar with specifics, it would seem unwise to equate automatically political efficacy with growing membership rosters. One could just as easily conclude from such numbers that a government has been resorting to the expedience of debasing the currency of party membership in order to achieve short-term goals. We should remember that the pace of Soviet economic growth has steadily slowed and that the fraction of economic projects completed has steadily dropped over the past generation, even as "recruitment rates" have steadily risen. In this consistent with Dellenbrant's assertion that his study "shows that the theory [of social mobilization formulated for Western societies] may also be used for studying a Communist nation like the Soviet Union"?

Although Smith generally avoids the examination of numbers, his interpretation of administrative events in the U.S.S.R. may also be called into question. Smith finds the notion that the U.S.S.R. is a totalitarian state to be both objectionable and misleading; more to his taste is the concept of a "pluralist" Soviet Union, in which contending interest groups compete for influence. Indeed, in his estimate, the model that Soviet public administration follows should be quite familiar to Western political scientists, for "Soviet administration bears striking resemblance to that in many developing countries."

One must wonder what Smith has in mind here. If he is referring to the "striking resemblance" of government processes in the U.S.S.R. and (say) Cuba, Ethiopia, or the People's Democratic Republic of Yemen, he is of course correct. Yet, this similarity is quite readily explainable. If on the other hand he means to equate the Soviet bureaucracy with those of (say) Nigeria, India, or Mexico, he is indulging in something close to fantasy. While it is true that "Third World" bureaucracies, like the U.S.S.R.'s own, frequently seem plodding and incompetent to their critics, it should be clear that inefficiency can be caused by a very wide variety of administrative practices and social conditions. It is not a guiding principle of governance.

Smith is right to be distrustful of the casual use of such terms as "totalitarian" and "democratic." Such terms can be marshaled not only for descriptive but also for abusive purposes; as with Socrates' ideal forms, no earthly political system can be a pure and crystalline manifestation of a single essence. There are always shadows, imperfections, contradictions, and exceptions. This should not prevent us, however, from attempting to give political phenomena their proper names. "Pluralism" may be an emotionally appealing way to describe the Soviet bureaucracy, but it is sadly lacking as a description of the essence that animates the Soviet *apparat*. By virtue of the fact that people are not machines, that modern societies are complex, and that governments can never be omniscient or omnipotent—try as they might—a certain amount of "pluralism" and "authority leakage" can be found in any political system.

A close reading of the reminiscences of any Gulag survivor will demonstrate that there was "pluralism" and "authority leakage," in some sense, even in the day-to-day operations of those terrible camps. Yet the search for "pluralism" is obviously of limited use in attempting to explain, let alone predict, the workings of a political prison. To the NKVD, "authority leakage" within the Gulag was a necessary evil—a limiting consideration, rather than a key to strategy. Though conditions of life in the contemporary U.S.S.R. are obviously different from those in Stalin's Gulag, very similar principles about organization and command still apply. For this reason, manifestation of "pluralism" must be analyzed with greater caution, and with more attention to strategic considerations, than Smith demonstrates.

Smith vigorously disputes Zbigniew Brzezinski's thesis (in *Dilemmas of Change in Soviet Politics*) that the Soviet political edifice is beset by degeneration and decay. He sees little evidence of political ossification in the U.S.S.R. today. Quite the contrary. In Smith's view, the U.S.S.R.'s problems are much like those of other countries in the Western world with which we are familiar:

> Soviet administration appears to be meeting successfully some of the most pressing needs of Soviet society. The most significant shortcomings of Soviet administration appear to be due to the less developed and less uniformly developed nature of its economy and the absence of universally held sociocultural attitudes that support hard work, efficiency, and professionalism.

One may of course take issue with Brzezinski's particular formulation of the U.S.S.R.'s "dilemmas of change." Still, in light of the evidence that has emerged over the past decade on the economic condition of the U.S.S.R.—the declining and now actually negative contribution of productivity to Soviet economic advance; the continuing failure of the agricultural sector despite massive and expensive efforts to set it straight; the rising death rates for nearly every age cohort in the Union; and the evident reluctance of the Politburo to make hard decisions about any of the serious domestic problems with which it is confronted—Smith's pronouncements sound somewhat eccentric.

Smith would have us treat the Soviet Union as if it were a "developing nation." The theory of nation building, however, was devised as an analytical construct, not an academic pardon; while it might be used to *excuse* some of the U.S.S.R.'s present difficulties, it can do little to *explain* them. Unlike Ghana, Tanganyika, or any of the other "new nations" upon which political scientists turned their attentions twenty years ago, the Union of Soviet Socialist Republics is a work that has been in progress for something like sixty years. Its current social, economic, and political problems, moreover, are not recurrent and familiar ones. They are fundamentally new.

To fit his picture of the Soviet administration and bureaucratic policy to the lenses he prefers, Smith finds it necessary to exclude a certain amount of background scenery. None of the essays in his collection deals with foreign policy or domestic economic policy, even though it may be argued that these are the overwhelming preoccupations of the Soviet political apparatus. Nor do they deal with the actual results of policies implemented. For the most part, these essays confine themselves to an examination or organizational "inputs"; some, in fact, do not go much beyond a perusal of official statements of intentions and an outline of the bureaucratic flowchart.

Smith's own chapter in *Public Policy and Administration in the Soviet Union* on the Soviet legal system, for instance, relies heavily upon a detailing of the Soviet legal system as it is meant to work, on paper, and takes some pains to inform the reader of changes in the recent Soviet constitution. Yet surely there is more to Soviet legality than this. To appreciate the workings of *any* legal system, one must know something not only about theory but also about praxis. In functional terms, this means finding out something about—to mention only a few things—the fraction of violations that are identified and followed up; the effects and repercussions of police activity, both official and unofficial; the flexibility of sentencing; the severity of punishment in practice; and the role that social status or political influence may have in altering legal outcomes. Smith does not seem to have considered any of these matters.

By the same token, while Carol Nechemias' chapter on social welfare in the U.S.S.R. notes that the Soviet health system has turned out ever-greater numbers of doctors and hospital beds, she does not even mention the fact that life expectancy in the U.S.S.R. is apparently growing shorter. In dealing at length with Soviet consumption policy, she ignores what would seem to be the critical question: can Soviet authorities live with the political consequences of sanctioning consumerism? It is not intuitively obvious that they can. After all, if consumers are the best judges of what should be provided, the leading role of the party would presumably be called into question. The Liberman proposals of the early 1960s have been dismissed from the Soviet economic agenda; indeed, the general direction of the U.S.S.R.'s economic policy has been toward state control and away from consumer preference for at least fifteen years. Consumerism has been associated with alarming disturbances on the Europeanized periphery of the Soviet empire—the Prague Spring, Solidarity's "renewal"—and has been dealt with in a fashion befitting a threat to national security. And yet, the question remains: if Soviet authorities will not motivate their workers to compete against their Western counterparts through consumer inducements, and if they cannot improve their system's productivity by tightening political screws, what are they to do?

Gordon Smith and his colleagues are on target on one important point. The image of the Soviet administrator as a bumbling incompetent *is* overplayed, and very largely inappropriate. Administrators in the U.S.S.R. are charged with satisfying an awesome—perhaps numbing—multiplicity of demands. To succeed in this requires truly impressive sophistication and competence. It is a tribute to the men in Moscow that their cumbersome machine creaks along as well as it does. We will soon see whether the next generation of leaders is as accomplished.

Originally published in *Society,* November/December 1983, Transaction, Inc. Reprinted with permission, all rights reserved.

Notes

1. Jan Ake Dellenbrant, *Soviet Regional Policy* (Atlantic Highlands, N.J.: Humanities Press, 1980).
2. Gordon B. Smith, ed., *Public Policy and Administration in the Soviet Union* (New York: Praeger Publisher, 1981).

5

Understanding, and Misunderstanding, Soviet Power

Ever since the establishment of Soviet power over a prostrate Russian Empire some sixty-five years ago, observers in the West have been attempting to understand the internal workings and external behavior of the Soviet state. The challenges prompting these observers to their work have been various.

On the purely intellectual plane, the allure to the disinterested analyst of the puzzle of Soviet communism was, and is, self-evident. The Soviet state constitutes a fundamentally new form of rule, intuitively unfamiliar in many respects to the mind tempered by the heritage of the European Enlightenment. Moreover, it has been the deliberate policy of the Soviet state to make itself unfamiliar to the outside world. Once in power, Soviet communism accorded urgent and immediate priority to the systematic effort (through information control, propaganda, and a variety of other activities) to deprive foreign observers of an independent basis by which Soviet communism might come to be known and understood.

From the practical standpoint, an accurate understanding of Soviet capabilities and intentions has become a matter of increasing consequence. The weapons available to the U.S.S.R. in its ongoing struggle against the forces it deems hostile have undergone considerable evolution over the past sixty-five years. In the early 1920s the newly established Soviet state's arsenal, in the view of its own directorate, was principally intellectual and ideological. Of all states, the U.S.S.R. alone was the repositor of a particular storehouse of ideas concerning political organization, economic forces and historical inevitability. Though these ideas were by and large untested, it was hoped that they might be used to overturn government and destroy society in the lands against which they would be directed. In the late 1980s, by contrast, the U.S.S.R. is the possessor of a vast military force. Of particular portent is the Soviet Union's reserve of nuclear weapons. Unlike the communist doctrine of an earlier day, these bombs and missiles have been scientifically tested.

Important though a basic understanding of the Soviet Union may be to the West, the actual ability of Western students of the Soviet Union to explain and predict events in the U.S.S.R. today is conspicuously limited. One commentator, himself a prominent interpreter of Soviet behavior, has stated that Anglo-American scholarship on the U.S.S.R. is in a condition of "intellectual crisis."[1] As it happens, the proof of this "crisis" to the writer in question seems to be that an insufficient number of his colleagues subscribe to his own particular interpretation of Soviet affairs. There are less idiosyncratic measures for demarcating the limits of knowledge in the field of "Soviet studies." Many of them suggest that the corpus of learning about the U.S.S.R. is still inadequate to answer some basic questions about the U.S.S.R.

Take, for example, the question of political succession in the Soviet Union. Because power in the Soviet system is concentrated in the hands of the men at the very top, and because the limits on their power are by no means clearly delineated, a change in leading personalities can have great significance for Soviet policy—much greater, in fact, than is possible within any framework of actual constitutional government. Unfortunately, the record of foreign observers in predicting shakeups and transitions within the Politburo is less than confidence-inspiring. Leo Labedz has written that the only Western source to predict Secretary General Khrushchev's ouster in 1964 was *Old Moore's Almanac*—an astrological yearbook. More recently, considerable attention was devoted to the "Brezhnev succession" over the long period during which the ruler's physical infirmity was becoming increasingly difficult to conceal. In 1980, two years before the ruler's eventual death, a study specifically devoted to the "Brezhnev succession" was published by one of the leading U.S. institutions specializing in foreign affairs.[2] Its author did not entertain even the possibility that either Yuri V. Andropov or Konstantin U. Chernenko might at some further date come to power.

The evident limitations of the field as a whole do not diminish the contributions of specific individuals in expanding the West's ability to understand the Soviet state, or argue against the possibility of improving such understanding. Quite the contrary. The work of such analysts as the young George F. Kennan and such scholars as the late Naum Jasny should testify to the range and depth of insights that could be gleaned by outsiders under even the least auspicious circumstances. The methods underpinning their early successes—painstaking attention to detail; comprehensive study of words, deeds, and the tension between the two; and the overarching priority accorded to the quest to understand the essence of what animates the Soviet regime—continue to distinguish those students of Soviet affairs who choose to master them, as the writings of Alain Besançon, Murray Feshbach, Boris Meissner, and Adam Ulam (to name a few) will demonstrate.

Still, if the task of attempting to understand the Soviet state is less daunting today than in the prime of Kennan's youth, this is not solely because of trails blazed and trodden by earlier explorers. Intervening events have also played their part in making the terrain more accessible to would-be observers in the West.

Three of these factors deserve special mention. The first is the gradual fragmentation and attrition that has taken place within an international communist movement over which Moscow's control had once been virtually complete. From the world of communist states, revealing information about the U.S.S.R. was to emanate from Yugoslavia, Albania, and China, where Leninist precepts about communication were turned to the tasks of freeing local directorates from Soviet influence. Even more important was the complete disaffection from Communism of such former agents of the Communist International as Franz Borkenau, Milovan Djilas, Boris Souvarine, and Betram Wolfe—writers who, more often than not, had had direct and intensive dealings in their day with the highest circles in Moscow, and who to a man understood the workings of the Soviet system in their bones.

A second factor has been the escape to the West of persons who lived under Soviet rule and who were therefore familiar with diverse aspects of the Soviet system. Despite the abiding efforts of Soviet authorities to prevent the unsanctioned departure of any person at any time from any and all Soviet territories, a great many refugees have made their way to the West since the days of Stalin; literally hundreds of thousands of them may be found today in the United States, West Germany, and Israel alone. Their memories constitute an immense, living library of information on economy, society, and political administration in the U.S.S.R. Although the testimony of resettled emigres has not been utterly ignored, strangely little use seems to have been made of it. Soviet emigres to the United States are not today routinely, much less systematically, interviewed; the last major study to survey Soviet refugees comprehensively on life in the U.S.S.R. was completed at the end of the 1940s.[3] Unsolicited observations about the U.S.S.R. by its former residents seem often to be treated with suspicion or even hostility by students of Soviet affairs. In dismissing refugee accounts, some students of Soviet affairs have explained that the reminiscence of 'malcontents'—people sufficiently dissatisfied with their native country to leave it forever—may suffer from pervasive bias, and may be riddled with untruths.

Nevertheless, taking Soviet emigres sufficiently seriously to talk with them has proved to be a valuable, if unfashionable, undertaking. In the past, for example, eyewitnesses had accurately described and detailed the workings of the Gulag to the West at least fifteen years before Khrushchev made his famous "secret speech"; by the late 1940s, at least half a dozen volumes on the workings of the Soviet secret police and their slave labor camps—based on eyewitness testimony—were available in English for anyone wishing to read them. Today, students of Soviet affairs in Tel Aviv and Munich seem to pay more attention to refugees than those in Washington and London; their assessments of current events in the U.S.S.R. do not seem any the worse for this.

A third factor—perhaps the most important of the three—has been the Soviet policy of "opening" to contact with Westerners, a policy which took body while Brezhnev was in power, and which has continued in the years following his death. The "opening" was reflected in the increase in cultural contacts and academic exchanges between the U.S.S.R. and Western countries, and in the rising number of non-communist tourists who were permitted to visit selected areas in the Soviet Union, but its most significant manifestation was in the unprecedented willingness of Soviet officials to meet and talk with politicians, journalists, and academics from the West. In the 1970s and 1980s, the top men in the Politburo made themselves available to Western visitors, and Western audiences, as they had never been before; at much the same time, less senior members of the Soviet hierarchy were entrusted to represent Soviet policy, express opinions, and conduct unrehearsed verbal exchanges, often under the glare of the camera, with interlocutors from Western countries. Symbolic of the impact of this policy of "opening" has been the rise to prominence of one of its chief representatives, Georgi Arbatov, the Director of the Institute for the Study of the U.S.A. and Canada. Today, Mr. Arbatov is a familiar personality on American and European television, where he expresses and defends an official Soviet viewpoint to foreign reporters under Western terms of journalistic engagement. He has also been elevated to membership in the Central Committee of the Communist Party of the Soviet Union (CPSU).

More than a few observers in the West have equated the Soviet "opening" with an attitude of openness. For those raised in truly open societies, this mistake may be only natural—but it is a mistake nevertheless.

Though the policy of "opening" began while Brezhnev was in power, the Brezhnev circle demonstrated no initial interest in making itself more accessible to the West. (One may remember, by contrast, that the Brezhnev group set itself immediately to reversing a number of other policies from the Khrushchev years.) In his first three and a half years as Prime Minister, Brezhnev's colleague, Aleksei Kosygin, granted a total of two interviews to reporters from the West; Brezhnev himself gave none at all.[4] The eventual increase in contact between Soviet officials and visitors from the West would seem to have been a matter of deliberate and very careful preparation.

The policy of "opening" was predated by the 23rd Party Congress in 1966, at which Secretary General Brezhnev called for an intensification of the international ideological struggle, an upgrading of the Soviet propaganda capability, and a greater role for social scientists and researchers in such work.[5] It coincided with several important changes within the Soviet hierarchy. One of these was the rise of Yuri Andropov. Another was the rise of Boris Ponomarev. Both of these men were proteges of the late Mikhail Suslov.

Andropov's ultimately successful quest for supreme power was related to the transformations he wrought on the Committee for State Security, the KGB, in his fifteen years of stewardship over it. To be sure, the organization he inherited was enormously powerful. It maintained a vast network of political police and international agents, commanded its own divisions of combat troops and motorized border guards, controlled its own factories and even industries; nuclear rockets could not be launched without its personnel. Even so, Andropov managed to expand the influence, and the sway, of the KGB by redrawing the boundaries of its contribution to the security of the Soviet state. While the KGB under Andropov remained an agency for enforcement and espionage, it became much more.

Six months after Andropov's appointment to the KGB, the U.S.S.R. Academy of Sciences announced the creation of the new Institute for the Study of the U.S.A. Its Director was to be Georgi Arbatov. Arbatov was an expert in ideological warfare; his principal book on the subject, *The War of Ideas In Contemporary International Relations,* remains in publication in the U.S.S.R. today. Under his direction, the U.S.A. Institute grew and thrived. Before assuming its directorship, Arbatov had worked for three years in the CPSU Secretariat under Andropov. In the early 1980s, Arbatov described Andropov to a Western reporter as a close personal friend. Whatever the precise institutional relationship may be between the KGB and the U.S.A. Institute, there can be little doubt that the product of the Institute would have been consistent with KGB chief Andropov's conception of "intelligence."

Boris Ponomarev, for his part, is the first, and current, head of the Central Committee's International Department. The International Department is an institutional descendant of the Communist International, or Comintern (which was formally disbanded in 1943 as a gesture of goodwill toward wartime allies). Ponomarev was actually a member of the Comintern's Executive Committee. The International Department appears to be entrusted with a broad range of foreign policy responsibilities; among many others, these apparently include the implementation of programmatic ideological warfare, the dissemination of propaganda overseas, and the supervision of "active measures" and "disinformation" designed to affect popular opinion and public policy in the west. In pursuing these and other tasks, the International Department appears to draw upon the resources of the U.S.S.R. Academy of Sciences and its specialized institutes; Ponomarev himself is a full member of the Academy. The fortunes of the International Department are in some measure reflected in the fortunes of its chief, who has been elevated to the Politburo as an alternate member.

Andropov and Ponomarev joined the Politburo in 1973 and 1972, respectively—in the heyday of "détente" with the United States, and at precisely the moment when the policy of "opening" to Westerners was seen to be decisively in progress. Characteristics of the "opening" have become clearer in the intervening years. On the one hand, after initial relaxations, emigration controls have been tightened to the point where voluntary emigration has today (1987) virtually ceased; direct dialing to the West, a privilege briefly available to ordinary households with telephones in key Soviet cities, was summarily interrupted in the early 1980s by "technical problems" which have apparently proven impossible to locate or resolve; and a series of edicts has been passed which can effectively make any spontaneous or unapproved conversation or contact with foreigners a formal criminal offense. At the same time, the Soviet state's capacity for processing contacts with selected audiences, academics, or policy shapers from or in Western countries has been systematically upgraded: the creation in the late 1970s of a special new unit of the Central Committee Secretariat—the International Information Department—is testimony to the support such efforts command.

It should not be presumed that the intention or effects of the "opening" to the West that Soviet authorities have so carefully constructed is to increase the insight of Western viewers into the workings of the Soviet system. A more plausible assessment might be that the purposes of the "opening" created in the 1970s and 1980s parallel those of the coterminous policy of "détente"—a policy which Ponomarev once described as "mark(ing) a new, important stage in the development of the international battle against imperialism."

Within the Anglo-American community of Soviet studies, the publication of Seweryn Bialer's new book, *The Soviet Paradox: External Expansion, Internal Decline,*[6] has been treated as an important event. Widely discussed within the academy, the book has also evoked extensive note and comment in the popular media. To students of Soviet affairs, it would come as no surprise that an analysis of the current situation in the U.S.S.R. by Seweryn Bialer should be accorded such attention and respect. In a variety of ways, Mr. Bialer might seem ideally qualified to contribute to the West's understanding of the Soviet state.

Professor Bialer is currently Director of Columbia's Research Institute on International Change (formerly the Research Institute on International Communism), and is on the Executive Committee of the W. Averell Harriman Institute for Advanced Soviet Studies (formerly the Columbia University Russian Institute). The Russian Institute, dating as it does back to 1946, was the first academic organization for the study of the Soviet Union to be established in the United States. Fortified by bequests from the family of the late W. Averell Harriman (who had been ambassador to Moscow from 1943 to 1946) and by additional grants from foundations and individuals, the Harriman Institute promises to be a major institutional force in American "Sovietology" in coming years.

Professor Bialer's activities and achievements set him apart in the field of Soviet studies. A prolific writer and frequent television guest, he also serves on the editorial board of such journals as *Soviet Studies* and *Foreign Policy*; acts as a director or adviser for such institutions as the Ford Foundation, the Center for Strategic and International Studies, the Social Science Research Council, the Lehrman Institute, and the United Nations Association of the United States; has been recipient of numerous Western awards and fellowships, including the first MacArthur Foundation prize ever granted to a student of Soviet affairs; and has functioned as an unofficial adviser to key figures in the leadership of the Democratic Party.

In an interview with *Der Spiegel* in 1983, Bialer is described as "(the man) America's academics consider the leading expert on questions of East-West relations." It is beyond dispute that Seweryn Bialer occupies an extraordinary—indeed, a unique—position among Western students of the Soviet state. More than any other Western scholar, Professor Bialer has been able to gain insight into the Soviet Union from the events which have made the U.S.S.R. more accessible to Western observers. Indeed, Professor Bialer's career has in no small degree been part of those very events.

Seweryn Bialer defected to the West in 1956. He was no ordinary refugee. Though only 29 at the time of his transit through West Berlin, he forsook in passage a brilliant career in the new Poland, where he was already a very important person.

In his testimony before the U.S. Senate's internal security sub-committee in the summer of 1956, Bialer stated that he joined the Polish Communist underground in 1942, at the age of 15, in Nazi-governed Lodz. In a very real sense, he would, by this dating, have been present at the creation of modern Poland. The Polish communist movement that had, at an earlier era, given the likes of Rosa Luxemburg and Feliks Dzerzhinsky to the world was, by the mid-1930s, virtually bereft of life. In 1938, Moscow ordered the Communist Party of Poland (KPP) to be dissolved; by early 1939, in the words of Jan de Weydenthal, "all traces of organizational existence of the KPP had been eliminated." The Nazi and Soviet invasion of Poland later that year, and the subsequent agreement between Germany and the U.S.S.R. to partition between themselves the entire territory of the erstwhile Polish state, seemed to augur ill for any organization that might attempt to proclaim, at one and the same time, its allegiance to Moscow and its commitment to Polish national integrity—as the old KPP had sought to do. But in June 1941, with Operation Barbarossa (and, inter alia, the Nazi occupation of Soviet-occupied Poland), the "objective conditions" for a rebirth of Polish Communism were established. In late 1941, an organization arose in Warsaw by the name of the Union of Friends of the U.S.S.R.; in 1942 its name was changed to the Polish Worker's Party (PPR). It was the precursor of the Polish United Worker's Party (PZPR), the party that holds power in Poland today. According to official Party history, the PPR had 4,000 members in July 1942. Very probably, this figure overstates their strength; the memoirs of the first chief of staff of the People's Guard (GL), the military force directed by the PPR, places the GL's numbers at 1,500 to 2,000 in mid-1942, and states that the PPR itself was even smaller. By either reckoning, however, Bialer would have been one of the very earliest members of the Communist *apparant* of modern Poland.

Nineteen forty-three and 1944 were years of political success for the PPR, but of severe travail for its armed units. Bialer states that he was interned in Auschwitz in July of 1944—the very month that the PPR, in conjunction with a committee of Polish Communists based in Moscow, established the so-called "Lublin government" over Polish territories controlled by the advancing Red Army. A communist and a Jew, Bialer's chances of surviving in Nazi hands would have been slim. That he did in fact survive Hitler's camps is testimony to his endurance, determination, and courage. It is also perhaps testimony to the remarkable performance of the communist networks in these concentration and extermination camps. Communist policy toward the camps during these terrible years was to encourage the collaboration of inmates from the Party with their SS overlords in the administration of these murder centers. Communists were heavily represented, for example, among the *Sonderkommando*, units in which prisoners temporarily postponed their own death by engaging in the selection process through which other prisoners were sent to the gas chambers and the ovens. The Auschwitz camps had a particularly effective Communist organization. Josef Cyrankiewicz, who became Poland's Prime Minister in 1948, survived three years at Auschwitz thanks to the camp's communist underground. When the Party made the decision to save them, it was even possible to keep alive important communist Jews. It is said, for example, that Leon Stasiak, who rose to prominence in Poland as a propagandist on the Central Committee the very year that Bialer defected to the West, owed his life to the efforts of the Auschwitz Communist network.

Bialer's exact terms of service to the Party during the war are unclear. In any case, upon his liberation in 1945, Bialer immediately assumed sensitive responsibilities within the Lublin government—duties which would most logically be entrusted to a cadre not only of complete ideological reliability, but also with considerable military expertise. For Bialer was assigned to be a political commandant within the new, and rapidly growing, security apparatus for People's Poland. By his Senate testimony, Bialer was part of the uniformed police machinery from 1945 to 1951. His rise within the Polish police was astonishingly rapid. By 1951, according to his testimony, Bialer was Chief of the Political Division of the Central Command of the Citizen's Militia—that is to say, political commissar of a nationwide security force which included not only tens of thousands of police, but also an 85,000-man military auxilliary known as the Reserve Organization of the Citizen's Militia (ORMO). Bialer would have been no more than 25 years old when he was political chief of the Polish police. This pace of advance through the ranks of the security apparatus of the New Poland knows no parallel. To get some sense of this achievement, one might compare Bialer's career with that of a contemporary who was also charged with political control within the security force—Wojciech Jaruzelski, currently (1987) Prime Minister of the Polish People's Republic. Like Bialer, Jaruzelski was, in his day, a bright and trusted young man. He had joined the Soviet sponsored Polish force in the U.S.S.R. when he was sixteen; fought against the Wehrmacht all the way to the Elbe; was redeployed (it is thought) to units suppressing the Ukraine's anti-Communist underground in 1946; and was heavily decorated for these and subsequent services. He was, in his day, the youngest two-star general in the Polish armed forces. Jaruselski nevertheless did not become political commissar of the People's Army until he was thirty-seven.

The political command within the Polish Citizen's Militia would have been an excellent vantage point from which to learn how power in a

Communist state is administered. In the years in which Bialer says he served in these capacities, it would also have been an excellent vantage point from which to learn how power in a Communist state is consolidated. In the late 1940s, after all, the Citizen's Militia was one of the principal instruments by which Poland's communist government achieved mastery over a nation that was overwhelmingly hostile to the prospects of its rule. The Citizen's Militia, for example, was intimately involved in the terror that preceded the rigged elections of 1947—the last election in which independent parties were permitted to participate. By 1948, in the words of one observer of Polish affairs, "all organized forces of actual or potential opposition (to the Communist regime) were gone"; in 1951, the year that Bialer left the militia, ORMO was completing its liquidation of the country's last bands of armed anti-communist resistance.

In 1951 Bialer was transferred from State to Party, where he was attached directly to the Central Committee. His new area of responsibilities, according to his Senate testimony, was "anti-Western and anti-American propaganda." Bialer fulfilled his obligations in a variety of fashions. He was made first secretary of the party organizations in what he called "the two most important Communist schools in Poland," the Central Committee's Higher Institute of Marxism-Leninism and its Institute of Soviet Sciences (where he was also appointed professor). He was made ideological adviser to Trybuna Ludu, the Party's daily journal. He wrote for a variety of intellectual and popular magazines, and, in his capacity with the Propaganda and Agitation Department of the Central Committee, lectured both extensively and intensively. At a time when Eastern European parties were kept on a particularly short tether, propaganda work required consultation with and approval from the Soviet apparatus for ideological warfare. These were not only extensive, but also, at times, intensive: by his testimony, for example, Bialer spent November and December of 1954 in Moscow.

The early 1950s would have been an interesting time for ideological work in Poland. With the consolidation of communist power an accomplished fact, attention turned to the inculcation of conformity amongst the general populace. The task of infusing "socialist content," as this was understood in Stalin's day, into all aspects of cultural and intellectual life was facilitated considerably by the creation, in 1951, of the Polish Academy of Sciences, which among other things coordinated such efforts for academic institutions. For the country as a whole, anti-American propaganda figured prominently within the overall schema of indoctrination; indeed, in the early 1950s it rose to a pitch it never previously registered, and never reattained. As the Korean war progressed, Moscow instructed Warsaw to ship ever greater fractions of the still impoverished country's output to the

Asian front; anti-American agitation was to help focus the public's blame for its privations on the United States. Anti-American propaganda also helped to set the stage for the purges and secret police campaigns of the early 1950s, many of whose victims were accused of being American spies.

Though Poland's propaganda apparatus was engaged in what it said was "ideological battle," only one side was allowed to fight. In late 1951, the Polish government asked the United States to close the U.S. Information Service office at its embassy in Warsaw. The perilous consequences of allowing uncensored information from the West to penetrate into Poland were vividly demonstrated in 1954. In that year, the Voice of America and Radio Free Europe broadcast to Poland a series of interviews with and reports by Josef Swiatlo, a defector who had been a lieutenant colonel in the Polish secret police. An upheaval within the government followed his public revelations, and in December 1954 the Ministry of Public Security was "abolished."

When Bialer defected to the West in 1956, he was, according to the contemporary accounts in *The New York Times,* one of Poland's top two hundred Party activists and functionaries. In open testimony before the U.S. Senate Judiciary Committee's internal security subcommittee, he recounted his memory of extremely sensitive Soviet documents that he had been privileged to see, including one of the few full stenographic transcripts of the CPSU's Central Committee Plenum from July 1955. In addition, he identified several persons, in Poland and the United States, as agents of Polish intelligence or influence.

The attitude of Moscow, and its satellites, toward former Soviet bloc security personnel who commit what the Soviets take to be acts of espionage—or counterespionage—is typically less than charitable. Nevertheless, Professor Bialer gained access to leading Soviet circles once the policy of "opening" toward the West was underway. Indeed, Bialer not only secured entry to the corridors of access in which Western academics are now permitted to tread, but has in fact succeeded in becoming one of their most consummate travellers. By his own estimate he has visited Moscow a dozen times in the early and mid-1980s alone. His past has apparently not been held against him, for many, if not most, of these visits have involved meetings and discussions with high ranking Soviet personnel.

The community of American students of Soviet affairs has awaited the arrival of Professor Bialer's book on the U.S.S.R. and the world with an anticipation seldom accorded to topical publications. In the scope and strategy of its execution, *The Soviet Paradox* not only acknowledges this compliment, but seeks as well to redeem the debt that such a compliment implicitly confers. For it is a book intended to be both important and influential.

"This book," Bialer states in the Preface, "is based not only on thirty years of research and writing on twentieth-century Soviet history and politics, but also on many hours of conversation with people active in international relations in the Soviet Union, the United States, Eastern Europe, China, and other countries." On the strength of even one of these qualifications—Bialer's four decades of privileged, and extraordinary, access to policy circles in both Western nations and Communist countries—its claim to importance would be established beyond any reasonable doubt. That the book is meant to be influential is indicated by its envisioned audience. *The Soviet Paradox,* Bialer implies, was not produced simply for specialists on the U.S.S.R.; rather, it "has been written for the interested reader in politics, government, business, journalism, and academia."

Even Bialer's critics will concede that *The Soviet Paradox* is a subtle and masterful work. Carefully if not always elegantly written and skillfully if not always convincingly argued, it attests to a powerful and analytical intellect with a wide range of knowledge at its command. *The Soviet Paradox* is informed by an extraordinary understanding of the Soviet state, but displays no less a grasp of the workings of the main non-communist countries with which the U.S.S.R. is currently locked in conflict. Though it is a book full of forceful judgments, these are presented in a manner that will not startle the American reader newly initiated into the mysteries of the Soviet studies. And while Bialer's narrative leads to the verge of a number of proposals concerning the conduct of U.S. policy toward the U.S.S.R., he leaves his audience to alight upon these consequential recommendations themselves.

The Soviet Paradox is not easily summarized. This is a sweeping opus: Bialer writes with an air of confidence and authority about an amazing range of topics in this book. His thesis, moreover, is anything but simple. Bialer's argument about the Soviet Union and its role in world affairs is so complex, so nuanced and extended, that its component parts often appear to be inconsistent, if not actually contradictory. It is an opus, therefore, which may be better served by an exposition of its highlights than by any attempt at comprehensive synopsis.

Bialer portrays the contemporary Soviet state as a power struggling furiously, but without avail, against the forces of history. "The twenty-first century," he writes, "may not be Chinese, but it certainly will not be Russian." Secretary General Mikhail Gorbachev, in his estimate, "is the best of what the Soviets have." Yet he implies that neither Gorbachev's team, nor any other possible leadership configuration, can secure for the

U.S.S.R. a position of international primacy, for "Soviet foreign policy resources prevent the Soviets from becoming a dominant power."

By Bialer's account, Soviet power is increasingly affected by a diverse array of unfavorably and possible irremediable trends. Its official ideology, Marxism-Leninism, is today a spent and corrupted force: "the old Bolshevik dream of authentic socialist revolution," he observes, "has been displaced by the commitment to direct military conquest as the only way to spread communism." Yet even the spread of communism may not ultimately betoken success for the Soviet state. In Bialer's ironic phrase, the U.S.S.R. is today a victim of "communist encirclement." On one hand, it is flanked by a China which "has audaciously attacked all phases and dimensions of the Stalin-type economy at once"; it is bordered on another frontier by expensive Eastern European "vassal states" that constitute (entirely apart from such communist dependencies as Cuba and Vietnam) an "external empire that has become an embarrassment and a handicap to pursuit of foreign political objectives."

Things are not said to look much better within the U.S.S.R.'s official borders. The hammer and the sickle, Bialer argues, are "in one specific sense" appropriate symbols for the U.S.S.R., for they represent "the Soviet Union's economic and technological backwardness, and the attachment of its leaders to ideas and policies which belong . . . to the past." In fact, "the cycle of rejuvenation in Russian history inaugurated by the Soviet seizure of power has exhausted its domestic potential." By Bialer's diagnosis, the Soviet Union is today in the grip of "systemic crisis"—a "crisis of effectiveness," of which the U.S.S.R.'s widely discussed economic slowdown, for all its importance, is but a single symptom. Indeed: "the stability of the social order is declining and will continue to decline." Bialer uses the term "internal decline" to describe the overall process he sees underway within the Soviet Union. And the U.S.S.R.'s problems, in Bialer's eyes, may not end even here. *The Soviet Paradox* appears to question whether the Russian people, and the other peoples of what he calls "the internal empire," are the stuff from which a world power could really ever be built. In evaluating what he calls "the different road to reform in contemporary China and Russia," he argues that "there is one aspect . . . of absolutely fundamental importance. It concerns the quality of the human material with which the leadership of the two countries have to deal in contemplating reforms."

But if the Soviet quest for supremacy is, in Bialer's depiction, consigned to virtually inevitable failure, the state itself is not about to be swept into the dustbin of history. The "Soviet paradox" to which Bialer wishes to call attention is this: "the internal decline of the Soviet Union coincides with the height of its military power . . . today and (for) the foreseeable future, internal decline (will be) coupled with awesome military power directed at external goals.''

By dint of a sort of decay, ''the Soviet Union has come to resemble the type of highly authoritarian system well known from the Russian past.'' Unlike the autocracies of the Russian yesteryear, however, ''Soviet security may be identified with the achievement of a Communist world. Only such a victory will provide final security for the state.'' Insofar as this is an impossible prospect, Bialer writes, Soviet foreign policy is characterized by enormous and ultimately irreduceable tensions. In recent years, these tensions have mounted, for the U.S.S.R. has come to redefine ''security'' to ''include the preservation of Soviet status''—this, in Bialer's view, at a time when the Soviet position in the world has been exposed as ''over-extended.''

But in an age of nuclear arsenals, Mr. Bialer suggests, the West cannot afford to ignore Soviet insecurities. Like it or not, he argues, the danger of nuclear war exposes all of humanity to unprecedented and incalculable risk. In the current situation, which Bialer sees as potentially perilous, the Soviet policy he seems to feel to be most appropriate for Western countries to adopt is one he calls ''containment.''

Bialer's containment differs substantially from George F. Kennan's now classic exposition of the concept, for it offers no hope of ultimately modifying Soviet behavior. ''It is not within the West's power,'' Bialer writes, ''to bring about significant changes in the Soviet system or to redirect radically the leadership's preoccupations from international to domestic concerns.'' It is, however, ''possible to frustrate the Soviet global ambitions that are the most threatening.'' Though he never says so explicitly, Bialer strongly implies that the Western world, and the United States in particular, should reconcile itself to waiting the Soviets out. Such a strategy, he seems to suggest, would be both consonant with the long-range objectives of the West (since 'objective' conditions so clearly indicate that history is against the U.S.S.R.) and responsible (since it would minimize the chance of a nuclear conflict with the U.S.S.R. during the long decline he has envisioned for it).

If The Soviet Paradox seems to be a work that seeks after commendation, it is also one that deserves to be commended on a number of counts. Passages of its text rank with the very best in Western analysis of the Soviet Union. Bialer's brief disquisition on the influence of Marxist-Leninist doctrine on the framing and execution of Soviet foreign policy, for example, may be a lasting contribution to the field. In other places, The Soviet Paradox offers informative discussions of current issues; one of these is its section on the prospects in the U.S.S.R. for ''economic reform''—a term Bialer rightly notes is not used by Soviet authorities themselves. Bialer's attention in this discussion to the extent that all Soviet domestic policies, and especially those suggestive of liberalization, are judged in Moscow for their possible political impact in the "external empire" demonstrated a feel for the workings of Soviet power which is lacking in so much of the current commentary on the topic. And though many of Bialer's recommendations for American policy are implicit, in his writing, he does not shrink from placing himself in explicit opposition to viewpoints currently influential among both students of Russian history and the community of Soviet dissidents and emigres. Bialer, for example, emphasizes the continuity between the messianic tendency in prerevolutionary Russian nationalism and the universalist claims of Soviet communism; in so doing he seems to make a sophisticated and controversial case that the Russian culture is "naturally" expansionist in outlook, irrespective of whatever political creed may possess its rulers. Informed readers may dispute this interpretation, but they will not heedlessly dismiss it.

Despite such specific virtues, *The Soviet Paradox* is a puzzling—indeed a troubling—document. For all the evident intelligence behind its intricate arguments and for all the diverse data that are summoned to the support of its judgements, the resulting product is something less than a reliable guide to understanding the Soviet Union and its current position in the world arena. In a variety of ways, in fact, *The Soviet Paradox* may be said to misinform the general reader to whom it is expressly directed.

The Soviet Paradox is full of factual errors. Some of these appear to be quite trivial, others less so. Bialer states, for example, that "the collectivization and communization of the Chinese countryside . . . was by and large nonviolent"; in point of fact, Chinese authorities themselves have stated that their "anti-landlord" campaign in the early 1950s liquidated 1.5 million persons (and this was but one of many campaigns attendant on "land reform"). Western demographers now think that as many as thirty million "excess deaths" may have occurred in the years following the "Great Leap Forward," the nationwide campaign in the late 1950s that enforced the commune upon all rural Chinese communities. By the same token, Bialer lists "the stalemate in Poland" as one of the features affecting what he describes as the "defensive" Soviet decision to invade Afghanistan; yet the strikes in the Lenin shipyards which were to give birth to the Solidarity movement began in August 1980, while the Soviet assassination of Afghanistan's puppet President Amin, and surprise attack against his country, took place in December of the previous year.

Factual errors apart, Bialer's text projects a serious misreading of the Soviet situation in three important and closely related areas: its government, its economy, and its military and external strategy.

Like many other works on the U.S.S.R., *The Soviet Paradox* argues that the key to understanding the Soviet state is its legacy of Stalinism. "The real Soviet Revolution, the transformation of Russian society," writes Bialer, "took place from 1929 to 1939. It was directed by Stalin." His words for Stalin are not kind: "During Stalin's rule . . . the social order was that of a cemetery." The Stalinist tendency in Soviet rule, in Bialer's view, was by no means extinguished by the dictator's death in 1953. To the contrary: "While the policy of mass terror was abolished in post-Stalin Russia, the apparatus was simply purged, not dismantled." Elsewhere he states that "the Soviet economic system remains virtually unchanged in its basic characteristics from the Stalinist model." Still elsewhere he remarks that "the survival of the police state, the permanent priority assigned to military growth, and the fusion of Leninist messianism with Great Russian nationalism are the most obvious Stalinist features of the contemporary Soviet Union." But Stalin's successors, according to Bialer, did not limit themselves to maintaining and preserving these fundamental pillars of Stalinism. "In the cultural field," he writes, "Brezhnev's policies, almost from the beginning, adhered rigorously to the old Stalinist approach." And after Brezhnev's death, in Bialer's view, Soviet policy was marked by a multifaceted "turn to neo-Stalinism." Today, in fact, "one cannot find evidence of any meaningful anti-Stalinist forces either in the establishment itself or in the various strata of Soviet society."

This depiction of Soviet rule would be commonplace were it not for one distinctive aspect: Bialer insists that the Soviet Union is not a totalitarian state.

Bialer refuses to use the term "totalitarian" to describe the Soviet government today. "The Soviet Union," he writes, "is no longer a totalitarian nation." His preference is for the term "authoritarian." Evidently, in Bialer's view, the U.S.S.R. has been something other than totalitarian for a long time. For as he explains it, "authoritarianism remains the only model of rule with which the population as a whole has had any experience." True: the Soviet Union today is in the midst of "mature Stalinism," and is an "intimidating police state." It is, however, "an *authoritarian* and intimidating police state" (emphasis added).

While Bialer strongly implies that the Soviet Union did at one time qualify as a totalitarian state, he does not explicitly explain the reasons that it no longer merits such a title. The reader is provided only hints of his argument. In one place, Bialer writes that: "The character of the political system differs from what it was in Stalin's day. There is less coercion. It is more predictable—one is tempted to say rational." At another, he expresses the conviction that Khrushchev was "the last true believer in the ideals of the original Bolsheviks to hold a leadership position. His successors care about their own and their country's power, not about communism." "The essence of the Brezhnev regime," Bialer observes, "was the substitution of a stable and conservative corporate entity for the personal dictatorship of Stalin." The Party, he writes, "wishes to hold on to its monopoly of power. That is the heart, the essence, of the Soviet system." As for Gorbachev and his circle, "These new leaders seem to be less ideological and more interested in efficiency in domestic policies"; in fact, "The men of the new Soviet leadership are often called technocrats. It is as good a description as any." Under Gorbachev, according to Bialer, "domestic problems have priority over foreign policy goals." In fact, such are their orientations that Bialer predicts the Gorbachev Politburo will "try to obtain an arms control agreement that will permit (them) to concentrate on more pressing domestic social and economic problems."

Bialer's assessment of the nature of the contemporary Soviet state is integral to the policies which he prompts his American readers to consider. In dealing with the "technocrats" ruling the "stable and conservative corporate entity" that he takes today's Soviet *apparat* to be, the natural policy for American statemen to pursue toward the U.S.S.R. is "realpolitik"—that is, the nineteenth-century European conception of a power politics that is informed only by "objective" considerations, and that explicitly eschews moral or ideological objectives. "If ever there was a time in the history of mankind to have the most powerful states conduct a *realpolitik*," Bialer warns, "that time is now."

A principal facet of the *realpolitik* Bialer envisions for the United States would be the avoidance of ideological confrontation with the U.S.S.R. Participating deliberately in an international battle of ideas against the Soviet Union, he suggests, would be counterproductive, and perhaps a bit unworthy. "It may be very tempting to give the Russians a taste of their own rhetorical medicine," he admonishes, "but by doing so we may undermine our own interests." To judge by Bialer's commentary, moreover, there is little purpose in attempting to do battle with the U.S.S.R. for hearts and minds, since "the United States enjoys an enormous and insurmountable superiority over the Soviets. The time when the Soviet model was attractive to other nations is gone." It is, by Bialer's account, only because the "authoritarian" Soviet state "is on the defensive" that it is engaged in disseminating propaganda on such a staggering international scale—"making up in volume and intensity what they lack in substance," in his verdict.

It should be said that Bialer is not alone in his judgement that the Soviet policy is no longer totalitarian. In the late 1960s and the early 1970s, under the influence of the argument that the Soviet and American systems were "converging," the notion even enjoyed a certain academic vogue. And it may be said that totalitarianism, to paraphrase the late Vlacheslav Molotov, is a matter of taste. If "predictability," "rationalism" and what political-science jargon currently terms "authority leakage" are taken to denote the absence of totalitarianism, then it may safely be stated that no society on earth has ever been totalitarian—and in fact, that none will ever be. The Nazi death camps, the Soviet Gulag, and the Communist Chinese "re-education centers" were all characterized by a certain amount of "predictability" and "authority leakage" in their daily operations; such qualities were not only unavoidable, but probably essential to their abilities to function. Yet this should hardly come as a surprise, for the limits of any governance, no matter how ambitious, are ultimately set by the very real limits to endurance of the flesh and blood of the human beings beneath it. In the words of Hans Buchheim, "The totalitarian claim to power is unrealizeable."

But as Buchheim also pointed out, decades ago, "the realization that the totalitarian regime sets limits to its own development through its unlimited claim to control is no comfort to those who must live within its frontiers." For those who live beyond these frontiers, it serves no good purpose to mistake the realities constraining the administration of power with the claim to power itself.

Communist rule, as Professor Bialer well knows, not only declares its intervention to be legitimate in every sphere of life, but also demands ultimate authority in each of these, no matter how intimate or important they may be. Lenin put it succinctly: "We recognize nothing private." Those words were written in 1920, long before it seemed likely that Stalin might emerge as his successor. Stalin has risen to power, and passed from the political scene. The exigencies of power and the aging of the system have, over the decades, thrust upon Soviet leadership changes in tactics, strategy, and some of the particulars of administration. But as Soviet authorities are themselves the first to emphasize, the Soviet Union, and the CPSU which commands it, have maintained unswerving commitment to Lenin's precepts in this regard.

A few facts overlooked in Professor Bialer's lengthy discourse on the nature of the Soviet state since Stalin's death may be pertinent here. The Soviet Union's 1936 constitution, formally ratified and adopted at the height of the Great Terror, served as the legal basis for Soviet administration not only for the remainder of the dictator's life, but for nearly a quarter of a century after his death.[7]

In the years since the new constitution has come into effect, the Soviet citizen's open dissatisfaction with, or disapproval of proclaimed Soviet policy has continued to be treated as a psychiatric disorder, and persons evidencing such symptoms have been entrusted to the joint custody of

Soviet medical and security services, who together supervise a therapy consisting of chemical injections and prolonged confinement.

Although the duration of imprisonment has been reduced since the days of Stalin, Soviet citizens may still be sent to jail for telling a joke that Soviet authorities do not consider funny; in the early 1980s, the sentence for such anti-state activity could be three years.

The early 1980s was also slated to see the completion of the U.S.S.R.'s mandatory internal passport system. (The completion of the internal passport system was to coincide with the adoption of the Master Plan of Population Distribution on Soviet Territory, which was approved for implementation by the State Planning Committee in late 1983.) A citizen's "nationality"—his ethnic heritage—must be inscribed on the internal passport. At all times, however, a Soviet citizen's "nationality" remains provisional. Long-established Soviet policy posts the eventual "fusion" of the peoples inhabiting Soviet territory into a single, new Soviet race. This race policy is by no means a purely hypothetical concern. In consultation with the Soviet Academy of Sciences, the Soviet state periodically updates the list of Soviet "nationalities" accorded official recognition, creating and eliminating entire peoples in the process. Even peoples whose official "nationality" status seems secure, however, are not permitted to regard their most basic cultural characteristics as inviolably their own. In 1978, for example, provisional drafts of new constitutions for the Armenian and Georgian Republics stripped the Armenians and the Georgians of their national languages. Only after the outbreak of riots were clauses inserted into the documents acknowledging these people's rights to speak their native tongues.

It may be that such ambitious policies of experimentation with human beings remind Professor Bialer of "the type of highly authoritarian system well known from the Russian past." And it would take the greatest temerity to deny Bialer's assertion that the Soviet system is "authoritarian." As the late Leonard Schapiro observed of this term, all governments base their rule on the exercise of authority.

Even so, one might have hoped that in dismissing the possibility that the contemporary Soviet state might be "totalitarian," Bialer would have provided a more precise adjective for an authority which denies its subjects not only the right to active political opposition, and the right to conduct an independent economic existence, but the right to move or travel, the right to tell jokes, the right to utter what one believes to be the truth in one's home, the right to worship, the right to raise one's children in accordance with one's preferences, and the right to one's own ethnic identity.

Bialer's insistence on describing the Soviet Union today as a society that is not totalitarian extends at times to peculiar lengths. Throughout its text, *The Soviet Paradox* forces Western terminology onto Soviet phenomena that they are patently ill-equipped to fit. The "Soviet middle class" is one such turn of phrase, repeated frequently. One need only remember that the "middle class" constitutes the elements of bourgeois society that are supposed to be expropriated and liquidated by Soviet-style socialist revolution to appreciate its awkwardness.[8]

While *The Soviet Paradox* contains lucid passages on the relation of Marxist-Leninist thought to the Soviet state, there are many points where Professor Bialer inexplicably trivializes the role of ideology in the conduct of Soviet affairs. He writes, for example, "that it is ridiculous, and can only be explained by ideological blinders and the old guard's inertia, that . . . Soviet leaders still fear the existence of private restaurants or repair shops. . . ." In point of fact, the Soviet regime's enduring hostility toward economic activities not directed and controlled by the state is not a matter of ridicule. It is a matter of principle. Buchheim wrote that "every independence must appear as resistance or sabotage in the face of the totalitarian claim to control"; so it is in the U.S.S.R. today. Though independent economic activity is as a practical matter often tolerated as an unavoidable evil, even the smallest private shop servicing willing customers is, in the official Soviet view, engaging in an assault against the government. This may help to explain why the death penalty is still regularly meted out to prisoners convicted of what are called "economic crimes."

Bialer's book scarcely mentions the role of propaganda in Soviet rule. While this virtual omission may be in keeping with a verdict declaring the U.S.S.R. no longer totalitarian, it does little to help the general reader understand the Soviet system, and in fact denies Soviet authorities one of their most significant accomplishments. For the Soviet government, in its relentless and systematic attempt to command media of communication and the very languages used to communicate, has succeeded in altering the meaning of words in ways that make the expression of certain thoughts extremely difficult.[9] There is, for example, no word in the Russian language today to express the concept we associate with the word "peace." The nearest approximation to our word "peace" would be the Russian word *"mir."* *"Mir,"* however, is now meant to describe a situation which can only exist with the full and final triumph of socialism over capitalism—an event which Soviet doctrine foresees as the culmination of a protracted and possibly furious struggle. Thus, the word that serves for "peace" might just as easily be defined as "destruction of the enemy."

Protestations about the "less ideological" men who came to power with Mikhail Gorbachev notwithstanding, there is no indication that the ruling circles of the U.S.S.R. are now prepared to alter longstanding Soviet policy concerning the state's command and uses of communications. Yegor Ligachev, the figure in the Gorbachev Politburo most frequently associated with ideological affairs, may have announced the domestic publication of a novel by the late Boris Pasternak, but he has also emphasized that "television and radio programs should serve one aim—propaganda, the clarification and implementation of party policy."

Professor Bialer's proposed portrait of the Gorbachev Politburo as "technocrats" ignores a number of basic facts. One is that the Politburo today gives representation to the Soviet police and security apparatus that is unprecedented since the days of Stalin. There are eighteen full or alternate members in the Politburo at this writing. One of them—Geidar Aliev—was the head of the KGB for the Azerbaijan Republic. Another—Victor Chebrikov—is the current head of the entire KGB. Yet another—Eduard Sheverdnadze, currently Minister for Foreign Affairs—was formerly the head of the Ministry of Internal Affairs, the MVD, for the Georgian Republic. Both Aliev and Shevardnadze's routes to power, incidentally, involved securing the post of first secretary of the party in their respective Republics; in each case the transition also involved the disgrace of the former occupant of the office, and in Azerbaijan, reportedly, his execution as well.

In describing the regimes of both Gorbachev and Andropov (who "regarded Gorbachev as his successor"), facilities for criticism seem at times to be held in abeyance. Bialer depicts as "greater candor in relations between the leadership and the population" the attacks in the media during Andropov's tenure on "pervasive bureaucratic footdragging"—that is, on the holdovers from the Brezhnev era who were preventing Andropov from securing full mastery over Party and State. By the same token, Bialer writes that "Gorbachev and his closest associates do not make a fetish of the reconciliation of institutional interests, as Brezhnev did"—neglecting to mention that a similar judgement could have been rendered for Brezhnev (or Khrushchev or Stalin) in his first months in power.

Professor Bialer's discussions of the Gorbachev faction are in many places extremely considerate. With Gorbachev's ascension to power, according to Bialer, "the mood within the Moscow Party establishment, and among Party aides and experts, can simply be described as exhilaration.[10] . . . The nightmare of the past several years has disappeared . . . the analysis of the Soviet policy is once again a fascinating enterprise. . . ." Gorbachev is described as "suave, witty, and vigorous," "a strong, influential, and respected leader," "by Soviet standards, 'liberal,' deliberate, and workaholic." Personalities leading factions rivaling Gorbachev's own enjoy less consideration. Konstantin Chernenko, for example, is "a weak party apparatchik," "a crony of Brezhnev's with an undistinguished career," a "living corpse." As for Grigori Romanov, who was forced from the Politburo several months after Gorbachev's ascension to First Secretary of the CPSU, he is "an especially brutal man, known for his ostentatious style of living"; "impulsive," "self indulgent," "an extreme hardliner."

The careful reader will notice other problems with Bialer's account of the Andropov-Gorbachev succession. At the beginning of its chapter on "The Chernenko Episode," for example, *The Soviet Paradox* states that "Moscow residents were subjected to an assault of primitive and offensive anti-American propaganda that recalled Stalin's attacks of the 1950s." Dates are not supplied, but the text strongly implies that this "assault" was coincident with Chernenko's rise to power. The reality of the situation was somewhat different. It is true that Soviet propaganda has in recent years fastened upon the theme of war scare. The theme, which emerged in Brezhnev's final years, has been made more prominent and more shrill as the 1980s have progressed. But the escalation of this anti-American campaign was by no means a steady process. To the contrary: as one analyst has noted, "with the ascension of Yuri Andropov to power in late 1982 . . . Soviet propaganda on the danger of a new war acquired a radical new prominence. For the first time since Stalin's death, the Soviet population was exposed to a campaign suggesting that the world was on the verge of a nuclear catastrophe."[11] Under Andropov, for the first time, Soviet propaganda instituted the practice of directly likening the President of the United States to Adolf Hitler. After the death of Andropov, according to the analyst previously quoted, the war scare campaign "softened." If it may be seen to have resumed and surpassed itself in the last months of Chernenko's life, this may not be unrelated to the fact, noted by Gromyko in March 1985, that Gorbachev was by that point already chairing meetings of the Politburo on a regular basis.

Gorbachev gave a definitive presentation of his own position in October 1985, at a Central Committee Plenum. In his words, "the actions of imperialism, and especially U.S. imperialism, ever more clearly elucidate the essence of (their) policy, which is one of social revenge. . . ." In the Soviet language, "revenge" and "revanchism" are formulations customarily applied to the elements in West German society, allegedly wielding vast power, which advocates a continuation of Hitler's programs. Thus, the General Secretary was actually making the equation between the United States and Nazi Germany for his public audience. This speech, it might be noted, was issued almost directly upon his return from the Geneva summit talks with President Reagan.

Such pronouncements are by no means incidental to the Soviet Union's external policies. To the contrary; even if specific tactics and goals may differ, propaganda is as integral to the U.S.S.R.'s quest for international power as it is to the task of mastering the Soviet Union's domestic populations. The current Soviet viewpoint of what is called the "ideological struggle" is stated in a variety of documents, but it is perhaps explained most clearly in the writings of Georgi Arbatov, a professional entrusted not only with codifying such doctrines, but also with its applications.[12] "Far from dying down," Arbatov writes, "the ideological struggle remains acute . . ."; in fact, "peaceful coexistence inescapably presupposes ideological struggle." "The two social systems" and the governments representing them, according to Arbatov, are locked in a duel; "this duel, which is unfolding in the economic, political, and ideological spheres . . . will not end until the more progressive system is completely victorious." As Arbatov explains it, the ideological battle is not only launched against the "imperialist" countries in the international arena, but will be waged against them within their own borders, for "the increased public influence on foreign policy is a process which is undermining the positions of imperialism. This process is irreversible."

Arbatov, other Soviet professionals, and the enormous apparatus at their disposal are actively attempting to 'bring the battle home,' not only to "the main enemy" (the United States), but also to America's allies. However much Professor Bialer may belittle the Soviet Union's international propaganda campaigns, Soviet authorities judge these to be vital, even decisive, activities. In 1978, for example, the Soviet Union is thought to have spent the equivalent of $2 billion in that year of its campaigns against the neutron bomb. Whatever the precise effect of this effort on Western politics, the ultimate Soviet objective was in fact secured. President Carter, acceding to both domestic and international pressures, permanently postponed his decision on deployment, effectively forestalling the possibility that the neutron bomb might be used to assist in the defense of Western Europe in the event of an action by the Warsaw Pact.

There is apparently no room for purposefully countering such Soviet initiatives in Professor Bialer's vision of an American policy toward the U.S.S.R. *The Soviet Paradox* does not acknowledge the increasing role of public diplomacy in the conduct of foreign affairs. It does not discuss the merits of beaming uncensored news reports to the populations of communist countries. Enunciating America's values and principles for international audiences is not said to serve any positive purpose. Professor Bialer even seems to caution Americans against direct criticism of the Soviet Union. Commenting on increased tension in Soviet-American relations in recent years, Bialer states that "Reagan's rhetoric injured the self-esteem and patriotic pride of the political elites. . . . A rekindled sense of insecurity fires an angry and defiant response, a desire to lash out, to reassert self-esteem, to counter the diminished respect of others." In its practical implications, Professor Bialer's analysis cannot be distinguished from a counsel for a unilateral American disengagement and retreat from the international arena of thought and words.

It is particularly unfortunate that such an analysis should be wed to a call for *realpolitik*. Whatever its proponents may say of it, *realpolitik* has a less than perfect record as a calming force in international relations. There are real questions, moreover, about the appropriateness of a policy which dismisses ethical concerns (as *realpolitik* is meant to do) for a nation like the United States, whose international exertions have so often been predicated on a popular understanding of the moral purposes they were meant to serve. Under the very best of circumstances, there may be limits to what could be expected of a *realpolitik* for the United States in the modern world. But even less may be expected from a *realpolitik* that is, in some of its most important respects, uninformed by reality.

The Soviet Paradox comments extensively upon economic questions, but only a small portion of this analysis pertains directly to American policy. Even so, these fragments are significant.

Bialer asserts that "even now Soviet dependence on the world trade market is marginal." Moreover, he states, "The Soviet Union is one of the few communist countries without a significant international debt (relative to its resources and volume of foreign trade)." In Bialer's view, the U.S.S.R.'s "financial soundness, backed by oil, lumber, gold, etc. is questionable." Recognition of these and other basic facts, Bialer argues, should disabuse Americans of the notion that they might use economic leverage against the Soviet Union in any effective fashion. In his words, "Through its economic policy the United States can have no more than marginal influence on Soviet military and foreign policy."

Bialer seems almost adamant on the topic. "Even if the West were able to impose extreme economic sanctions (on the Soviet Union)," he writes, "the system would not crumble, the political situation would not disintegrate, the economy would not go bankrupt, the leadership would not lose its will to rule internally or its will to be a global power." So insistent is Bialer to make the case against the use of Western economic sanctions, as to claim that the Soviet Union "boasts enormous, unused reserves of political and social stability"—directly contradicting one of the principal arguments made earlier in the book.

Bialer implies that any practical attempt to limit contacts with the Soviet Union would have damaging repercussions for the Western alliance. In a subtle and interesting argument, Bialer suggests that Western European countries will need to seek greater outlets for trade in future years, in part to forestall reform of their cherished public welfare systems, and that

"Eastern markets will be of growing importance" as a result. "Basic differences," Bialer warns, "remain between the United States and Europe on the issue of East-West trade and credits." He leaves little doubt whose posture should be amended; as he puts it, "these differences may grow in importance unless there is a change in the American position."

The precise change in the American position that Bialer has in mind appears to be spelled out quite carefully in the last pages of *The Soviet Paradox*. Describing the general sorts of steps which might be taken to "normalize" Soviet-American relations, he mentions specifically one measure, which he describes as a "trade-off." This "would be improvement in Soviet policies on human rights and emigration tied tacitly (but not through an Act of Congress) to American readiness to grant the Soviets Most Favored Nation status." Bialer does not offer hopes that this might improve the "human rights" situation in the Soviet Union. Instead, he explains that "the privilege is important as an expression of equality" by the United States toward Moscow.

Many things might be said of Bialer's analysis; one of the first is that his factual premises appear to be factually incorrect. Bialer would have it understood that the Soviet economy is very largely autarkic, a self-encased construction that is only marginally affected by the world economy. This is a shopworn fiction, and is recognized as such by most serious observers of the Soviet economy. Five years ago the U.S. Bureau of the Census published a careful and thorough study on the role of foreign trade in the Soviet economy.[13] Its conclusions were unambiguous: "Valued in domestic prices, the Soviet Union's participation in world trade relative to its national income is in fact two to three times higher than has been recognized. . . . The notion that Soviet foreign trade is unusually small for an industrialized nation should be discarded." According to the study, "Foreign trade has clearly played an increasingly significant role in the Soviet economy. . . ." By the calculations in the study, total trade turnover equalled about 12 percent of the Soviet "national income" in the 1960s; this had risen to 17 percent by the early 1970s, and had climbed to 25 percent by 1978. Although the report does not provide estimates for later years, there is good reason to believe that the Soviet Union's ratio of foreign trade to national output has risen still further.[14] While no single index or approach can assign a definitive "free market" value to the output from a communist command economy, it is just as clear that the Soviet Union's economy commands a significant, and rapidly growing, portion of its resources from abroad. Indeed, valued against its own state-imposed prices, the U.S.S.R. appears to import twice as much as it exports—and to have done so for many years. By 1978, according to the Census Bureau calculations, imports amounted to over a sixth of the "value" of the U.S.S.R.'s "national income." Today that fraction would be even higher.[15]

Bialer's assertion that the Soviet Union's "financial soundness" is "unquestionable" merits scarcely greater credence. If the Soviet Union is in fact "financially sound," one might wonder why its currency cannot be freely converted into any other currency in the world at anything like the exchange rate that Soviet authorities officially assign to it.

It is true, of course, that Moscow has for many years permitted (or compelled) its Eastern European satellites to expose their economies to Western lending to a much greater degree than for the U.S.S.R. itself. This policy was born of a multiplicity of concerns, not the least of which was the necessity to defray the escalating financial burden attendant to assuring social peace in the "external empire." It is also true that certain Eastern European countries have in recent years adopted a stance of wholesale inability to honor their full financial and commercial obligations to Western countries, and that others have demanded comprehensive "renegotiation" of repayment schedules for the loans they contracted from Western countries, whereas the Soviet Union has reneged upon its contracted commercial obligations to the West in a much more precise and politically selective fashion.[16] But such distinctions are hardly sufficient to invest the Soviet Union with a reputation for solvency, much less reliability.

Despite its extensive and growing need for imported goods and services, many of them from the West, the Soviet Union's ability to generate hard currency is not great. Although hard currency earnings are treated by Moscow as a state secret, and therefore never accurately divulged, it is thought that hard currency exports may have earned the Soviet Union a bit more than the equivalent of $30 billion in 1985. (By way of comparison, this would have been about the same as for Hong Kong, or about a third as much as Canada.) Hard currency debt for the Soviet Union is also a closely guarded state secret. The International Monetary Fund, in one of its exacting exercises in deconstruction and reconstruction, suggests that the Soviet Union's net hard currency debt in 1985 may have been in the range of $14–15 billion U.S. dollars, and its gross hard currency debt about $26 billion. These numbers, however, may understate the actual dimensions of the Soviet debt to the West. A former analyst for the National Security Council has warned that Soviet banking facilities in Western countries may play havoc with such estimates by taking advantage of the accounting rules and regulatory laws under which they operate.[17] (Recycling money through its international network of banking facilities, for example, could make funds originally borrowed from the West appear to be Soviet assets.) Attempting to correct for such financial legerdemain raises this estimate of Soviet gross debt to the West for 1985 by over a third in comparison with the IMF estimate, and nearly doubles the U.S.S.R.'s net debt to the West, which by this calculation would have been $25–28 billion.

Nineteen eighty-six, as it happens, was not a good year in Moscow for hard currency earnings. Prices for the Soviet Union's main exports, oil and gas, continued their downward slide of the previous several years. As a secondary consequence of weak international energy markets, "Third World" cash purchases of Soviet weaponry—another mainstay of earnings for the U.S.S.R.—are also thought to have been down. As Soviet hard currency earnings decline, so the borrowing of Western funds must rise if import targets are to be maintained.

Final figures for debt of the U.S.S.R. for 1986 have yet to be presented by any of the Western institutions capable of reliably attempting such estimates. And there may be limited utility in calculating the ratio of export earnings to net foreign debt, as is customary on Western lending circles, when a government's creditworthiness so directly depends upon its precise intentions about honoring the obligations it has legally contracted. For these qualifications, it is worth noting that the Soviet Union's ratio of earnings to debt may today be approaching the level of Eastern Europe in the late 1970s and early 1980s—a time, it will be recalled, when this region caused great alarm (and ultimately cost a great deal of money) to Western creditors. It is in fact quite possible that the U.S.S.R. today (1987) would be forced into unpleasant economic dislocations, were it not that the Soviet Union and its subsidiary financial organizations enjoy such unimpeded access to Western markets for capital and credit.

In short, Professor Bialer's analysis of the Soviet Union in these points seems about as far off the mark as might be managed. The self-contained and creditworthy economy of which Bialer speaks is in reality more reliant upon Western produce and Western funds today than at any time since the lend-lease program. To no inconsiderable degree, the Soviet Union today augments its might by the benefits it derives from an international order it is doctrinally committed to destroying.

In focusing so carefully on whether foreign economic pressure can force Soviet leaders to relinquish or reverse a specific policy, Bialer totally ignores that impact that foreign economic pressure might have on the U.S.S.R.'s *overall economic might*—a factor that underwrites all Soviet policies. This oversight seems all the more striking in light of Bialer's interests in and enthusiasm for *realpolitik*.

One must wonder what Bialer has in mind by *realpolitik* if it is consonant with the simultaneous repeal of the Jackson-Vanik (and other) "human rights" legislation and extension to the Soviet Union of Most Favored Nation privileges. From the standpoint of power politics, granting Most

Favored Nation status (and all that could reasonably be expected to come with it) to the U.S.S.R. can be expected predictably to strengthen the Soviet Union, and to weaken the position of the United States.

First, contrary to the claims of so many proponents, liberalizing trade with the Soviet Union cannot be expected to liberalize the Soviet regime. To the contrary, increasing trade and credit benefits from the West typified a period of recent Soviet history that Bialer himself has characterized as evincing "a turn to neo-Stalinism." Liberalizing trade with the U.S.S.R. may be more likely to forestall than to sponsor what Westerners call "reform," for it pre-emptively grants to Soviet rulers economic benefits which they otherwise have to seek through the adjustment of domestic and international policies.

Second, increasing trade and credits for the U.S.S.R. would materially ease Moscow's financial burden for its operations abroad. Eastern Europe, Cuba, Vietnam, Nicaragua, Ethiopia and other Soviet dependencies are heavily subsidized by the U.S.S.R., and maintaining them constitutes a real expense for the Soviet state. By one estimate, subsidies to the "external empire" amounted to 2 to 3 percent of the U.S.S.R.'s "GNP" in the early 1980s.[18] Contributing to the Soviet Union's ability to draw resources from the West can only help make this burden less onerous, and therefore extend the scope of Soviet influence abroad, both through proxies and on its own account. Because so many transactions can be made with hard currencies that cannot be managed with rubles, trade and credit from the West ease constraints on Soviet international action out of direct proportion to nominal increases in turnover or loan positions.

Third, thanks to administrative intricacies of the Soviet financial system, it appears that trade with the West directly empowers the Soviet state. It would take us far afield to review the complexities of the Soviet trade and budget systems. In essence, however, one must understand that all rubles are not created equal. A 'tradeable' ruble's worth of grain purchased abroad, upon reaching home port, may automatically be "sold" for (say) three 'domestic' rubles; in a such self-dealing transaction, the Soviet state would pick up a 'profit' of two rubles. Contrary to the view of many Western economists, the Soviet Union appears to run a steady, and growing, budget deficit.[19] 'Profit' on the trade from the West appears to be a major means by which this deficit is financed. In the words of Igor Birman, the emigre economist who has done so much to elucidate this process, "by selling grain to the U.S.S.R., the U.S., besides feeding Soviet cattle, plugs a huge hole in the State budget."[20] It is not impossible that the sale of Western goods to the U.S.S.R. may, in administrative terms, directly finance the Soviet military buildup. Defense expenditures, after all, are an item always kept low on official Soviet ledgers, and thereby particularly suited to "off budget" financing.

Fourth, increasing trade with the Soviet Union is likely to be an expensive proposition for the American taxpayer. Far from offering economic opportunity to Western Europe, the "Eastern markets" of the Warsaw Pact have to date been kept in good repair by the willingness of Western governments to lose money on them. In Western Europe an elaborate and highly inefficient subsidy to endangered domestic economic sectors has been provided by "Osthandel"—in effect, transferring resources from the national legislature to the local farmer, union member or state-owned corporation by way of Karl Marx, Stadt or Kama. Through loan guarantees, subsidized credit, federal export insurance, and a host of other arrangements consistent with Most Favored Nation status, the cost (and risk) of doing business with the Soviet Union would in large measure be charged to the American public. To the extent that the U.S.S.R.'s enhanced economic potential were channelled into increased military expenditures, increased trade with the U.S.S.R. would also require new and possibly significant additions to the American defense budget.

Fifth, relaxing restrictions on trade with the U.S.S.R. would almost necessarily result in a hemorrhage of American military technology, to say nothing of technology with military uses. Part of this loss could be expected to occur through revisions in the guidelines of CoCom, the consultative group, representing most Western nations, that reviews and in theory enforces the embargo of strategic exports from member states against communist countries. If the United States were to treat the U.S.S.R. as a Most Favored Nation, this new position would not only alter the nature of the consensus on the Committee, but might also encourage some members to press for relaxations on Soviet trade that they had not even dared propose in the past. But only part of an increased flow of technology would pass to Moscow by legal means. As is well known, the Soviet Union devotes high priority to efforts to steal Western technology; industrial espionage, in fact, is thought to account for the vast majority of KGB activity in the West. Increased trade privileges for the Soviet Union would seem to argue in favor of an even greater presence of, and access for, Soviet personnel—especially technical specialists—in the United States.

Illegal technology leakage to the Soviet Union is already far from insignificant. To cite but one example, it has been reported that it took less than two years for the radar system invented for the American F-18 fighter jet to appear as a standard feature in the next generation of Soviet MiGs. And more ambitious projects are already in progress. It is reported, for example, that the FBI in 1985 thwarted a Soviet attempt to purchase three banks in Silicon Valley.[21] How such purchases would be prevented once the Soviet Union enjoyed enhanced legal privileges and protections is an unanswered question.

All of these considerations, however, pale by comparison with the sixth. For the relaxation of trade and credit restrictions against the Soviet Union that is envisioned by Bialer would grant Moscow an effective license to intervene in American politics, and to lobby for an American international policy more to the Soviet Union's liking.

Purposeful insinuation of the Soviet agenda into the American political process through the agency of bilateral trade is more than merely an abstract possibility. There is good reason to believe that such an objective is an active aim of Soviet foreign policy—and in fact has been for quite some time. It is worth recalling, for example, that the official representing the U.S.S.R. at the exploratory meetings preceding the creation of the U.S.-U.S.S.R. Trade And Economic Council (an organization dating from the Nixon era, composed on its American side solely of business leaders, and dedicated to the promotion of Soviet-American commerce) was none other than Georgi Arbatov—a professional whose responsibilities lay distinctly outside the fields of trade and economics.

Soviet authorities may have even more reason to look longingly for an expansion of economic ties with the West than this summary suggests. For in the months since Gorbachev's ascension to power, relations in the Soviet press have indicated that the Soviet economy is in more serious straits than had previously been admitted. (It is now [1987] indicated, for example, that real investment levels in the mid-1980s were lower than they had been a decade before; per capita output probably also fell betwen the mid-1970s and mid-1980s.) Under such circumstances, it may not be too much to state that the commercial and economic policies Bialer favors for the United States have never before held the possibility of such strategic advantage—for the U.S.S.R.

Much of *The Soviet Paradox* focuses on Soviet foreign policy. Unlike certain Western observers, Bialer does not feel that Soviet foreign policy can be understood in isolation from other factors pertaining to Soviet power. In particular, Bialer's analysis of Soviet foreign policy is reinforced by, and interwoven with, his evaluation of Soviet military policy. The necessity of examining Soviet military policy and foreign policy conjointly is one of the precepts supporting Bialer's entire exposition. For as he explains it, military power is today the Soviet Union's principal "foreign policy resource," and has served as the engine of "external expansion" for a regime otherwise undergoing "internal decline."

This is a promising point of departure. Unfortunately, Bialer's analysis of Soviet external policy is marked by a tension that does not derive entirely from the difficulty of wielding his theoretical construct. On matters bearing on the conduct of American policy, Bialer's judgments are often inconsistent, sometimes seriously so. Much of Bialer's book, for example, takes the stance that Americans have little chance of altering the Soviet Union's domestic or external policies through their own international action. Yet in discussing the prospective policies of the Gorbachev Politburo, Bialer suggests that "whether concilliatory or aggressive tendencies (in Moscow) prevail (will) depend to a large degree upon Western policies."

If Professor Bialer's reasoning about Soviet external policy appears at times to be (as it were) dialectical, it may also be said to have a main thesis, and one germane to American policy. Though he depicts the Soviet Union as a power obsessed with military strength, and likens the Soviet production system to a "war economy," Bialer nevertheless insists that most Western observers seriously exaggerate the 'Soviet threat' (a phrase he does not use). According to Bialer, in fact, "the American government consistently and continuously overestimate(s) the military strength of its adversary."

Bialer implies that American officials have been moved by something other than intellectual integrity in assessing Soviet military capabilities. He notes pointedly that CIA estimates of Soviet weapons procurements in the late 1970s—estimates, he says, that have since conclusively been proved too high—"created a seemingly solid factual basis for a public mood receptive to the need to rearm America." He leaves the suggestion that important circles in the United States would not be averse to deceiving the public about the nature of the 'Soviet threat,' since "the only way the American military can get increased appropriations is by convincing the people and the Congress of Soviet advances . . ." Bialer indicates that official misperceptions of the Soviet military "have been reinforced under the Reagan Administration." Laboring as it does under the illusion that the U.S.S.R. is a totalitarian state, he writes, the current Administration fails to appreciate what he describes as obvious differences between the Soviet and the Nazi military postures. "Unlike the Nazis," Bialer writes, "the Soviets do not want war with their adversaries"; moreover, "they do not propagandize or glorify offensive military action as the means by which to achieve their international goals."

By Bialer's account, American officials are also guilty of an important misreading of Soviet politics: they ascribe undue consequence to the Soviet military. According to Bialer, "the military establishment" in the Soviet Union "is not today a central actor on the political state." "Tentative new conclusions," Bialer says, are in order about the Soviet planning system: among them, that "the importance of the military priority in

Soviet economic planning may have declined and may continue to do so." Bialer is sufficiently confident in his "tentative" conclusion to base categorical predictions upon it. Surveying the Soviet horizon, he insists that "in any case there will be no return to high growth rates (of military expenditure or defense investment) even in the 1990s in the absence of major improvement in labor productivity." Given Bialer's gloomy prognosis for the Soviet economy, rapid growth of Soviet military expenditures between now and the end of the century would be made to seem a remote possibility indeed.

The slow growth that Bialer foresees for the Soviet military effort fits together with another important component of his vision of Soviet policy: this is the desire of Soviet authorities to achieve a secure "arms control" treaty with the United States. In part, Bialer suggests, a Soviet interest in "arms control" may be "economically determined." In part, he implies, it may be related to the Gorbachev faction's reassertion of control over the Soviet military, a sign of which he sees in the transfer of Marshal Nikolai Ogarkov, the outspoken military theoretician, from his position as Chief of the General Staff of the Red Army to a less conspicuous command. But to a great degree, in Bialer's view, the Soviet impetus for "arms control" emanates from Moscow's appreciation of the reality of "mutually assured destruction" which the present nuclear balance is said to enforce.

In Bialer's view, the need for an "arms control" agreement between the United States and the Soviet Union can scarcely be understated. As Bialer explains it, mankind today lives with the threat of a nuclear holocaust; the danger is so severe, in Bialer's judgement, as to merit the rewriting of the rules of international affairs. According to Bialer, these should now read: "Politics is the avoidance of nuclear war without surrendering one's core values and interests." An "arms control" agreement with the Soviet Union, Bialer writes, will reduce the risks of nuclear catastrophe not only to the principals, but to the rest of the human population. So important does Bialer take the task of "arms control" to be that he urges it to be isolated from all other aspects of Soviet-American relations: in his words, "an arms control accord . . . ought to be reached regardless of confrontation on other issues." Bialer's attention to the need for "arms control," in fact, is so encompassing that it leads him to sound a warning that "those (in the United States) who entertain the idea that (the Soviets) will be unable to match (any increased American defense) efforts have learned nothing from past experience." Professor Bialer's feelings on this matter seem to be so fervent that he neglects to notice that his claim directly conflicts with his earlier forecast of almost immutably low growth rates for Soviet military expenditures until the year 2000.

Bialer seems particularly disconcerted by the American military program known as the Strategic Defense Initiative (SDI). In his view, the United States and the Soviet Union are currently at a "strategic parity" in nuclear weaponry. There are, he implies, no rational reasons why either power would wish strategic superiority, since such superiority could confer no realistic benefit upon its possessor. Bialer describes SDI as a program undertaken in the quest for strategic superiority—one thus by inference destabilizing and irrational. In an analysis phrased much like a recommendation, Bialer explores the merits of using SDI as a negotiating chip to press the Soviets "for concessions with regard to offensive (nuclear) weapons that will make the superpower military balance more equitable and stable." Relinquishing the SDI program, however, would be but a single action in the service of a broader strategic perspective. "The United States," in Bialer's words, "should reconcile itself to strategic parity and abandon illusions that its technological advantages can produce strategic superiority and attain a level of security available in the past but no longer possible in the nuclear age, especially when facing such a determined and powerful opponent."

Professor Bialer's view of Soviet-American military relations frames his view of relations between the two powers overall. The possibility he seems to find most desirable is one he calls "competitive coexistence," a modus vivendi that seems different mainly in name from what Americans once called "détente." The collapse of "détente," Bialer explains, was due in part to a Soviet impulse to exact destabilizing advantages from agreements designed to promote stability. But it was also, he says, in large measure the fault of the United States, for *"in the 1970s no policy toward the Soviet Union would have worked. American paralysis denied credibility to any coherent policy"* (original emphasis). In fact, according to Bialer, "without détente, Soviet actions probably would have been even less restricted and more adventurous."

Bialer dismisses what some people have interpreted as the success to date (1987) of the Reagan Administration in containing the expansion of Soviet influence in the world. "The Reagan administration policies," he writes, "enjoyed some success because they coincided with Soviet overextension, with leadership succession, and with a phase of retrenchment in foreign policy." "In the longer run," he warns, "the United States will fail unless its goals and expectations . . . are significantly readjusted. . . .'' "Competitive coexistence," with its "military détente," increased bilateral trade ties, and de-emphasis of ideological confrontation, is what Professor Bialer offers to avert this impending American failure.

Bialer indicates forthrightly his preferred American responses to the Soviet Union's external policies. He states that "the amount of budgetary growth" that the Defense Department enjoyed in the last year of the Carter Administration and the first term of the Reagan Administration "was probably excessive." He describes the Reagan Administration's new military programs as "a shopping list with no clear priorities." He criticizes specifically the MX missile program, claiming that "nobody has yet found a rational mode of deployment for them." While Professor Bialer characterizes himself as a proponent of a strong American defense, he has nothing but criticism for particular increases in the U.S. military budget, finds no single American weapon system worthy of explicit praise or support, and offers no suggestions for alternative programs that might better contribute to American national security.

As best can be told, the overwhelming majority of the American public would prefer to limit U.S. military spending to the absolute minimum that is consistent with our security and defense needs. Under such circumstances, the identification and assessment of security risks takes on a special importance. Viewed from this perspective, Professor Bialer's exposition on Soviet external policy, written as it is for the general reader seems particularly wanting.

Bialer's claim that Soviet propaganda does not "glorify offensive military action," for its part, relies on the central fact that Soviet doctrine stipulates that any Red Army action by definition *cannot* be aggressive. As Soviet accounts of the recent histories of such places as Afghanistan, the Baltic Republics, Czechoslovakia, Hungary, and Poland repeatedly emphasize, these areas and their peoples have been the beneficiaries of Soviet efforts to defend "peace" and promote international socialism.

Orwellian wordplay notwithstanding, there is little evidence that the Soviet Union's officially crafted cult of militarism is less vibrant, or less comprehensive than was the one in Nazi Germany in the 1930s. Bialer himself notes that nearly a third of the places in Soviet higher education in the 1970s were to be found in military institutions. Perhaps a more vivid illustration of the state of militarization of Soviet society is one he does not mention. This is the "Summer Lightning"/"Little Eagle" exercise held in the U.S.S.R. every year. These mandatory programs gather schoolchildren across the country every summer. Boys and girls are then instructed in and prepared for fighting and winning wars—including nuclear wars. The Soviet press put the number of boys and girls drilled in "Summer Lightning" and "Little Eagle" at about 30 million each year. Children as young as seven are routinely inducted into these preparations.[22]

Professor Bialer's depiction of an American government that "consistently and continuously overestimates" Soviet military spending is equally questionable. Judged by its own figures, the CIA appears to have spent much of the postwar era *underestimating* Soviet military spending. In the early 1970s, for example, CIA estimates of Soviet outlays on weapons were only about a third of what the Agency now believes them actually to have been. It is true that, in retrospect, American officials seem to have overestimated Soviet military outlays for most of the 1950s. Then as now, Soviet authorities prohibited independent inspection of their military facilities; estimates of their military efforts then, as now, had to be based on inference and outside assessment. In those days, however, Soviet authorities were actively interested in exaggerating Soviet military capabilities. The famous "missile gap" of the Eisenhower and Kennedy years to which Bialer derisively refers did indeed mark a failure of American intelligence. What he does not mention is that it also heralded success: the success of Soviet efforts to deceive American analysts.

Today, Soviet military deceptions have a very different purpose. Moscow currently has an active interest in disguising the full extent of its military effort. Soviet budget figures, which depict the U.S.S.R.'s defense expenditures over the course of the 1970s and the early 1980s as *declining,* are but the most evident facet of a more elaborate and far-reaching program of action. Under such conditions, it might seem reasonable to wonder whether American estimates of Soviet defense outlays adequately compensate for the U.S.S.R.'s programmatic attempt to understate its military effort. Professor Bialer's expresses no such concern.

Professor Bialer takes great interest in the revised CIA estimates of Soviet defense expenditures that were released in the early 1980s. Those figures reduce the Agency's previous estimate of growth rates for overall military spending by about half (from about 4 percent to about 2 percent in inflation adjusted U.S. dollars), and give Soviet weapons procurement a zero rate of growth. Bialer takes these new numbers to mean that the American government now acknowledges it had been overstating the extent of the Soviet military buildup, and that its earlier figures had been "faulty." His interpretation is somewhat misinformed. The new consensus about Soviet military spending that Bialer describes in some detail does not, in fact, exist. For example, the CIA and the Defense Department's intelligence unit (the DIA) have not only been involved in a continuing dispute over the revised CIA estimates for the mid-1970s, but are today in public disagreement on the period 1982–1984, with the CIA putting the rate of growth of Soviet weapons spending in those years at zero, the DIA at 3 to 4 percent. The CIA currently (1987) estimates that the U.S.S.R. devotes something like 12 to 14 percent of its GNP to the military effort. There are, of course, a variety of difficulties with these estimates: among them, that the Soviet Union publishes no reliable estimates of its military spending, and no estimates whatsoever of its GNP (a concept peculiar to "bourgeois" economic thinking). For all the caveats appropriate to economic comparisons between the U.S.S.R. and Western societies, one must ask whether the CIA's proposed share of Soviet GNP allotted to the military does not seem strangely low. Perhaps it does not strike American analysts as odd to ascribe to the U.S.S.R. today an only marginally greater "defense burden" than that shouldered in the United States in the mid-1950s (when something like 9 to 11 percent of measured GNP went to defense). Such estimates, however, are taken as totally implausible by many Soviet emigres. According to Igor Birman, the notion that the U.S.S.R. might spend as little as 12 to 14 percent of its GNP on defense is rejected by "practically all" of "the former and present Soviets who have spoken on the subject." These speakers include Academician Andrei Sakharov, who has stated as his view that fully forty percent of Soviet output is devoted to the military.

Bialer appears to be quite comfortable with the 12 to 14 percent figures proposed by the CIA, adjustments of which, he states, would be "irrelevant" to the "indisputable fact of Soviet military strength." Bialer's equanimity in the face of potential instabilities in these CIA estimates is noteworthy for its contrast with his caustic attitude toward presumed errors in other CIA numbers—upon which these figures are in fact necessarily based. His equanimity is all the more striking because of what would portend for U.S. policy if the CIA's assessment were to turn out to be broadly incorrect. For if it were the case that the Soviet military effort absorbed a larger share of the output of that troubled economy than is commonly believed in the West, both the Soviet Union's immediate objectives, and its longer range prospects and needs, might vary significantly from those that Western policymakers are accustomed to anticipating.

This would not mean, of course, that Soviet rulers would secretly be staking their state's future on some imminent surprise attack against the West. This is a notion which is easily ridiculed. But neither the fury with which some observers set at this straw man, nor the obvious relish that they take in dispatching it, can in any way dispose of the more serious issue from which they compose so assailable a caricature. What they avoid discussing—and what many other observers neglect to consider—is the extent to which the threat of force figures in Soviet statecraft, and the extent to which Soviet statecraft is dependent on this threat.

It is not clear that Professor Bialer, for all his attention to the Soviet military, has taken the time to consider its commitment to producing credible force. He notes, for example, that the stock of machine tools is roughly twice as great in the U.S.S.R. as in the United States, but only to emphasize the inefficiency of Soviet industry. It might equally be mentioned that machine building and metal working tools are the equipment with which heavy weaponry is wrought, and that the inventory of such machines determines not only the sort of "surge" in military output that may be produced during the short period, but also the base of any long-term production buildup.

The threat of force depends in part for its impact on the sorts of threats contemplated. Bialer assures his readers that Soviet authorities are "committed consciously and deliberately to the prevention of nuclear war"; such, indeed, is their commitment that they are "prepared to prevent nuclear war for any reason whatsoever." Thoughts of this sort, of course, have been expressed by Georgi Arbatov and other professionals engaged in the battle to influence Western opinions and policies. But these sentiments are not entirely consistent with the actual doctrine that guides the Red Army. Though Marshal Ogarkov is no longer Chief of the General Staff, his writings on military affairs continue to be published. Ogarkov is, for example, the editor of the eight volume 1979 edition of the *Soviet Military Encyclopedia*. His article in that work on "Military Strategy" is particularly informative:

> It is taken into account that with modern means of destruction world nuclear war might be comparatively short. However . . . it is not excluded that it might be protracted also. . . . The Soviet Union and fraternal states in this event will have, in comparison with imperialist states, definite advantages. . . . This creates for them objective possibilities for achieving victory. However, for the realization of these possibilities it is necessary to prepare the country and the armed forces thoroughly and in good time.[23]

Professor Bialer does not entirely exclude Marshal Ogarkov's thinking from his presentation of Soviet military views, but his presentation of the Marshal's writing seems strangely selective. His summary of Ogarkov's writings, in fact, centers on an interview and an article, both from April 1984, where the Marshal expressed his longstanding interests in augmenting and modernizing the procurement of conventional weaponry, and seemed less concerned with bolstering Soviet nuclear forces. Bialer takes these words not only to mean that Ogarkov favors "reform," but additionally makes them mean that Ogarkov might "be opposed" to arguments propounding "the crucial nature of strategic weapons." Even with so narrow a citation of such a prolific author, it is by no means easy to use his words to sponsor the impression that Soviet strategists take nuclear war to be unthinkable—much less unwinnable. After all, if a nuclear war were indeed the protracted engagement that Ogarkov has speculated it might become, ultimate victory might well depend upon the reserves of non-nuclear materiel that a combatant had accumulated for this eventuality. Far from betokening a renunciation of the instrument of nuclear war, the articles Bialer carefully synopsizes are fully consistent with an interest in *perfecting* it—or in Ogarkov's own words, with "preparing the country and the armed forces thoroughly and in good time" in order to establish "the objective possibilities of achieving victory" in "world nuclear war."

An interest in posing a credible threat of nuclear destruction to any and all chosen enemies does not appear to be peculiar to the Soviet Union's military leadership. To the contrary, it is reflected in the viewpoint of the Party ruling the Soviet state, and has been for quite some time. Thus Leonid Brezhnev's toast at the Soviet Embassy in Washington in 1973:

> Our planet is big enough for us to live in peace (e.g., "mir"), but too small to be subjected to the threat of nuclear war . . . everything must be done for the peoples of the world to live free from war, to live in security, cooperation, and communication with one another.[24]

Though the phrasing of Brezhnev's toast is somewhat elliptical, its logic is clear enough. Even at a time of rough strategic balance, the possessor of an enormous nuclear arsenal can "subject the world to the threat of nuclear war." Under such circumstances, "Doing everything for the peoples of the world to live free from war" would have to include propitiating a power that was wielding, or might choose to wield, the threat of global destruction. In short, Brezhnev's formula is a thinly veiled endorsement of diplomacy by blackmail.

It is hardly a coincidence that Brezhnev's professed concern with "the threat of nuclear war" found its public expression at a time of heretofore unprecedented Soviet military power. Nor is it a coincidence that these sentiments colored the early phases of the Soviet policy of "détente" with the United States.

Professor Bialer criticizes equally the United States and the Soviet Union for entertaining unrealistic notions about "détente." He leaves the impression that the Soviet penchant for seeking one-sided gains under the umbrella of U.S.-U.S.S.R. détente—the proximate cause of the policy's collapse—was an idiosyncratic (and thus perhaps correctable) error on Moscow's part. It is an impression that can only be sustained at the cost of ignoring the Soviet Union's official statements on the topic. In Soviet political doctrine, "détente" is understood to be a policy in the service of "peaceful coexistence." Leonid Brezhnev's words on "peaceful coexistence" at the 25th CPSU Congress in 1976 may be taken as the definitive interpretation for the 1970s: "Peaceful coexistence," he warned, "does not in the slightest abolish, and it can not abolish or alter, the laws of class struggle"—the international advance against the forces of "imperialism" that the "worker's state" was historically destined to lead. Regarding negotiations and treaties, Brezhnev stated in 1973 that "the revolution, the class struggle, and Marxism-Leninism cannot be abrogated by order or agreement"; in other words, whatever documents it might sign, the Soviet state, which represents those irresistable forces, could not be expected to restrain their articulation on the world stage, or be held responsible for the consequences. In short, far from being remediable under "détente," the aggressive pursuit of unilateral advantage is integral to the Soviet understanding of the term. "Détente," as the Soviets understand it, is simply a policy by which to make the quest for international power safer and surer. For any state that dares to resist the Soviet Union's international will must now reconcile itself with the certainty that it will be "heightening the threat of nuclear war."

Engaging in "détente" with the Soviet Union does not spare a foreign state from Soviet efforts at nuclear extortion. If more evidence of this were needed, the Western European experience of the early 1980s should surely attest to this. After the demise of "détente" with the United States, the Soviet Union's "détente" with Western Europe continued. Yet during the INF negotiations preceeding NATO's decision to deploy Cruise and Pershing missiles, Western European governments were subjected to the most explicit and violent nuclear threats by ranking Soviet officials. From the Soviet standpoint, there is nothing paradoxical or extraordinary about issuing such threats during a period of "détente." To the contrary: as it is currently conceived, it would be more accurate to suggest that the Soviet policy of "détente" cannot be pursued without the possibility of subjecting foreign states to atomic blackmail.

"Arms control" is foremost among the many items on the Soviet agenda for "détente." What, however, is the objective of such negotiations from the Soviet standpoint? One may best appreciate the Soviet interest in arms control by considering why Soviet authorities have reacted with such undisguised hostility and alarm to the Reagan Administration's Strategic Defense Initiative.

The official Soviet position on the SDI program has been carefully and repeatedly outlined in the Soviet media and by Soviet professionals abroad. It would not matter, from the Soviet perspective, if the resulting American defense system against incoming missiles were less than completely effective (or that the Soviet Union were in the midst of furious development of its own version of the system, as happens to be the case). It would not even matter if the United States were to donate to the U.S.S.R. a system identical to the one it would ultimately install for its own defense.

From the Soviet standpoint, what matters is that the system of strategic defense that the Reagan Administration has embarked upon promises to restrict the Soviet Union's ability to conduct a foreign policy based upon nuclear blackmail. For any policy or invention that would serve to deprive Soviet authorities of the threat of nuclear war would correspondingly push the Soviet Union toward an international position more consistent with its economic base. Not surprisingly, this is a prospect that Soviet rulers are loath to accept.

There is an additional danger to Soviet interests in the U.S. Strategic Defense Initiative. Unlike the current process of "arms control," the technical system the United States promises to devise affords no opportunities for summary violation. For all its attention to arms control, *The Soviet Paradox* neglects to inform its readers about the issue of Soviet violation of existing arms treaties—much less the evidence that such violations are systematic and premeditated. In contrast to the current arms-control process, a strategic system of the sort envisioned by SDI would afford no such opportunities for summary violation. The very existence of the system would be its own "verification"—in this case, a verification which would relieve the United States of any need to presume that the Soviet Union was honoring treaty obligations.

In an interesting exercise in logic, Bialer argues that the Strategic Defense Initiative would increase the threat of nuclear war. But Bialer's position is perhaps not so inconsistent as it would at first appear. He has simply chosen to elevate "the prevention of nuclear war" to the top priority of American foreign policy. From this decision, and his particular interpretation of "preventing nuclear war," many consequences inexorably follow. The United States, he writes, must learn to live with a level of insecurity it would have found intolerable in the past, one which cannot help but make the nation uncomfortable. It must accept not only "strategic parity" with the U.S.S.R., but realize that the Soviet Union has obtained superiority in conventional forces in a number of important regions (Bialer mentions Europe and parts of the Far East). When Soviet actions imperil American "vital interests," it is permissible to attempt to offset their moves, but Bialer leaves "vital interests" conspicuously undefined, and thus subject to ongoing amendment.

Thus, *The Soviet Paradox* leads its readers to the verge of a most unusual bargain. In return for the assurances it offers of inexorable Soviet decline in the years to come, Bialer's analysis seems to request from the United States a purposely diminished, and largely reactive, role in international affairs today. Bialer warns that the alternatives to the "readjustment" he prefers would be "American failure" in the world arena. But the failure that *The Soviet Paradox* would protect America against, and the role it would have America assume, are both in some sense artificial. Both are based not only upon a misreading of key aspects of Soviet military and foreign policy, but require as well subscription to the notion of the threat of nuclear war as it has been defined by the Soviet Union.

Bialer evidently ascribed little value to the *principle* of resisting nuclear blackmail, and sees little benefit to be derived from attempting to cleanse international relations of the poison with which the programmatic introduction of blackmail has necessarily infused them. But to embrace these attitudes, it may be argued, would by itself constitute a vast sacrifice of the American interest in the world, and would only be occasion for even further diminution of the institutions and values in the world that Americans hold dear.

Soviet policy is today at a critical juncture. At issue is not whether the Party will "democratize," or whether the economy will "reform." These hardy perennials of hopeful discussion in the West have survived sixty-five winters with the Soviet state, and will doubtless last a good many more. In Moscow itself, what is at issue today are instead the steps necessary to halt and reverse what is taken to be a relative decline in Soviet power. In Soviet parlance, the "correlation of forces" in the world seem unexpectedly, but unmistakeably, to have shifted against the U.S.S.R. The Gorbachev Politburo is resolved to embark upon a path that will restore a more favorable trend of events.

One may appreciate the enormity of the difficulties Soviet rulers face in this task. Their official ideology, while perhaps integral to the effort to preserve and expand the sway of their state, today appears to have little emotive power of its own. Their economy is troubled and in comparison with the array of countries against which Soviet rulers may envision themselves in conflict, getting weaker. By itself, even the military option may offer little opportunity, for even so directed an economy as the U.S.S.R.'s may only pursue the quest for military ascendancy at a long-range cost. And one cannot count on chance to reverse a trend in the "correlation of forces"; for even in a state with historical inevitability on its side, luck may prove to be an unreliable ally.

The Soviet Union does, however, have one intricate but nevertheless promising option for regaining its lost momentum in the international arena—and indeed for achieving an ascendancy there that it has not yet enjoyed. This is to rely upon the power of the West to promote the Soviet Union's own objectives. If it were possible to channel Western policies in directions and into activities that would serve the Soviet purpose, the U.S.S.R. could prop itself on the backs of its enemies, and elevate itself through their exchange. Through such *jujitsu*, the Soviet Union might even use the very strength of its foes to help achieve their own diminution, or even subjugation.

What such a strategy would require, of course, would be to convince the public and the government of the Soviet Union's most powerful enemies that those things the Soviet Union so dearly wished of them were actually in their own best interest. This would involve an ambitious and complicated battle for the hearts and minds of the enemy, a battle for the commanding heights of Western political will. For any hope of success it would have to be waged relentlessly and one which could only be on many fronts at once.

The Soviet Union wishes Westerners to believe it is not a totalitarian state. It wishes them to believe that Western leaders, for reasons of their own, exaggerate the 'Soviet threat.' It wishes them to believe that the Soviet Union has an active interest in "preventing nuclear war." It wishes them to believe that engaging in "ideological confrontation" can only sour international relations.

The Soviet Union needs greater access to Western trade and credit to aid its own economy. It needs an "arms control" agreement with the United States that will maintain its "strategic parity." It needs somehow to eliminate the system of strategic defense that the United States is currently attempting to develop.

In accepting these arguments and policy preferences, Bialer is by no means unique. Many ordinary Americans, and even a good number of political figures, subscribe to an interpretation and viewpoint very similar to the one expressed in *The Soviet Paradox*. But in the case of Seweryn Bialer, there is a difference. Active as he was in the transformation of Poland into a Soviet satellite; active as he was in the Soviet bloc security apparatus and in the preparation of East bloc propaganda against the United States; familiar as he was, and once again is, with the cadre that is now leading the Soviet Union's "ideological struggle" against the United States and the West—in this case, one can only say: he should know better.

An abridged version of this essay appeared in *Commentary*, May 1987. Reprinted with permission, all rights reserved.

Notes

1. Stephen F. Cohen, *Rethinking The Soviet Experience* (New York: Oxford University Press, 1985).
2. Jerry F. Hough, *Soviet Leadership in Transition* (Washington, D.C.: The Brookings Institution, 1980).
3. Fortunately, such research is once again underway. Initial results are now becoming available on a major survey supervised by Professors Gregory

Grossman of Berkeley and Vladimir Treml of Duke, and Professor James Millar of the University of Illinois.

4. John Van Oudenaren, "Interviews by Soviet Officials in the Western Media: Two Case Studies," The Rand Corporation, October 1985.

5. *23rd Congress of the Communist Party of the Soviet Union,* Novosti Press Agency Publishing House, pp. 142–44, 151–53.

6. Seweryn Bialer, *The Soviet Paradox: External Expansion, Internal Decline* (New York: Alfred A. Knopf, 1986).

7. The newest Soviet Constitution, ratified and adopted in 1977, amends and expands upon Stalin's Constitution (173 articles vs. the previous Constitution's 146). While many of the articles pertaining to the economic life of the Soviet citizen are basically unchanged from the 1936 Constitution, the section on the Soviet citizen's civil rights is laid out in greater detail. The 1977 Constitution, for example, affirms "the right to unite in public organizations"—"in accordance with the goals of communist construction" (Art. 51); "freedom of speech"—"in accordance with the working people's interests" (Art. 50); "the right to conduct atheistic propaganda" (Art. 52); and the obligation of government officials "to take necessary steps" when citizens "criticize shortcomings in work" (Art. 49). It establishes the duty of all Soviet citizens "to prepare (children) for socially useful labor" (Art. 66), and of all able-bodied citizens to "conscientious labor in one's chosen field of socially useful activity" and to "strict observance of labor and production discipline" (Art. 67). While the phrase "enemies of the people" does not appear in the current Soviet Constitution, Articles 59 and 39 specify that "the exercise of rights and liberties is inseparable from the performance by citizens of their duties" and that "the exercise of rights and liberties by citizens must not injure the interests of society and the state"—qualifications which do not totally deprive authorities of administrative and juridical flexibility.

8. In certain passages, Bialer's attempt to describe Soviet events with the American political vernacular amounts to a rewriting of history. Describing Khrushchev's rewriting of history, Bialer states that "He turned over agricultural machinery . . . to the peasants themselves, to be used in accordance with their local needs." The event to which he is apparently referring was the decree to "sell" the equipment from the Machine Tractor Stations which Stalin had devised to the collective farms into which the U.S.S.R.'s peasants had been forcibly gathered.

9. On this score, see Ilya Zemtsov, *Lexicon Of The Soviet Political Language* (Fairfax, VA: Hero Books, 1985).

10. Some comrades, however, appear to have been more exhilarated than others. In his March 11, 1985 nominating speech for Gorbachev, Andrei Gromyko noted that the Central Committee was "solidly in favor" of his candidacy. For Chernenko, and Andropov before him, the term that had been used at the time was "unanimous."

11. Vladimir E. Shlapentokh, "Moscow's War Propaganda and Soviet Public Opinion," *Problems Of Communism,* September/October 1984.

12. The following quotations come from his book, *The War of Ideas in Contemporary International Relations* (Moscow: Progress Publishers, 1973).

13. Vladimir G. Treml and Barry L. Kostinsky, *Domestic Value of Soviet Foreign Trade: Exports and Imports in the 1972 Input-Output Table,* Bureau of the Census Foreign Economic Report #20, 1982.

14. See, for example, the figures presented in Alex Nove, "Some Statistical Puzzles Examined," *Soviet Studies*, January 1986.
15. The extent of Soviet reliance on world markets may be indicated in an area vital to the Soviet economy: food. In 1981, over a fifth of the calories in the Soviet food system is estimated to have come from foreign countries. On this point, see Vladimir G. Treml, "Soviet Foreign Trade In Foodstuffs," *Soviet Economy*, January–March 1986.
16. As when in 1986 it chose to ignore the provisions of its long-term grain purchase agreement with the United States. It should be noted that most discussions of solvency problems in the Soviet bloc have to date confused inability to pay and unwillingness to pay. It can hardly make sense, after all, to argue that an indebted "socialist" government has no saleable assets to apply against its foreign debts when *by definition* it owns the "means of production" of the entire country.
17. Roger W. Robinson, "Soviet Cash and Western Banks," *The National Interest*, Summer 1986.
18. Charles Wolf et al., "The Costs Of The Soviet Empire," The Rand Corporation, September 1983.
19. See Igor Birman, *Secret Incomes of the Soviet State Budget* (Boston: Martinus Nijhoff, 1981).
20. Igor Birman, "The Soviet Economy: Alternative Views," *Survey*, Summer 1985.
21. Richard C. Thornton, "Nuclear Superiority, Geopolitics, and State Terrorism," *Global Affairs*, Fall 1986.
22. Norman M. Naimark and David E. Powell, "Moscow's Cult Of Militarism," *The National Interest*, Summer 1986.
23. Quoted in R.V. Daniels, ed., *A Documentary History of Communism* (Hanover, NH: University Press of New England, 1984).
24. *A Documentary History of Communism, op. cit.*

Part II

Communist China

6

What We Now Know About China

The late 1970s and early 1980s were, quite literally, a time of self-discovery in China. From the 1949 liberation onward, China's Communist leaders had striven to secure unchallengeable power to transform the society beneath them, but they had not shown the same steady interest in familiarizing themselves with the problems and needs of the populace whose lives they intended to transform. As a result, ambitious and delicate "social experiments" were routinely performed with very little knowledge of the conditions, or even the specific afflictions, of the hundreds of millions of patients in question.

As one might expect, this approach to "planning" exacted a high human toll: Chinese officials now say, for example, that over *10 million* people died of hunger in the wake of the "Great Leap Forward" of 1958–59, and non-official estimates by Western scholars run much higher. From the standpoint of the socialist technocrats, perhaps no less shameful was the fact that this kind of "scientific socialism" left the Chinese state apparatus backward and weak. In 1978, frightened by how little they had inherited from their Maoist legators and worried by an increasingly menacing international situation, the group that rose to power with Deng Xiaoping sought to bring events more fully under its command through a campaign of "truth from facts". Like previous Communist Chinese campaigns, this one involved a massive settling of old scores. What set it apart from the two decades of campaigns before it was its nominal goal: learning about the condition of the Chinese people.

Statisticians and academic experts, long considered suspect "bourgeois elements," were rehabilitated and set to work mapping out the nation's social and economic problems; a general documentation of past policy failures was systematically assembled; and a tactical "opening" to the West was effected, through which technicians and know-how might be made to pass. In these early years of the post–Mao "readjustment," it did not serve the purposes of China's new directorate to keep its findings completely out of the public domain; nor would this have been fully possible. Thus, as the new leaders educated themselves about their nation, they also let escape to the West substantially more information about everyday life in modern China than had previously been available. A new body of scholarly literature has taken life from these revelations.

The most eagerly awaited of the new books on life in People's China is without doubt Steven W. Mosher's *Broken Earth: The Rural Chinese*.[1] Even before the book appeared, the Mosher case had become a cause celebre: an issue in U.S.–China relations, and a focal point for arguments about academic freedom and scholarly responsibilities. The Mosher case is highly involved and still (1984) only partly a matter of public record; only the briefest exposition of its outlines (upon which Mosher and his detractors often disagree) can be given here.

In 1979, at the height of "truth from facts" fervor and just after the establishment of diplomatic relations between the U.S. and China, Mosher was awarded a highly coveted Committee on Scholarly Communications (CSC) fellowship to live in and study his then-wife's native village in Guangdong province. Mosher had been a star student in anthropology at Stanford University, and by all accounts was a tireless and highly resourceful investigator of Chinese life during his year-long research visit. The Chinese government lodged no complaints against Mosher at any point during his stay, but when he began writing up and publishing his findings, a far-reaching and relentless campaign to discredit and punish him seems to have been launched. In meetings with Western scholars, Chinese diplomats and scholars would almost invariably bring up the "Mosher incident" and fix upon it, denouncing the man and lecturing their guests on his alleged transgressions. Mosher was—unofficially—accused of bribing local cadres, profiting from graft, smuggling gold and art work out of the country, living with prostitutes in his study village, and other violations of scholarly mores and Chinese law.

At the crescendo of this campaign, Chinese officials directly threatened an executive director of the Social Science Research Council (SSRC), one of CSC's sponsors, that American scholars' access to China would be "reexamined" if the Mosher case were not "resolved." The impact of such threats is unclear: Mosher and Stanford give substantially different accounts of subsequent events. After the start of the anti-Mosher campaign, however, two of Mosher's advisers resigned from his doctoral committee—a highly unusual circumstance in academia—and the Stanford anthropology department began an investigation of Mosher's ethical conduct. After several months of deliberation, the department voted unanimously to expel Mosher. No student in the department had ever been punished so severely.

With much yet to be released, including the faculty report upon which Mosher's expulsion was presumably based, it is too early to comment conclusively on the incident. It seems that Stanford's anthropology faculty believes Mosher was duplicitous in his dealings with them. On the other hand, what seems equally clear at this point is that neither the SSRC, the quasi-governmental sponsor of so much research in the social sciences, nor Stanford University made any great effort to protect or support a young scholar who had come under attack from a government which explicitly rejects the principles both of free speech and of academic freedom. (Since relations with the United States are a topic of great sensitivity in Peking, it seems reasonable to assume that the campaign against Mosher could only have been approved at a fairly high level.) In China, men who "know too much" can be purged without much ado; it would be a disturbing reflection on the American educational system if Chinese cadres were to learn that they could count on scholars in this country to do their punishing and disgracing for them.

Broken Earth: The Rural Chinese is Mosher's testimony of what he saw during his fateful year in China. There is much in this volume which the men in Peking would surely rather not see in print. Mosher writes that the peasants in Sandhead Brigade (village), his temporary home, have come to terms with socialism by circumventing its rules as best they can, much as peasants before them responded to capricious or inexplicable edicts from their emperors. Peasants saved their strength (and their nightsoil) in their obligatory hours in the communal fields, hurrying home to do real work on their private plots. In a system where cadres could award benefits and privileges without even a passing nod to merit, corruption was endemic, and many peasants seemed to have honed the buying of favors down to a science. Local cadres, faced with the options of accomplishing the impossible or incurring wrath from on high, had grown adept at doctoring reports and numbers to please their higher-ups; Mosher mentions one brigade which actually hired educated peasants from nearby communes to take local tests so they could "prove" they had totally eliminated illiteracy.

Not all rules, however, could be dodged or twisted to advantage. While the Chinese government bureaucracy that Mosher saw was often lost in torpor, it was periodically energized by marching orders from Peking that required it to reach into peasants' lives and shake them to their foundations. During these periods there was no hope of escaping the directives of the state, even though these might have disastrous consequences. Mosher was in China at the start of a population-control campaign. The Deng group had decided that its modernization program was being threatened by "excessive" childbearing in the provinces (the role of the government in depressing the production of food or restricting the expansion of consumer industries was not a subject for public discussion). Even as agricultural policy was changing to make peasants more dependent on the labor of their family, a second set of orders was suggesting that parents limit their families to a single child (the so-called "one-child norm").

Mosher described what these orders meant in practice for the women of Sandhead. All who had already borne their "quota" of babies were brought into commune headquarters for a meeting with top commune cadres and party members:

> From Sandhead Brigade there were eighteen women, all from five- to nine-months pregnant, and many red-eyed from lack of sleep and crying. They sat listlessly on short plank benches in a semicircle about the front of the room, where He Kaifeng [a top cadre and party member] explained the purpose of the meeting in no uncertain terms. "You are here because you have yet to 'think clear' about birth control, and you will remain here until you do." . . . Looking coldly around the room, he said slowly and deliberately, "None of you has any choice in this matter. . . ." Then, visually calculating how far along the women in the room were, he went on to add, "The two of you who are eight or nine months pregnant will have a Caesarean; the rest of you will have a shot which will cause you to abort."

Later, Mosher visited the commune health center where these "voluntary" abortions were being performed:

> [One woman], already looking beyond a present in which she had been given an injection of what she called "poison," . . . seemed under the circumstances to be bearing up amazingly well. The woman in the far bed was clearly in much worse shape. Her swollen and blood-flecked eyes . . . took no notice of my presence. . . . I thought at first that she was under medication for pain, but the woman's work cadre informed me that, aside from the "poison shot," she had received no medicine. . . . Nevertheless, the cadre hastened to add, the woman was not in any pain.

There was more. Mosher reports of a woman who was given the "poison shot" *after* she had begun labor, and tells the heart-rending story of a would-be mother who had been successful in concealing her pregnancy from the authorities almost until the end:

> They are so strict now," she continued, tears welling up. "I just want to have this one more baby, and then I'll be glad to have a tubal ligation. In the village there is no way to survive if you don't have a son." . . . She was sobbing heavily by this time. . . . "I will agree to anything they want if they only let me have my baby."

Scenes like these, replicated by the hundreds of thousands, appear to be the human essence of the current Chinese "family-planning" campaign. Although this campaign may seem especially horrifying to foreigners, Mosher argues that it is neither more arbitrary nor more cruel than dozens of other campaigns that have been forced forward in China since the liberation. Indeed, Mosher's conversations with adults who lived through the Cultural Revolution suggest that part of the price of growing up in modern China is coming to expect, and preparing to endure, recurrent periods of state-inflicted suffering.

Few Westerners have seen what Mosher was able to see, and fewer still have had the courage to make their observations public. On these grounds alone *Broken Earth* is assured a place as an important book. Nevertheless, it is not without shortcomings. Mosher is clearly convinced that life in China today is worse than before the liberation; in his final chapter, however, he attempts to convince us of this through the nostalgic reminiscences of the old folks in Sandhead village. Of all people, an anthropologist should be aware that respondents' casual recollections are a highly imperfect means of documenting the past. If life in fact was better under Chiang Kai-shek, the warlords, and the Japanese expeditionary army than it is today, there should be a more persuasive and comprehensive way of showing it.

There are other difficulties with Mosher's approach. At more than one point it appears that Mosher, who is fluent in Cantonese and Mandarin, is not above stretching a translation to fit whatever point he is trying to make. And he has a peculiar habit of winking through the typewriter at his readers, as if there were things he wished he could tell us, but cannot. There may indeed be reasons for Mosher to keep many of his best stories to himself, if only to protect the villagers in Sandhead. Yet his coyness does not serve the cause of clear exposition, nor does it bolster his assertion that an anthropologist on location in a Chinese village can tell us vastly more about Chinese life than a reporter locked up in a hotel in Peking. Fox Butterfield *(China: Alive in the Bitter Sea)*, Richard Bernstein *(From the Center of the Earth: The Search for the Truth About China)*, and Jay and Linda Mathews *(One Billion: A China Chronicle)* have all recently (1984) written reports based on their experiences in China; paradoxically, though these journalists had much less access to "real life" within China than did Mosher, they seem generally more informative about it, and at times even appear to do a better job of conveying its flavor.

As it happens, recent revelations in the Chinese press and scholarly journals have made it possible to paint fascinating pictures of life in modern China without ever setting foot in the country, as two recent works demonstrate. The first is *The Bad Earth: Environmental Degradation in*

China, by Vaclav Smil.[2] Smil, a Czech emigre now teaching in Canada, has laid to rest forever the vision of China as a low-tech ecological paradise. His masterful study, relying almost exclusively on Chinese–language materials, demonstrates that China's path to development has been followed at the cost of serious environmental disruption. Past policies, he suggests, have caused considerably more pollution than one would expect in a poor country that is on its way to industrializing.

Smil is not an environmentalist hysteric: he seems to have no philosophical problems with harnessing nature to serve man's needs. His ecological objections are to inefficient, impractical, or self-defeating policies, and if his account is correct, these have been the rule rather than the exception in China since the liberation.

For much of the past generation, for example, China has pursued the line of "taking grain as the key link" in the rural economy. In practice, this has meant converting forest, hillside, and pastureland into rice paddies and wheat fields, irrespective of the consequences for the local environment, or even for the production of food. According to Chinese scholars, the single-minded preoccupation with grain did not lead to an expansion of arable acreage. Available farmland appears to have declined since the liberation: what overplanting has added to production, resultant erosion and desertification have more than taken away. Despite highly vaunted reforestation programs, China's afforested area has apparently shrunk by more than a third since the early 1950s, with mountains and hillsides correspondingly less capable of retaining water, cycles of drought and flooding have become an increasing plague upon the Chinese farmer.

Smil notes that about a fifth of China's farmland was stricken each year by floods in the early 1950s; today, the fraction is said to be closer to a third. In the centuries before the Revolution, southerly Yunnan province experienced serious flooding about once a decade; today the cycle of disaster recurs every three years. In the arid north, the fragile environment appears to have been even more seriously destabilized. The agricultural outskirts of Peking, which were hit by an average of three sandstorm days a year in the early 1950s, were seeing twenty-six sandstorm days a year by the late 1970s. In Inner Mongolia, overgrazing and overfarming led to a steady decline of agricultural production in the 1970s. And by 1978, Smil notes, Chinese agricultural experts were writing that "production levels and living standards of the masses in quite a number of places are still lower than during the early post–liberation period or *during the War of Resistance against Japan*" (emphasis added). It is only when one considers the magnitude of the disruptions attendant on that all-out war that the meaning of these words can be fully appreciated.

Agricultural problems seem often to have been compounded rather than relieved through the state's use of water resources. The Chinese government seems to have a penchant for giant irrigation and flood-control projects; unfortunately, many of these, like the enormous Sanmenxia reservoir on the Yellow River, turn into useless basins of silt through poor planning and mismanagement, squandering water in the nation's thirsty regions in the process. Smil argues that prudent water management at the local level could meet the needs of China's fields, factories, and families, but the government seems to prefer to solve water problems through constructing new projects, and pays little attention to maintaining, let alone upgrading, the projects it has already completed.

Inattention to water pollution has also left its mark on the People's Republic. By 1978, China's inland fish catch was only half as great as in 1954. The same water that kills the fish must be consumed by the people. Over 90 percent of the waste water from the cities, Chinese authorities report, is totally untreated. This might lead to problems when a main city sewage grate is located forty meters upstream from a main intake duct for drinking water, as it is in Shanghai. Due in part to the diversion of river water to inefficient irrigation projects in the country, the ratio of sewage water to fresh water in Shanghai's Huangpu River during the summer months has been dropping in recent years: by the 1970s, the mix at the drinking taps was six parts fresh water, one part sewage; during the drought of 1979 it fell briefly to one-to-one. If the Huangpu looks to be a public-health hazard, the Ba River of Peking may not be far behind: it caught fire and blazed out of control in late 1979.

Air pollution has also proved to be a serious problem in modern China, and not only from the standpoint of aesthetics. China's industries, motor vehicles, and homes appear to be flagrantly inefficient users of fuel. The magnitude of the waster is suggested by Smil's estimate that reaching Western (i.e., U.S.) levels of energy efficient *in industry alone* would save China the equivalent of 60 million tons of coal a year. The World Bank is now suggesting that China burns twice as much fuel per unit of economic output as the United States, and nearly half again as much as India.

A poor nation can ill afford such reckless use of scarce resources. Chinese officials have stated that 500 million of China's 800 million rural residents suffer from "serious" shortage of fuels for three to five months a year. Deprived of the wherewithal to warm their homes and their food by the profligacy of industry, they must get by as best they can: stripping trees, cutting up turf, and otherwise undermining the productive base of the soil which must sustain them.

Environmental degradation is hardly unique to China. But it may be more difficult to reverse the process in China than in other less-developed countries. In China's planned economy prices are not intended to reflect market scarcities. There may be little financial incentive, or pressure, for factories to consume less energy, or for communes to use water more carefully. In China's monolithic political system, moreover, it is difficult— and risky—for groups which suffer from pollution to stand in opposition to policies officially embraced. If China is to escape from the net of environmental troubles it has cast over itself since the liberation, Smil concludes, it will only be through a radical and sustained redirection of priorities from the very top.

The extent to which China's leadership has trapped itself in problems of its own making is also a theme running through Nicholas R. Lardy's *Agriculture in China's Modern Economic Development.*[3] This superb study, based on a painstaking analysis of Chinese reports on agriculture and industry, is easily the best book on China's food economy in fifteen years. A short volume, it provides not only a history of Chinese agriculture since the onset of "planning," but the best exposition to date of the mechanics of the system that must feed a billion people, and of the effects a generation of revolutionary management has had on its ability to function.

The agricultural system the Chinese Communist party inherited, writes Lardy, is reputed to have been primitive and subsistence-oriented; in fact, though it did have many failings, these were not among them. Though battered by almost twenty years of war and civil disorder, China's farm economy was specialized and complex, with over half of all farm produce finding its way to eventual users through a dynamic network of markets. The revolutionaries who came to power after 1949 attributed the social ills of the old rural China in no small part to the markets themselves, and to the competitive forces which propelled them. After overturning rural society through land reform, they resolved to improve the rural economy by freeing it, to the maximum extent feasible, of marketing infrastructure and independently determined prices.

These reforms had unanticipated consequences. By forcing agriculture to be less commercialized, Chinese authorities necessarily backed farmers into unnatural patterns of subsistence production. "Self-sufficiency" turned out to mean that farmers could not produce what they were best at, and thus led to rising costs of production and declining efficiency in a nation which desperately wanted more food. As Lardy writes, "Self-sufficiency was a chimerical goal except to the extent that it could be achieved by reductions in consumption and income."

Distrust of markets, for its part, unavoidably resulted in a diminished capacity to cope with the disasters which regularly befell the Chinese countryside. By 1978, for example, interprovincial transfers of grain had fallen to one-tenth of a percent of national output—a considerably lower fraction than had been achieved in the 17th century. As a practical matter, such a meager volume of trade could not provide for relief operations for even one stricken province: needy and desperate regions had in effect been cut off from those who might help them in times of hardship.

Although slogans like "agriculture first" implied that the development of the countryside ranked high in the hierarchy of official concerns, Lardy argues that economic policies proved otherwise. Much as the government reversed itself on other matters, it held steady in keeping farm prices low and the prices of farmers' necessities unnaturally high; moreover, the government budget consistently denied the farm sector an economically rational share of national investment funds. Since the mid 1950s, Lardy claims, agriculture has been soaked to build industry, but the industrial structure that has been erected through these regressive transfers is highly inefficient, in effect dependent for its future growth upon continued uneconomic transfer of resources from countryside to city. The process has seriously distorted the entire Chinese economy. "China is probably the only country in modern times," he concludes, "to combine, over twenty years, a doubling of real per-capita income and a constant or even slightly declining average food consumption."

In human terms, Lardy writes, socialist reconstruction of the countryside appears to have been a mixed blessing even for the poor and the hungry. While land reform and the redistributionist policies of the early 1950's incontestably improved the diet of many disadvantaged groups, this appears to have been a once-only gain. "Tentatively," Lardy reports, "it would appear that two decades of collectivized agriculture failed to raise, and may even have reduced, the level of consumption of the poorest quintile [fifth] of China's population." For the nation as a whole, there seems to have been a deterioration in both quantity and quality of foods between the late 1950s and the late 1970s. As one observer has noted, "grain first" worked out in practice to mean "grain only"; per capita grain availability failed to rise, and consumption of the more highly valued foods—vegetable oil, sugar, vegetables, fruit, fish—all went into decline.

If food availability did not grow over these years, inequality in distribution did. According to Chinese sources, per-capita grain availability fell in the countryside by 6 percent between 1957 and 1978; yet it rose by over 10 percent in the cities. Vegetable oil—indispensable to Chinese cooking—dropped by 9 percent over those same years in the cities, but by 43 percent in the rural regions. China's cities have become enclaves of nutritional privilege; their protected status is insured by laws that prohibit country people from traveling to town except under specific and highly restricted circumstances.

Since 1978, China's planners have relaxed some of the rules against rural markets, and have moved to bring agricultural prices more in line with production costs. Agricultural production has responded vigorously to these reforms, but Lardy warns that there may be sharp limits to how much further this regime can "liberalize" its agricultural policies. Since urban food prices are heavily subsidized, raising prices for farmers "would require even larger subsidies for the Ministry of Food that would come at the expense of other government expenditures. That constraint inhibits setting rational farm-level prices and increasing the commercialization of Chinese farming."

But the pressures to return to previous policies do not emanate solely from the budget. Regardless of the sentiments Westerners may choose to ascribe to it, the entire spectrum of leaders high in modern China appears to have a fundamental distrust of policies that remove choices from its immediate grasp. Punitive, even catastrophic, farm policies of the past cannot be written off as aberrations on the learning curve. Lardy writes:

> Policy appears to reflect a consensual process, not the dictates of one man or small group. . . . The fundamental shortcomings of agricultural development policy stem not from the Cultural Revolution, when the so-called leftists were in ascendancy. They stem rather from the introduction of compulsory procurements of farm products in the fall of 1953 and the collectivization of agriculture in 1955–56. . . . In some periods party intervention was moderate . . . but the use of price incentives rather than direct control always has had consequences that have proven unacceptable to China's ruling coalition, whatever its composition. That coalition proclaims frequently its affinity for the peasantry but, except for brief interludes, has adopted policies that promote urban and industrial development, even at the expense of the vast majority.

If the new literature on China answers many questions about the well-being of the Chinese people under three decades of radical social experimentation, it should also raise a number of questions here in the United States. In a society like ours, where information carries certain moral obligations, revelations of the distress of broad segments of the Chinese population—much of it caused by policies deliberately undertaken by a continuum of governmental leaders—raises the issue of what the proper American attitude toward the Chinese state should be. At present (1984), for example, the United States is spending over $10 million, through United Nations conduits, to fund "population activities" in China—presumably efforts not too different from the ones that Steven Mosher witnessed in 1979. China is lobbying for a substantial increase in development assistance from the World Bank so that it might, among other things, undertake new water-works projects and strengthen its "agricultural-management infrastructure"; the United States is reportedly considering underwriting the request. Last, but certainly not least, the Reagan administration appears to have entangled itself in a commitment to shut off the sale of defensive weapons to Taiwan, and may be on the verge of an even more significant strategic decision, which would include the provision of military and nuclear technology to the Mainland.

The new literature on China should leave little doubt in our own minds about the credibility of our nation's commitment to human rights if we should press forward in this relationship. There is, after all, an old Occidental adage that you can judge people by the friends they choose.

Originally published in *Commentary*, March 1984. Reprinted with permission, all rights reserved.

Notes

1. Steven W. Mosher, *Broken Earth: The Rural Chinese*, (New York: The Free Press, 1983).
2. Vaclav Smil, *The Bad Earth: Environmental Degradation in China*, (White Plains, N.Y.: M. E. Sharpe, 1983).
3. Nicholas R. Lardy, *Agriculture in China's Modern Economic Development* (New York: Cambridge University Press, 1983).

7

Material Poverty in the People's Republic of China in International Perspective

From the start of the Great Leap Forward in 1958 through the conclusion of the Third Plenary Session of the Chinese Communist Party's Eleventh Central Committee in December 1978, the material situation of the Chinese people was, at best, a matter of informed speculation in the outside world. The political and social changes witnessed in the Chinese mainland over these two decades were profound, but the statistics which might have borne witness to the impact of various policies and events on the living standards of China's peoples were first systematically falsified, and in later years often simply not published. Despite painstaking and assiduous research by a small number of Western scholars,[1] statistical reconstructions of macroeconomic trends in China during those years were necessarily tentative, and depictions of the material circumstances of the populace itself were all the more conjectual.

Much more is known today (1985) about poverty in China, and its patterns. The "period of readjustment"—which began with the Third Plenum in 1978, and whose duration continues to be extended—has seen the reintroduction of data and statistics into the process of formal policy discourse within the People's Republic of China (P.R.C.). A wide range of numerical information, much of which had been unavailable for decades, is now being released not only through specific speeches, broadcasts, and official pronouncements, but also through increasingly regularized communication with international institutions, by the increasingly systematic publication of statistical compendia, and through the pages of domestic journals devoted to research in the social or natural sciences. These new data make it possible to examine China's achievements in limiting and alleviating material deprivation since the founding of the P.R.C. in 1949, to assess the scope and nature of material poverty on the Chinese mainland today, and to compare the communist Chinese government's performance in improving the material circumstances in the society beneath it with that of other states.[2]

It should go without saying that China's new data on economy and society must be handled with care. The accuracy of statistics depends upon the capabilities of the agencies which generate them, and China's current capabilities for gathering representative and timely data should not be exaggerated. The State Statistical Bureau was a casualty of the Great Leap Forward; it was purged again during the Cultural Revolution. According to Yu Guangyuan, vice president of the P.R.C.'s Academy of Social Sciences, there was a point when "statistical work in China [at the State Statistical Bureau] was performed by only 14 persons".[3] Data-gathering capabilities also suffered at the provincial and the local levels during these upheavals. In Shanghai—China's foremost industrial center—all statistical work is now said to have "virtually ceased" during one period[4]; statistical units were apparently disbanded, even down to the factory level. The extent of the damage to China's statistical apparatus is suggested by the recent revelation by a leading Chinese health statistician that "population and mortality statistics were largely destroyed during the period 1966–1972."[5] Rebuilding a largely shattered national statistical apparatus could only be a formidable task—and a slow one. In 1981, more than two years after the "historic Third Plenary Session," the staff of the State Statistical Bureau was only half as large as it had been in 1965, and less than a third of its size in 1956.[6]

Even as China's statistical system recuperates from earlier injuries and develops new abilities to gather, process, and analyze information, data on poverty are likely to remain a problem area. Li Chengrui, currently director of the State Statistical Board, seemed to acknowledge as much in an article in 1983, when he noted pointedly that, "Our statistics on social affairs, including such areas as population, labor, wages, education, cultural activities, public health, physical education, politics and law . . . are still insufficient as a comprehensive and systematic representation of our country's social developments."[7] Three factors in particular complicate efforts to produce accurate numbers on living conditions in the P.R.C. The first is falsification of data at the lower levels. Deliberate misrepresentation of local conditions has been something of a tradition in the new China: planners recognized the problem well before the Great Leap Forward and have dealt with it ever since.[8] As was dramatized by the "Dazhai [Tachai] brigade incident," even flagrant and continuing falsification of local data may go unnoticed or unchallenged for years. Though recent directives have recognized the fact of falsifications at the local level, they have done little to reduce the pressure on local cadres to doctor figures. A 1984 State

Council "Resolution On Strengthening Statistical Work," for instance, states that "Insuring the accuracy of data is a basic demand of statistical work," but at the same time stipulates that "local statistical bureaus of all levels are under the dual jurisdiction of the people's governments at their particular levels and the statistical bureau at the higher levels . . ."[9]—an arrangement which could all too easily result in conflicting obligations and responsibilities for statisticians in units whose performance is feared to be unsatisfactory. In the past, cadres seem to have felt pressure to adjust local statistics most acutely during political campaigns, or on topics of special political sensitivity. With the resolution at the CCP's 12th National Congress in September 1982 that "we must firmly adhere to the principle of 'first feeding the people and second building the country,' "[10] there can be little doubt in any cadre's mind that poverty is currently a politically sensitive issue.

A second problem, perhaps even more germane to the analysis of poverty, is that China's statistical agencies have apparently never developed an ability to conduct genuinely random sample-surveys.[11] Sample surveys in the P.R.C. typically appear to overestimate local or national output, income, and consumption.[12] This upward bias reflects systematic underrepresentation of poorer localities and population groups in chosen samples. As Chinese authorities explicitly recognize, the devolution of the commune and the rise of the currently (1985) favored "production responsibility system" in the countryside significantly reduces the usefulness of the production brigade as a unit for gathering economic information about the rural population.[13] Direct investigation of conditions through sample surveys of household units is the only practical alternative. Local reports have frankly admitted that the pace of social change in rural areas has exceeded the statistical apparatus' abilities to adjust methods to the new requirements incumbent upon it.[14] Until this gap is closed, figures on living standards for the vast majority of China's population may be beset by margins of sampling error larger than the annual changes that such figures presume to measure.

The third problem concerns the question of indexing, which among other things, permits measurement of changes in real purchasing power. The construction of index systems by which to adjust for or standardize economic changes is theoretically complex under the best of circumstances (see Chapter 11), and is even more troublesome in China's current circumstances. As a recent article in China's leading statistical journal put it, ". . . we have not yet formulated a complete and scientific system of index. Soon after the index of the economic results was set up [a few years ago], some interrelated indices failed to link together or to complement each other. . . . It was even difficult to link up the related statistical index of commodity prices with the statistical index of the overall balance in the national economy. . . . The problems that urgently need to be solved at present include: . . . how to link up . . . the price index of daily expenses of the staff members and workers . . . with the survey of the livelihood of the staff members and workers. . . ."[15] Until the trouble with indices is better resolved, data on economic change, whether pertaining to living standards or any other issue, may easily mislead the observer who wishes to invest them with great significance and meaning.[16]

The task of constructing a statistical apparatus which can render an accurate and timely depiction of social and economic conditions in China, then, is by no means completed. Nor is it seen as such by China's highest authorities. China's National Statistics Law, enacted in 1984, will require "six transformations" in data gathering, processing, and analysis from the various organs responsible for the collection of numbers; some provincial statistical bureaus have set themselves the target of two years to meet these new standards.[17] For the time being, however, it is said that "the development of statistical work is very uneven in the country as a whole" and that it "falls behind the need of the Four Modernizations program."[18] Chinese policymakers, quite naturally, are sensitive to the shortcomings of the statistical system upon which they must depend in their current attempts to create "socialism with Chinese characteristics"; yet their criticisms should not prompt foreign observers to discount the competence which Chinese statistical authorities have demonstrated in given areas. Independent analyses of the Chinese censuses of 1964 and 1982, for example, have suggested that these mass exercises in enumeration achieved a high level of coverage and unusually good accuracy in response.[19] (This accomplishment seems all the more impressive when compared with census results from low-income nations with more technically qualified, and less politically vulnerable, statistical apparatuses.[20]) "Mobilization," in the view of some students of comparative political development,[21] has been Peking's long suit since 1949, and, at least to date, this seems to hold true in statistics as well as politics: modern China appears to be in the anomalous position of often being able to assess national conditions more accurately through mass data-gathering exertions than through the infinitely less taxing procedure of the independent, investigative sample survey. We should keep this in mind in our evaluations.

Even under the best of statistical circumstances, material poverty is imperfectly reflected in national statistics. The problem is intrinsic to poverty itself, and thus may be attenuated but never resolved. The very characteristics which define material deprivation mean that poor people can be expected to leave fainter statistical trails than richer people, even in technically advanced or tightly regimented societies. Moreover, material poverty is not a single, homogeneous, and fixed phenomenon but instead a very human problem: variable, behavioristic and (thus) at least partly attitudinal.[22] Any single set of criteria for measuring poverty will, unavoidably, exclude useful and important information.

While all statistical assessments of poverty, unfortunately, must be arbitrary, some may be less arbitrary than others. Certainly some can be less misleading than others. The difficulties in using such economic measures as income per capita and income distribution, for instance, are legion.[23] Very often these measures are misused. In the case of China, the problem of extracting meaning from economic data is more than ordinarily complex, insofar as one cannot expect either prices or wages to be in equilibrium, or even heading in the direction of equilibrium.[24] In general, it may be argued that physical and behavioral measures provide more insight into conditions of poverty than do financial or economic measures, since, in general, the former are easier to quantify, less sensitive to valuation, and thus more able to transcend the profound differences in political and social systems which separate many of the peoples of the world today. (Economic data, to be sure, have their place in describing poverty, but often seem most useful in highlighting patterns of behavior rather than characterizing levels or standards of income.[25])

In the pages that follow, we will try to use national statistics to speak to four distinct, but overlapping, aspects of material poverty: health, nutrition, literacy and the status of women.

Health

Health conditions provide a primary and basic perspective on poverty within any community or population. They are the clearest and most literal reflection of a group's life chances, in large part because good health comes as close to being a universally desired attribute as any other personal characteristic over which individuals and households may exercise choice.

The least ambiguous indicator of a population's health is its mortality rate. Expectation of life at birth is perhaps the most comprehensive of the many different measures of mortality within a population. For nations with accurate data on age–sex structures and near-complete registration of births and deaths, the calculation of life expectancy is a fairly straightforward arithmetic procedure. When data on population distribution are inadequate or inconsistent, or when registration systems undercount births or deaths to any significant degree, the construction of "life tables" (which give the pattern of mortality for every age group within a population, and thus also the expectation of life at birth) requires that assumptions guide results.

China's vital registration systems, though more complete than those of many other low-income nations, are inadequate for the task of direct estimation of life expectancy.[26] Fortunately, three comparatively reliable censuses (conducted in 1953, 1964, and 1982) and a retrospective nation-wide fertility survey (1982) have made it possible for analysts to reconstruct mortality patterns in China with some confidence. Even so, differences among these estimates suggest the extent to which results remain sensitive to alternative assumptions and techniques.[27]

The most comprehensive analysis of China's newly released population data is perhaps the one undertaken by Banister.[28] According to her estimates, life expectancy at birth in China rose by over twenty years between the early 1950s and 1970. Her estimates suggest that it increased over the 1970s as well, rising by almost another four years (Table 7.1).

Placing a country's record in international perspective requires comparisons with other countries. For China, this presents special problems. In terms of population, diversity, history, and administrative requirements, mainland China is unique. With life expectancy, as with other criteria, China's performance might best be highlighted by contrast against a variety of nations and populations with which it can be said to share certain specific characteristics.

Overseas Chinese populations provide one obvious yardstick for mainland China's performance. Taiwan and Hong Kong would serve in such a comparison; it might also be useful to include Singapore, whose population is about three quarters ethnic Chinese, and Peninsular Malaysia, where a sizeable minority of the population is of Chinese origin.[29] Around 1980, life expectancy is estimated to have been in the mid-60s in China, and in the low-to-mid-70s for these overseas Chinese populations. The pace of improvement over the 1970s is estimated to have been roughly the same in China and the overseas Chinese populations, even though it is presumably more difficult to raise life expectancy by any given amount in the nation where it is already higher. On the other hand, these overseas Chinese populations began the 1950s with an enormous lead in life expectancy over the mainland: in Hong Kong, for example, that difference may have exceeded twenty years. Between the early 1950s and 1970, estimated life expectancy rose very much more rapidly in China than in any of these other territories. The fact is striking for at least two reasons. First, each of these overseas populations was experiencing rapid social and economic development in the 1950s and the 1960s; their performance has been recognized as exceptional in both historical terms and by the standard of contemporary lower-income nations. Second, the administrative problems

TABLE 7.1
Estimated Expectation of Life at Birth for the P.R.C. and Other Selected Regions,
c. 1950–c. 1980 (both sexes in years)

	(1) 1950	(2) 1960	(3) 1970	(4) 1980
1. *People's Republic of China*	40	25	61	65
2. *Overseas Chinese Populations*				
a. Republic of China (Taiwan)	55	65	69	72
b. Hong Kong	(61)	67	71	75
c. Singapore	(60)	64	67	71
d. Peninsular Malaysia	(52)	57	66	70
3. *Populous Asian Nations*				
a. India	32	41	47	52
b. Indonesia	(36)	40	45	51
4. *Other Asian Benchmarks*				
a. Sri Lanka	58	62	65	68
b. South Korea	48	52	63	66
5. *Eurasian Industrial Powers*				
a. Soviet Union	64	68	70	68
b. Japan	60	68	72	76

Notes: Parenthetical figures are projections not based directly on census or survey results. Sources indicate year of estimate when this differs from column heading.

Sources:
Line 1: Banister, "Recent Data on the Population of China," *Population and Development Review*, June 1984; column 1 estimate is for 1953.

Line 2:
a: Directorate-General of Budget, Accounting and Statistics, *Statistical Yearbook of the Republic of China, 1981* (Taipei: Executive Yuan, 1981). Column 1 estimate is for 1951.
b: Column 1: United Nations, *Demographic Indicators of Countries: Estimations and Projections as Assessed in 1980* (New York: UN Department of International Economic and Soviet Affairs, 1982); projection is for 1950–55. Columns 2–3: United Nations, *Model Life Tables for Developing Countries* (New York: UN Department of International Economic and Social Affairs, 1982); estimates are for 1960–62 and 1970–72. Column 4: *Hong Kong Life Tables* (Hong Kong: Census and Statistics Department, November 1982); estimate is for 1981.
c: Column 1: *Demographic Indicators;* projection is for 1950–55. Columns 2–4: Saw Swee-Hock, *Demographic Trends in Singapore* (Singapore: Department of Statistics, 1982); estimate for column 2 is for 1956–1958.
d: Column 1: *Demographic Indicators;* projection is for 1950–55. Columns 2–3: Dorothy I. Fernandez, Amos H. Hawley, and Silvia Predaza, *The Population of Malaysia* C.I.C.R.E.D. Series, 1975; estimate in column 2 is for 1957. Column 4: United Nations, *Demographic Yearbook 1982* (New York: United Nations, 1984); estimate is for 1979.

Line 3:

a: Column 1: Census of India, *Actuarial Reports for the Census, 1881, 1891, 1901, 1911, 1921, 1931, and 1951* (New Delhi: Registrar General, 1960); estimate is for 1941–50. Column 2: Census of India, *1961 Census Life Tables*, 1951–60; *Expectation of Life in the Various States* (New Delhi: Office of the Registrar General, n.d.); estimate is for 1951–60. Column 3: *Model Life Tables for Developing Countries;* estimate is for 1970–72. Column 4: Government of India, *Health for All by the Year 2000 A.D.* (Delhi: Ministry of Health and Family Welfare, 1981); estimate is for 1978.

b: Column 1: *Demographic Indicators;* projection is for 1950–55. Column 2: U.S. Bureau of the Census, *Levels and Trends of Mortality in Indonesia 1961 to 1970* (Washington, D.C.: Department of Commerce, Bureau of the Census, n.d.). Column 3: *Estimates of Fertility and Mortality in Indonesia Based on the 1971 Population Census* (Jakarta: Biro Pusat Statistik, January 1976); estimate is for 1971. Column 4: U.S. Bureau of the Census, *Country Profile: Indonesia* (Washington, D.C.: Department of Commerce, Bureau of the Census, August 1984); estimate is for 1976.

Line 4:

a: Columns 1–3: *Model Life Tables for Developing Countries;* estimates are for 1952–54, 1962–64, and 1970–72. Column 4: Sri Lanka, *Statistical Pocketbook 1983* (Colombo: Department of Census and Statistics, 1983); estimate is for 1979.

b: Columns 1–2: Kwon Tai Hwan, *Demography of Korea: Populations Change and Its Components, 1925–66* (Seoul: Seoul National University Press, 1977); estimates are for 1950–55 and 1960–65. Columns 3 and 4: National Bureau of Statistics, *The Life Table of Korea* (1978–79) (Seoul: Economic Planning Board, July 1982); estimate in column 4 is for 1978–79.

Line 5:

a: Columns 1–3: United Nations, *Levels and Trends of Mortality Since 1950* (New York: UN Department of International Economic and Social Affairs, 1982); estimates are for 1954–55, 1958–59, and 1968–71. Column 4: Christopher Davis and Murray Feshbach, *Rising Infant Mortality in the U.S.S.R. in the 1970s* (Washington: Department of Commerce, Bureau of the Census, September 1980).

b: Column 1: See note 37, columns 2–4: *Japan Statistical Yearbook 1983* (Tokyo: Statistical Bureau, Prime Minister's Office, 1983).

inherent in managing social change within a population of two million (as in Singapore) or even twenty million (e.g., Taiwan) are of an entirely different order from those facing a government responsible for the well-being of a billion people. The administrative challenges incumbent in attending to a population as diverse and simply as large as China's should never be forgotten in any assessment of state performance, past or present.

China might, then, invite comparison with other populous Asian nations. The second and third most populous nations in Asia are India, which has slightly over two-thirds as many people as China, and Indonesia, whose population is less than a sixth of China's, but is distributed across a diverse and expansive archipelago. Life expectancy estimates for both nations involve some conjecture. Neither as yet has a reliable system of death registration, and Indonesia's first census after independence did not take place until 1961. With these limitations in mind, we can see that it appears as if life expectancy in China may have been a decade higher in China than in either India or Indonesia in recent years. At the same time, China's life expectancy in the early 1950s may also have been higher than life expectancy in either India or Indonesia. The pace of progress in raising life expectancy, moreover, appears to have been more rapid in India and Indonesia than in China during the 1970s.

The records of Sri Lanka and South Korea may also be usefully contrasted with China's. While these countries are small, and not populated by Chinese peoples, each is regarded by its admirers as an exemplar of a specific style of successful socioeconomic development. Sri Lanka, it has been said, has managed to reduce extremes of poverty within its borders despite a low overall income level[30]; Korea, by contrast, is sometimes said to have made "trickle down" development work.[31] By 1980, China's estimated life expectancy was only a couple of years lower than either country's, even though a sizeable gap may have separated China from these nations in the early 1950s.

A final glimpse at China's performance may be afforded by contrasting the Chinese experience against life expectancies in the leading Communist and noncommunist nations on China's periphery, the Soviet Union and Japan. Life expectancy may still be several years lower in China than in the U.S.S.R., but for the period in question as a whole, China's life expectancy may have increased by two and a half decades, while life expectancy in the U.S.S.R. since the mid-1950s seems to have risen by only four years. (Soviet life expectancy appears to have fallen for both men and women since the early 1970s[32]; a "freeze" on Soviet health and mortality data, which began in the mid-1970s and has not yet (1985) relented, has made it increasingly difficult both to specify current levels of mortality in the U.S.S.R., and to account for the factors underlying the deterioration in health conditions for broad segments of the national population.[33]) In contrast to both the U.S.S.R. and China, Japan has seen improvements in overall levels of national health which were both rapid and steady. While China has narrowed the gap in life expectancy between itself and Japan since the early 1950s, it is worth remembering that Japan's pace of advance was about twice as fast in the 1950s as was China's in the 1970s, even though China and Japan began those respective decades with similar estimated lifespans.

If China's progress in raising life expectancy could be judged by the endpoints in Table 7.1 alone, evaluation of the country's performance would be a straightforward task. There is, unfortunately, a terrible deviation from trend in the middle of this period. By Banister's estimate, life expectancy in China dropped by half between 1957 and 1960—from almost 50 years to under 25 years.[34] It would take a catastrophe of extraordinary proportions to depress life expectancy for an entire population so radically. The estimated decline in life expectancy in China during those years would be both more rapid and more substantial than the drop in life expectancy for Japanese men over the course of World War II.[35] That drop in life expectancy in China appears to be largely a consequence of the implementation of policies sanctioned by the leadership of the Chinese Communist Party: specifically, the Great Leap Forward. While adverse weather may well have affected agriculture in China in the years following the Great Leap Forward, as China's official commentators still insist (albeit with less conviction than in the past),[36] purposeful governmental action can prevent bad weather from determining the national death rate, even in a low-income society. In India, for example, regional and even national harvest failures have occurred on several occasions since the 1960s, but government policies have consistently checked the increase in mortality during these food shortfalls, and have often prevented death rates in afflicted areas from rising measurably.[37]

The communist Chinese government is in an unusual position. The same state apparatus (and many of the same officials) to oversee modern China's impressive long-term increase in life expectancy also approved decisions which drove short-term health conditions to alarming and unnecessary depths. In other nations, the reduction of mortality levels typically has coincided with the stabilization of mortality. Revolutionary China's mortality trends diverge from this pattern. For the period in question, taken as a whole, it would appear that instability in mortality levels and the pace of improvement in long-run mortality levels were *positively* related.

Infant mortality rates (the number of children to die before their first birthday from every thousand born) are another important measure of health conditions. The rate is significant not only because infants are more vulnerable than adults to the physical insults associated with poverty, and because parents and societies typically place high value on seeing their young survive, but because much of the difference in lifespan between low-income nations and more affluent societies is attributable to differences in the death rates of infants and children.[38] Significant though the infant mortality rate may be, infant mortality itself is especially prone to underregistration. Only a few countries in Asia come close to a complete registration of infant deaths, and China is not one of them. *Chinese Health Care*, a recent compendium compiled under the direction of the Committee of Medical Sciences of the Ministry of Public Health, puts infant mortality in China in 1982 at 13.2 per thousand in cities and 27.2 in rural areas, implying a nationwide infant mortality rate of about 24.3 per thousand.[39] Subsequently, Chinese researchers have produced a "life table" for 1981 in which infant mortality was estimated at 34.68 per thousand.[40] The difference between these estimates is about 30 percent. More sophisticated analyses of Chinese data, using indirect techniques to correct for underreporting of infant deaths, would suggest that as many as half of all infant deaths in China in recent years may have gone unregistered,[41] although the precise fraction cannot be determined. Reconstructions of infant mortality rates are sensitive to the assumptions implicit in the indirect techniques employed. Thus, where infant mortality is high, its exact level is also likely to be in doubt. We should keep this in mind in perusing Table 7.2.

Tables 7.2 and Table 7.1 seem to tell consistent stories. Unlike other countries, where reduction and stabilization of infant mortality typically occurred simultaneously, China appears to have achieved long-term reduction in infant mortality after experiencing a dramatic upsurge. Though infant mortality rates in India and Indonesia remain a matter of informed speculation, there is little doubt that they are at least twice as high in these nations today as in China; quite possibly the disparity may be even greater than that. China's long-run progress in reducing infant mortality compares favorably with Sri Lanka's and South Korea's, countries sometimes cited for their strides in improving popular health. A large gap still seems to separate estimated infant mortality rates in China from those of the overseas Chinese populations and Japan (areas where registration of infant mortality is now complete, or close to complete). Interestingly, China's estimated decline in infant mortality during the 1970s was slower than the declines in Japan, Taiwan, or Singapore in the 1950s, even though infant mortality rates were at roughly similar estimated initial levels.

Regional differences in life expectancy are common to all nations; the more populous and diverse the country, the larger the differences that may be expected. (Within the United States, a developed nation where regional diversity is no longer so pronounced, the difference in life expectancy between Hawaii and South Carolina in 1970 was nevertheless almost six years.[42]) Chinese scholars have attempted to compute life expectancy by province in China on the basis of a "national" cancer epidemiology survey covering mortality during the years 1973–1975.[43] Their computations appear in Table 7.3. Their estimates exclude five provinces or autonomous regions, accounting for over a fifth of China's population. Three of the excluded regions—Gansu, Ningxia, and Shandong—were characterized by an incidence of chronic agricultural poverty in the late 1970s which was well above the national average, according to Ministry of Agriculture investigations.[44] Among those provinces, autonomous regions, and munic-

TABLE 7.2
Estimated Infant Mortality Rates for the P.R.C. and Other Selected Regions,
c. 1950–c. 1980 (deaths per 1000)

	(1) 1950	(2) 1960	(3) 1970	(4) 1980
1. *People's Republic of China*	175	284	70	42
2. *Overseas Chinese Populations*				
a. Republic of China (Taiwan)	91	42	27	22
b. Hong Kong	100	42	19	12
c. Singapore	82	35	21	12
d. Peninsular Malaysia	95	65	40	25
3. *Populous Asian Nations*				
a. India	(190)	(157)	(133)	(129)
b. Indonesia	(166)	(145)	(112)	(99)
4. *Other Asian Benchmarks*				
a. Sri Lanka	81	66	52	38
b. South Korea	116	93	52	38
5. *Eurasian Industrial Powers*				
a. Soviet Union	75	32	26	36
b. Japan	67	31	11	8

Notes: Parenthetical figures are projections. Sources indicate year of estimate when this differs from column heading.

Sources:
Line 1: Banister, "Recent Data on the Population of China"; column 1 estimate is for 1953.

Line 2:
a: *Social Welfare Indicators, Republic of China, 1982* (Taipei: Manpower Planning Committee, Executive Yuan, 1982); column 1 estimate is for 1953.
b: Columns 1–2: *Hong Kong Statistics 1947–1967* (Hong Kong: Census and Statistics Department, 1969). Columns 3–4: *Hong Kong 1981 Census Main Report Volume 1: Analysis* (Hong Kong: Census and Statistics Department, December 1982). Estimates are for 1971 and 1981.
c: Saw Swee-Hock, *Demographic Trends in Singapore.*
d: Columns 1–2: *Monthly Statistical Bulletin of the State of Malaya,* September 1965. Columns 3–4: *Monthly Statistical Bulletin, Peninsular Malaya,* March 1983.

Line 3:
a: United Nations, *Demographic Indicators.* Projections are for 1950–55, 1960–65, 1970–75, and 1975–80.
b: *Ibid.* Projections are for 1950–55, 1960–65, 1970–75, and 1975–80.

Line 4:
a: Columns 1–3: United Nations, *Model Life Tables for Developing Countries.* Estimates are for 1952–54, 1962–64, and 1970–72. Column 4: United Nations, *Demographic Yearbook 1982.* Estimate is for 1979.

b: Columns 1–2: Kwon Tai Hwan, *Demography of Korea;* estimates are for 1950–
55 and 1960–65. Columns 3–4: National Bureau of Statistics, *The Life Table of
Korea (1978–79);* estimate in column 4 is for 1978–79.

Line 5:
a: Column 1: *Population Index,* July–September 1968. Estimate is for 1950–1954.
Columns 2–4: Adjusted from *Rising Infant Mortality in the U.S.S.R. in the
1970s;* estimates are for 1960–61, 1970–71, and 1975–76.
b: *Japan Statistical Yearbook 1983.*

ipalities for which life expectancy estimates were presented, it seems
likely that underregistration of deaths, and thus overestimation of expectation of life at birth, was most common in the least developed areas. In
Tibet, for example, a recent report has stated that infant mortality in the
early 1980s was 190 per thousand, and that this level represented a
significant improvement over earlier years.[45] It is virtually impossible to
reconcile an estimate of expectation of life at birth of over 61 years—the
Chinese author's estimate for Tibet for 1973–1975—with an infant mortality rate of 190 per thousand, let alone any higher figure. Thus, the
interprovincial differences in Table 7.3 may safely be presumed to present
a minimum estimate of actual disparities.

The regional differences in life expectancy computed for China are
contrasted with corresponding estimates of disparities in India and Brazil,
two other populous and diverse nations, in Table 7.4. (Figures for India
and Brazil make an effort to adjust for the underreporting of deaths, and
thus can be expected to depict the gap between advanced and more
impoverished regions with less understatement.) In the mid-1970s, the
difference in life expectancy between China's Manchurian provinces of
Liaoning and Heilongjiang and its "southeastern" provinces of Sichuan
and Guizhou was at least ten years. In India in the 1960s, the difference
between the healthiest state (Kerala) and the state with the lowest estimated life expectancy (Uttar Pradesh) was put at over twenty years, and
for Brazil in 1970 the estimated difference between the highest and lowest
state was placed at almost thirty years. Even accounting for the likely
differential in underregistration of deaths in China's less developed areas,
it would appear that regional disparities in life expectancy in China were
unlikely to be greater than in India or Brazil and may well have been
considerably smaller.

While interprovincial differences in life expectancy do not appear to be
extreme when placed in this international perspective, disparities within
provinces do seem to be pronounced. The cleavage between rural and
urban areas is particularly striking. Recent analysis by Chinese scholars
has estimated the gap in life expectancy between the cities and the
countryside to be on the order of 3–4 years[46]; these computations, how-

TABLE 7.3
**Unadjusted Chinese Estimates of Life Expectation at Birth in the P.R.C. by Province,
1973–75 (both sexes)**

Province	Life Expectancy (Year)
Southeast Region	
Sichuan	60.1
Guizhou	59.3
Yunnan	60.6
Tibet (autonomous region)	61.3
Northwest Region	
Shaanxi	64.6
Gansu	NA
Qinghai	61.3
Ninxia (autonomous region)	62.5
Xinjiang (autonomous region)	62.5
Central South Region	
Henan	66.9
Hubei	NA
Hunan	62.5
Guangxi (autonomous region)	NA
Guangdong	NA
East Region	
Shanghai (autonomous region)	72.0
Jiangsu	67.2
Zhejiang	68.4
Anhui	65.7
Fujian	67.3
Jiangxi	63.2
Shandong	NA
North Region	
Peking (municipality)	69.5
Tianjin (municipality)	70.9
Hebei	68.6
Shaanxi	66.6
Nei Monggol (autonomous region)	66.3
Northeast Region	
Liaoning	69.2
Jilin	65.8
Heilongjiang	70.4
National Average	64.9

Notes: NA: Not available. Figures rounded to nearest tenth. Figures do not adjust for underreporting of deaths.

Source: Rong Shoude et al, "Analysis of Life Expectancy in China, 1973–75," *Renkou Yu Jingji,* 1981, No. 1, quoted in International Bank for Reconstruction and Development, *The Health Sector in China* (Washington: IBRD, 1984).

TABLE 7.4
Estimates of Regional Differences in Life Expectation at Birth in the P.R.C., India, and Brazil for Selected Years (both sexes)

	Period	Estimated Life Expectation at Birth (years)
1. *People's Republic of China*		
Urban Areas		
Shanghai municipality	1973–75	72
Tianjin municipality		71
Peking municipality		70
Provinces		
Heilongjiang	1973–75	70
Liaoning		70
Sichuan	1973–75	60
Guizhou		59
(National Average)	1973–75	(65)
2. India		
States		
Kerala	1961–71	61
Punjab		54
Orissa	1961–71	43
Uttar Pradesh		40
(National Average)	1961–71	(46)
3. Brazil		
State		
Rio Grande de Sol	1970	65
Goias		60
Santa Catarina		60
Alagoas	1970	43
Paraiba		42
Rio Grande do Norte		36
(National Average)	1970	(53)

Sources:
Line 1: Table 7.3, this article.
Line 2: P. N. Mari Bhat, Samuel Preston, and Tim Dyson, *Vital Rates in India, 1961–1981* (Washington, D.C.: National Academy Press, 1984).
Line 3: *Anuario Estatistico do Brasil 1983* (Rio de Janeiro: IBGE, 1984).

ever, do not seem to take the disproportionate underregistration of deaths in rural areas into account. A World Bank mission on rural health and medical education for China, by contrast, has estimated that the difference in lifespans between urban and rural areas at the time of the cancer survey may have been on the order of twelve years.[47] This would be a greater inequality between city and countryside than in India in 1971 (an estimated 8 years),[48] or Indonesia in 1971 (an estimated 6 years),[49] and would be much wider than the difference in Brazil (an estimated 2–3 years).[50] No other nation which has reached China's estimated level of overall national life expectancy has such a pronounced difference in life expectancy separating its urban and rural population.[51]

City people have always lived comparatively privileged lives in China.[52] On the eve of the Communist victory, for example, life expectancy in Shanghai may have been eight years higher than for the nation as a whole.[53] What is striking about modern China's development strategy is that this seems to have preserved a demographic inequality which has tended to diminish over time in other countries.[54]

Government policy appears to contribute actively to this pattern of inequality in modern China. Since the late 1950s, comprehensive administrative restrictions and controls against what is termed "blind migration" have made it difficult for rural people to move to the cities on their own, and still harder to gain official sanction for an unscheduled change of residence.[55] Even with the relaxation of anti–urban mobility policies since the Third Plenum in 1978,[56] the apparatus for impeding or preventing voluntary movement to the cities remains extensive, imposing, and active.[57] Modern China, moreover, has seen the dramatic expansion of a system of subsidies which maintains and even increases the difference in consumption between agricultural and non-agricultural populations.[58] (Although these subsidies usually are not explicitly directed to the cities, being generally conferred instead on the households of "staff and workers at public and state enterprises," in practice the overlap between the two categories is very substantial; in 1980, for example, over five-sixths of the workers entitled to subsidized food lived in cities, and virtually all households legally registered in the cities were entitled to subsidized food.[59]) According to the World Bank's health sector mission in China, state expenditure on medical care on a per capita basis in 1981 was over nine times greater in urban areas than rural areas[60]; while the Chinese rural population does in some measure benefit from urban health expenditures thanks to the medical referral mechanism, the gap in health subsidies for rural and urban peoples is nevertheless profound. Per capita food subsidies work out to be well over ten times higher on average in urban areas than for rural ones in 1981.[61] Extending to China's rural population the nutritional and medical services currently underwritten by subsidy in urban areas would be an awesomely expensive proposition for the Chinese state. For 1981, for example, it would have cost the central government over 90 billion yuan to raise per capita subsidies for medical care and food in rural areas up to the urban level; state revenues for that year totaled just under 109 billion yuan.[62] Matching per capita urban subsidies on all services for the rural population for that year would have required a tripling of total government expenditures.[63]

Between the early 1950s and the early 1980s, China's overall improvement in life expectancy was, by any historical or international measure, very rapid. (Even with the disparity between life expectancy in urban and rural areas, life expectancy in the Chinese countryside in the early 1970s would have been over 60; in the period before "liberation," it has been estimated to have been under 25.[64]) China's pace of health improvement, however, seems to have slowed dramatically over the course of the 1970s. A slowdown of increments in life expectancy at higher overall levels of health is a pattern common among nations, since the locus of health problems tends to shift toward diseases which are more difficult to prevent and more expensive to cure.[65] The tendency toward slowdown in mortality reduction, however, is far from an iron rule. In the United States, for example, life expectancy increased by less than one year between 1955 and 1965, but it rose by almost two and a half years between 1965 and 1975, and by over three years between 1973 and 1983.[66] At any given level of national income or national mortality, social and economic policies strongly influence the prospects for continued improvements in national health.

China's slowdown in life expectancy improvements in the 1970s appears to have been more pronounced than the slowdown for other, overseas Chinese populations when they were at similar levels of life expectancy. While China's sheer size undoubtedly presents administrators with special problems in attempting to implement uniform social policy for the nation as a whole, it seems quite possible that policies chosen may themselves have contributed to the slowdown in health improvements. The system of fiscal subsidies to improve living standards, which has evidently grown vigorously during the "period of readjustment" for urban and state employee households, would seem to have distinct limits in a low-income nation as a vehicle for sustained improvements in health levels for the population as a whole. At the same time, some of the recent policy measures enacted in the hope of raising overall income levels may exert an unanticipated pressure on health conditions for many households.

Transition to a "responsibility system" of household-oriented agricultural management in the countryside, for example, has led to the dismantling of administrative apparatuses previously connected with the commune and the production brigade—including both preventative and curative health services. With the fading of the work–point system, collective mechanisms for insuring the financial cost of medical treatment have also atrophied. In the late 1970s, according to Chinese sources, over 80 percent of the rural population was covered by cooperative medical guarantees of various sorts.[67] By 1981, the fraction is said to have declined to less than 60 percent of the rural population; for 1983, according to Hsiao, "senior public health officials (say that) the latest survey shows that only 40 to 45 percent of the rural population has such coverage."[68] With a decreasing proportion of the rural population covered by health insurance guarantees, and an increasing fraction of the rural population serviced on a flat, pay-as-you-go basis, health care treatment in China would be predicted to reflect economic disparities between households and regions more fully than it did in the past. The ongoing population control campaign, with its aggressive emphasis on limiting parents in rural areas to a single child, appears to have accidentally set the stage for the reemergence of female infanticide in the Chinese countryside as a widespread phenomenon.[69] China's 1982 census, in any event, indicates an abnormally high ratio of boys to girls for those aged under one years, and the Chinese press has carried a continuing stream of articles, editorials, and official directives focusing on and exhorting against the practices of "abandoning and killing baby girls"[70] and "maltreating or persecuting women who give birth to baby girls."[71]

In China's present policy context, it may be difficult to translate economic gains into improvements in health for the population as a whole. If Banister's estimates are accurate, the first years of the "period of readjustment" may have seen stagnation or even decline of health conditions in China by several meaningful indices, despite significant increases in many reported measures of economic and social consumption (see Table 7.5).

Nutrition

For all its importance to individual well-being, nutritional status is not easily assessed through social or economic statistics. Margins of error in data on the availability or consumption of foodstuffs are very often greater than the differences between groups or the changes over time such statistics are used to measure.[72] Moreover, considerable uncertainties remain over the criteria by which dietary adequacy should be judged.[73] (The recent Health and Nutrition Examination Survey in the United States, for example, determined that actual median per capita intake of the American

TABLE 7.5
Estimated Indices of Economic and Demographic Change in the P.R.C. during the
"Period of Readjustment," 1978–1982

	1978	1982	Percentage Change
1. National Income Per Capita (RMB)	315	421	+34 (+21)
2. Consumption Per Capita (RMB)	175	266	+52 (+32)
3. Grain Consumption Per Capita (Kg)	195.5	225.5	+15
4. Doctors Per 10,000 Population	10.8	12.9	+19
5. Infant Mortality Rate (deaths per 1,000)	37	46	+24
6. Life Expectation at Birth, both sexes (years)	65.1	64.7	−1

Notes: National Income Figure refers to P.R.C. conception of "national income."
Parenthetical figures indicate inflation-adjusted changes, as estimated by P.R.C.
State Statistical Bureau.

Sources:
Lines 1–4: State Statistical Bureau, *Statistical Yearbook of China 1983* (Hong
Kong: Economic Information And Agency, 1983).
Lines 5–6: Banister, "Recent Data on the Population of China."

population in the late 1970s was about 1,800–1,850 calories per day[74]—well
below the recommended daily allowances set by the UN Food and Agriculture Organization and the World Health Organization, and lower than
some estimates of per capita availability in Bangladesh.) At present,
clinical examination provides the only basis for conclusive assessment of
an individual's nutritional well-being; since it is not feasible to subject
entire national populations to detailed clinical assessments, it is necessary
to use imperfect proxies in their place.

A first step in assessing a nation's food situation might be to estimate
the overall availability of food per person. National availability per capita
of food cannot provide insight into two of the processes that are decisive
in linking the national food situation to individual well-being: the distribution of available food, and the consumption patterns of the food that is
distributed. National food availability per capita is, thus, a measure of the
maximum potential standard of nutritional comfort that a population may
enjoy rather than a direct measure of the deprivation affecting the least
advantaged elements within society.[75]

In 1981 China released detailed estimates of output for a variety of
agricultural products for selected years in the past; estimates for the
output of "grain," the principal component in mainland China's diet,
extended back to 1950. Using these data, figures on China's international

food trade compiled by the UN Food and Agriculture Organization and the U.S. Department of Agriculture, and recent estimates for the changes in China's population since "liberation," Alan Piazza has attempted to construct "food balance sheets" for China for the years 1950 to 1981.[76] Using the standard caloric valuations for the various foodstuffs represented, it is possible to derive estimates of national caloric availability per capita from these food balance sheets. Table 7.6 presents Piazza's caloric estimates for selected years—generally years in which data output were most comprehensive.

Piazza's estimates are subject to a number of qualifications. They cannot adjust for fluctuations in national grain reserve stockpiles, which may raise or lower national caloric availability per capita in any given year. They use conservative estimates for both the extent of the feedstock economy and the conversion factors within it, thus possibly adding an upward bias to more recent estimates of caloric availability per capita. And they make virtually no allowance for the growth in industrial demand of foodstuffs for non-food use. Taken together, these methodological specifics are likely to exert an upward bias on estimates for more recent years. Upward bias would be consistent with the discrepancy between Piazza's estimates and Chinese estimates of changes in national grain consumption per capita. By Piazza's computations, national caloric availability per capita rose by nearly 15 percent between 1957 and 1978. According to Chinese sources,

TABLE 7.6
Estimated Daily Per Capita Caloric Availability in the P.R.C., for selected years
1952–1981

Year	Estimated Caloric Availability	Index (1957 = 100)
1952	1,917	93
1957	2,065	100
1960	1,462	71
1965	1,997	97
1970	2,092	101
1975	2,226	108
1977	2,247	109
1980	2,496	121
1981	2,526	122

Note: Caloric availability estimated by food balance sheet approach. Calorie estimates to four places reflect computation process, not implicit accuracy.

Source: Alan Piazza, "Trends in Food and Nutrient Availability in China, 1950–1981," World Bank Staff Working Papers, No. 607 (1983).

per capita consumption of grains—which provide the overwhelming bulk of calories on the mainland China diet—*declined* by about 3 percent over this same period.[77] The discrepancy, of course, speaks not only to possible upward bias in Piazza's calculations, but possibly also to changing grain reserve policies, and to changing patterns of loss and wastage within the transportation, storage, and marketing processes—factors which cannot be taken into account in these calculations. Thus, even with these broad national estimates, we should be careful in divining trends.

According to Piazza's estimates, national caloric availability per capita rose by about 7 percent during the First Five-Year Plan (1953–1957). It fell precipitously after the Great Leap Forward, dropping by almost 30 percent between 1958 and 1960. The availability level indicated for 1960, less than 1,500 calories per person per day, would be significantly lower than the FAO estimate of 1,700 calories per day for Ethiopia during the famine years of 1972–1974, if those latter estimates were indeed accurate.[78] (Interestingly, Chinese sources suggest that the cities were spared the nutritional catastrophe which befell the rest of the nation during these years: according to these data, per capita grain consumption in urban areas dropped by less than 2 percent between 1957 and 1960.[79]) National availability per capita appears to have recovered to its 1957 level by 1970, and to have increased substantially since then, with the bulk of the increase occurring after 1977.

The years since the "period of readjustment" may be the first time since "liberation" that national per capita caloric availability has stayed above the level it maintained in the late 1920s and early 1930s. Buck's surveys of farm households, conducted between 1929 and 1933, indicated that per capita caloric availability in rural areas was over 2,500.[80] Though his estimates were corroborated by other contemporary surveys[81] it is generally believed that Buck's surveys and others tended to oversample more prosperous households. Adjusting Buck's estimates downwards to 2,100–2,300 calories per day, it would nevertheless appear by Piazza's computations that national caloric availability per capita would not have clearly exceeded the earlier period's until after 1978. Even then, overall margins of improvement are uncertain, since patterns of both industrial demand for foodstuffs for non-food use and patterns of loss and wastage within the food economy may have changed dramatically since prerevolutionary days. What these figures seem to emphasize is that China's recent and rapid improvements in health and life expectancy were achieved on a level of national food availability which may have been consistently lower than the prerevolutionary norm.

Broad-based improvements in health conditions of the kind which China has experienced would be virtually impossible to achieve without increasing the nutritional security of the more vulnerable strata within the nation. When overall caloric availability is comparatively low, and increasing only slowly or irregularly, nutritional advance must be principally a matter of narrowing differentials in consumption within society, and, perhaps more importantly, of establishing minimum consumption guarantees. China's rising expectation of life at birth would seem to speak to the effectiveness of such minimum guarantees, although in practice these are known to vary widely from one region to the next.[82] Even so, modern China remains a nation of marked disparities in estimated caloric availability per capita, as Table 7.7 suggests. In 1980, by Piazza's calculations, overall per capita caloric availability was scarcely half as great in Inner Mongolia as in the Manchurian province of Heilongjiang. Piazza's figures do not adjust for interprovincial differences in age structure or in industrial demand for foodstuffs for non-food use, two factors which might narrow these ostensible inequalities. Actual differences in availability may also be overstated to some extent because these estimates do not adjust for interprovincial transfers of food. That trade, however, accounted for only a small fraction (barely 1 percent) of foodgrain output in the late 1970s.[83] Directives since that time have aimed at freezing interprovincial transfers at these (historically speaking) extremely low levels.[84] For all these reservations, regional inequalities in per capita caloric availability at the provincial level would nevertheless seem unmistakeably pronounced in modern China.

Table 7.8 puts these geographic disparities in international perspective. For the years 1979 and 1980, overall per capita caloric availability, by Piazza's estimates, was almost 70 percent higher for China's top three provinces (representing about one-eighth of China's population) than in the bottom three (which accounted for about 7 percent of China's population). In India, despite its regional diversity, consumption differences between states were lower than this. (India's figures separate urban and rural consumption for each state, and thus highlight rural disparities; regional differences in food consumption typically tend to be greater in rural than in urban areas throughout the low-income world.[85]) In Indonesia, differences in average consumption per capita between high and low availability areas were estimated to be considerably less extreme than in China. Somewhat surprisingly, the same appears to be true for Brazil.

No less striking than modern China's regional caloric disparities is its pattern of nutritional differences between urban and rural areas. According to the State Statistical Bureau, average caloric availability per capita was 18 percent higher in cities than in the countryside for the years 1979 and 1980. In India, Indonesia, and Brazil, per capita caloric consumption was estimated to be 4 to 12 percent lower in cities than in the countryside in different surveys conducted during the 1970s. (In those three societies,

TABLE 7.7
Estimated Daily Per Capita Caloric Availability in the P.R.C. by Province or
Autonomous Region, 1980

Province	Estimated Caloric Availability	Index (National Average–100)
Nei Monggol	1,577	69
Guizhou	1,631	71
Shanxi	1,764	77
Guansu	1,815	79
Shaanxi	1,832	80
Yunnan	1,895	83
Hebei	1,998	87
Xizang	2,061	90
Henan	2,115	92
Anhui	2,190	95
Xinjiang	2,191	95
Ningxia	2,226	97
Liaoning	2,226	97
Hubei	2,299	97
Guangxi	2,381	104
Fujian	2,384	104
Guangdong	2,387	104
Sichuan	2,389	104
Shandong	2,482	108
Jilin	2,495	109
Jiangxi	2,578	112
Zhejiang	2,679	112
Hunan	2,763	120
Jiangsu	2,793	122
Heilongjiang	3,084	134

Note: Estimates derived from food balance sheet approach. Figures exclude all interprovincial and international trade in food crops. Caloric estimates to four places reflect the computation process, not implicit accuracy.

Source: Piazza, "Trends in Food and Nutrient Availability in China, 1950–81."

and in other low-income nations, the tendency for rural caloric consumption to exceed urban consumption speaks not to deprivation in the cities— but at least in part to the higher caloric requirements of an active rural life.[86]) Part of the difference in urban–rural caloric availability patterns between China and other low-income nations may be explained by the differences in age composition between urban and rural areas in China. Due in part to governmental migration and fertility control policies, China's cities have a markedly lower fraction of children under fifteen years of age in total population (26 percent) than its villages (35 per-

TABLE 7.8
Variation in Estimated Caloric Availability Within the P.R.C., India, Indonesia, and Brazil

	Estimated Calories/Person/Day	Ratio
1. People's Republic of China, 1979–80		
a. Urban Areas	2,901	
Rural Areas	2,453	
(Urban to Rural)		1.18
b. *High Availability Provinces*		
Heilongjiang	2,986	
Jiangsu	2,841	
Hunan	2,934	
Unweighted Average	2,887	
Low Availability Provinces		
Gansu	1,786	
Nei Monggol	1,730	
Guizhou	1,604	
Unweighted Average	1,706	
(High Provinces to Low Provinces)		1.69
2. India, 1971–72		
a. Urban Areas	2,067	
Rural Areas	2,184	
(Urban to Rural)		0.95
b. *High Consumption States, Rural*		
Punjab	2,969	
Haryana	2,922	
Madhya Pradesh	2,829	
Unweighted Average	2,907	
Low Consumption States, Rural		
Tamil Nadu	1,879	
West Bengal	1,849	
Kerala	1,618	
Unweighted Average	1,792	
(High to Low Consumption States, Rural)		1.63
c. *High Consumption States, Urban*		
Rajasthan	2,405	
Madhya Pradesh	2,280	
Himachal Pradesh	2,258	
Unweighted Average	2,314	
Low Consumption States, Urban		
Karnataka	1,898	

Tamil Nadu	1,791	
Kerala	1,682	
Unweighted Average	1,790	
(High to Low Consumption States, Urban)		1.29

3. Brazil, 1974

a. Metropolitan Areas	2,006	
Urban Areas	2,012	
Rural Areas	2,283	
(Urban to Rural)		0.88

b. *High Consumption Regions*		
Region III (The South)	2,361	
Region III (The South), rural	2,847	
Low Consumption Regions		
Region V (The Northeast)	1,899	
Region V (The Northeast), rural	1,980	
(Ratio, Region III to Region V)		1.24
(Ratio, Region III rural to Region V, rural)		1.44

4. Indonesia, 1978

a. Urban Areas	1,912	
b. Rural Areas	2,002	
(Urban to Rural)		0.96

c. *High Consumption Regions*		
Kalimantan	2,431	
Sualwesi	2,408	
Unweighted Average	2,420	
Low Consumption Region		
Central Java	1,605	
East Java	1,584	
Unweighted Average	1,594	
(High to Low Consumption Regions)		1.52

Note: Estimates for China, Line b, derived from food balance sheet approach; figures exclude all interprovincial and international trade in food crops. All other figures derived from consumption surveys. Caloric estimates to four places reflect the computation process, not implicit accuracy.

Sources:
Line 1: a. State Statistical Bureau, *Statistical Yearbook of China 1983;* b. Piazza, "Trends in Food and Nutrient Availability in China, 1950–81."

Line 2: National Sample Survey Organization, *The National Sample Survey, Twenty-sixth Round: July 1971–June 1972 Number 238 Volume I* (New Delhi: Department of Statistics, Ministry of Planning, 1976).

Line 3: Vinod Thomas, "Differences in Income, Nutrition and Poverty Within Brazil," *World Bank Staff Working Papers,* no. 505 (1982).

Line 4: Dov Chernichovsky and Oey Astra Meesook, "Patterns of Food Consumption and Nutrition in Indonesia: An Analysis of the National Socioeconomic Survey, 1978," *World Bank Staff Working Papers,* no. 670 (1984).

cent)[87]—a disparity wider than is found in other low-income nations, and one which would tend to raise average nutritional requirements for urban areas. In the recent past, China's extensive rural health care system may also have lowered rural caloric needs by reducing the prevalence and extent of caloric malabsorption due to infectious or parasitic disease.[88] Adjusting for such factors, however, would not appear to account fully for the difference in urban–rural caloric availability patterns between modern China and other low-income nations. The pattern of preference for the cities is not only distinct from consumption patterns of other nations, but from China's own pattern in the past. Fragmentary survey results from the prerevolutionary period suggest that average caloric consumption was higher in rural than in urban areas during the Republican era.[89] Per capita grain consumption also appears to have been higher in rural areas than in urban areas in China during the First Five-Year Plan.[90] The distinct, new pattern for modern China apparently did not emerge until after the Great Leap Forward.[91]

If the gap in food availability between urban and rural areas in contemporary China seems unusually large, the quality of the overall diet seems unusually low. This can be seen in Table 7.9. By Piazza's estimate, national per capita caloric availability in China rose by almost a third between 1952 and 1981, or by over six hundred calories per person per day. Over this same period there is estimated to have been very little change in the composition of the Chinese diet. In 1952, China derived about seven-eighths of its available calories from "grains"—cereals, starchy root crops, and pulses. This fraction is similar to the fraction derived from similar low-cost calories sources in the extremely poor populations listed together as "Group 3" in Table 7.9. By 1979–1981, when China's national per capita caloric availability was estimated to be similar to that of the overseas Chinese populations in "Group 1," its dietary composition remained much as it had been in earlier periods. China's estimated composition of caloric output is notably different today from those countries listed in "Group 2," all of which have estimated life expectancies similar to China's.

Like the wish for good health, the preference for a tasty and diversified diet appears to be virtually universal. Surveys since the nineteenth century have consistently revealed a preference on the part of consumers for higher-cost, higher-quality foodstuffs (fruits, meats, sugars, oils, leafy vegetables) at higher levels of income or caloric satiation, irrespective of nationality, culture, or social class.[92] It is noteworthy that China's dietary composition seems to have conformed to patterns dictated elsewhere by extreme poverty or lack of purchasing power at a time when overall national caloric availability per capita is estimated to have risen signifi-

TABLE 7.9
Estimated Fraction of Total Caloric Availability Derived from "Grain": P.R.C. and Selected Other Areas

	Period	Total Caloric Availability	Percent from "Grain"
1. P.R.C.	1952	1,917	88.3
	1957	2,065	88.4
	1960	1,462	87.0
	1970	2,092	89.5
	1975	2,226	89.0
	1979–81	2,531	87.1
Group 1			
2. Hong Kong	1972–74	2,596	48.4
3. Peninsular Malaysia	1972–74	2,428	62.3
4. Singapore	1972–74	2,787	49.8
Group 2			
5. Brazil	1972–74	2,471	52.9
6. Mexico	1972–74	2,625	58.6
7. Sri Lanka	1972–74	2,071	65.3
8. Thailand	1972–74	2,297	78.4
Group 3			
9. Bangladesh	1972–74	1,949	86.0
10. Ethiopia	1972–74	1,879	82.9
11. Java, Poorest 40%	1978	1,747	80.2

Note: Caloric availability given in estimated calories P.R.C. per person per day. "Grain," after standard official Chinese usage of the term, is taken to include not only cereals, but roots and tubers, and pulses and legumes. All estimates but line 11 are from food balance sheet approach; line 11 is derived from a nutrition survey. Caloric estimates to four places reflect computation process, not implicit accuracy.

Sources:
Line 1: Piazza, "Trends in Food and Nutrient Availability in China, 1950–81."

Lines 2–10: FAO, *Provisional Food Balance Sheets 1972–74 Average* (Rome: FAO, 1977).

Line 11: Chernichovsky and Meesook, "Patterns of Food Consumption and Nutrition in Indonesia."

cantly. The inflexibility of dietary composition in the early years of the "period of readjustment"—the seeming resistance of output to patterns of consumer taste as witnessed in other Chinese populations—would seem to testify to the limited impact of the "market mechanism" in the Chinese food economy today, even after the advent of the "production responsibility system".

"Bennett's Law"—the tendency for higher-quality food to replace starchy staples at higher levels of caloric consumption[93]—seems to have been suspended, or at least highly qualified, in modern China. "Engel's Law"—the tendency for expenditures on food to account for a smaller fraction of the household budget at higher levels of affluence—by contrast, may still be in effect, since this is a preference revealed directly by the behavior of individual households. As can be seen from Table 7.10, China's city people today seem to devote about the same fraction of their measured incomes to food expenditures as the urban residents of India in the mid–1970s or the city people in Indonesia in the late 1970s. Urban China's "Engel coefficient" is significantly higher than was Hong Kong's in the early 1960s, even though Hong Kong then and China today would appear

TABLE 7.10
Estimated Fraction of Household Expenditure Allocated to Food in Urban and Rural Areas: P.R.C. and Selected Other Regions

	Period	Estimated Fraction Allocated to Food
A. Urban Areas		
1. People's Republic of China (Staff and Workers in Cities)	1982	58.7%
2. Peninsular Malaysia	1973	30.1%
3. Hong Kong	1963–64	46.8%
4. Pakistan	1971–72	49.3%
5. India	1964–65	60.7%
6. Indonesia	1978	59.7%
B. Rural Areas		
7. P.R.C. (Peasant Households)	1982	60.5%
7a. (Liaoning Province)		(54.7%)
7b. (Anhui Province)		(63.8%)
7c. (Guizhou Province)		(65.6%)
7d. (Kansu Province)		(67.8%)
8. Peninsular Malaysia	1973	41.2%
9. Pakistan	1971–72	57.5%
10. India	1964–65	70.5%
11. Indonesia	1978	69.6%

Note: Survey methodologies differ among countries compared in this table.

Sources:

Lines 1 and 7–7d: State Statistical Bureau, *Statistical Yearbook of China 1983.*

Lines 2–5 and 8–10: FAO, *Review of Food Consumption Surveys 1977* (Rome: FAO, 1979).

Lines 6 and 11: Chernichovsky and Meesook, "Patterns of Food Consumption and Nutrition in Indonesia."

to be at roughly similar levels of life expectancy. Comparisons of Engel coefficients between urban areas in China and other nations, however, are compromised by a number of factors, not the least of which are the hidden subsidies which do so much to shape actual consumption patterns in China's cities.[94] The Engel coefficient may be a somewhat more meaningful measure in the Chinese countryside, where the level of state subsidy is dramatically lower. For 1982, survey results indicated that about three-fifths of China's peasant household's expenditures were devoted to food, although the fraction varied noticeably between more affluent and more impoverished provinces. (Since Chinese survey techniques appear to underrepresent poorer households, we may take the figures produced in these expenditure studies as providing a lower boundary for the actual likely Engel coefficient for these regions, and for the nation as a whole.) For China's overall agricultural population, the Engel coefficient for 1982 was estimated to be similar to that of Pakistan's rural population for the early 1970s; for certain provinces, it was estimated to be closer to that of rural Indonesia in 1978, or rural India for 1964–1965.

Judged by their health levels, the Chinese people would be predicted to live in modest comfort (or, in the case of the cities, perhaps even in an environment approaching mass affluence). Judged by available statistics on their consumption patterns for food, China's people might be expected to live in poverty—possibly in extreme poverty. The contradiction speaks to the extent to which nutritional patterns in contemporary China have been separated from consumer preference. This contradiction, in one sense, might represent a policy success, since the isolation of consumer preference from economic results is one of the objectives of central economic planning.

In physical terms, the nutritional results of China's food policies are represented in Tables 7.11 and 7.12. These provide estimates, respectively, for mortality of children aged 1 to 4—a cohort thought to be particularly sensitive to nutritional setback[95]—and of heights and weights for children between the ages of 7 and 16.

China's estimated child death rate appears to have fallen dramatically between 1957 and 1975, and to have fallen further by 1981, although at a much slower pace. By this singularly important measure, China would appear to have made notable progress in controlling and reducing the worst effects of malnutrition on its population. At the same time, anthropometric data indicate that significant nutrition-related differences separate the populations of prosperous and less prosperous provinces, to say nothing of rural areas and the cities. By the criteria of height and weight differences of children, nutritional inequalities between regions appear to be similar in China today and the Brazil of the mid-1970s. Interprovincial differences in

TABLE 7.11
Estimated Mortality Rates for Children from 1 to 4 Years of Age in the P.R.C. and
Selected Other Regions, c. 1950–c. 1980 (deaths per 1000)

	(1) 1950	(2) 1960	(3) 1970	(4) 1980
1. *People's Republic of China*	25	NA	6	5
2. *Overseas Chinese Populations*				
a. Republic of China (Taiwan)	17	8	3	1
b. Hong Kong	NA	4	1	—
c. Singapore	NA	4	1	—
d. Peninsular Malaysia	12	8	4	2
3. *Populous Asian Nations*				
a. India	40	24	17	15
b. South Korea	NA	28	26	18
4. *Other Asian Benchmarks*				
a. Sri Lanka	17	10	6	3
b. South Korea	21	16	4	3
5. *Eurasian Industrial Powers*				
a. Soviet Union	NA	4	3	3
b. Japan	9	2	1	—

Notes: NA: Not available; — = Less than 1 per 1000.

Sources:
Line 1:
Columns 1 and 3: Based on Ling, Rui-Zhu, "30 Years' Mortality of Chinese
Population." *World Health Statistics Quarterly* (1981). Figures given are for 1957
and 1975, and are adjusted for presumed 20 percent undercount of mortality rates
both sexes. Adjustments based on age distribution data and urban-rural population
distribution data from State Statistical Bureau, *Statistical Yearbook of China 1983*.
Column 4: based on Jiang and Zhu, cited in note 40. Mortality estimates are
adjusted for presumed 15 percent undercount of child deaths for each sex.

Line 2:
a: *Statistical Yearbook of the Republic of China 1981*. Estimate in column 1 is for
   1953.
b: Columns 2–3: United Nations, *Model Life Tables for Developing Countries;*
   estimates are for 1960–62 and 1970–72. Column 4: *Hong Kong 1981 Census
   Main Report Volume 1: Analysis;* estimate is for 1981.
c: Columns 2–4: Derived from Saw Swee-Hock, *Demographic Trends in Singapore;* estimates for column 2 are for 1956–58, and in column 3 for 1969–71.
d: Columns 1–2: *Monthly Statistical Bulletin of the States of Malaya,* September
   1965; estimate for column 1 is for 1955. Columns 3 and 4: *Monthly Statistical
   Bulletin,* Peninsular Malaysia, March 1983.

Line 3:
a: Column 1: Census of India, *Actuarial Reports for the Census* (1960); estimate is
   for 1941–50. Column 2: Census of India, *1961 Census Life Tables;* estimate is
   for 1951–61. Columns 3–4: Derived from Bhat, Preston, and Dyson, *Vital Rates
   in India;* estimates are for 1972 and 1971–81.

b: Columns 2–3: U.S. Bureau of the Census, *Levels and Trends of Mortality for Indonesia 1961 to 1971;* column 3 estimate is for 1971. Column 4: U.S. Bureau of the Census, *Country Profile: Indonesia;* estimate is for 1976.

Line 4:

a. Columns 1–3: *Model Life Tables for Developing Countries;* estimates are for 1952–54, 1962–64, and 1970–72. Column 4: United Nations, *Demographic Yearbook 1982;* estimate is for 1979.

b: Columns 1–2: Kwon Tai Hwan, *Demography of Korea;* estimates are for 1950–65. Columns 3–4: National Bureau of Statistics, *The Life Table of Korea (1978–79);* estimates in column 4 are for 1978–79.

Line 5:

a: Columns 2–4: Derived from *Rising Infant Mortality in the U.S.S.R. in the 1970s;* estimates are for 1960–61, 1970–71, and 1975–76.

b: *Japan Statistical Yearbook 1983.*

the height and weight of children may be greater in China than the disparities between the most prosperous and the least prosperous areas of South Korea. These anthropometric differences indicate areas of nutritional and health disadvantage within China, and thus priority areas for nutritional improvements in the future.

Literacy

Attaining literacy does not in and of itself protect an individual against the risks of poverty, but command of reading and writing skills can be used to reduce systematically the risk of suffering from material deprivation.[96] By placing the world of written knowledge at the disposal of an individual or household, literacy can increase both productivity and security for those who are willing to use it to do so. In the modern world, education and literacy bear strong positive association with earnings,[97] strong negative association with infant mortality,[98] and seem to increase the ability of households to cushion themselves against adverse fortune in times of hardship.[99]

Literacy has no fixed definition. It is a functional concept, and its requirements thus depend upon the society, the occupation, and the era. In China, where the writing system is not phonetic, the definition of literacy becomes particularly problematic. Full mastery of the Chinese calligraphic system was commonly said to require twenty years' study for the literati in the days of the imperial examinations, yet intensive training courses sponsored by the "Mass Education" reformers in the early twentieth century could provide a knowledge of Chinese writing sufficient for the basic demands of village life in four to six weeks.[100] Educational reformers in Republican China set the standard for functional peasant

TABLE 7.12
**Media Heights and Weights for Children in the P.R.C., Brazil,
and South Korea**

	Height by Age (cm)				Weight by Age (kg)			
	7	10	13	16	7	10	13	16
1. P.R.C.								
A. Urban Shanghai								
males 1979	118.0	131.0	145.0	162.0	20.0	26.0	34.9	49.1
males 1959	114.9	125.6	139.5	157.8	18.7	23.7	31.8	44.9
females 1979	117.3	131.5	146.6	155.4	19.6	25.8	36.0	46.7
females 1959	111.2	123.6	141.0	152.4	18.3	22.9	31.9	44.8
B. Schoolchildren, Peking and rural Gansu, 1980								
Peking males	125.3	136.4	156.0	—	24.3	28.9	41.4	—
Rur. Gansu males	114.5	124.6	140.2	—	25.6	26.5	34.1	—
Peking females	122.4	136.3	156.0	—	22.4	28.6	42.0	—
Rur. Gansu females	112.5	125.3	143.1	—	22.4	26.5	35.0	—
C. 16 Province Survey, 1979								
Urban males	121.2	—	—	—	21.3	—	—	—
Rural males	117.3	—	—	—	20.3	—	—	—
Urban females	120.4	—	—	—	20.6	—	—	—
Rural females	116.3	—	—	—	19.6	—	—	—
Rural Liaoning males	118.8	—	—	—	21.1	—	—	—
Rural Sichuan males	113.5	—	—	—	19.2	—	—	—
Rural Liaoning females	117.3	—	—	—	20.3	—	—	—
Rural Sichuan females	112.9	—	—	—	18.5	—	—	—
Urban Liaoning males	121.6	—	—	—	21.1	—	—	—
Urban Sichuan males	118.7	—	—	—	20.5	—	—	—
Urban Liaoning females	121.0	—	—	—	20.5	—	—	—
Urban Sichuan females	118.0	—	—	—	19.6	—	—	—

2. Brazil, 1975

A. Sao Paolo vs. The Northeast
   (Region II vs. Region V)

Sao Paolo males	120.0	135.5	155.5	166.3	22.2	29.5	40.1	54.0
Northeast males	114.0	128.7	142.2	158.9	19.8	26.0	34.1	47.9
Sao Paolo females	119.6	135.8	151.8	157.3	22.0	30.5	42.9	51.0
Northeast females	114.4	128.8	146.2	153.2	19.7	26.2	38.5	47.8

3. South Korea

A. Schoolchildren, 1980 v. 1965

males 1980	120.0	134.4	150.4	165.6	22.2	29.3	40.0	55.5
males 1965	112.5	128.3	143.4	162.5	19.1	25.4	34.7	50.7
females 1980	119.6	134.8	150.7	156.5	21.4	29.4	42.7	51.5
females 1965	112.0	128.6	144.9	154.7	19.1	25.2	36.2	47.6

B. Schoolchildren, Seoul vs. Chollanam Province, 1980

Seoul males	121.8	135.4	153.2	167.7	22.6	30.2	41.6	55.1
Chollanam Do males	119.0	132.8	148.4	164.2	21.9	28.6	37.8	54.5
Seoul females	120.7	137.6	152.2	156.1	21.6	31.2	43.9	50.1
Chollanam Do females	118.7	133.1	148.8	155.5	20.7	28.2	41.5	52.3

Sources:
Line 1: World Bank, "The Nutritional Status of Children in China: A Review of the Anthropometric Evidence: *PHN Technical Notes, GEN–17*, August 1983.

Line 2: *Anuario Estatistico do Brasil 1980* (Rio de Janeiro: IBGE, 1980).

Line 3: For 1965: Ministry of Health and Soviet Affairs, *Yearbook of Public Health and Social Statistics, 1980* (Seoul: Ministry of Health and Soviet Affairs, 1980). For 1980: Ministry of Education, *Statistical Yearbook of Education, 1981* (Seoul: Ministry of Education, 1981).

literacy at recognition of about 1,200 characters; [101] Communist Chinese authorities set the standard for peasants at 1,500 characters ("enough to read simple publications, to keep accounts, and to write informal notes") and at 2,000 characters for workers. [102] Chinese authorities distinguish between "illiterates" and "semi-literates" in accordance with the number of characters they can command. [103] At the same time, China's educational tabulations place "illiterates" and semi-literates together in a single category—perhaps not an unreasonable classification, considering the limitations of semi-literacy in a non-phonetic system.

At least as much as with reducing disease or malnutrition, direct governmental interventions have an instrumental role in reducing illiteracy. Communist China has made well-noted efforts to eliminate illiteracy, both through expansion of primary schooling and promulgation of adult education campaigns.[104] The results of these efforts are reflected in the 1964 and 1982 censuses, both of which included questions on literacy. Table 7.13 presents these data. (The findings are presented in terms of the estimated extent of illiteracy, since its shadings may be fewer in the Chinese context, and its pertinence to poverty is more direct.)

Changes in the estimated incidence of adult illiteracy and semi-literacy in China are contrasted with changes in estimated rates of illiteracy in other regions in Table 7.13. These comparisons must be approached with special care, since definitions of and standards for literacy vary so widely among the nations surveyed. Hong Kong, for example, treats anyone with formal education as literate; Singapore requires the respondent to write a specified sentence; India simply asks its adults if they can read.

The overseas Chinese populations began the 1950s with significantly lower rates of illiteracy than the Chinese mainland, and seem to have kept them significantly lower. India's illiteracy rate may have been somewhat higher than China's in the early 1950s, but it appears to be dramatically higher today. On the other hand, it is not clear that China's performance in reducing illiteracy is superior to Indonesia's. For comparable age groupings (i.e., adults over 15 years of age), China's measured rate of illiteracy and semi-literacy in 1982 was higher than Indonesia's measured rate of illiteracy for 1980 (35 percent vs. 32 percent). Though data on literacy and schooling in Indonesia are spotty before 1961, it appears that before 1949 non-enrollment and illiteracy were at least as prevalent in Indonesia as in China.[105] Japan, on the other hand, had virtually eliminated adult illiteracy by 1949, and while adult illiteracy is thought to be a continuing problem in the U.S.S.R., especially among its populations of Muslim descent, the peculiarities of Soviet presentations of information of education qualification and illiteracy reduce the information which foreign analysts may draw from them and limit their comparability against data from other countries.[106]

There are substantial regional variations in illiteracy in China today, as can be seen in Table 7.14. In general, these variations are consistent with measured regional disparities in health and nutrition. Estimated rates of illiteracy and semi-literacy are almost twenty points higher in rural than in urban areas. This disparity is wider than the corresponding differences in Peninsular Malaysia, Taiwan, South Korea, or Sri Lanka, but it is about the same as in Indonesia, is somewhat narrower than in Brazil, and is noticeably narrower than in India. China's interprovincial differences in

TABLE 7.13
Estimated Adult Rates of Illiteracy in the People's Republic of China and Other
Selected Regions, c. 1950–c. 1980 (percentage)

	(1) 1950	(2) 1960	(3) 1970	(4) 1980
1. *People's Republic of China* (12+) (Illiterates and Semi-literates)	(70–80)	59	NA	31

2. *Overseas Chinese Populations*
    a. Republic of China (Taiwan)
        (15+)
	43	27	22	14

b. Hong Kong (15+)	NA	29	23	16
c. Singapore (15+)	54	50	31	17
d. West Malaysia (15+)	61	53	42	24
3. *Populous Asian Nations* a. India (15+)	80	72	66	(60)
b. Indonesia (15+)	NA	61	43	32
4. *Other Asian Benchmarks* a. Sri Lanka (15+)	32	25	22	14
b. South Korea (15+)	NA	29	12	(7)
5. *Eurasian Industrial Powers* a. Soviet Union (9–49 only)	NA	—	—	—
b. Japan (15+)	2	2	—	—

Notes: NA = Not Available: — = less than 2%: Definitions of illiteracy vary by
country and by the given census.
Parenthetical figures are projections.

Sources:
Line 1: Column 1: taken from Evelyn S. Rawski, *Education and Popular Literacy
in China.* (Ann Arbor: University of Michigan Press, 1979). Estimates for pre-1949.
Column 2 and 4: Calculated from State Statistical Bureau, *Statistical Yearbook of
China 1983;* estimates are for 1964 and 1982.

Line 2:
a: Directorate-General of the Budget, Accounting and Statistics. *Statistical Yearbook of the Republic of China. 1981* Taipei: Executive Yuan; estimate in column
   1 is for 1951.
b: *Hong Kong Census Main Report Volume 1: Analysis.* (Hong Kong Census and
   Statistics Department, December 1982). Estimates are for 1961, 1971, and 1981.
c: Columns 1 and 3: UNESCO, *Statistics of Educational Attainment and Illiteracy
   1945–1974.* (Paris: UNESCO Statistical Reports and Studies #22, 1977). Estimates in columns 1 and 2 are for 1947 and 1957. Column 4: Khoo Chian Kim,
   Census of Population 1980 Singapore Release #1. (Singapore: Department of
   Statistics, 1981).
d: Column 1: M. V. de Tufo, *A Report on the 1947 Census of Population* (Kuala
   Lumpur: The Government Printer, 1949); estimate is for 1947. Columns 2 and 3:
   Statistics of Educational Attainment, op. cit., estimate for column 2 is for 1957.

Column 4: *Population and Housing Census of Malaysia 1980 General Report on the Population Census, Volume 2* (Kuala Lumpur, Department of Statistics Malaysia, n.d.)

Line 3:

a: Columns 1 and 3: *Statistics of Educational Attainment, op. cit.,* estimates are for 1951, 1961, and 1971. Column 4: UNESCO, *Estimates and Projections of Illiteracy.* (Paris, UNESCO, Division of Statistics, September 1978).

b: Columns 2 and 3: *Statistics of Educational Attainment, op. cit.,* estimates are for 1961 and 1971. Column 4: *Results of Sub-Sample of 1980 Population Census Preliminary Tables,* (Jakarta: Biro Pusat Statistik, 1982).

Line 4:

a: Columns 1 and 3: *Statistics of Educational Attainment, op. cit.,* estimates are for 1953, 1963, 1971. Column 4: Census of Population and Housing Sri Lanka 1981 *Population* Table based on a *Ten Percent Sample.* (Colombo: Department of Census and Statistics, February 1982). Estimate is for 1981.

b: Columns 2 and 3: *Statistics of Educational Attainment, op. cit.* Column 4: *Estimates and Projections of Illiteracy, op. cit.*

Line 5:

a: Central Statistical Board of the U.S.S.R., *The U.S.S.R. In Figures for 1979.* (Moscow: Statistika Publishers, 1980).

b: Column 1 and 3: *Statistics of Educational Attainment, op. cit.,* column 1 is for 1948. Column 4: UNESCO, *Statistical Yearbook 1982.* (Paris: UNESCO, 1982).

literacy, however, seem exceptionally wide. In 1982, Liaoning and Tibet were separated by a gap of almost sixty points. In India, a country often cited for its regional disparities in educational attainment, the difference between the highest and lowest illiteracy rate among its states in 1971 was more than ten points less than this.

To some extent, any government intent upon reducing illiteracy is hostage to the past. Adult illiterates are typically resistant to the transition to a lifestyle shaped by the written word, and require constant reinforcements if the change is to hold.[107] China may have been no more successful with its adult illiterates than other low income nations. According to the 1982 census, the rate of illiteracy and semi-literacy for people then over 55 (i.e., 22 years old or older in 1949) was above 75 percent—not too different, perhaps, from the national level of the prerevolutionary period.

China's record in inculcating literacy in cohorts which grew up under the revolutionary order is shown in Table 7.15. Among those who were of the proper age for primary schooling after 1949, the measured rate of illiteracy of semi-literacy is put at 19 percent. This would be far lower than India's estimated rate of illiteracy for younger adults in 1971. China's 1982 rate of illiteracy and semi-literacy for teenagers (15 to 19) was similar to Indonesia's illiteracy rate for 1980 (9 percent vs. 13 percent). Its rate for people in their twenties was close to Brazil's estimated illiteracy rates for

TABLE 7.14
Regional Variations in Estimated Adult Illiteracy: People's Republic of China, India,
Indonesia, and Brazil

	Illiteracy Rate
1. *People's Republic of China, 1982* (12 +) (Illiterates and Semi-literates)	
A. Urban Areas	16
Rural Areas	35
B. Liaoning Province	17
Guizhou	48
Xizang (Tibet) Autonomous Region	75
2. *India, 1971* (15 +)	
A. Urban Areas	40
Rural Areas	73
B. Kerala State	31
Bihar	76
Rajasthan	78
3. *Indonesia, 1980* (15 +)	
A. Urban Areas	17
Rural Areas	36
4. *Brazil, 1978* (15 +)	
A. Urban Areas	16
Rural Areas	42
B. Sao Paulo (Region II)	14
The South (Region III)	16
The Northeast (Region V)	44

Notes: Definitions of illiteracy and urban areas differ among surveys and censuses presented in this table.

Sources:
Line 1: *Economic Daily,* December 19, 1983 quoted *China News Analysis,* 1256, March 12, 1984.

Line 2:
a: UNESCO, *Statistical Yearbook 1983* (Paris: UNESCO, 1983).
b: Government of India, *A Handbook of Education, and Allied Statistics* (New Delhi: Ministry of Education and Culture, 1980).

Line 3: *Results of the Sub-Sample of 1980 Population Census Preliminary Tables* (Jaharta: Biro Pusat Statistik 1982).

Line 4: UNESCO, *Statistical Yearbook 1984* (Paris: UNESCO 1984). Anuario Estatistico do Brazil—1980. (Rio de Janeiro: IBGE, 1980).

TABLE 7.15
Estimated Rates of Illiteracy for Younger Age Cohorts: People's Republic of China,
India, Indonesia, and Brazil

	Estimated Illiteracy Rate (percent)
1. *China 1982* (age 12–44) (Illiterates and Semi-literates)	
Beijing	3
Liaoning	4
Jiangxi	19
Guizhou	38
Xizang (Tibet) Autonomous Region	69
National Average	19
2. *India 1971* (age 15–35)	
Kerala	19
Tamil Nadu	48
Punjab	53
Madhya Pradesh	66
Bihar	71
Rajasthan	72
All India	58
3. *Indonesia 1980* (age 15–19)	
Urban	5
Rural	16
National Average	13
4. *Brazil 1978* (age 20–29)	
Rio de Janeiro (Region I)	6
Sao Paulo (Region II)	6
The South (Region III)	9
The Northeast (Region V)	33
National Average	15

Notes: Definitions of illiteracy vary among surveys compared in this table.

Sources:
Line 1: *Economic Daily,* December 19, 1983, quoted in *China News Analysis,* 1256, March 12, 1984.

Line 2: Government of India, *A Handbook of Educational and Allied Statistics* (New Delhi: Ministry of Education and Culture, 1980).

Line 3: *Results of the Sub-Sample of 1980 Population Census Preliminary Tables* (Jakarta: Biro Pusat Statistik, 1982).

Line 4: *Anuario Estatistico do Brazil—1980.* (Rio de Janeiro: IBGE, 1980).

the same age cohort in 1978 (17 percent vs. 15 percent). China's national rate for younger people, however, conceals dramatic regional disparities. In such places as Peking and Liaoning, illiteracy and semi-literacy for younger adults seem close to being eliminated, while in Tibet the measured incidence of illiteracy and semi-literacy was placed at 65 percent. In Guizhou, a poor province but one which unlike Tibet is overwhelmingly Han Chinese in ethnicity, illiteracy and semi-literacy among the younger adult population is put at 38 percent—twice the national average.

Further reductions of illiteracy and semi-literacy rates in China will depend largely on the education of rising generations. As Table 7.16 shows, the net enrollment ratio for primary schooling in China in 1981 was put at about 93 percent. On its face, this would seem to indicate a much greater access to primary school for Chinese than for Indian children. It would be a rate of access similar to that of Indonesia and somewhat below that of other East Asian nations. A net enrollment ratio of 93 percent would indicate that 7 percent of those children of the age group for which primary schooling is designated (in China, the years 7 through 11) are not enrolled. Non-attendance, however, is a problem above and beyond non-enrollment. In rural areas of Peking municipality, for example, the average attendance rate for primary schools was reported to be 75 percent in the early 1980s.[108] Attendance rates may well have been lower in less developed rural locales. Unfortunately, there are no reliable data on school attendance rates for either China as a whole, or many of the nations against which we might wish to compare her.

Ultimately, a cohort's literacy rates may be either higher or lower than its primary school net enrollment ratio, depending (among other things) on the quality of education provided, the correspondence between enrollment and attendance, the economic returns and social advantages to attaining literacy, and the rhythms and requirements of daily life in the milieu where education may be taking place. It is perhaps significant, however, that China's net primary school enrollment ratio is reported to have fallen since the beginning of the "period of readjustment." In 1977 and 1978, according to Chinese reports, net primary school enrollment ratios were over 95 percent.[109] By 1981, the rate was put at 93 percent.[110] It was said to remain at 93 percent in 1982.[111] In 1983 it was reported to have risen, but only to 94 percent—a level lower than reported six years earlier.[112]

The reasons for this decline—which has been widely discussed not only in Chinese educational journals but also in the Chinese press—may differ among the various localities for which this has emerged as a problem. By all accounts, however, it appears to be a rural rather than a strictly national problem, and while it undoubtedly reflects ongoing official efforts to raise local educational standards, it seems partly to be related to the transition

TABLE 7.16
Estimated Gross and Net Primary Enrollment Ratios for the People's Republic of China and Selected Other Regions, c. 1980

	(1) Gross Enrollment	(2) Net Enrollment
1. *People's Republic of China* (1981)	118	93
2. *Overseas Chinese Populations*		
a. Republic of China (1980)	NA	100
b. Hong Kong (1980)	109	97
c. Singapore (1980)	107	98
d. Malaysia (1980)	92	NA
3. *Populous Asian Countries*		
a. India (1978)	85	66
b. Indonesia (1980)	112	92
4. *Other Asian Benchmarks*		
a. Sri Lanka (1981)	100	NA
b. South Korea (1980)	109	100
5. *Eurasian Industrial Powers*		
a. Soviet Union (1980)	106	NA
b. Japan (1980)	100	100

Notes: NA = Not Available. Duration of and age norms for, primary schooling varies among the countries compared in this table.

Sources:
Line 1: Column 1: UNESCO, *Statistical Yearbook 1983* (Paris: UNESCO, 1983). Column 2: Ji Hua, "Education in China" in Xue Muqiao, ed., *Almanac of China's Economy 1981* (Hong Kong: Modern Cultural Company, Ltd., 1982).

Line 2:
a: *Social Welfare Indicators Republic of China 1981* (Taipei: Manpower Planning Committee, Executive Yuan, 1982).
b: *Statistical Yearbook, 1983*, loc. cit.
c: *Ibid.*
d: *Ibid.*

Line 3:
a: Column 1: Government of India, *Selected Educational Statistics, 1978–79* (New Delhi: Ministry of Education and Culture, 1980). Column 2: *Fourth All-India Educational Survey* (New Delhi: National Council of Educational Research and Training, 1980).
b: *Statistical Yearbook, 1983*, loc. cit.

Line 4:
a: *Statistical Yearbook, 1983*, loc. cit.
b: *Ibid.*

Line 5:
a: *Statistical Yearbook, 1983*, loc. cit.
b: *Ibid.*

to a "production responsibility system" in the countryside. Some reports, for example, suggest that the "production responsibility system," in increasing the value to the household of family members' labor, has prompted some parents to withdraw their children from the classroom and place them in the field.[113] Others have suggested that changes in the system of financing primary schooling have brought new, theretofore unfelt, pressures on poorer households, and that some parents have responded by selective non-enrollment of their children.[114] Still others have noted that with the decline of the work–point system, school teachers in some places are now responsible for growing their own food, and do so during class hours.[115] It may also be that education policies at the national level have put pressure on primary enrollment at the local level. Higher education in China is an extremely expensive proposition by any comparative measure: the cost for a year of schooling at the tertiary level is estimated to be over seventy times higher than at the primary level.[116] Tertiary education, as of 1979, is estimated to have cost China almost as much as primary education, even though it accounted for only about one percent of China's total student population.[117] The Sixth Five-Year Plan envisions a dramatic expansion on tertiary enrollment; university enrollment, in the meantime, had increased by almost half between 1978 and 1981. In the context of an education budget with growing but nonetheless limited resources, China's policymakers may perceive a conflict between the objective of universalizing primary schooling and the objective of technical and scientific modernization.[118] Whatever its causes, the apparent drop in net primary school enrollment ratios since the Third Plenum in 1978 would seem to suggest that China's new development policies cannot automatically be assumed to accelerate the pace at which China heads toward the eventual elimination of national illiteracy.

Status of Women

Discrimination against women figures prominently in the patterns of poverty in many low-income societies. Both social custom and legal norm in various nations consign women to a life in which social opportunity and economic reward are systematically restricted and diminished. In many regions, moreover, it is the accepted lot of women to shoulder a disproportionate fraction of society's harsh physical toil, and to live without many of the protections men might expect against physical abuse. Discrimination against women means that the incidence of material poverty within any given society can be considerably higher for its women than its men. For future generations, discrimination against women can serve as a transmission belt for poverty, since a mother's health and education directly affect the life chances of her children.

Analysis of the role of women in contemporary Chinese society is beyond the scope of this paper. It will suffice here to present some of the recent data pertaining to the differential physical impact of poverty on men and women in China, and to set these differences in international perspective.

Differentials in literacy, important in and of themselves, may also speak to differences in productive capabilities, social opportunities, and physical security in times of hardship. According to the 1982 census, the difference between male and female rates of illiteracy and semi-literacy was 26 points for adults over age 12 (see Table 7.17). In absolute terms, the spread between female and male illiteracy and semi-literacy in China would appear to be the largest in East Asia. It would also seem that the difference in literacy rates between men and women in China is unusually great for a nation at China's estimated level of overall adult literacy. Substantial differences in male and female literacy, of course, are characteristic of Asia's Muslim societies, but it is interesting to note that, in absolute terms, the measured gap for China's population over the age 15 appears to be greater than in Bangladesh (where the measured gap in 1974 was 24 points), Iran (1976: 24 points), Bahrain (1981: 23 points), Saudi Arabia (1980: 22 points), or Pakistan (1981: 21 points)—though it may be slightly lower than in Jordan in 1979 or Turkey in 1980, where the gaps were estimated at 30 points.[119]

Enrollment ratios for primary schooling shape the literacy rates of the future. China's estimated gross enrollment ratios for boys and girls are presented in Table 7.18. Again, the absolute gap in China appears to be unusually large, being exceeded only by India's in the sample of countries in Table 7.18. No other East Asian nation has nearly so large a disparity in gross enrollment ratios at the primary level between boys and girls. While the estimated absolute difference in China's rates is lower than for a number of contemporary Asian Islamic societies (Oman, Iran, and the two Yemens among them) it is considerably greater than for some others, including Turkey, Jordan, Syria, Bahrain, Kuwait, and Iraq. In societies with expanding primary school systems or rising levels of general educational attainment, the gap between male and female enrollment rations typically narrows. In China, the disparity appears by contrast to have widened noticeably in recent years. In 1979 male gross primary enrollment ratio was 20 points higher than that estimated for women.[120] By 1982—the latest year for which UNESCO has made computations—the disparity was put at 25 points. Such numbers suggest that social and economic changes in China since the Third Plenum in 1978 have widened the gap in basic

TABLE 7.17
Differences in Estimated Male and Female Illiteracy Rates for the People's Republic
of China and Selected Other Regions, c. 1980 (percent)

	Male Illiteracy Rate	Female Illiteracy Rate	Difference
1. *People's Republic of China* (1982, 12 +) (Illiterates and semi-literates)	19	45	− 26
2. *Overseas Chinese Populations*			
a. Republic of China (Taiwan) (1982, 15 +)	5	18	− 12
b. Hong Kong (1981, 15 +)	8	26	− 18
c. Singapore (1980, 15 +)	8	26	− 18
d. Peninsular Malaysia (1980, 15 +)	14	33	− 19
3. *Populous Asian Nations*			
a. India (1971, 15 +)	52	81	− 28
b. Indonesia (1980, 15 +)	22	41	− 19
4. *Other Asian Benchmarks*			
a. Sri Lanka (1981, 15 +)	9	19	− 10
b. South Korea (1970, 15 +)	6	19	− 13
5. *Eurasian Industrial Powers*			
a. Soviet Union (1979, 9–49)	—	—	0
b. Japan (1980, 15 +)	—	—	0

Notes: — = less than 2%. Definition of illiteracy vary among the censuses
represented here. Figures may not add up due to rounding.

Sources:
Line 1: *Economic Daily*, December 19, 1983, quoted in *China News Analysis*, 1256,
March 12, 1984.

Line 2:
a: *1982 Taiwan-Fukien Demographic Fact Book Republic of China* (Republic of
China: Ministry of the Interior, December 1983).
b: *Hong Kong 1981 Census, Main Report, Volume 1: Analysis*, Hong Kong: Census
and Statistics Department, December 1982).
c: UNESCO, *Statistical Yearbook 1983* (Paris: UNESCO, 1983).
d: *Population and Housing Census of Malaysia 1980, General Report of the
Census, Volume 2* (Kuala Lumpur: Department of Statistics, Malaysia, n.d.).

Line 3:
a: *Statistical Yearbook 1983*, loc. cit.
b: *Results of the Sub-Sample of 1980 Population Census Preliminary Tables*
(Jakarta: Biro Pusat Statistik, 1982).

Line 4:
a: *Statistical Yearbook, 1983*, loc. cit.
b: *Ibid.*

Line 5:
a: *Statistical Yearbook, 1983*, loc. cit.
b: *Ibid.*

TABLE 7.18
Differences Between Estimated Male and Female Gross Primary Enrollment Ratio in
the People's Republic of China and Selected Other Regions, c. 1980 (percent)

	Year	Male	Female	Difference
1. *People's Republic of China*	1981	130	106	− 24
2. *Overseas Chinese Population*				
a. Republic of China	1981	99 +	99 +	0
b. Hong Kong	1981	108	104	− 4
c. Singapore	1981	108	105	− 3
d. Malaysia	1982	94	91	− 3
3. *Populous Asian Nations*				
a. India	1980	93	64	− 29
b. Indonesia	1981	123	110	− 13
4. *Other Asian Benchmarks*				
a. Sri Lanka	1981	106	100	− 6
b. South Korea	1981	108	105	− 3
5. *Eurasian Industrial Powers*				
a. Soviet Union	NA	NA	NA	NA
b. Japan	1981	100	100	0

Note: NA = Not Available.

Sources:
Line 2:
a: *Social Welfare Indicators, Republic of China 1982* (Taipei: Manpower Planning
    Committee, Executive Yuan, 1982).

All others: UNESCO, *Statistical Yearbook 1983* (Paris: UNESCO 1984).

educational opportunities between boys and girls, although it is not possible to tell from these data whether girls have borne a disproportionate share of the decrease in net primary enrollment.

Data on the distribution of food within the household are scarce for any society, and are not to be had as yet for China.[121] Even so, the death rate for children aged 1 to 4 may provide some insight into the difference in nutritional odds facing boys and girls. Table 7.19 presents the ratio of female to male mortality for children aged 1 to 4 in the People's Republic of China and elsewhere.

China's data on death rates for boys and girls are taken from vital registration sources for 1957 and 1975, and from the recently released life table for 1981. Though it is believed that underestimation of deaths affects all of these figures, it is not evident that they should be affected by differing rates of underregistration for boys and girls. Even so, figures

TABLE 7.19
Estimated Ratio of Female to Male Mortality Rates for the Ages 1–4, People's
Republic of China and Selected Other Regions, c. 1950–c. 1980 (deaths per 1000)

	(1) 1950	(2) 1960	(3) 1970	(4) 1980
1. *People's Republic of China*	1.09	NA	1.01	1.11
2. *Overseas Chinese Populations*				
a. Republic of China	1.09	0.92	0.89	0.85
b. Hong Kong	NA	1.02	0.79	—
c. Singapore	NA	NA	0.86	—
d. West Malaysia	1.03	1.03	0.99	0.96
3. *Populous Asian Nations*				
a. India	1.22	1.18	1.31	NA
b. Indonesia	NA	0.87	0.88	0.89
4 *Other Asian Benchmarks*				
a. Sri Lanka	1.22	1.19	1.18	NA
b. South Korea	0.91	0.78	0.88	1.89
5. *Eurasian Industrial Powers*				
a. Soviet Union	NA	NA	NA	NA
b. Japan	1.0	0.85	0.73	—

Notes: — = death rates for both sexes under 1 per 1,000.
NA = not available

Sources: See Table 7.11.

based on incomplete coverage must always be treated with caution. We may note that death rates for female children appear to have been higher than for male children in modern China in each of the periods for which we have data. The disparity between death rates for girls and boys does not appear to have narrowed between the late 1950s and the early 1980s, despite improving levels of national health; the gap, in fact, may have widened since the mid-1970s.[122]

China's patterns appear to be in marked contrast with those of other Chinese populations. In those other societies, there has been a tendency for the disparity in death rates between female and male children to diminish as overall mortality decreases, and for female mortality in the 1 to 4 age group to slip below that of males. The ratio of female to male child deaths appears to be significantly higher in China today than in Taiwan, Hong Kong, Singapore, or Peninsular Malaysia when they were at China's present estimated level of life expectancy. China's pattern appears to be closer to Sri Lanka's, a society where, despite overall health improvements, death rates for female children continue to be high in comparison to those for male children. In the Sri Lankan case, preferential care for sons and selective neglect of daughters is often said to account for this continuing and unusual disparity.[123]

Chinese authorities believe that discrimination against women has been intensifying in the period since the historic Third Plenary Session in 1978. In a televised address to a national audience in early 1984, Zou Yu, Justice Minister for the People's Republic, flatly stated that "discrimination against women and incidents of humiliation, mistreatment, and injury to women and children have been on the rise in the last few years".[124] The theoretical and political journal of the Communist Party of China, *Red Flag*, had noted a few months earlier that investigations had revealed that "in some rural brigades the malpractice of killing and abandoning female babies has been so serious that the ratio of female babies to male babies has already dropped to 1:4 or 1:5."[125] That general problem has evidently not yet been resolved in at least some regions of China, for as recently as late 1984, an "Announcement from the Standing Committee of the 6th Shaanxi Provincial People's Congress" included the stipulation that "drowning or abandoning infants and other activities to cruelly injure or kill infants are prohibited." Although little has appeared in the Chinese press or in Chinese research journals on differential disadvantages for women in education, China's leading sociologist, Fei Xiaotong, recently stated in the pages of the *People's Daily* that "(in the countryside) the number of 'drifting students' is continuously increasing" and warned "of the appearance of new illiteracy"[126]—this at much the same time that educational statistics supplied to UNESCO were revealing a widening gap in gross primary school enrollment ratios between boys and girls.

It is clear enough that the proximate medium for the physical sorts of discrimination against women outlined in this paper is the family. It is parents who choose to enroll their children in school or to withdraw them from it, just as it is parents who are responsible for the incidents of "drowning or abandoning baby girls" that have been decried in the Chinese press. It is husbands and in-laws who do the "hounding to death of women" that has been condemned in the Chinese Communist Party's official and theoretical journal. It is usually the case with social problems, however, the proximate causes are easier to identify than underlying causes and motivating factors. The impact of the "production responsibility system," the population control program, and other specific manifestations of government policy since the Third Plenum of 1978 on family relations in rural China is a subject which is only just beginning to be investigated.[127] It may be premature to posit a conclusive link between China's "new development strategy" and increasing physical discrimination against women. Physical discrimination against women is not unique to China; to the contrary, it shows up in the statistics of many low-income nations.[128] What is noteworthy about recent events in China, however, is that a generalized increase in economic activity, a substantial increase in measured economic output per capita, and ostensibly broadbased increases in personal consumption—all changes which would typically be taken to indicate increasing national prosperity—have coincided with a measureable and significant rise in physical manifestations of severe discrimination against the female population.

Concluding Remarks

Great transformations in material living conditions have taken place on the Chinese mainland since the victory of Communist forces in 1949. The Marxist–Leninist Party which assumed command of Chinese society at the time of "liberation" claimed to have special insight into the problem of mass poverty, and constructed an elaborate and far-reaching administrative apparatus, reaching directly into the Chinese household and affecting its most basic decisions, in the name of benefiting the poor. The policies implemented by this apparatus, and engineered by this Party, have been characterized by a number of important and fundamental changes over the past three and a half decades; not a few of these have been radical reversals of directives and directions previously embraced. An overall record of performance against manifestations of material poverty has emerged for these years.

Assessment of this record depends strongly upon what one chooses to emphasize. The assessment of material welfare is, after all, in no small degree a philosophical and ideological question, whether or not it is treated as such explicitly. There is no empirical basis by which one may decide whether short-run or long-run implications of policies are more important, even though these can and often do differ in important ways. By the same token, there is no preordained answer to the question of whether "individual rights" or the radically different conception of "people's rights" provides the more satisfactory standard by what to measure human well-being. Rather than issue judgements on the appropriate vision of self, society, and virtue—for it is differing perspectives on these three issues which account for so much of the variety in assessments of social performance in any given situation—it may be more useful to conclude with some observations about the distinctive characteristics of material poverty in modern China, and some speculations about the prospects for further and continued alleviation of China's material deprivations.

When placed in international or historical perspective, Communist China's performance in alleviating material poverty, and its current patterns of material deprivation, present the observer with a number of seeming paradoxes and contradictions. Within three and a half decades of planned socialist development, for example, China has reached a level of national life expectancy enjoyed by few other low-income nations, but in the course of this ascent appears to have experienced catastrophic loss of life from famine and nutrition-related diseases. While China's current per capita caloric availability and mortality level appear to be similar to those of countries where caloric satiation (as reflected by consumer behavior) has been generally achieved, China's pattern of food output and its patterns of consumer behavior are more characteristic of nations where caloric satiation remains an unresolved problem. Though the demand for education, both as an investment and a consumer good, tends to rise with individual and national income, educational enrollment at the primary level has evidently fallen in China since the surge in national income that began in 1978. And whereas social and economic development typically reduce the mortality disadvantage of both the rural and the female fractions of any national populations, modern China sees striking gaps in lifespans between city and countryside, and (at least for certain age cohorts) between men and women; these gaps may actually have increased in recent years or decades.

These discrepancies between modern China's pattern of poverty and those witnessed elsewhere in the world are explained best not in terms of culture or history, but rather in terms of the policy tools chosen and developed by the Chinese government. In modern China, social and economic changes have been directed by a command planning system. The purpose of command planning, in an operational sense, is to divorce economic and social results from the preferences of individuals. China's patterns of poverty reflect this separation. Intermittent experimentation with decentralization notwithstanding, the distinctiveness of patterns of poverty in modern China is testimony to the success of the Chinese command planning apparatus in superimposing state-designated "social preferences" over the ordinary preferences of individual consumers and producers in the determination of economic and social outcomes.

Because successful implementation of command planning divorces economic and social results from those results which would be expected if individual economic actors were allowed to move toward what they would perceive as the maximization of their welfare, social and economic conditions in communist China are exceedingly difficult to forecast. If command planning can free a nation from the confines of historical "pattern of development," it will simultaneously make the fate of the poor a less predictable matter, for predictions are based in large part on the pool of historical experience that is taken to be generalizeable.

If prospects for alleviating poverty in China are in some sense intrinsically less predictable than in other low-income nations, there are nevertheless important indications for the future which may be taken from the recent past. One of these concerns the sustainability of Mao-era strategies credited with the alleviation of material poverty.

Apart from the redistribution of existing wealth (which may have a profound and immediate impact on the lives of the poor) and foreign assistance, reduction of national poverty must be financed by generalized and sustained increases in income and output, and hence by improvements in productivity. Whatever else the communist government may have accomplished in its first three decades of power in China, it found no solution to the problem of regularizing productivity increase. Measurement of productivity change, to be sure, is not a straightforward affair, even under the best of circumstances.[129] Exercises in "growth accounting" for China are further complicated by the fact that output and economic "inputs" in the P.R.C. are valued by prices which give primacy to political decisions, not articulated demand or market scarcity. Inexactitudes notwithstanding, several analysts have attempted to trace patterns of productivity in the modern Chinese economy; their findings are all broadly consistent. Tang, for example, used rough computations to estimate that total factor productivity in Chinese agriculture dropped by 15 percent or more between 1952 and 1977.[130] Dernberger has suggested that total factor productivity in Chinese industry may have dropped by over a third between 1952 and 1979.[131] In perhaps the most comprehensive of such exercises to date, Yeh has calculated that total factor productivity for the Chinese economy as a whole fell on average by 1.5 percent a year between 1957 and 1978, implying that overall efficiency of resource use declined by over 25 percent during this period.[132]

If such calculations are even roughly accurate, modern China's pattern of development was indeed distinctive. Of all nations for which such computations have been attempted, no other economy, be it market-oriented or centrally planned, has been thought to suffer such a profound, and secular, erosion of productivity.[133] It would appear from such calculations that economic growth in China, from the early 1950s until the Third Plenary Session of the CCP's Eleventh Central Committee in 1978, depended exclusively on the mobilization of additional factors of production (augmentation of investment, expansion of the workforce and lengthening of the workday)—and that even so, increments in output did not match the increments in resources mobilized for growth. China's economy was set on a precarious trajectory during those years: it would approach overall stagnation as it approached full mobilization of social resources. Such an economic framework would appear to be manifestly unsustainable; yet it

174   The Poverty of Communism

was within this framework that modern China's achievements against poverty were scored, and upon this framework that the anti-poverty strategy of the Mao era ultimately relied.

If China's current leadership believes there is scope for increasing the efficiency of resource use in China today, it would seem hard to disagree with its assessment. Tables 7.20 and 7.21 may provide some perspective on the challenge that faces them as they attempt to move the Chinese economy in a "new direction." It is often said that modern China's levels of health and literacy are unusually high for its level of national income, yet the inescapable converse of this observation is that China's level of national income is unusually low for its given level of "human resources." Even allowing for the perhaps considerable errors and distortions contained or concealed in the figures in Tables 7.20 and 7.21,[134] it would appear

TABLE 7.20
World Bank Estimates for GDP Per Capita and Life Expectation at Birth for
Countries with Life Expectations at Birth Similar to That of the P.R.C., c. 1982

	Life Expectation, c. 1982	World Bank Estimated GDP Per Capita, 1982 (current U.S. dollars)
El Salvador	63	700
Thailand	63	790
Philippines	64	820
Ecuador	63	1,350
Turkey	63	1,370
Columbia	64	1,460
Paraguay	65	1,610
Syria	66	1,680
Jordan	64	1,690
Malaysia	67	1,860
South Korea	67	1,910
Brazil	64	2,240
Mexico	65	2,270
1. Unweighted Average	64	1,520
2. P.R.C.	65	310
3. Ratio, 1-2	1.00	4.90

Note: World Bank estimates may differ from other sources.
Figures and ratios reflect rounding.

Sources:
Life expectancy estimate for the P.R.C. from Banister, "An Analysis of Recent Data on the Population of China." All other estimates from the World Bank, *World Development Report 1984* (New York: Oxford University Press, 1984).

TABLE 7.21
World Bank Estimates for GDP Per Capita and Adult Illiteracy Rates for Nations
with Estimated Adult Illiteracy Rates Similar to that of the P.R.C., c. 1982

	World Bank Estimated Adult Illiteracy Rates (Percent) c. 1977	World Bank Estimated GDP Per Capita, 1980 (Current U.S. dollar)
Burma	30	170
Tanzania	34	280
Indonesia	38	430
Honduras	40	560
El Salvador	38	660
Dominican Republic	33	1,160
Tunisia	38	1,310
Jordan	30	1,420
Turkey	40	1,470
1. Unweighted Average	36	830
2. P.R.C.	35	310 (1982)
3. Ratio, 1-2	1.03	2.67

Note: World Bank estimates may differ from other sources.
Figures and ratios reflect rounding.

Sources:
For the P.R.C.: literacy estimate from UNESCO, *Statistical Yearbook 1984* (Paris: UNESCO 1984); GDP per capita from World Bank, *World Development Report 1984*. All other estimates from World Bank, *World Development Report 1982* (New York: Oxford University Press, 1982).

that economic and social arrangements in other less developed countries have made it possible for other societies to register substantially higher levels of per capita product than those achieved in China on seemingly comparable "human capital" bases.

At present, China's leadership seems to believe that improvements in living standards must be linked more closely with improvements in productivity. Improvements in productivity, however, may be more difficult to regularize than the current leadership may anticipate. Recent efforts to recast China's economic policies do appear to have had a positive impact on overall efficiency; by Yeh's estimate, total factor productivity increased in China by about one percent a year between 1979 and 1982.[135] Though this would represent a distinct improvement on earlier performance, such a rate of productivity progress would appear quite modest, not only in the context of other East Asian economies,[136] but even in comparison with the Soviet economy's overall postwar record.[137] Further improvements in economic efficiency in China will depend not only on technological transfer and allocative efficiency—both of which fall within the jurisdiction of China's planners—but also on what Leibenstein has called "X–efficiency,"[138] which concerns motivation, incentive, and other aspects of "microeconomic" performance. If X–efficiency is related to household purchasing power, improvements in X–efficiency would seem to be directly related to changes in the mechanisms by which consumer goods are produced, distributed, and priced—and thus to the allocative mechanism in the command economy itself.[139] There would be far-reaching implications for China in allowing purchasing power to correspond more closely to consumer preference and market signals; it is not clear that these would be acceptable to any fraction within China's Marxist–Leninist leadership if they were fully articulated.

The ascent of household purchasing power as an economic force in modern China would have important implications for the formulation of patterns of national poverty. If household purchasing power assumes a more prominent role in the determination of economic events in China, disparities in purchasing power would also more fully shape the contours of material deprivation within the nation. This could, in theory, expose a significant fraction of the national population to new risks of poverty. Yet it would not necessarily mean that China would replicate more closely the patterns of poverty seen in other low-income nations. "Reform" and "readjustments" notwithstanding, China's leaders have not renounced the principle of command planning of economy and society, nor have they relinquished the practice of it, as the ongoing population control campaign should vividly demonstrate. "Readjustments" in the context of command planning could all too easily leave many households in China caught between a reduction in the social guarantees which had previously supported living standards, and official directives and restrictions which prevent actions to protect or improve family welfare.

Seven years ago, at the start of the "period of readjustment," I speculated that "what will happen to the vast number of poor people in China remains an open question."[140] Much has changed in China since those days, and much more is known now about changes which have taken place. For better or worse, neither intervening events nor the great amounts of additional information which have become available in the meantime would seem to date to argue for an alteration of that earlier assessment.

A shorter version of this essay originally appeared in U.S. Congress Joint Economic Committee, *China's Economy Looks Toward the Year 2000* (Washington: Government Printing Office, 1986). Reprinted with permission.

Notes

1. A list of such works would include, for example, John S. Aird, *The Size, Composition, and Growth of Mainland China* (New York: AMS Press, 1973); Kang Chao, *Agricultural Production in Communist China, 1949–1965* (Madison: University of Wisconsin Press, 1971), and *idem, Capital Formation in Mainland China, 1952–65* (Berkeley: University of California Press, 1974); Nai-ruenn Chen and Walter Galenson, *The Chinese Economy Under Communism* (Chicago: Aldine Publishing Company, 1969); Alexander Eckstein, Walter Galenson, and Ta-chung Liu, eds., *Economic Trends in Communist China* (Chicago: Aldine Publishing Company, 1968); and Robert Michael Field, Nicholas R. Lardy, and John Philip Emerson, *A Reconstruction of the Gross Value of Industrial Output by Province in the People's Republic of China, 1949–73* (Washington, D.C.: Department of Commerce, Bureau of Economic Analysis, 1975).
2. This paper will deal only with *material* poverty. Spiritual and cultural poverty may be no less real than material poverty, and may in ways do more to shape the quality of life for individuals and nations, but these are questions which are far beyond the scope of the present discussion.
3. Quoted in S. Ivanov, "Statistics and Politics," in the Soviet journal *Far Eastern Affairs*, 1982, no. 3:27.
4. International Bank for Reconstruction and Development (IBRD), *China: Socialist Economic Development* (Washington, D.C.: IBRD, 1983), vol. 1, Annex A.
5. Ling Rui-zhu, "A Brief Account of 30 Years' Mortality of Chinese Population," *World Health Statistics Quarterly* 34, no. 2 (1981).
6. See *China: Socialist Economic Development*; Choh-ming Li, *The Statistical System of Communist China* (Berkeley: University of California Press, 1962).
7. Li Chengrui, "Initiating New Aspects of Statistical Work," *Tongji*, 1983, no. 7, trans. in Joint Publication Research Service, (hereafter JPRS), no. 84564 (October 19, 1983).
8. Li, *The Statistical System of Communist China*; see also John S. Aird, "Recent Demographic Data from China: Problems and Prospects," in U.S. Congress Joint Economic Committee, *China Under the Four Modernizations* (Washington, D.C.: Government Printing Office, 1982), vol. 1.
9. "State Council Resolution on Strengthening Statistical Work, January 6, 1984, Reference 'Guofa (1984) #7,' " *Bulletin of the State Council of the People's Republic of China [P.R.C.]*, 1984, no. 1, trans, in JPRS, CEA–84–085 (October 16, 1984).
10. "Text of the Sixth Five-Year Plan (1981–85)," *Bulletin of the State Council of the PRC*, 1983, no. 9, tans. in JPRS, CEA–84–005 (January 25, 1984).
11. This problem is discussed at greater length in *China: Socialist Economic Development*. See note 4 above.
12. See, for example, S. Lee Travers, "Bias in Chinese Economic Statistics: The Case of the Typical Example Investigation," *China Quarterly*, no. 91 (September 1982): 478–85.
13. For a detailed discussion of this problem, see "New Lesson for Agricultural Statistics," *Shansi Daily*, August 7, 1983, trans. in JPRS, no. 84770 (November 17, 1983).

14. "Agricultural Statistical Work to be Restructured," *Shansi Daily*, August 7, 1983, trans. in JPRS, no. 84770 (November 17, 1983).
15. Zhang Yigeng, "We Must Have a New Improvement in Statistical Work Concerning Commodity Prices," *Tongji* 1983, no. 5, trans. in JPRS, no. 84356 (September 19, 1983).
16. A recent indication of the seriousness of the problem comes from Chinese trade statistics. The Ministry of Foreign Economic Relations and Trade has announced that trade increased by 38 percent for the first six months of 1984 in comparison with the previous year. The International Monetary Fund, of which China is a member, and to which China is thus obliged to provide certain basic and often confidential data, has also made an estimate for the increase in trade in China between the first half of 1983 and the first half of 1984. By the IMF's calculations, the increase was 6 percent. *The Economist*, February 16, 1985.
17. "State Council Resolution on Strengthening Statistical Work," *Bulletin of the State Council of the PRC*, 1984, no. 1, trans. in JPRS, CEA–84–042 (June 5, 1984).
18. Huang Hai, "Problems in the Reform of Statistical Work," *People's Daily*, July 8, 1983, trans. in *Chinese Economic Studies*, Spring 1984.
19. Ansley J. Coale, *Rapid Population Change in China, 1952–1982* (Washington, D.C.: National Academy Press, 1984).
20. China's estimated rate of under-enumeration, for example, was several times lower in its 1982 census than was India's in its 1981 census. See U.S. Bureau of the Census, *World Population: 1983* (Washington, D.C.: Department of Commerce, 1983).
21. See, for example, Lucian W. Pye, *The Dynamics of Chinese Politics* (Cambridge, Mass: OGH Books, 1981).
22. Some of the philosophical and ontological problems in measuring and quantifying human poverty are touched upon skillfully in Amartya K. Sen, "Poor, Relatively Speaking," *Oxford Economic Papers*, October 1982. Some of the practical questions which arise in measuring poverty are treated in Michael Lipton, "The Poor and the Poorest" (Washington, D.C.: IBRD, unpublished manuscript, 1982).
23. See, for example, Chapter 11 and Mark Lilla, "Why the 'Income Distribution' is so Misleading," *The Public Interest*, Fall 1984.
24. For a careful elaboration of this point, see Gavin Peebles, "Inflation in the People's Republic of China, 1950–82," *Three Banks Review*, June 1984.
25. See, for example, V. V. Bhanoji Rao, "Measurement of Deprivation and Poverty Based on the Proportion Spent on Food," *World Development*, April 1981, and C. H. Shah, "Food Preferences and the Poor," *Society/Transaction*, September 1980.
26. For an exposition of the workings of the registration system at the grassroots level, see William H. Lavely, "China's Population Statistics at the Local Level," *Population Index*, Winter 1982.
27. These differences can be seen in comparing the reconstructions in Judith Banister, "An Analysis of Recent Data on the Population of China," *Population and Development Review* 10, no. 2 (June 1984), with those in Kenneth Hill, "Demographic Trends in China, 1950–81," Supplementary Paper 1 to International Bank for Reconstruction and Development, "The Health Sector in China" (Washington, D.C.: IBRD, unpublished paper, 1983). For 1970, for

example, Banister estimates expectation of life at birth in China at 61 years, and infant mortality at 70 per thousand. Hill's computations result in a life expectancy estimate of 55 years, and an infant mortality rate of 109.

28. Banister, "Recent Data on the Population of China"; see also Judith Banister, "Population Policy and Trends in China, 1978–83," *China Quarterly*, no. 100 (December 1984).
29. Approximately one-third of the population of Peninsular Malaysia were self-identified ethnic Chinese in the latest census. Unofficial evidence suggests that with the continuation and intensification of discriminatory *bumiputras* policies, increasing numbers of people of Chinese origin are now identifying themselves as "Malaysian," and even "Malay."
30. See, for example, James P. Grant, *Disparity Reduction Rates in Social Indicators* (Washington, D.C.: Overseas Development Council, 1973).
31. For a particularly sanguine version of this argument, see Jon Woronoff, *Korea's Economy* (Seoul: Si-sa-yong-o-sa Publishers, 1983).
32. Stephen Rapawy and Godfrey Baldwin, "Demographic Trends in the Soviet Union, 1950–2000," in U.S. Congress Joint Economic Committee, *Soviet Economy in the 1980s: Problems and Prospects* (Washington, D.C.: Government Printing Office, 1983).
33. Christopher Davis and Murray Feshbach, *Rising Infant Mortality in the U.S.S.R. in the 1970s* (Washington, D.C.: Department of Commerce, Bureau of the Census, September 1980); Murray Feshbach, "Issues in Soviet Health Care," in *Soviet Economy in the 1980s, loc. cit.*
34. Banister, "Recent Data on the Population of China."
35. Institute of Population Problems, *The 22nd Abridged Life Tables* (Tokyo: Ministry of Health and Welfare, Research Series #194, July 15, 1970).
36. Continuing, if attenuated, emphasis on the role of adverse weather on economic conditions in the wake of the Great Leap Forward may be found in such recent works as Ma Hong, *New Strategy for China's Economy* (Peking: New World Press, 1983).
37. See, for example, Alan D. Berg, "Famine Contained: Notes and Lessons from the Bihar Experience" (Washington, D.C.: Brookings Institution, Reprint #211, 1971).
38. International Bank for Reconstruction and Development, *Health: A Sector Paper* (Washington, D.C.: IBRD, 1980). The paper suggests that as much as two-thirds of the difference in life expectancy between "developed regions" and "developing regions" may be accounted for by differences in the mortality of children under 5 years of age.
39. Chen Haifeng and Zhu Chao, eds., *Chinese Health Care: A Comprehensive Review of the Health Service of the People's Republic of China* (Lancaster, England: MTP Press Limited, 1984).
40. Jiang Zhenghua and Zhu Limei, *Renkou Yu Jingji*, 1984, no. 3, trans. in JPRS, CPS–84–075 (November 1, 1984).
41. Banister's estimate of infant mortality for China for 1982 was 46 per thousand, suggesting an underregistration of infant deaths for that year of over 47 percent. See Banister, "Recent Data on the Population of China." Jiang and Zhu note that in a Wuxi county experiment, "complete" infant mortality checking in 1981 produced a measured rate of infant mortality some 60 percent higher than that of selected reporting counties in 1982 (see note 40 above).
42. *State Life Tables: 1969–71* (Washington, D.C.: U.S. Department of Health, Education, and Welfare, National Center for Health Statistics, June 1975).

43. Rong Shoude et al., "Analysis of Life Expectancy in *China, 1973–75,*" quoted in *China: Socialist Economic Development* (see note 4 above). For more information on this survey, see Judith Banister and Samuel H. Preston, "Mortality in China," *Population and Development Review*, March 1981.
44. Ministry of Agriculture Commune Management Bureau, "Poor Counties in China, 1977–79," *Xinhua Yuebao*, 1981, no. 2, cited in Nicholas R. Lardy, *Agriculture in China's Modern Economic Development* (New York: Cambridge University Press, 1983). In this survey, chronic poverty was defined as "per capita distributed collective income averaging less than 50 yuan in each of three years 1977–79."
45. *NCNA*, September 21, 1984, trans. in JPRS, CPS–84–066 (October 5, 1984).
46. See note 40 above.
47. International Bank for Reconstruction and Development, *The Health Sector in China* (Washington, D.C.: IBRD, 1984).
48. Morris K. Morris and Michele McAlpin, "Physical Quality of Life in India by State" (unpublished paper, 1981).
49. Lee-jay Cho et al., *Population Growth in Indonesia* (Honolulu: University of Hawaii Press, 1980).
50. *Anuario Estatistico Do Brasil 1978* (Rio de Janeiro: IBGE, 1978).
51. For some benchmarks, see United Nations, *Levels and Trends of Mortality Since 1950*, and *idem. Demographic Yearbook 1982.*
52. For more information, see G. William Skinner, ed., *The City in Late Imperial China* (Stanford: Stanford University Press, 1977); see also Jacques Gernet, *Daily Life in China On the Eve of the Mongol Invasion 1250–1276* (Stanford: Stanford University Press, 1962).
53. Derived from *NCNA*, May 24, 1984, trans. in JPRS, CPS–84–045 (June 28, 1984), and Chen and Zhu, *Chinese Health Care.*
54. On mortality convergence, see *The Determinants and Consequences of Population Trends* (New York: United Nations, 1973).
55. See Martin K. Whyte and William L. Parish, *Urban Life in Contemporary China* (Chicago: University of Chicago Press, 1984); see also Parris H. Chang, "Control of Urbanization—the Chinese Approach," *Asia Quarterly*, 1979, no. 3.
56. Perhaps the most important official relaxation of rules concerns the rustication of urban youth; since 1980 the Chinese government has announced no new quotas for the settlement of city people in the countryside. See Banister, "Population Policy and Trends in China."
57. In the examination in Wuxi city in 1981, for example, scarcely 1 percent of the people covered were not registered to live in Wuxi, a fact which may speak to the tight and continuing nature of restrictions on voluntary immigration to the cities. Investigative results cited in Lavely, "China's Population Statistics."
58. Nicholas R. Lardy, "Agricultural Prices in China," *World Bank Staff Working Papers*, No. 606 (1983).
59. *Ibid.*
60. See note 47 above.
61. Calculated on the basis of Lardy, "Agricultural Prices in China," and State Statistical Bureau, *Statistical Yearbook of China 1983* (Hong Kong: Economic Information & Agency, 1983).
62. *Statistical Yearbook of China 1983.*

63. Calculated on the basis of Lardy, "Agricultural Prices in China," and *Statistical Yearbook of China 1983*.
64. George W. Barclay *et al.*, "A Reassessment of the Demography of Traditional Rural China," *Population Index*, October 1976.
65. Samuel H. Preston, *Mortality Patterns in National Populations* (New York: Academic Press, 1976).
66. U.S. Bureau of the Census, *Statistical Abstract of the United States 1984* (Washington, D.C.: Department of Commerce, 1984).
67. William C. Hsiao, "Transformation of Health Care in China," *New England Journal of Medicine*, April 5, 1984. See also note 47 above.
68. Hsiao, "Transformation of Health Care in China."
69. See Wong Siu-lun, "Consequences of China's New Population Policy," *China Quarterly*, no. 98 (June 1984).
70. *Red Flag*, 1983, no. 5, trans. in JPRS, no. 83318 (April 22, 1983).
71. *Red Flag*, 1983, no. 17, trans. in JPRS, no. 84595 (October 24, 1983).
72. This problem is addressed at greater length in Nick Eberstadt and Clifford M. Lewis, "World Hunger and the Global Food Economy" (unpublished paper).
73. Michael Lipton, "Poverty, Undernutrition, and Hunger," *World Bank Staff Working Papers*, no. 597 (1983).
74. *Dietary Intake Source Data: United States, 1976–80* (Hyattsville, MD.: U.S. Department of Health and Human Services, National Center for Health Statistics, March 1983).
75. See note 72 above.
76. Alan Piazza, "Trends in Food and Nutrient Availability in China, 1950–81," *World Bank Staff Working Papers*, no. 607 (1983).
77. See note 44 above.
78. Food and Agriculture Organization, *Provisional Food Balance Sheets 1972–74 Average* (Rome: FAO, 1977).
79. See note 44 above.
80. John Lossing Buck, *Land Utilization in China* (Chicago: University of Chicago Press, 1937).
81. See Herbert Day Lamson, *Social Pathology in China* (Shanghai: The Commercial Press Limited, 1935).
82. See Kenneth Walker, *Food Grain Procurement and Consumption in China* (New York: Cambridge University Press, 1984).
83. See note 44 above.
84. See note 58 above.
85. See, for example, Rajaram Dasgupta, "Nutritional Situation in India: A Statistical Analysis," in the Indian journal *Economic and Political Weekly*, August 25, 1984.
86. See, for example, Food and Agriculture Organization, *Review of Food Consumption Surveys 1977* (Rome: FAO, 1979). See also Nick Eberstadt and Clifford M. Lewis, "Food Security" (Washington, D.C.: IBRD, unpublished paper, 1982).
87. Wu Cangping, "Characteristics of Age Composition of China's Population," *Renbou Yenjiu*, 1984, no. 4, trans. in JPRS, CPS–84–077 (November 20, 1984).
88. For the nutritional potential of such measures, see John Briscoe, "The Quantitative Effect of Infection on the Use of Food by Young Children in Poor Countries," *American Journal of Clinical Nutrition*, March 1979.
89. See note 81 above.

90. See note 44 above.
91. *Ibid.*
92. For discussion of these patterns, see C. Peter Timmer, Walter P. Falcon, and Scott R. Pearson, *Food Policy Analysis* (Baltimore: Johns Hopkins University Press, 1983). For a classic discussion of these issues, see H. S. Houthakker, "An International Comparison of Household Expenditure Patterns, Commemorating the Centenary of Engel's Law," *Econometrica*, October 1957.
93. See Merrill K. Bennett, *The World's Food* (New York: Arno Press, 1976).
94. Interestingly, the measured ratio of household expenditures on food to disposable income has been rising steadily in China's urban areas in recent years. In 1981, the "Engel coefficient" for urban working families was put at 56.7 percent; in 1983, it was estimated to be 59.2 percent. See *China's Statistical Abstracts*, July 1984, trans. in JPRS, CEA–84–103 (December 18, 1984). That the "Engel coefficient" should rise during a period of ostensible increase in real per capita income is a measure of the extent of disequilibrium in consumer markets in urban regions of China.
95. See J. E. Gordon et al., "The Second Year Death Rate in Less Developed Countries," *American Journal of Medical Science*, September 1967, for the original formulation of this argument.
96. For a fuller discussion, see John Oxenham, *Literacy: Writing, Reading and Social Organization* (London: Routledge & Kegan Paul Ltd., 1980).
97. George Psacharopoulos, *Returns To Education: An International Comparison* (San Francisco: Jossey–Bass Publishing Company, 1973).
98. See, for example, Susan H. Cochrane, *The Effects of Education on Health* (Washington: IBRD, 1980) See also J. C. Caldwell, "Education as a Factor of Mortality Decline: An Examination of Nigerian Data" *Population Studies*, November 1979.
99. For evidence on these matters, see Paul R. Greenough, *Prosperity and Misery In Modern Bengal* (New York: Oxford University Press, 1982), and Amartya K. Sen, *Poverty and Famines* (New York: Oxford University Press, 1981).
100. Evelyn S. Rawski, *Education and Popular Literacy in Ch'ing China* (Ann Arbor: University of Michigan Press, 1979).
101. *Social Pathology in China, loc. cit.*
102. *Xinhua*, October 4, 1982, translated in JPRS, No. 82226, November 16, 1982.
103. Juergen Henze, "Alphabetisierung in China," in the German journal *Bildung Und Erziehung*, September 1983.
104. International Bank For Reconstruction and Development, *China: Socialist Economic Development* (Washington: IBRD, 1983), Volume III.
105. For available data, see Republic of Indonesia, *Development of Education in Indonesia 1957* (Jakarta: Ministry of Education, 1957), and Department van Ekonomishe Zaken, *Onderwijsstatistiek Over Het Schooljaar 1938–1939* (Batavia: August 1941).
106. On this score, see Rosemarie Crisostomo, "Soviet Education and Language Policy in the USSR's Southern Tier," U.S. Bureau of the Census, Center for International Research (forthcoming).
107. *Literacy: Writing, Reading, and Social Organisation, loc. cit.*
108. *Renmin Jiaoyu*, No. 2, 1981, cited in Billie L.C. Lo, "Primary Education: A Two-Track System for Dual Tasks", in Ruth Hayhoe, ed., *Contemporary Chinese Education* (London: Croom Helm, Ltd., 1984).
109. Cited in Jan-Ingvar Loefstedt, *Chinese Educational Policy* (Stockholm: Almqvist and Wiksell, 1980).

110. "Education in China," in Zue Muqiao, ed., *Almanac of China's Economy, 1981* (Hong Kong: Modern Cultural Company, Ltd., 1982).

111. "Education in China," in Zue Muqiao, ed., *Almanac of China's Economy, 1983* (Hong Kong: Modern Cultural Company, Ltd., 1984).

112. *Xinhua*, September 17, 1984, translated in JPRS, CPS–84–067, October 12, 1984.

113. Rong Siping, "Why Do Communes, Production Brigades, and Teams Get Rich While Elementary Schools Fall into Disrepair?" *Wenhui Bao*, July 4, 1983, translated in *Chinese Education*, Fall 1984.

114. Yi Mu, "Attention Must Be Paid To Rural Students Who Unlawfully Leave School" *Shanxi Ribao*, October 26, 1982, translated in JPRS, No. 82440, December 10, 1982.

115. See, for example, Liaoning Provincial Broadcast Service, November 27, 1982, translated in JPRS, No. 82540, December 27, 1982.

116. Han Zongli, "An Inquiry into the Investment in Universalizing Primary Education", *Jiaoyu Yanjiu*, No. 12, translated in *Chinese Education*, Fall 1984.

117. *China: Socialist Economic Development, loc. cit.* Volume III.

118. See, for example, "An Inquiry into the Investment in Universalizing Primary Education," op. cit.

119. UNESCO, *Statistical Yearbook 1984* (Paris: UNESCO, 1984).

120. *Ibid.*

121. For a first effort in this direction, see Elisabeth J. Croll, *The Family Rice Bowl* (London: Zed Press, 1982).

122. Ansley Coale's reconstructions of Chinese mortality patterns in the post–Liberation period are consistent with an interpretation that sees rising differentials in death rates for girls versus boys in the cohort of children aged 1 to 4. By Coale's calculations, the ratio of female to male mortality for ages 1–4 was 1.10 for the period from 1953 to 1964; for the period from 1964 to 1982, by his estimate, the differential had increased to 1.14. See *Rapid Population Change in China, 1952–1982*, loc. cit.

123. But on this argument, see T. Nadarajah, "The Transition from Higher Female to Higher Male Mortality in Sri Lanka," *Population and Development Review*, June 1983.

124. "Resolute Protection of Women and Children's Legitimate Rights," January 16, 1984, translated in JPRS, CPS–84–031, April 24, 1984.

125. "Overcome the Outworn Prejudice That Men are Superior to Women," *Honggi*, No. 5, 1983, translated in JPRS, No. 83318, April 22, 1983.

126. Fei Xiaotong, "Close Attention Should be Paid to the Development of Cultural Resources," *Renmin Ribao*, June 25, 1983, translated in JPRS, No. 83966, July 25, 1983.

127. See, for example, *The Family Rice Bowl*, loc. cit., and Margery Wolf, *Revolution Postponed: Women in Contemporary China* (Stanford: Stanford University Press, 1984). In a slightly different vein, see Marlyn Dalismer and Laurie Nisonoff, "The New Economic Readjustment Policies: Implications for Chinese Urban Working Women," *Review Of Radical Political Economy*, Spring 1984.

128. See, for example, Jocelyn Kynch and Amartya Sen, "Indian Women: Well-Being and Survival," *Cambridge Journal of Economics*, September/December 1983; see Ester Boserup, *Women's Role in Economic Development* (New

York: St. Martin's Press, 1970), for a more generalized argument about the status of women in the course of "modernization."

129. The problem is perceptively discussed in Mark Blaug, *Economic Theory in Retrospect* (New York: Richard D. Irwin, Inc., 1962).

130. Anthony M. Tang and Bruce Stone, *Food Production in the People's Republic of China* (Washington, D.C.: International Food Policy Research Institute, May 1980).

131. Robert F. Dernberger, "Communist China's Industrial Policies: Goals and Results," *Issues & Studies* 17, no. 7 (July 1981): 34–75.

132. K. C. Yeh, "Macroeconomic Changes in the Chinese Economy During the Readjustment," *China Quarterly*, no. 100 (December 1984.)

133. Recent estimates suggest that total factor productivity may have been negative in the U.S.S.R. during the 1970s, and in Yugoslavia during the early 1970s. See Chapter 3, and Mieko Nishimizu and John M. Page, Jr., "Total Factor Productivity Growth, Technological Progress and Technical Efficiency Change: Dimensions of Productivity Change in Yugoslavia 1965–78," *Economic Journal*, December 1982. In these cases, however, productivity decline was neither as dramatic nor as prolonged as in China. Total factor productivity estimates have not yet been produced for socialist Vietnam or the more economically troubled regions of sub–Saharan Africa.

134. See, for example, Irving B. Kravis et al., *World Product and Income: International Comparisons of Real Gross Product* (Baltimore: Johns Hopkins University Press, 1982).

135. See note 132 above.

136. Edward K. Y. Chen, "Factor Inputs, Total Factor Productivity, and Economic Growth: The Asian Case," in the Japanese journal *The Developing Economies*, March 1977.

137. See Herbert S. Levine, "Possible Causes of the Deterioration of Soviet Productivity Growth for the Period 1976–80" in U.S. Congress Joint Economic Committee, *Soviet Economy in the 1980s: Problems and Prospects* (Washington: Government Printing Office, 1983).

138. Harvey Leibenstein, "Allocative Efficiency vs. X–efficiency," *American Economic Review*, June 1966.

139. See, on this score, Janos Kornai, *The Economics of Shortage* (New York: Academic Press, 1978).

140. Nick Eberstadt, *Poverty in China* (Bloomington: International Development Institute, 1979).

Part III

Other Experiments

8

The Cost of Pax Sovietica

Since the death of Stalin, the Soviet Union's treatment of its allies and friends has followed a broad pattern of trading economic support for political control—that is, of accepting financial loss as the price of empire. In recent years the costs of this system of governance have multiplied, even as the Soviet Union itself has entered a period of increasing economic difficulty. The consequences of the dilemma first became apparent in the most expensive region of the empire, Eastern Europe—and specifically in Poland. Today (1981) we see the Soviet Union trying to reassert its political control over the Polish people while simultaneously decreasing its economic support. Over the next two decades, the men who rule the U.S.S.R. are likely to face this kind of situation repeatedly. Whatever the eventual outcome in Poland, it will very likely become a precedent that will loom over the Soviet Union's relations with its allies.

The Soviet Union has three kinds of allies. The first are governments it has installed in contiguous nations, and now supports through armed occupation. These are Mongolia, Afghanistan, and the Warsaw Pact nations. The second are Marxist–Leninist countries overseas. Some of these, such as Cuba and Vietnam, are ruled by regimes that came to power on their own terms, and largely by their own exertion; others, such as the ruling cliques in Angola and Ethiopia, have always depended on the support of Soviet bloc troops. Finally, there are "radical" but non-Leninist leaders in the poor world: included in this category would be Hafez Assad, Muammar Qaddafi, and Yasir Arafat. Without the help of these countries and men, the Soviet Union could not achieve many of its military and diplomatic ends. Yet these political allies and ideological friends also present Moscow with a number of strategic and economic problems.

The Third World radicals with whom the Soviet Union allies itself are very often consummate politicians—and, as the adage has it, politicians cannot be bought, only rented. For the Soviets, the terms of lease often have proved to be exorbitant, and repossession has often come unexpectedly. The waning of the era of decolonization has sharpened Soviet disappointment in the Third World. Although it is obvious that the Soviet Union could benefit from an alliance with, say, guerrilla leader Robert Mugabe in his fight for control of Rhodesia, it may not be quite so clear to President Robert Mugabe of Zimbabwe how the Soviets can help him in the more complex task of raising the living standards of his people while assuring the sovereignty of his regime. In fact, the Soviet Union cannot offer very much. As the International Institute for Strategic Studies observed in the 1980 edition of *Strategic Survey*, the Soviet Union finds it difficult to compete with the West in providing aid, technology, and anything more than the tools of war. "In 1980 alone," the *Survey* observed, "Western economic assistance to the Third World surpassed total Soviet non-military assistance for the 25 years previous to 1979."

The men in the Kremlin possess an enormous distrust of their friends in poor nations. This is not unreasonable. More often than not, Soviet investment in "radical" Third World leaders who were not avowedly Marxist–Leninist has not paid off. No matter how mutually advantageous the Soviets' relations with the Third World leaders have been at times, such alliances ultimately have proven neither stable nor reliable. Sekou Toure, Sukarno, Nkrumah, Sadat, and, in his own way, Siad Barre, must be weighed against Arafat, Qaddafi, and, in her own way, Indira Gandhi. Faced with this political deficit, Soviet leaders have drawn back from Khrushchev's policy of extending help to the Third World's anti–colonialist "nationalist bourgeoisie" (Sukarno, for example) in favor of a return to the Stalinist practice of trusting important work to solidly "socialist" regimes.

Colonel Qaddafi may harbor a hatred for the United States, but he is in power today because in 1969 the U.S., aware of his then undisguised anti–Soviet sentiments, did not oppose his revolution against King Idris. In any event, Qaddafi rules in a region where political supremacy is best measured in months. Arafat's aims are supported today by the Soviet Union, but eventually they may be better served by aid that is at once anti–Zionist *and* anti–Soviet, be it from Riyadh, Peking, or even Lagos. And although Gandhi has been driven into the Soviet embrace by her anti–Americanism and her fear of China, the Politburo knows that others in her nation do not share her specific fears and prejudices, and that she has been rejected by her people once already.* When other independent nations make overtures

*Prime Minister Indira Gandhi was assassinated on October 31, 1984.

toward the Soviets, as Mexico seems to have done in accepting "cooperation country" status in Comecon (the Soviet bloc economic organization),
it is because they expect to glean certain specific, and usually short-term,
advantages from the move. Although Mexico's maneuverings have encouraged the U.S. to discuss questions of oil and emigration, it would be highly
unrealistic to expect Mexico to move from quiet observation to sympathetic participation in Comecon.

Yet the view from the Soviet Foreign Ministry is not entirely bleak.
Moscow's search for allies is shaped by the knowledge that a nation's
interests are not always the same as those of all its politicians, and that it
is politicians, not nations, who shake hands, deliver orations, and sign
agreements. The men who direct Soviet foreign policy know how easy it
is to find Third World statesmen who believe their people are incapable of
discerning their own best interests. It is the nature of politics and opposi-
tions that in most nations, at any given time, factions can be found within
the political elite who will deem it in the "objective" interest of the nation
to accept foreign slush funds or military hardware, or who will even
acquiesce in outside military intervention. In the Afghanistan of 1979, out
of approximately 15 million people, there were fewer than 10,000 Marxists,
and not even all of them wanted to see the Red Army move in. But a small
fraction did, and that was enough. Nevertheless, quisling relationships, if
not cemented by Soviet troops or Soviet proxies, are likely to be transient,
for an unoccupied people can find means of impressing its interests upon
an unresponsive regime.

For their part, overseas Marxist–Leninist regimes may have goals different from those of their Soviet patrons, but observed conflicts of interests
have been relatively minor. Cuban hesitancy about participation in an
assault on Eritrea may have been annoying, but it was hardly insurmountable; Vietnamese occupation of Cambodia may not have been exactly
what the Soviet Union would have wanted at a time when it was pressing
for acceptance of an increased Soviet presence in the Far East, but it did
have its advantages.

The gravest Soviet difficulty with its friends is not political but financial.
The economies of the Soviet Union's Marxist–Leninist friends have demonstrated a troubling inability to make themselves self-sufficient. Cuba and
Vietnam (to say nothing of the territories they occupy) are not economically viable. The external subsidies they require are likely to grow during
the 1980s, precisely when the U.S.S.R., with growth rates lower than at
any point in its peacetime history (and still falling), is apt to be least able
to increase its aid.

In both Cuba and Vietnam, the deepening of "socialism" has not
brought prosperity. In Cuba, rigid controls and economic mismanagement

seem to have succeeded in bringing the economy to a precarious halt. According to one set of World Bank figures Cuba's per capita GNP is smaller now than it was under Batista. If those numbers are accurate, Cuba has joined Cambodia and South Yemen in that exclusive club of countries whose economic output per person is lower today than it was 25 years ago. One startling indication of the state of Cuban affairs, Sovietologist Jiri Valenta recently wrote, is that "in 1980, for the first time in its history, Cuba . . . had to import a large quantity of sugar instead of exporting it." At the moment, Moscow's subsidy to Havana (in the form of concessionary trade arrangements and lapsed loans) amounts to about $4 billion a year. This amount is approximately half as large as Cuba's own internally generated GNP is thought to be. Military aid to support the 40,000 or so Cuban troops and advisers abroad comes in addition to this amount. It currently runs at perhaps $2 billion.

Vietnam is even worse off. Contrary to expectations, the end of the war and the subsequent program of "socialist reconstruction" have lowered output and living standards. Although statistics on Vietnam are not entirely reliable, a 1978–1979 World Bank mission reported that in post–collectivization Vietnam, basic consumer goods such as grain, cloth, and cooking oil were as scarce as in India and Bangladesh. Sympathetic observers such as William Shawcross report that conditions have worsened since that time. The Soviet Union has found it necessary to ship several million tons of grain to Vietnam in each of the past few years to alleviate the difficulties caused by "bad weather." State Department estimates suggest that the total Soviet grant to Vietnam now exceeds $1 billion a year; others have put the figure at two and even three times that level. This would mean that Soviet money accounts for at least an eighth of Vietnam's economic consumption, and perhaps as much as a quarter.

The Soviet Union's sub–Saharan friends have fared no better. Angola's per capita food production is now at about half the 1970 level. And in Ethiopia (according to the U.S. Department of Agriculture), per capita food output is 30 percent lower today (1981) than it was when Colonel Mengistu's Dergue ousted Emperor Haile Selassie in the midst of a famine in 1974.

Two and a half years after the original appearance of this essay, reports began to reach the West that a major famine was under way in Ethiopia. The Marxist–Leninist Dergue, then preparing the celebration of its tenth anniversary in power, attempted to suppress this news. It is now thought that hundreds of thousands of persons may have died in this famine, although exact numbers will never be known. Dergue policies appear to have seriously exacerbated the loss of life once the famine had commenced, and may also have played a role in precipitating the famine in the first place.

Over the next few years, the cost of supporting Vietnam, Cuba, Ethiopia, and the Soviet Union's other economically inefficient but militarily useful clients is likely to increase. So, it seems, will the Soviets' domestic economic problems. If the Politburo chooses to continue to bankroll its impoverished surrogates, surely it will also look for new ways to use them. There is evidence that that search is on. Edward Luttwak has reported in *Commentary*, for example, that Soviet advisers have been training Cuban forces in combat methods appropriate to conditions of the desert. Similarly, 50,000 Vietnamese "guest workers" are now laboring in the factories of Warsaw Pact countries, according to a *Christian Science Monitor* account printed in November 1981. Cuban troops and Vietnamese coolies are unlikely to assume new burdens solely on the basis of their admiration of the Soviet Union; every new job they take on will require that much more in client support from the Soviet government.

As measured by the unreliable medium of international foreign exchange, the Soviet Union may spend some $10 billion a year on its proxies in the Third World. High as these costs seem, they are small when compared with the expense of maintaining the Soviet Union's European allies.

Soviet control in Eastern Europe is decisive, but it is also subject to a number of limitations. The task of mobilizing unwilling captives for competition against one's adversaries is not an easy one. Since the death of Stalin, total terror has been ruled out as impractical in Soviet dealings with Eastern Europe. To cope with the bourgeois aspirations and nationalist sentiments of their European protectorates, the Soviets have engaged in a delicate game of coax and menace, backing up their suggestions with the 30 Red Army divisions stationed west of the Soviet border.

This modus operandi, so unhappy for the peoples of communist Europe, is also far from ideal for Moscow's leaders. In order to cow Eastern Europe, the Soviet Union must be assured of military predominance over its subject nations. From this political necessity flows both strategic and economic consequences. Soviet occupation of these nations must be tempered by the reality that, left to their own devices, the soldiers of the Warsaw Pact could not necessarily be relied upon to point their rifles westward. Thus the armies of the Eastern states can never be more than police forces—and we are now seeing whether they can be relied upon to play even that role in Poland. The prospect of sharing their most sophisticated weaponry with the governments of Eastern Europe is, and must remain, out of the question. As Adam Ulam noted in *Expansion and Coexistence*, the Soviets' repossession of the Czechoslovakian government from Alexander Dubček would have been incalculably more risky if deliverable nuclear warheads had been in Dubček's possession.

As a result of its uneasiness with its involuntary allies, the Soviet Union is obliged to assume almost the full cost of the military competition with NATO, accounting for 80 percent of the Warsaw Pact budget. (The United States, by comparison, pays as little as 40 percent of NATO's expenses according to some calculations.) Though the economies of Eastern Europe are more productive than the Soviet Union's, their share in the defense of "socialism" is far lower. According to most official Western estimates, the military absorbs somewhere between 10 percent and 18 percent of the Soviet Union's GNP; in Eastern Europe, the average fraction is estimated at about 3 percent, ranging from an estimated 1.4 percent in Romania to an estimated 6.3 percent in East Germany. It is unlikely that the Soviet government, acutely aware of financial constraints and always eager to cut costs, would have taken upon itself the full costs of the military race unless the risks of distributing the expense seemed forbidding.

The Soviets' relationship with Eastern Europe depends upon rewards as well as tanks. The peoples of Eastern Europe were somewhat sensitive to comfort when they came under Soviet rule. They have shown, for example, that they are bourgeois in the sense that they will revolt *before* they are starving. To keep them complacent, the Soviets have allowed something to arise that would never be sanctioned in the motherland: a fragile and tenuous, but nonetheless unmistakable, consumerism. The peoples of Eastern Europe were granted (albeit tacitly) the right to expect material conditions to improve and creature comforts to multiply.

Encouraging prosperity under the Soviet mode of economic organization is, of course, a problematic task. In an effort to increase growth while maintaining stability in Eastern Europe, the Soviet Union relaxed some of its rules of "socialist" organization, though never to the point where control of the system came into question. Yet simply tinkering with the Soviet model has proven insufficient, so the Soviet Union has also attempted to encourage economic growth with actual subsidies. This is a fact that is generally ignored by Western observers. The common notion about East bloc trade with the Soviet Union conforms to the Polish joke: "We give them our meat, and in return they take our coal." In the days of Stalin, when control over the satellites was absolute and the dictator's first task was to rebuild his shattered economy, this may have been so. But today the joke is wrong: During 1979, Poland's per capita meat consumption was officially reported to be nearly twice that of the Soviet Union.

The fact is that Eastern Europe registers as a deficit on the Soviet ledgers. Because trade within Comecon is valued at artificial prices, the size and rate of growth of the deficit have not been generally recognized.

In terms of rubles, the Soviet Union runs a slight profit in its trade with Eastern Europe.

But when Comecon trade is valued by prevailing world prices, a different picture emerges. Soviet trade patterns with Eastern Europe are those of an undeveloped area's relations with the advanced economies: in return for Soviet oil, gas, and timber, Eastern Europe provides the U.S.S.R. with machinery and finished consumer goods. Eastern Europe, of course, is hardly the ideal supplier of precision products. In the hot-house of Eastern Europe's economy, plants that could not survive elsewhere can foist their fruits on captive markets. Comecon trade overvalues the worth of its sorry creations by a factor of two or three, if compared with what might be bought on the world market. At the same time, the Soviet Union, which during the 1970s became the world's largest oil producer, supplies the Warsaw Pact nations with raw materials at prices that are the stuff of nostalgia in the West. The discrepancy between Comecon prices and world prices is most apparent in oil, which the U.S.S.R. now (1981) sells to its captive states at half or less of what it might fetch on the free market. Currently the Soviet Union is obliged not only to deliver more than 75 million tons of oil annually—the equivalent of over 1.5 million barrels a day—but also to provide something like 15 billion thousand cubic feet of natural gas. On December 11, 1981, Czech officials confirmed to Michael Dobbs of the *Washington Post* that the Soviet Union is planning to break that obligation and reduce energy supplies to Eastern Europe by 10 percent. The openness of the announcement can be taken as an indication of the severity of Soviet economic difficulties; its timing should be taken as a lesson, for it seems to be an economic complement to the political crackdown in Poland.

All told, according to calculations made by economists Jan Vanous and Michael Marrese, the Soviet Union's 1980 subsidy to Eastern Europe comes to roughly $20 billion. This is not an inconsiderable factor in the economic health, such as it is, of Eastern Europe. If the World Bank's reckoning of the GNP for the Warsaw Pact nations at about $400 billion is correct, then the Soviet subsidy constitutes 5 percent of the total "output" of the Eastern bloc. And if, as many experts believe, standard economic accounting methods overstate output in these countries by exaggerating the quality of their goods, then the Eastern Bloc's economic dependence on the Soviet Union is even greater than these comparisons would suggest.

As oil prices rose and the quality of goods in Western markets improved, the financial costs of maintaining Eastern Europe and its inflexible, inefficient economies increased. These are hardly unbearable costs: $20 billion a year is a small price even for a faltering Soviet economic machine to pay for control over the lives of more than 100 million people. This de facto socialist Marshall Plan for Eastern Europe, provided grudgingly to unwilling recipients, may cost the Soviet Union no more than 2 percent of its GNP in foregone earnings. Centrally planned economies, moreover, aim for political control rather than efficiency; if the second can be had, all well and good, but it is the first which Communist systems strive for.

It would be a mistake to overlook the role Western Europe has played in underwriting the economic prosperity of the Soviet satellites. During the 1970s, much of the increase in Eastern European economic growth was financed by Western European loans, resulting in a debt of nearly $70 billion. It is not clear how much more will be forthcoming. A fundamental financial crisis seems to be pending, with a frightened but financially prudent Western Europe unwilling to further finance Soviet domination of Eastern Europe even as the Soviet Union scrambles to reduce the strain on its own economy.

For 20 years Soviet leaders have directed their diplomatic efforts at achieving political "détente" with Western Europe. But much to their displeasure, they have not been able to forestall pressures for a true détente with their own Eastern European subject states—that is, for a relaxation of Soviet control over social policies. To some extent, this is actually a consequence of the Soviet bloc's pursuit of détente with the West during the 1970s. Twenty years ago, Soviet consideration of an invasion of Poland would have been a simple matter of examining logistical difficulties. Today, even if the U.S.S.R. decides to risk the military aspect of an anti–Poland operation, it will also need to think about potential financial and technological sacrifices, and possible political and economic setbacks. Can the Soviet Union assume most of the $20 to $30 billion Polish debt to the West, on top of the 8 billion rubles Poland already owes the U.S.S.R.? Can the Soviet economy survive a cutoff of vital technology and trade from the West? Can the Soviet government afford to go on demonstrating to its Third World allies that to be a friend of the Soviet Union means to risk invasion?

However, most of the pressures for this détente emanate not from Moscow or Paris or London, but from Eastern Europe itself. It has been possible to find technocrats willing to rule and direct the Warsaw Pact nations for the Soviets, but the peoples of Eastern Europe have no great love for either the men in the Kremlin or their troops. In most, though not all, Eastern European countries, the forces of patriotism and of government are in fundamental opposition. The conflict between the two was easier to suppress in the late 1940s and early 1950s, when Eastern Europe's societies were exhausted and its politics Stalinized. Stalin's successors decided that these nations would only remain pacific under a delicate and controlled program of economic development. This required certain free-

doms of thought and movement, and of contact with the West to an extent
unthinkable in the Soviet Union. Even more than the Soviets, the Eastern
European regimes have felt the pressure of the post–Stalin contradiction
of not being able to continue in the dictator's path, yet not being able to
stray far from it, of presiding over a system dangerous either to continue
or to reform. The Brezhnev era attempt to alleviate their client states'
difficulties with economic palliatives has only made the dilemma more
immediate.

If the Western nations were to do nothing, pressures for détente in
Eastern Europe would mount anyway; perhaps not in Bulgaria, where
Todor Zhivkov can speak of his people as the "loyal younger brothers to
the great Russians," and perhaps not in Romania, where Nicolae Ceau-
şescu has managed to blend nationalism and "Brezhnevism" into a unique
Transylvanian variant of totalitarianism. But in East Germany, Hungary,
Czechoslovakia, and Poland, pressures for economic and political independence from the Soviet Union can be expected to grow stronger no
matter what the West does.

Constraint breeds constraint; for reasons of ideology and "security,"
Soviet leaders feel unable to withdraw from Eastern Europe. In light of
current Soviet economic difficulties, and of the strong likelihood of their
becoming more severe during the 1980s, it is nearly as improbable that the
Soviet leadership could attempt to increase the Soviet presence in, or
subsidy to, Eastern Europe. Thus it seems likely that the Soviets will
attempt to muddle through—that is, mount a desultory attempt to contain
and minimize a continuing crisis. Such a half-hearted strategy is really no
strategy at all, for brushfire responses can only slow, not reverse, the
political drift of much of Eastern Europe. Eventually there might come a
flashpoint crisis that demands (in the Soviet view) a military response. Yet
the peoples of Eastern Europe appear to have learned well the lessons of
Hungary and Czechoslovakia, and now know how to probe without
provoking an invasion. For many Warsaw Pact citizens, such a standoff,
no matter how uneasy, would bring them close to victory, far closer than
they have been for decades.

The West is in a position to help move the Eastern Europeans beyond a
mere stalemate. Soviet–East European relations do not exist in a vacuum.
Given the situation developing in the Warsaw Pact countries, Western
Europe and the United States might, despite recent events in Poland, be
able to encourage a gradual relaxation of the Soviet grip on the economies
and people of Eastern Europe. This is not to be confused with updated
versions of the 1952 Republican Party platform's call for "rolling back"
the Soviets to the Ukraine. (As John Spanier has noted, that plank "seems
to have been devised primarily to roll back the Democrats in the United

States," and it was all too easy to move from that kind of blustering for domestic consumption to Radio Free Europe's false encouragement of Hungarian hopes in 1956.)

For the West, the advantages of "Finlandizing" Eastern Europe are self-evident. Although in Soviet eyes Finlandization is something to be foisted upon one's enemies, the Finlandization of Eastern Europe could well prove to be the least undesirable outcome for an empire facing the problems that the U.S.S.R. seems likely to encounter in the coming decades. After all, as William Pfaff has observed, of the 12 nations on the Soviet periphery, the one causing the least worries for the Politburo, the one whose border with the Soviets is most peaceful, is Finland, which was beaten by the Soviet Union during World War II but was never fully occupied. Finland sustains its own economy, and indeed, through its trade deals, has been made to play a disproportionately large role in sustaining the Soviet empire. With its army of 40,000 men—100 times smaller than the Soviet armed forces—Finland poses no military threat to the U.S.S.R. And Finland tacitly allows the Soviet Union a veto over its foreign policy.

Yet, as the *Economist* has noted, Finland is the only democracy on the east of the Baltic. It has a nominally free press and holds free elections; its citizens enjoy freedom of speech and movement, and make changes in their lives more or less as they see fit. The American mind recoils at the notion of settling for a life that is half-free. But this is surely more satisfactory to the people of Finland than the situation of the Warsaw Pact nations is to the peoples of Eastern Europe.

What can American policymakers do to encourage rather than frustrate this possibility? Simply recognizing the possibility would be a step in the right direction. At bare minimum, our responsibility to the Poles and to other Eastern European peoples is not to get in their way, and, especially, not to mislead them; there should never again be a situation in which American promises are given with no intention of their being kept, as seems to have happened with Radio Free Europe in 1956.

Americans could further help the people of Eastern Europe by keeping an eye on Western bankers. Only one side in East–West relations has ever attempted to separate business from politics. Western governments must scrupulously examine the loans being granted to the Warsaw Pact nations by Western financial institutions. If loans are dispensed carelessly or out of fear of losing funds already expended, we not only run the risk of subsidizing the inefficient systems which retard economic progress, but also of suffocating political progress by underwriting regimes which would otherwise themselves be forced by economics to liberalize. Commercial loans could, under certain specific conditions, be granted explicitly as rewards to follow each successful step in economic liberalization. Consideration of creditworthiness notwithstanding, that can happen only if Western banks act both as a consortium and as stewards of Western interests; right now it is not clear that they can do either.

Finally, the West must stop subsidizing the Soviet imperium. Currently, Japanese, European, and even American corporations and governmental bodies make the Soviet task of controlling its allies far easier than it might otherwise be by granting Moscow financial room to maneuver. In Angola, to take one case, Soviet proxies are now making the jungles safe for the MPLA's variant of "socialism." This is an expensive task: by some estimates, it costs as much as $3 million per day. The U.S.S.R. has been spared the necessity of footing this bill. Instead, Gulf Oil has stepped smartly into the breach, and is currently paying $5 million a day in royalties to the Luanda government. But it is not necessary to look to exotic regions of the world for further examples. Western corporations are competing against each other to participate in the 3,000-mile-long gas pipeline from Western Siberia to Western Europe, which during the next decade is expected to increase the Soviet Union's hard currency receipts by 50 percent, even as it gives the men in the Kremlin a foot on the oxygen line of the nervous patients in Western Europe.

Readers of the Soviet journal *International Affairs* are familiar with the Marxist-Leninist portrait of the West, in which every economic and social disturbance is held to be an auspicious outcropping of economic crisis, another indication that the decrepit West is slouching toward the end of an era. This assessment is wrong; indeed, it is far more descriptive of the Soviet predicament. This is not to say that all is well in the West. Both the Soviet empire and the Western Alliance are pained, but by entirely different afflictions. Systemic economic difficulties and anti–state patriotism are the hallmarks of modern totalitarianism. The Western malaise is not precisely economic, but spiritual and moral. Among its many manifestations are, on the one hand, the evident unwillingness of the adherents of the European peace movement to defend their own societies, and, on the other hand, the evident willingness of Western industrialists and financiers to reap short-term profits at the expense of Eastern freedom and Western security.

The ailments of the superpowers are chronic, but not necessarily terminal. Whether East or West will emerge the more successful from this long-term competition depends largely upon their recuperative abilities. These are as yet unknown.

Originally published in *The New Republic*, December 31, 1981. Reprinted with permission, all rights reserved.

9

Literacy and Health: The Cuban "Model"

It is widely believed that Fidel Castro's revolutionary government in Cuba has achieved major successes in the fields of health and education since it came to power 27 years ago. It is not merely admirers of the "Cuban experiment" who subscribe to this notion. A study prepared by President Reagan's Commerce Department in 1982, for example, stated that "Cuba has succeeded in almost totally eliminating illiteracy," and reported that Cuba's health care system "rivals that of most developed nations."[1] By the same token, a recent report prepared under the aegis of the Organization of American States, while sharply criticizing Cuba's human rights violations, remarked that "Cuba has been notably effective in meeting the basic needs of its population."[2] Irrespective of their political inclinations, it seems, the consensus of virtually all informed observers is that Cuba has made model progress against disease and ignorance, those two basic scourges of low-income countries.

This opinion is fundamentally unsound. It is not based on an examination of Cuban data, or of statistics from countries with which Cuba might most reasonably be compared. If Cuba's social progress is accurately reflected in its statistics, it has fared not better in improving health and reducing illiteracy than most other affluent Caribbean and Latin American societies. There is reason, moreover, to wonder whether Cuba has done even this well. Since the early 1970s, substantial inconsistencies have emerged in Cuban social statistics—inconsistencies that would be readily explainable only if Cuba's records were being deliberately falsified.

Literacy

In 1977, a U.S. Congressional delegation visiting Havana was told that Cuba's literacy rate had risen to 99 percent from 25 percent during the

Castro years.[3] This claim is directly contradicted by Cuba's own statistics. Cuba's literacy rate, as measured by its censuses, passed the 25 percent mark long before 1900.[4] By 1953, the date of the last prerevolutionary census, the literacy rate for those 15 and older was put at 76 percent—over three times what modern Cuban authorities claim it was.[5] Despite the misrule of the dictator Fulgencio Batista and the disruption attendant to the revolutionary struggle for power, Cuba's literacy rate appears to have risen, albeit slowly, through the 1950s. Professor Carmelo Mesa-Lago of the University of Pittsburgh, an expert on the Cuban economy, has suggested that Cuba's literacy rate might have been about 79 percent when Castro gained control of the government.[6] This would have been one of the very highest rates of literacy for a non-industrial country in that era.

Surveys and censuses since the revolution show that illiteracy in Cuba is far from being "almost completely eliminated." According to the 1970 census, about 13 percent of Cubans over 15 were illiterate. For those 35 and older, the rate was put at 21 percent—as against a national average of 24 percent in 1953.[7] A decade and more of highly vaunted mass literacy campaigns and adult education programs appears in practice to have had only a marginal impact on the reading and writing skills of those who were already out of school.

According to a nationwide survey, Cuba's illiteracy rate was under 5 percent in 1979.[8] Much of the improvement implied by this drop, unfortunately, comes from a change in definitions. The 1970 census, like all previous Cuban censuses, gave the illiteracy rate for the entire population over 15 years of age. The 1979 number, by contrast, covered Cubans between 15 and 49—the adults most likely to be literate. By excluding people 50 and older, more than a quarter of Cuba's adult population was left out of the literacy count. In 1979, illiteracy rates for the group 45 to 49 years of age were over 12 percent.[9] For the population over 50, rates were presumably higher. Adjustments would raise Cuba's nominal rate of illiteracy to something like 7 percent to 10 percent at the end of the 1970s.

If these Cuban figures are correct, illiteracy may have fallen to about 7 to 10 percent from 13 percent in 1970, and 24 percent in 1953. Clearly, this record entails progress; yet just as clearly it is unexceptional by the standards of other Caribbean and Latin American states. Instead of "starting practically from zero," as Mr. Castro has sometimes claimed, prerevolutionary Cuba was one of the hemisphere's more developed and literate tropical societies. Revolutionary Cuba should be compared with other comparatively affluent Caribbean and Latin American societies—not with impoverished Haiti, Guatemala or El Salvador.

A check of the historical record is instructive. In the late 1940s or in the 1950s nine other Caribbean or Latin American societies had literacy rates roughly comparable to Cuba's. Of these, three seem to have reduced illiteracy much more rapidly than Cuba did. Dominica, Grenada, and Trinidad–Tobago all began the 1950s with illiteracy rates equal to Cuba's, or higher.[10] By 1970 they had reduced their measured rates of illiteracy to 6 percent, 3 percent, and 8 percent, respectively—rates that Cuba not only had failed to attain then, but may not have attained yet.[11] Martinique and Puerto Rico had slightly higher illiteracy rates in the early 1950s; by 1970 their illiteracy rates were lower. Three nations—Chile, Costa Rica, and Panama—seem to have more or less matched Cuba's performance. For one nation—Jamaica—evaluation is as yet impossible; since 1960 Jamaica's censuses have not produced useful or reliable data on literacy. Cuba's rate of progress against illiteracy appears unambiguously favorable only next to Argentina's. Argentina led Cuba in literacy by more than 10 points in the late 1940s, but by only 5 points in 1970. Those familiar with postwar Latin American history will know how modest any Cuban claim to success on this last ground would be.[12]

To be sure, literacy figures must be treated with caution. The definition of literacy is functional, not absolute; it depends upon requirements which can vary between or even within societies, and which may change over time. Moreover, the evaluation of literacy, a tricky business even under controlled and standardized circumstances, is complicated considerably when procedures and criteria employed in quick mass surveys differ from one such exercise to the next. Such complexities, however, may argue for caution in the interpretation of literacy numbers, but they do not necessarily bias these numbers in any systematic direction.

As best as can be told from these numbers, revolutionary Cuba's performance in dealing with illiteracy has been no better than that of its peers in the Western hemisphere. Such a conclusion, moreover, would be consistent with indications from other educational statistics with less scope for alternative interpretations. Revolutionary Cuba's gross primary enrollment ratios suggest that something approaching universal elementary education for children of the appropriate ages was not achieved until about 1975—about the same time as for Chile.[13] (For 1981–82, Cuba estimates that slightly over 97 percent of its children of primary school age were in fact enrolled in school.[14]) Even a decade after the revolution, Cuba appears to have been far from the goal of guaranteeing its youth a full six years of basic education. In 1970, for example, 30 percent of Cuba's primary school students were enrolled in first grade, but only 8 percent were in sixth grade; other things being equal, the proportions would be expected to be relatively steady from one grade to the next in a universal enrollment society.[15] Moreover, the efficacy of the schooling process for those who actually did enroll may not have been distinctly superior to that of neighboring societies. In 1970, the repeater rate for Cuba's primary schools was registered as 22 percent: the same rate as for the Dominican Republic that year, only slightly lower than the 24 percent recorded in Haiti in 1970, and significantly higher than Mexico's 11 percent figure for 1975.[16] Performance may also have been affected by truancy and non-attendance: on a visit in 1977, for example, reporters from the *New York Times* were informed that something like a quarter of the students enrolled in primary schools had not been attending regularly.[17] This may not be so different from the situation in many contemporary Latin American or Caribbean societies; that, however, would be precisely the point.

Cuba has recently released a new set of numbers pertaining to illiteracy. Preliminary reports on the 1981 census say that less than 2.2 percent of the adult population are unable to read or write. These new numbers are strangely inconsistent with the results of the 1979 nationwide survey. The 1979 survey placed the total number of illiterates in Cuba between ages 15 and 50 at 218,358. The 1981 census states that there were 105,901 adult illiterates in Cuba; the 1981 census, moreover, presumes to count illiterates of all ages, not just those between 15 and 50. According to preliminary reports, 30,434 persons over 45 were identified as illiterate in the 1981 census. This would mean 75,467 persons between 15 and 45 were identified as illiterates. In the 1979 survey, about 180,000 adults in those same age groups were identified as illiterate. The discrepancy is by a factor of about 2.4. Definitions of illiteracy, of course, can vary from one survey to another, but there is no formal indication that Cuba has changed its criteria for identifying illiteracy. It is not immediately apparent, moreover, how a shift in questionnaire criteria would result in the diminution of the number of identified illiterates by about 60 percent among a young adult population.[18]

Health

Many of the Castro government's proudest claims concern the transformation of health conditions in Cuba. Thanks to radical social reforms and people-oriented health care, it is argued, Cuba's infant mortality has been cut by more than 75 percent since 1959, and its life expectancy has come up to European and North American levels. Such reports have convinced many foreign observers that Cuba is a "socialist showcase," as a chief of staff of the Senate Foreign Relations Committee once described it.[19]

The Cuban health record should be examined with greater care. As with education, the Cuban government did not have to start from scratch. Prerevolutionary Cuba's last smallpox epidemic was in 1897; its last outbreak of yellow fever was in 1905.[20] On the basis of its 1953 census,

Cuba's life expectancy in the early 1950s has been calculated at 59 years.[21] This may sound low today, but in the early 1950s it placed Cuba above most Latin American nations. It also placed Cuba above such nations as Spain, Portugal, Greece and Japan.[22] Far from being an especially stricken nation, prerevolutionary Cuba was in fact one of the developing regions' healthiest societies. Interestingly, the 1950s appear to have been a decade of solid health progress in Cuba. Demographers in Cuba today suggest that their nation's life expectancy had risen to 64 years by 1960—before new policies would have borne many results.[23]

According to Cuban statistics, health progress in Cuba's first decade of revolutionary government was in important respects problematic. In 1958, Cuba's registered rate of infant mortality was about 38 per thousand births. In 1969, it was 46 per thousand—an increase of over 20 percent. To some extent, this jump in death rates may have been a statistical artifact. Cuba was tightening up its vital registration system during those years, and improvements in enumeration could in theory make it seem as if death rates were rising when they were really falling. On the other hand, death and birth statistics were reasonably reliable before the revolution. A recent study by the National Academy of Sciences in Washington, for example, suggests that the registration system was catching over 80 percent of all infant and child deaths by 1953.[24] Moreover, revolutionary Cuba's statistics on "morbidity," or sickness, go through the same sort of rise in the late 1960s as the infant mortality rate does. Between 1965 and 1968, for example, Cuba's reported incidence of acute diarrhea rose 11 percent; measles was up 20 percent, chicken pox and hepatitis were up by more than 70 percent.[25] These diseases are closely related in infant mortality in developing countries.

Social policy in Cuba in the 1960s appears to have cut two ways. Cuban children may have gained from their government's rationing of foods and subsidization of medical care, but they may have lost by their government's negative-growth economic policies and the change in conditions that led a third of the country's doctors to flee their native land.

According to revolutionary Cuba's vital statistics, infant mortality did not begin to decline until the 1970s. Once the decline began however, it seemed extremely rapid. According to these official figures, infant mortality fell from 46 per thousand in 1969 to 19 per thousand in 1979—a drop of 60 percent in barely a decade.

By 1982, Cuba's officially reported infant mortality rate was 17.3 per thousand births. While this would represent a comparatively advanced level of infant health in the context of today's developing regions, it is not dissimilar from the infant mortality rates of a number of islands and societies in Central America and the Caribbean, including Costa Rica

(1981 infant mortality rate: 18.0 per thousand), Dominica (1978: 19.6), Grenada (1979: 15.4), Guadeloupe (1982: 15.5), Puerto Rico (1983: 16.0), St. Lucia (1977: 19.2), Martinique (1977–81: 16), the Cayman Islands (1981: 14), and Bermuda (1979: 15).[26] (These are all places which the World Health Organization designates as having essentially complete registration of births and deaths.) And while a 60 percent reduction in infant mortality in a decade would incontestably represent an impressive accomplishment, such feats are, apparently, not unknown in the rest of Latin America. According to data from vital registration systems, the Latin American nation with the fastest pace of infant mortality decline since 1970 has not been Cuba. Instead, it appears to have been Chile. In 1973, Chile's registered rate of infant mortality was 66 per thousand births. In 1982, Chile's infant mortality rate was recorded as 24 per thousand—a 64 percent drop in nine years. Although Chileans may have lost political liberty under the Pinochet dictatorship, the junta which installed itself was apparently not insensitive to the political significance of appearing to "meet the basic human needs" of the population beneath it.[27]

Cuba's accomplishments in infant health, however, appear to be undercut by factors more compromising than external comparisons alone. For Cuba's purported achievements are directly contradicted by another set of its own infant mortality estimates.

Infant mortality estimates can come from two different sources. The first is the official figures from the birth and death registration system. Their accuracy depends upon the extent of under-reporting. The second source is from indirect methods, such as those incorporated in the construction of "life tables", which apply demographic techniques to census data and vital registration statistics to correct for under-reporting of deaths, and to present internally consistent estimates of survival probabilities by age group. Unless registration of births and deaths is universal and complete, infant mortality estimates from such indirect methods as adjusted life tables will be the more reliable.

Cuba produced two life tables in the early 1970s. The first put the nation's infant mortality rate at 40 per thousand in 1970. That squared with the registration system's estimate of 39 per thousand. For 1974, Cuba's registration system put the infant mortality rate at 29 per thousand: a 25 percent drop in four years. The 1974 life table, however, indicated that infant mortality had not dropped at all. To the contrary: these figures suggested it had risen by more than 11 percent, to over 45 per thousand.[28]

This anomalous inconsistency has been noted by foreign demographers. Kenneth Hill of the National Academy of Sciences recently completed a careful analysis of Cuban population data. For the most part, he found their reliability to be very good, and getting better. He found only one exception to this rule: Cuban infant mortality statistics. According to Hill:

> "From the early 1970s on, the consistency between the indirect and official [estimates of infant mortality] disappears. The indirect estimates indicate constant or even rising child mortality, while the official figures show a continued rapid decline. . . . The sharp drop from the mid–1970s to 1980 is not supported by the available child survivorship data."[29]

Interestingly, the reported rapid decline in infant mortality is also inconsistent with Cuban morbidity data. Infant mortality, by the registration system's tally, is said to have dropped more than 45 percent between 1969 and 1977, yet over those same years the reported incidence of acute diarrhea was up 15 percent; chicken pox rose 35 percent; hepatitis was up 44 percent, and measles almost doubled. Table 9.1 compares reported incidences of various infectious parasitic diseases in Cuba between 1970 and 1982. Over those years the official estimate states that infant mortality dropped by well over half. Yet the incidence among the general population of most diseases listed in Table 9.1 actually rose between 1970 and 1982: acute diarrhea, acute respiratory infection, chicken pox, hepatitis, malaria, measles, and syphillis all appear to have become more prevalent at a time when infant mortality is said to have been falling sharply. The paradox is sharpened in Table 9.2, which compares reported incidences of certain infectious and parasitic diseases in Cuba in 1982 and the U.S.S.R. in 1974. In many categories, the incidence appears to be higher in Cuba: these include acute respiratory infection, malaria, measles, meningococcal infections, mumps, and possibly acute diarrhea. Yet in 1974, the last year for which the U.S.S.R. published its infant mortality data, the U.S.S.R.'s adjusted infant mortality rate was almost twice as high as Cuba's stated infant mortality rate in 1982. Morbidity and mortality statistics generally correspond in national populations; the uncoupling of Cuba's morbidity and infant mortality trends since the early 1970s is a puzzle, the answer to which is yet to be supplied.

If Mr. Hill's estimates are accurate, Cuba's vital registration system was missing only about 2 percent of the nation's infant deaths in 1970, but would appear to have been missing fully 44 percent by 1978. Such a deterioration in statistical coverage would be extraordinary—not only because of the high priority Cuba says it gives to health care, but because the reliability of vital statistics for all other age groups continued to rise.

The sloppiness that seems to have allowed reported infant mortality rates to fall when actual rates may have been stationary, or even possibly rising, sounds increasingly suspicious as one learns its background. Since

TABLE 9.1
Reported Incidence of Selected Infectious and Parasitic Diseases in Cuba, 1959–1983 (per 100,000)

Year	Acute Diarrhea	Acute Respiratory Infections	Chicken Pox	Diptheria	Hepatitis	Malaria	Measles	Polio	Syphillis	Tetanus	Tuberculosis	Typhoid
1970	7.694	10.162	150.1	0.1	102.6	—	105.2	—	7.8	2.6	30.8	5.0
1982	8.732	27.441	191.5	—	208.4	3.4	238.8	—	38.5	0.2	8.3	1.3
Index (1970 = 100)												
1970	100	100	100	100	100	—	100	—	100	100	100	100
1982	113	270	128	—	203	200	227	—	494	8	27	26

Notes: "—" = less than .1% per 100,000

Sources: Republic of Cuba, *Annuario Estadistico de Cuba* (Havana: Comite Estatal de Estadisticas), various issues.

TABLE 9.2.
Reported Incidence of Selected Communicable or Infectious Diseases: Cuba 1982 and U.S.S.R. 1974 (or more recent previous year)
(incidence per 100,000 population)

Disease	Cuba, 1982	U.S.S.R., 1974	Ratio, U.S.S.R. = 100
Acute Diarrhea	8,732	(409) (1966)	NA
Acute Respiratory Infection	27,441	18,623	147
Brucellosis	0.6	5.6 (1966)	11
Chicken Pox	191.5	419.4	46
Diptheria	—	—	NA
Hepatitis	208.4	223.6	93
Malaria	3.4	.1 (1969)	2,830
Measles	239	149	160
Meningococcol Infections	8.2	6.7	122
Mumps	261	247 (1966)	106
Polio	—	—	NA
Scarlet Fever	2.3	146.2	2
Tetanus	0.2	0.2	100
Typhoid	1.3	6.6	20

Notes: "—" = less than .1 per 100,000; "NA"—not applicable; "( )" parenthetical figure for USSR for acute diarrhea refers incidence of bacterial dysentery.

Sources: Republic of Cuba, *Anuario Estadistico de Cuba 1983* (Havana: Comite Estatal de Estadisticas, 1984)

Murray Feshbach, *A Compendium of Soviet Health Statistics* (Washington: U.S. Bureau of the Census, Center for International Research, January 1985).

1972, all infant mortality figures have been treated as "preliminary"—subject to revision at any time. This proviso has been used to make major alterations in official figures far in the past: the 1973 infant mortality rate for Isla de Juventud, for example, was lowered by almost a quarter between the 1977 and the 1982 editions of Cuba's Statistical Yearbook.

Changes in the Cuban statistical system in the early 1970s, moreover, relieved the precursor of Cuba's present State Statistical Committee of authority to check on the accuracy of infant mortality numbers. Figures are now provided directly by the Ministry of Health, whose performance they also implicitly measure. Perhaps most interestingly, the preliminary results of the 1981 census, which would help overseas demographers to check the reliability of recent Cuban infant mortality numbers, have been strangely garbled. Instead of giving the customary population by age and sex, this preliminary report lumps all people under 16 into a single undifferentiated category. No foreign observer can say with certainty why this was done; it does have the effect, however, of confounding indirect techniques of estimating Cuba's infant mortality rate.

Are Cuban authorities deliberately falsifying statistics on their nation's infant mortality rate? No outsider can answer this question definitively. It is, however, worth remembering Cuba's past treatment of statistics designated as important by the revolutionary authorities. In the 1960s Cuba altered and deleted reports on the all-important sugar harvest to impede "the enemies of the revolution," as President Castro explained at the time. In 1983, documents uncovered in the invasion of Grenada show Maurice Bishop, the late prime minister, praising "the Cuban experience of keeping two different sets of records in the bank," and recommending that "comrades from Cuba . . . visit Grenada to train comrades in the readjustment of the books".[30]

According to Cuba's own life tables, infant mortality fell by about 32 percent between 1960 and 1974. Over roughly that same period, according to their life tables, infant mortality fell 40 percent in Panama, 46 percent in Puerto Rico, 47 percent in Chile, 47 percent in Barbados, and 55 percent in Costa Rica. If Mr. Hill's National Academy of Sciences reconstructions are correct, infant mortality in Cuba would have fallen by only 25 percent between 1960 and 1978. If his estimates are reliable, the revolutionary Cuban experience would represent not the most rapid, but instead virtually the slowest, measured rate of progress against infant mortality in Latin America and the Caribbean for that period.[31]

Originally published in *Caribbean Review*, 1986. Reprinted with permission, all rights reserved. The essay is based upon an article which first appeared in *The Wall Street Journal*, December 10, 1984.

Notes

1. Lawrence W. Theriot, "Cuba Faces the Realities of the 1980's," Office of East–West Policy and Planning, Commerce Department; quoted in the *New York Times*, April 4, 1982.
2. Inter-American Commission of Human Rights' 7th report on Cuba, as quoted in the *New York Times*, December 21, 1983.
3. Cf., Norman Luxenburg, "Social Conditions Before and After the Revolution," in Irving Louis Horowitz, ed., *Cuban Communism* (New Brunswick: Transaction Books, 1984).
4. *Fertility Determinants in Cuba* by Paula E. Hollerbach and Sergio Diaz-Briquets, with an appendix by Kenneth H. Hill (Washington, D.C.: National Academy Press, 1983).
5. UNESCO, *Statistical Yearbook 1980* (Paris: UNESCO, 1981).
6. Carmelo Mesa-Lago, *The Economy of Socialist Cuba: A Two-Decade Appraisal* (Albuquerque: University of New Mexico Press, 1981).
7. *Ibid.*
8. UNESCO, *Statistical Yearbook 1982* (Paris: UNESCO, 1983).
9. *Fertility Determinants in Cuba,* op. cit.
10. UNESCO, *Statistical Yearbook 1967* (Paris: UNESCO, 1967).
11. UNESCO, *Statistical Yearbook 1980* (Paris: UNESCO, 1981).
12. Statistics for all countries mentioned in this section come from various issues of UNESCO, *Statistical Yearbook.*
13. See UNESCO, *Statistical Yearbook*, 1980 and 1978.
14. Comite Estatal de Estadisticas, *Anuario Estadistico, de Cuba 1982.*
15. UNESCO, *Statistical Yearbook* (Paris: UNESCO, 1984).
16. UNESCO, *Statistical Yearbook,* various issues.
17. *New York Times*, December 18, 1977.
18. Data are from United Nations, *Demographic Yearbook 1983*, UNESCO, *Statistical Yearbook 1984*, and *Fertility Determinants in Cuba.*
19. *New York Times*, December 1, 1974.
20. Hugh Thomas, *Cuba* (Boston: Little, Brown, 1971).
21. UN, *Demographic Yearbook 1967.*
22. *Ibid.*
23. A. Farnos Morejon, "Cuba: tablas de motalidad estimadas por sexo, periodo 1955–1970," *Estudios Demograficos*, Series 1, Number 8.
24. Kenneth Hill, "An Evaluation of Cuban Demographic Statistics, 1930–80," in *Fertility Determinants in Cuba.*
25. Mesa-Lago, op. cit.
26. Data from UN, *Demographic Yearbook 1983, World Health Statistics Annual 1983*, and U.S. Bureau of the Census, *World Population 1982.*
27. Chilean infant mortality data from Peter Hakim and Giorgio Solimano, *Development, Reform and Malnutrition in Chile*, (MIT Press, 1978), and *World Health Statistics Annual 1983.*
28. Figures cited in United Nations Department of Economic and Social Affairs, *Levels and Trends of Mortality Since 1950* (New York: United Nations, 1982).
29. Hill, "An Evaluation of Cuban Demographic Statistics, 1930–80."
30. *Granma*, January 2, 1965, cited in Carmelo Mesa-Lago, "The Availability and Reliability of Statistics in Socialist Cuba," Part 2, *Latin American Research Review*, No. 2, 1969; *Wall Street Journal*, December 16, 1983.
31. *Levels and Trends of Mortality Since 1950; World Population 1983.*

10

Health of an Empire: Poverty and Social Progress in Eastern Europe, Mongolia, Vietnam, and Cuba

The problem of human poverty is of considerable rhetorical and practical concern to contemporary Marxist–Leninist governments. Indeed, to no small degree, these states have defined their political and economic programs, their mode of social organization, and even their justification for existence in terms of their conception of the issue of poverty. The diverse writings of Marx are animated and unified by their attention to material deprivation and social injustices, and by their insistence that these failings were systemic—remediable only by the utter transformation of social order with which he identified them. Lenin and his successors, who built upon the rubble of the Russian Empire the first of the many state apparatuses explicitly committed to the interpretation and application of Marxism, made it their stated goal to construct and promote a system of governance which would serve human needs. The eradication of material poverty was professed to be integral to both the revolutionary struggle and the quest for "scientific" socialist construction. Such an outlook informs Stalin's dictum that "human beings are the most important and decisive capital in the world," a statement which has been repeated with only slight modifications by Marxist–Leninist rulers around the globe for the past half century.

The performance of Marxist–Leninist states in alleviating and overcoming mass poverty in the territories under their administration was understood, in some formulations of Marxist–Leninist thinking, to affect directly the "correlation of forces" between the "socialist" and capitalist" camps, insofar as it would alter the confidence in, support for, and ultimately the legitimacy of existing non-communist states in the eyes of the workers and voters living under them. No less importantly, the elimination of undernutrition, ill health, illiteracy and other manifestations of physical poverty would relieve constraints against enhancing national production, thereby accelerating "socialist construction" and augmenting the resources the state might harness in either domestic campaigns or "international struggle."

Western nations have offered their own response to the problem of poverty. Its articulation includes the tradition of private and voluntarily supported charities, the evolution of the "welfare state," and the invention of a form of government-to-government resources transfers known as "foreign aid." Though there are similarities between Western and Marxist–Leninist strategies to alleviate poverty—not least because certain programs, actions, and approaches in the West have taken their cue from the Marxist–Leninist attacks on mass poverty—efforts in the two systems are governed by distinct and largely incompatible conceptions of what "poverty" actually is. The attenuation of poverty, from the liberal Western standpoint, is linked to the extension of human choice. Planned progress in a socialist command economy, by contrast, is meant to occur precisely by subordinating these many individual choices to a single "social preference function" according to which resources are allocated, and prices set.

Insofar as the liberal humanist and the Marxist–Leninist traditions express antithetical attitudes about the relationship between the individual, society, and the state, it would seem unrealistic to expect from them a unanimity on what "progress against poverty" actually means.

These irresolveable philosophic differences do not vitiate the need for an understanding of the comparative performance of Marxist–Leninist states and non-communist societies in their respective efforts to deal with poverty. For better or worse, this understanding is of operational significance because of the enduring contest between Marxism–Leninism and the political philosophies to which it is hostile. Intellectually, attempts to further such an understanding need not be doomed to complete frustration, for despite the profound differences in their outlook on poverty, there are aspects of poverty which both communist and non-communist states take to be meaningful—aspects, moreover, which are subject to unambiguous measurement and quantification.

Reliability and Usefulness of Official Communist Data

In theory, if not always in practice, central economic planning requires data. To meet the claims of efficacy made for it by its proponents, centrally planned economic systems actually require *more* data, and *better* data, than a market-oriented system, for the political authorities directing such a command economy assume direct responsibility for disseminating economic information and managing economic adjustments throughout society—functions that markets perform spontaneously and impersonally through the price mechanism. Many Soviet-style economies generate considerable amounts of data on economic and social conditions, some of which is published with regularity. Table 10.1 collects some of the indicators of macroeconomic performance for the 1970s and 1980s that have been released by the U.S.S.R. and some of its allies.

In an economy whose governance is explicitly predicated on and ideologically justified by the quest to meet human needs, one might expect that macroeconomic indicators would provide an especially accurate measure of the material prospects for the populations in question. In reality, such numbers provide at best an opaque lens through which to attempt to divine the material welfare of local populations. A number of problems come into play. Morris Bornstein has summarized some of them:

> First, statistics are not published on many internal and external economic activities of interest. Second, the statistical concepts used may give an incomplete picture of economic activity; for example, figures for national income in terms of net material product (NMP) exclude most services. Third, statistical methodologies—and changes in them—often are not fully explained. Fourth, administratively set non-scarcity prices are used to aggregate physical output series. Also, the uneven incidence of indirect taxes and subsidies on different categories of goods and services distorts the relative shares of different end-uses of national product. Commonly, the share of consumption is higher, and the shares of investment and defense are lower, at the officially established than at factor cost excluding indirect taxes and subsidies.[1]

Some other important limitations may also be noted. Soviet-style statistical systems are typically ill-equipped to measure activity in the informal or private sectors of the economy, even though such activity may be considerable, and may bear directly on the material well-being of substantial fractions of the local population. Accounting procedures for the socialist sector of the planned economy are problematic when it comes to assessing net value added through economic activity, and tend to bias statistical series upwards as an economy becomes more complex. Time series data of a socialist planned economy are further affected by the problem of intertemporal indexation; the political administration of prices severely compromises any efforts to use price series to derive "real changes in economic activity." Finally, as Charles Wolf has noted, the statistical publications of Soviet-style economic systems are often construed by leadership as an instrument of policy. Hence, they are subject to political "adjustments," as well as to concealments. Release of data, therefore, need not necessarily imply accuracy.[2]

TABLE 10.1
Estimates and Indices Pertaining to Economic Performance for Certain Soviet Bloc Countries, 1971–1985

A) Official Estimates of Changes in Net Material Product (percent per annum)

COUNTRY	1971–75	1976–80	1981–83
Bulgaria	7.8	6.1	4.0
Czechoslovakia	5.7	3.7	0.6
East Germany	5.4	4.1	3.2
Hungary	6.2	3.2	1.7
Poland	9.8	1.2	−4.3
Romania	11.2	7.3	2.7
Unweighted average	7.1	4.3	1.3
U.S.S.R.	5.6	4.2	3.7

B) Official Estimates of Changes in Material Product Used for Consumption (percent per annum)

COUNTRY	1971–75	1976–80	1981–83
Bulgaria	7.0	4.0	4.2
Czechoslovakia	5.3	2.5	1.3
East Germany	5.3	2.5	1.6
Hungary	4.7	3.1	1.3
Poland	8.7	4.5	−4.7
Romania	NA	7.1	0.7
Unweighted average	NA	4.2	0.7
U.S.S.R.	5.8	4.7	2.6

C) Official Estimates of Changes in Net Material Product Used for Net Investment (percent per annum)

COUNTRY	1971–75	1976–80	1981–83
Bulgaria	12.9	0.1	1.7
Czechoslovakia	8.4	1.4	−10.4
East Germany	2.9	3.0	−4.2
Hungary	8.1	−2.0	−11.1
Poland	18.1	−11.8	−9.8
Romania	NA	6.6	−10.3
Unweighted average	NA	−0.5	7.4
U.S.S.R.	3.3	3.2	5.1

D) Unofficial Estimates of Net Hard Currency Debt
(Billions of U.S. Dollars)

COUNTRY	1971	1975	1980	1983
Bulgaria	0.7	2.3	2.8	1.1
Czechoslovakia	0.2	0.8	3.5	2.7
East Germany	1.2	3.5	12.3	9.5
Hungary	0.8	2.2	7.7	7.0
Poland	0.8	7.4	24.5	25.8
Romania	1.2	2.4	9.3	8.0
Subtotal	(4.9)	(18.7)	(59.9)	(54.0)
U.S.S.R.	0.6	7.5	9.7	9.1
Total	.5.5	26.2	69.8	63.1

E) Indices of Economic Change for Selected Soviet Bloc Countries (1970 = 100)

COUNTRY	Net Social Product		Gross Industrial Output		Turnover In Foreign Trade	
	1980	1984	1980	1984	1980	1984
Bulgaria	194	229	206	247	383	576
Czechoslovakia	159	169	124	191	300	423
East Germany	162	180	174	204	303	439
Hungary	159	174	159	169	386	570
Poland	169	157	207	202	385	415
Romania	230	262	290	336	481	467
U.S.S.R.	167	192	178	206	426	633
Cuba (1975 = 100)	125	186	176	245	364	537
Mongolia	195	259	234	359	345	600
Vietnam (1975 = 100)	114	154	113	199	160	233

Sources: Panels A–C: Jan Vanous, "Macroeconomic Adjustment in Eastern Europe in 1981–1983: Response to Western Credit Squeeze and Deteriorating Terms of Trade with the Soviet Union," in U.S. Congress Joint Economic Committee, *East European Economies: Slow Growth in the 1980s* (Washington: Government Printing Office, 1985).

Panel D: Columns 1 and 2: Joan Parpart Zoeter, "Eastern Europe: The Hard Currency Debt," in U.S. Congress Joint Economic Committee, *East European Economic Assessment,* (Washington: Government Printing Office, 1981) and *idem,* "U.S.S.R.: Hard Currency Trade and Payouts," in U.S. Congress Joint Economic Committee, *Soviet Economy in the 1980's: Problems and Prospects* (Washington: Government Printing Office, 1983). Columns 3 and 4: Vanous, op. cit.

Panel E: Soviet Economicheskoi Vzaimopomoshchi, *Statisticheskii Ezhegodnik Stran-1985* (Moscow: Finansy i Statistika, 1985).

In and of themselves, these problems greatly complicate any attempt by independent observers to understand the economic changes represented in economic statistics produced by Soviet-style economies. The degree of such difficulties may be suggested from situations where Soviet bloc authorities and non-communist agencies have access to roughly the same data, and employ the same theoretical constructs. Hungary, a member of the International Monetary Fund, is obligated by its membership to share a wide array of financial and economic data with the Fund to which international agencies customarily have no access. By the reckoning of Hungarian authorities, "net material product" rose at a rate of 3.2 percent per year in the 1976–1980 period. IMF data, however, indicate the rate of growth to have been 1.9 percent—two fifths lower than Budapest's computation. By the same token, Hungarian accounts put the real rate of change in gross fixed investment at over those same years at 2.4 percent, while the IMF data suggest it was − 0.2 percent—a difference not only in magnitude, but also in a sign![3]

Thus, while the official economic data in Table 10.1 are suggestive of economic slowdown in the Soviet Bloc between the 1960s and the 1980s— a phenomenon which has been accorded much discussion and analysis— they are not fully capable of portraying its dimensions accurately. They are not comparable with purportedly comparable statistics from non-communist countries. They are still less useful in suggesting the impact that economic changes in these Marxist–Leninist countries have on the material well-being of local populations.

This does not mean, however, that there are no data by which one can reliably assess changes in the material well-being of these populations. Alternative indicators do exist.

The most important of these is arguably the health of the population. There are a number of reasons to use health conditions for the comparison of poverty among nations. First, improved health for the populations over which they preside is a goal all modern states profess to champion. Second, better health comes close to being a universally desired personal attribute; indifference to one's own health, or to the health of family and friends, is considered pathological in a wide array of cultures with little else in common. Third, health conditions may be objectively and precisely measured. As Oskar Morgenstern noted more than a generation ago, economic statistics are subject to an irreducible margin of uncertainty, owing to the specificities of the valuation process.[4] Demographic statistics circumvent that problem: in principle, there is no difficulty in determining whether a person is alive or dead. The meaning of such determinations, moreover, is quite independent of the ideology or social system of the society such numbers depicts. Fourth, health conditions are directly shaped by the social, economic, and political factors which prescribe the material limits of daily life, and thus reflect indirectly upon such things as nutrition, sanitation, public hygiene, education, housing, and the varieties of social stratification. Fifth, improved health, and the conditions which make it possible, are widely thought to be handmaidens to the process of modern economic growth. Finally, good health is widely viewed as a valuable good by those who enjoy it. On the basis of some arbitrary but nonetheless plausible assumptions, Dan Usher calculated that the early postwar economic growth rate for Sri Lanka would be doubled by an imputation to account for the increased utility to consumers of their own extended lifespans.[5] Indeed, it is almost tautological to assert that good health is an important component of one's quality of life, or standard of living.

For a first foray into the measurement of poverty in the "Soviet Empire", we may do worse than to examine levels and trends in national health, and to compare result with those achieved in non-communist nations. In this essay we will examine health conditions in the member states of the Council for Mutual Economic Assistance (CMEA, also known as COMECON). Full and active CMEA membership currently extends to Warsaw Pact Europe, Mongolia, Vietnam and Cuba. This definition of the "Soviet Empire" excludes many states dominated by, dependent upon, or apparently sympathetic to Soviet power: for example, Afghanistan, Angola, Cambodia, the Democratic People's Republic of Korea, Ethiopia, Laos, Libya, Mozambique, Nicaragua, People's Democratic Republic of Yemen, and Syria. There are reasons for excluding each of these places from our survey. This diverse group includes governments of dubious Marxist–Leninist credentials, states with Marxist–Leninist aspirations which have yet to achieve mastery over the society and economy within their claimed territory, and regimes with minimal ability or inclination to release statistics pertaining to the life of the peoples they rule. By contrast, full and active CMEA membership implies acceptance in Moscow of the state's interpretation of Marxism–Leninism, and requires, at least officially, the compilation and exchange of an array of accurate data on social conditions. Let us examine health conditions in each of the CMEA regions in turn.

Eastern Europe and the U.S.S.R.

The phenomenon of secular deterioration in health conditions in the Soviet Union is examined in detail elsewhere in this volume.[6] The phenomenon is remarkable, and anomalous, for an industrial country during peacetime. Industrial development and conscious social policy have typically been expected to stabilize the death rate, and to reduce it. But the Soviet experience may no longer be unique. Mortality data from the U.S.S.R.'s Eastern European allies indicate that improvements in overall life expectancy came to a halt in many of these societies during the 1970s. In several, overall life expectancy has declined slightly in recent years. Although their patterns of mortality change are still in important ways distinct from the Soviet Union's, Warsaw Pact Europe is now evidencing certain health trends which would be exceptional among Western nations, but which appear quite familiar in the Soviet context.

Like the U.S.S.R., Eastern Europe enjoyed rapid improvements in health in the 1950s and the early 1960s. Between the early 1950s and the early 1960s the unweighted life expectancy at birth for the six active European member states in the Warsaw Pact (Bulgaria, Czechoslovakia, East Germany, Hungary, Poland, Romania) rose by nearly six years; by contrast, the life expectancy of the twelve European NATO states rose by less than three and a half years.[7] In the early 1950s, lifespans were nearly six years shorter in Warsaw Pact Europe than in NATO Europe; by the second half of the 1960s, that gap had been narrowed to two and a half years. Since the mid 1960s, however, that gap has once again widened; by the early 1980s lifespans were nearly five years longer in NATO Europe than Warsaw Pact Europe. In part, this reflected changes in the West: while Western Europe's health improvements had been slowing down in the late 1950s and early 1960s, they sped up, for a variety of reasons, in the 1970s and early 1980s. But the rapidly growing gap also reflected Eastern European health trends. After rapid strides, health improvements suddenly had come to a halt. Indeed, for the region as a whole, life expectancy may have dropped slightly in recent years. As Table 10.2 points out, five of the six countries of Warsaw Pact Europe have registered a decline in national life expectancy in their most recent "life tables." Poland's life expectancy appears to be slightly lower today than in the mid-1970s; Hungary's was somewhat lower in 1982 than in 1972; and in Czechoslovakia it seems that overall life expectancy may have been slightly lower in the early 1980s than two decades earlier. Only East Germany has recorded steady gains in life expectancy, but in recent years even these have been modest. Over the course of the 1970s, for example, life expectation at birth in the German Democratic Republic rose by less than a year.[8]

Eastern Europe's stagnation, and even decline, in health can be better understood by decomposing the problem. Life expectancy at birth may be considered the product of survival chances during the first year of life, and survival chances thereafter. Table 10.3 depicts infant mortality in Eastern Europe. In contrast to the Soviet Union, there has been no sustained

TABLE 10.2
Declines in Life Expectancy at Birth in Eastern Europe, 1960–1984 Period

Country	Period	Change in E° (Years)	Change in Male E°	Change in Female E°
Bulgaria	1970–1980	−0.2	−0.7	+0.3
Czechoslovakia	1964–1983	−0.1	−0.9	+0.7
Hungary	1972–1983	−0.6	−1.8	+0.4
Poland	1975/78–1984	−0.3	−0.5	0
Romania	1976/78–1981	−0.2	−0.6	+0.2

Sources: Bulgaria: United Nations, *World Population Trends, Population and Development Interrelations and Population Policies: 1983 Monitoring Report Volume 1* (New York: United Nations, 1985).

Czechoslovakia: United Nations, *Demographic Yearbook 1969* (New York: United Nations, 1970); *Statisticka Rocenka 1985* (Prague: Federalny Statisticky Urad, 1985).

Hungary: *Demografaia Evkonyv 1983* (Budapest: Kozponti Statisztikai Hivatal, 1984).

Poland: *Rocznik Statystyczny 1985* (Warsaw: Glowny Urzad Statystyczny, 1985).

Romania: United Nations, *Demographic Yearbook 1983* (New York: United Nations, 1985); World Health Organization, *World Health Statistics Annual 1983* (Geneva: WHO, 1983).

recorded rise in infant mortality for the region as a whole (although registered rates did increase slightly in Czechoslovakia in the early 1960s). For the region as a whole, measured infant mortality rates fell by nearly two thirds between 1960 and 1983. Even so, such measured improvements do not compare favorably with achievements in Western Europe during the same period. Although infant mortality in Eastern Europe in 1960 was almost twice as high as in Western Europe, and thus presumably easier to reduce, the decline recorded between 1960 and 1983 was only slightly higher in Warsaw Pact Europe than in NATO Europe (65 percent vs. 64 percent). Moreover, NATO Europe's pace of infant mortality improvement has been the more rapid since 1965 (a 56 percent decline between 1965 and 1983, versus 47 percent in Warsaw Pact Europe).

Table 10.4 shows the expectation of life at one year of age for European countries between 1960 and 1981. By this measure, Eastern Europe was worse off in 1980 and 1981 than it had been in the mid-1960s. For the region as a whole, life expectancy at age 1 was more than half a year lower in 1980–1981 than in 1964–1966. Only East Germany registered improve-

TABLE 10.3
Recorded Infant Mortality in Warsaw Pact Europe and NATO Europe, 1980–1983
(deaths per 1000 births)

	1960	1965	1980	1983
Bulgaria	45	31	20	17
Czechoslovakia	24	26	18	16
German Democratic Republic	39	25	12	11
Hungary	48	39	23	19
Poland	55	42	26	23
Romania	75	44	29	24
Unweighted Average Warsaw Pact Europe	51	35	22	18
Unweighted Average 9 NATO Europe Countries	27	23	13	10
Ratio, Warsaw Pact Europe to NATO Europe	1.89	1.48	1.65	1.78

Percentage Decline in Recorded Mortality Rates

	1960–65	1965–80	1965–85
Unweighted Mean Warsaw Pact Europe	−33	−38	−47
Unweighted Mean 9 NATO Europe Countries	−19	−44	−55

Note: Figures only presented to two places, thus may not add or average due to rounding.

9 NATO Countries: Belgium, Denmark, Federal Republic of Germany, France, Greece, Italy, Netherlands, Norway, United Kingdom.

Sources: World Bank, *World Development Report,* (New York: Oxford University Press) various years.

TABLE 10.4
Estimated Expectations of Life at Age 1, 1960–1981

	1960	1964	1965	1966	1970	1975	1980	1981
Bulgaria	71.7	72.4	72.2	72.3	72.3	71.7	71.7	71.7
Czechoslovakia	71.2	71.2	71.0	71.1	70.2	70.9	70.7	71.0
German Democratic Republic	70.7	71.3	71.3	71.4	71.0	71.4	71.2	71.6
Hungary	70.9	71.8	71.4	72.2	71.2	71.1	70.2	69.9
Poland	70.6	71.1	71.5	71.9	71.7	71.9	70.7	71.5
Romania	70.3	70.8	71.0	71.3	70.6	71.3	70.4	70.1
Mean, Eastern Europe	70.9	71.5	71.5	71.7	71.1	71.4	70.7	71.1
U.S.S.R.	71.4	72.1	71.4	71.6	70.0	69.5	69.3	69.3
Mean, Northern Europe	72.1	71.9	72.2	72.0	72.3	72.9	73.7	(74.4)
Mean, Southern Europe	70.5	71.1	70.9	71.4	71.9	72.2	72.7	(73.7)
Mean, Western Europe	71.3	71.2	72.0	71.6	71.8	72.7	73.7	73.7

Source: Jean Bourgeois-Pichat, "Mortality Trends in Industrialized Countries," in
United Nations, Mortality and Health Policy (New York: United Nations,
Department of International Economic and Social Affairs, 1984).

ment by this measure, and it was miniscule (0.06 years between 1964–1966
and 1980–1981). All other countries experienced declines; Hungary lost
nearly two years. In contrast, Western European nations are estimated to
have gained about two years in life expectancy for its population above
the age of one during this period.

Eastern Europe's current health problem is principally an adult problem,
as can be seen in Table 10.5 Between the mid-1960s and the early 1980s,
life expectancy for those 35 and older fell throughout Eastern Europe,
including East Germany. These changes may be contrasted with the record
of NATO Europe, where 35 year old men gained over a year, and women
almost two and a half years, during the same period.

Health trends among Eastern European adults are further decomposed
in Table 10.6. Between the mid-1960s and the early 1980s death rates for
men over 30 not only rose in total in each of these nations, but also rose
for nearly every age group in each country. For the region as a whole,
death rates for men in their forties jumped by over two-fifths, and by over

TABLE 10.5
Life Expectancy at Age 35 for Eastern and Western European Populations, Mid-
1960s and Early 1980s

	Eastern Europe				
	Mid-1960s		Early 1980s		Change
Bulgaria					
Male	38.39	(1965–67)	37.3	(1981)	−1.1
Female	41.2		41.8		+0.6
Czechoslovakia					
Male	36.3	(1966)	35.07	(1981)	−1.2
Female	41.15		41.46		+0.3
German Democratic Republic					
Male	37.58	(1965–66)	36.76	(1982)	−0.8
Female	41.45		41.74		+0.3
Hungary					
Male	37.10	(1964)	34.36	(1982)	−2.7
Female	40.67		40.89		+0.2
Poland					
Male	37.11	(1965–66)	35.77	(1981)	−1.3
Female	41.69		42.49		+0.8
Romania					
Male	38.08	(1963)	36.3	(1981)	−1.7
Female	40.94		40.9		0

	Western Europe (Selected Countries)				
	Mid-1960s		Early 1980s		Change
Italy					
Male	37.66	(1960–62)	38.4	(1978)	+1.7
Female	41.67		44.3		+2.7
U.K. (England and Wales)					
Male	36.6	(1965–67)	38.3	(1981)	+1.7
Female	42.1		43.7		+1.6
West Germany					
Male	36.48	(1965–67)	37.7	(1981)	+1.2
Female	41.27		43.7		+2.4
Norway					
Male	39.22	(1961–65)	39.6	(1981)	+0.4
Female	43.01		45.9		+2.9
Netherlands					
Male	38.9	(1967)	39.6	(1981)	+0.7
Female	43.4		45.9		+2.5
Greece					
Male	38.73	(1960–62)	41.2	(1981)	+2.5
Female	41.38		45.0		+3.6

Sources: United Nations, *Demographic Yearbook,* various issues, World Health
Organization, *World Health Statistics Annual 1983* (Geneva: WHO 1983).

TABLE 10.6

Mortality Change for Adults in Eastern and Western Europe Between the Mid–1960s and the Early 1980s
(percentage change)

Eastern Europe

Males

Age Group	30/34	35/39	40/44	45/49	50/54	55/59	60/64	65/69	70/74	75/79	80/84
Bulgaria (1966–1983)	13	27	56	41	35	37	15	17	27	21	14
Czechoslovakia (1965–1983)	−5	12	27	44	35	29	13	11	7	13	9
G.D.R. (1965–1981)	−11	5	16	27	10	−1	−7	−5	3	7	1
Hungary (1966–1982)	39	56	85	102	74	54	31	23	22	18	12
Poland (1965–1982)	5	10	28	33	33	23	6	2	0	2	−3
Romania (1966–1983)	16	24	49	55	37	27	10	7	—	14	—
Unweighted Average	10	22	44	50	37	28	11	9	(11)	(13)	(9)

TABLE 10.6 (cont.)

Eastern Europe

Females

Age Group	30/34	35/39	40/44	45/49	50/54	55/59	60/64	65/69	70/74	75/79	80/84
Bulgaria											
(1961–1983)	−11	−31	−19	0	2	−3	−5	−6	4	−4	4
(1972–1983)	−11	−25	−10	−7	4	−4	−11	−11	−2	−3	−6
Czechoslovakia											
(1965–1983)	−13	−15	−10	0	2	5	3	3	−3	−3	0
(1972–1983)	−13	−15	−5	−6	−6	2	0	7	0	1	1
G.D.R.											
(1965–1981)	−27	−31	−17	−9	−8	−6	−8	−5	−7	−7	−7
(1972–1981)	−11	−21	−5	−6	−4	−6	−9	−4	−6	−7	−8
Hungary											
(1966–1982)	22	20	17	27	17	21	10	7	−1	−3	−2
(1972–1982)	22	20	12	11	11	11	1	3	−7	−10	−7
Poland											
(1965–1982)	−28	−25	−14	−9	−2	−3	−8	−16	−18	−9	−10
(1972–1982)	−11	−8	−5	0	2	1	3	−3	−8	−9	−3
Romania											
(1966–1983)	−15	0	0	0	2	1	−4	6	−3	NA	NA
(1972–1983)	−11	−6	4	9	6	2	1	3	−5	−3	0
Unweighted Average Mid-1960s–early 1980s	−12	−14	−7	2	3	3	−1	−3	−4	(−6)	(−3)
Unweighted Average 1972–early 1980s	−5	−9	−2	0	2	1	−3	−1	−5	−2	−4

TABLE 10.6 (cont.)

Western Europe/Selected NATO Countries

Males

Age Group	30/34	35/39	40/44	45/49	50/54	55/59	60/64	65/69	70/74	75/79	80/84
U.K. and Wales (1966–1982)	−17	−28	−23	−21	−18	−16	−21	−18	−15	−12	−11
Greece (1966–1981)	−27	−13	−19	−22	−12	−8	−6	−7	−7	−5	5
Italy (1966–1979)	−31	−33	−23	−9	−3	−8	−13	−14	−12	−12	−7
Netherlands (1966–1981)	−18	−19	−23	−14	−13	−13	−10	2	3	2	−3
Norway (1965–1982)	−33	−21	−16	0	−5	−3	−6	−5	0	−1	−5
West Germany (1965–1982)	−22	−9	−6	−2	−7	−18	−22	−18	−12	−7	−8
Unweighted Average	−25	−21	−18	−11	−10	−11	−13	−10	−7	−8	−5

TABLE 10.6 (cont.)

Western Europe/Selected NATO Countries

Females

Age Group	30/34	35/39	40/44	45/49	50/54	55/59	60/64	65/69	70/74	75/79	80/84
U.K. and Wales (1966–1982)	−25	−31	−29	−29	−17	−6	−8	−14	−18	−20	−19
Greece (1966–1981)	−25	−30	−25	−28	−18	−22	−11	−23	−11	−16	6
Italy (1966–1979)	−33	−36	−33	−26	−19	−24	−28	−31	−28	−18	−14
Netherlands (1966–1981)	−20	−20	−22	−12	−12	−17	−20	−24	−29	−28	−27
Norway (1965–1982)	−64	−44	−45	−47	−41	−35	−34	−41	−42	−37	−33
West Germany (1965–1982)	−20	−27	−26	−24	−21	−22	−27	−27	−29	−24	−22
Unweighted Average	−31	−31	−30	−26	−21	−20	−21	−26	−27	−26	−19

Sources: United Nations, Demographic Yearbook (New York, United Nations), various issues; World Health Organization, World Health Statistics Annual 1983 (Geneva: WHO, 1983); Statisticka Godischnik no Narodna Republika Bulgariya 1984 (Sofia: Komitet po Edinna Systema za Sotsialna Informatsiya Pri Ministerksiya S'vet, 1984); Statisticka Rocenka Ceskoslovenskoe Socialisticke Republiky 1985 (Prague: Federalny Urad, 1985); Anarul Statistic al Republicii Socialiste Romania 1984 (Bucharest: Directia Centrala De Statistica, 1984); Rocznik Statystyczny 1985 (Warsaw: Glowny Urzad Statystyczny, 1985).

a third for men in their fifties. For Eastern European women, stagnation and reversal of health progress was evident in some age groups in some countries in the 1960s, and became more widespread in the 1970s. Health trends for adults in Eastern and Western Europe contrast starkly. Taken as a group, the decline in cohort death rates for these Western women range from 31 percent (early thirties) to 17 percent (over 85). Thus, the "worst" age–specific mortality improvement for this Western European group is greater than the "best" of Eastern Europe's. The same is true for men, where the Western group's "worst" performance (a decline in mortality of 5 percent for men over 80) is distinctly superior to the Eastern European group's "best" (a rise in mortality of 9 percent for men in their late sixties).

It is true that health improvements for adults were modest in certain Western nations between the mid 1960s and the early 1980s; Norway offers a case in point. For certain specific cohorts in the West, death rates may actually have risen slightly (for example, Dutch men between the ages of 65 and 79). Even so, the downward trend in mortality among Western European adults has been unmistakeable, as has been the upward trend among the Warsaw Pact states in the East. Indeed, performance has been so distinct that there are only a few age categories for either women or men in which the "best" health results of any of the Warsaw Pact states is better than the "worst" of the six NATO nations selected in Table 10.6.

Table 10.7 compares the Eastern European health decline with the Soviet Union's earlier decline, and with contemporary changes in some of the countries of NATO Europe. Though decline in adult health occurred earlier, and more rapidly, in the U.S.S.R., Eastern Europe's experience seems largely faithful to the pattern. The correspondence is closest for men. Eastern Europe's women have not, at least to date, suffered the same broadbased reversal in health that Soviet women experienced in the 1960s and early 1970s. Even so, the Eastern European pattern for women looks like a reflection of the Soviet experience, albeit a paler one: health progress in both cases is greatest for women in their thirties, and setbacks are most pronounced for women in their fifties. Against a Western European backdrop, the health problems of Eastern Europe's women and men looks like a less virulent, but distinctly nonetheless recognizeable, strain of the recent "Soviet malaise".

How is this pattern of broad health reversal to be explained? Some analysts have suggested that rising adult mortality may be a delayed aftereffect of war. Rainer Dinkel, for example, has argued that male cohorts which have passed through a major war may be expected to have unusually high mortality rates in their later years, since the healthiest portion of the cohort will have been initially selected for active combat,

TABLE 10.7
Mortality Change for Adults in the U.S.S.R., Eastern Europe, and Selected Western European NATO Countries (percent)

Age Group	Males											
	30/34	35/39	40/44	45/49	50/54	55/59	60/64	65/69	70/74	75/79	80/84
(1960s–1974)	19	20	37	29	26	22	20	25	—	27	—
Eastern Europe, (mid-1960s– early 1980s)	10	22	44	50	37	28	11	9	(11)	(13)	(9)
Western Europe, six countries (mid-1960s– early 1980s)	−25	−21	−18	−11	−10	−11	−13	−10	−7	−8	−5

Females

	30/34	35/39	40/44	45/49	50/54	55/59	60/64	65/69	70/74	75/79	80/84
U.S.S.R. (early 1960s–1974)	−6	−5	5	6	13	15	4	12	—	11	—
Eastern Europe, (mid-1960s–early 1980s)	−12	−14	−7	2	3	3	−1	−3	(−4)	(−6)	(−3)
Eastern Europe, (1972–early 1980s)	−5	−9	−2	0	2	1	−3	−1	−5	−2	−4
Western Europe, six countries (mid-1960s–early 1980s)	−31	−31	−30	−26	−21	−20	−21	−26	−27	−26	−19

Sources: For Eastern and Western Europe: see Table 6

For U.S.S.R.: Murray Feshbach, *A Compendium of Soviet Health Statistics* (Washington: U.S. Bureau of the Census. Center for International Research, 1985).

and since the group surviving the war will include the wounded, the disabled, and those whose health may have been permanently damaged.[9] Shiro Horiuchi, in an examination of mortality patterns for the generation which passed through World War I, noted that death rates in later life seemed to be increased for men, but not for women. Boys who were in their early teens during World War I, he wrote, seemed to have the greatest health troubles in later life; he suspected that they were particularly affected by the stress of wartime conditions, particularly by the nutritional shocks of reduced availability of foods.[10]

Are today's health problems in Eastern Europe and the U.S.S.R. a consequence of shocks sustained during the Second World War? It is certainly true that civilian and military casualties were both higher on Nazi Germany's Eastern Front than on its Western Front. Nutritional distress was also more pronounced in Eastern Europe, not only during the war but in the years following the National Socialist Army's surrender. Consequential though these differences may have been, they can provide only limited assistance in explaining the differences in health patterns in Eastern and Western Europe today. For one thing, Horiuchi's studies indicated that mortality in later life was largely unaffected by wartime stresses for the women who survived them, yet rising female mortality has been an integral part of the recent Soviet and Eastern European health pattern of health problems. For another, the timing of the rise in death rates in the Warsaw Pact is inconsistent with the European pattern after World War I, or the Western experience after World War II. Whereas increases in male mortality in Western Europe were specific to the cohorts which passed through a great war as teenagers, recent increases in Soviet and Eastern European mortality have beset those who would have been middle aged at the end of World War II, and those who were not yet born. Finally, a difference in adult health trends is apparent among the East and West Germans, even though they experienced World War II as a single nation. As can be seen in Table 10.8, adult male mortality has fallen in West Germany since the mid 1960s, even as it has risen for certain age groups in East Germany. The gap in mortality performance between East and West Germany, moreover, is roughly the same for both men and women over forty—the only adults in the early 1980s who would have been alive during the Second World War.

Eastern Europe's health problems are to be understood less in the stresses of the past than in the stresses of the present. Certain predictably injurious habits, for example, have been broadly embraced by adult populations of the Warsaw Pact. One of these is smoking. As Table 10.9 illustrates, cigarette smoking rose sharply in Eastern Europe between the mid 1960s and the early 1980s. Between 1965 and 1985, cigarette consump-

TABLE 10.8
Adult Mortality Change in East and West Germany, 1965–early 1980s (percentage change)

Age Group	30/34	35/39	40/44	45/49	50/54	55/59	60/64	65/69	70/74	75/79	80/84
Males											
East Germany (1965–1981)	−11	5	16	27	10	−1	−7	−5	3	7	1
West Germany (1965–1982)	−22	−9	−6	−2	−7	−18	−22	−18	−12	−7	−8
Females											
East Germany (1965–1981)	−27	−31	−17	−9	−8	−6	−8	−5	−7	−7	−7
West Germany (1965–1981)	−20	−27	−26	−24	−21	−22	−27	−27	−29	−24	−22
Differences. *East Germany minus West Germany*											
Males	11	14	22	27	17	17	15	13	15	14	9
Females	−7	−4	9	15	13	16	19	22	22	17	15

Source: Table 10.5

TABLE 10.9
Estimated Annual Cigarette Consumption Per Person Fifteen Years
of Age or Older

Selected Eastern and Western European Nations

Country	1960	1965	1970	1975	1980	1985 (or latest year)
Poland	2252	2458	2897	3245	3489	3157
Hungary	2117	2371	2745	3070	3389	3189
German Democratic Republic	1360	1473	1574	2039	2291	2390
Federal Republic of Germany	1637	2147	2531	2608	2588	2419
United Kingdom	2756	2767	3066	3124	2746	2141
Sweden	1186	1361	1724	1902	1956	1781

Source: U.S. Department of Agriculture databank; United Nations, Demographic Indicators of Countries: Estimates and Projections as Assessed in 1980, (New York: United Nations Department of International Economic and Social Affairs, 1982).

tion per adult rose by nearly a third in Poland, by over a third in Hungary, and by over 50 percent in East Germany; by contrast, it rose by about 20 percent in Sweden, by about 15 percent in West Germany, and actually fell by over 20 percent in the United Kingdom. In Western Europe, moreover, the nicotine content of cigarettes was falling over those two decades. By the mid 1980s over 150 packs of cigarettes a year were consumed per adult in both Poland and Hungary; this was nearly half again as many as in the United Kingdom, and well over half again as many as in Sweden. In most of Western Europe, cigarette consumption per adult began to fall in the 1960s or early 1970s. No such trend has been evident for Eastern Europe. Dips in consumption in Poland and Hungary in the early 1980s were synchronous with economic difficulties, and thus may represent changes in purchasing power or availability rather than changes in attitudes or preferences.

As Table 10.10 indicates, the use of hard liquor also rose sharply in Eastern Europe during the 1960s and 1970s. The increase in the drinking of hard liquor was particularly pronounced in the "Northern" Warsaw Pact countries: Czechoslovakia, Hungary, East Germany, and Poland. In those countries, per capita consumption of hard spirits was two and a half times the Western European level in 1980. There appears, moreover, to be

TABLE 10.10
Estimated Per Capita Consumption of Distilled Spirits, Eastern European Nations,
1960–1980 (in liters of pure alcohol)

	1960	1970	1980
Bulgaria	0.8	1.9	2.0
Czechoslovakia	1.1	2.5	3.5
G.D.R.	1.4	2.5	4.3
Hungary	1.4	2.8	4.3
Poland	2.4	3.1	5.9
Romania	1.1	2.4	2.2
Unweighted Average Eastern Europe	1.4	2.5	3.7
Index (1960 = 100)	100	183	271
U.S.S.R.	4.7	6.2	6.8*
Index	100	131	144*
Unweighted Average 8 NATO Europe Countries	1.2	1.8	2.2
Index	100	153	187

Note: * = 1979

Sources: M. Harvey Brenner, "International Trends in Alcohol Consumption and Related Pathologies," in National Institute on Alcohol Abuse and Alcoholism, *Alcohol and Health Monograph No. 1,* (Washington, D.C., Department of Health and Human Services, 1981).

Werner K. Lelbach, "Continental Europe," in Pauline Hall, ed., *Alcoholic Liver Disease: Pathology, Epidemiology and Clinical Aspects,* (New York: John Wiley and Sons, 1985).

Vladimir G. Treml, *Alcohol in the USSR: A Statistical Study* (Durham, N.C.: Duke Press Policy Studies, 1982).

some convergence between the "Northern" Warsaw Pact patterns and the U.S.S.R.'s. In 1960, these "Northern" countries consumed about a third more hard liquor per capita than Western Europe; intake levels were recognizeably European rather than Soviet. Today their intake level stands almost exactly halfway between Western Europe's and the U.S.S.R.'s. Moreover, hard liquor has emerged as the alcohol of choice throughout the "Northern" Warsaw Pact, as Table 10.11 demonstrates.

Just as in the Soviet Union, the heavy drinking of hard liquor has become an accepted and chosen feature of daily life for a substantial and

TABLE 10.11
European Countries Where Distilled Spirits Accounts for More Than One Third of Total Consumption of Alcohol

1980	
Country	**% of Totals**
Poland	69.0
Soviet Union*	59.7
Iceland	57.7
Sweden	48.2
East Germany	46.4
Finland	43.6
Hungary	39.1
Czechoslovakia	36.7

Note: * = 1979

Source: In Europe: Werner K. Lelbach, "Continental Europe," in Pauline Hall, ed., *Alcoholic Liver Disease: Pathology, Epidemiology and Clinical Aspects* (New York: John Wiley and Sons, 1985).

In U.S.S.R.: Vladimir G. Treml, *Alcohol in the USSR: A Statistical Study* (Durham, N.C.: Duke Press Policy Studies, 1982).

growing fraction of the national populations of Warsaw Pact Europe. In Hungary, recent studies have suggested that over 10 percent of the "typical" household's disposable income is spent on alcohol.[11] By contrast, alcoholic beverages in 1980 accounted for about 4 percent of private consumption in Sweden, something like 2.2 percent in France and the United Kingdom, and under 2 percent in the United States.[12] In Poland, it has been estimated that the 1979 expenditures on alcohol accounted for a third of all expenditures on "food," and equalled the sums spent on clothing;[13] around the same time, French and Portuguese households spent three times as much on clothing as on drink; American spent four times as much, and in Spain the ratio was nine to one.[14] (Such comparisons, of course, are limited by the problematic relationship between nominal incomes, prices, and household purchasing power in a system where markets are neither necessarily in equilibrium, or even heading toward equilibrium.) Poland's Ministry of Labor Wages and Social Affairs has estimated that, in the late 1970s, one employee out of 39 "is drunk while working"; even more interesting was the suggestion that "one professional driver out of every 26 in public transportation enterprises operates his vehicle while drunk."[15] Dangerous drinking may be considered a male predilection, but Eastern European data detail a progressive "feminization" of alcohol abuse since the mid-1960s. In Hungary, the Eastern European nation with the most comprehensive data on causes of death, the incidence of mortality from cirrhosis was higher for women in 1980 than it had been for men only fifteen years earlier. For the entire adult female population, the death rate from cirrhosis more than tripled between 1964–1966 and 1980; for women in their late thirties and their forties, the cirrhosis death rate jumped by a factor of five.[16]

Eastern Europe's adult population may well be more susceptible to serious health threats—many of these lifestyle related—today than they were two decades ago. Increased health risks, however, do not inevitably lead to a deterioration in national health conditions. Properly framed and implemented, state social policies and other government-led interventions can prevent health deterioration even during periods of seriously increased health risks. Indeed, the most basic objective for social policy, from the nineteenth century to the present day, has typically been to protect and maintain the physical well-being of the national population. Eastern Europe's secular increase in adult mortality over the past twenty years argues incontestably that the measures undertaken by Eastern European states have not been adequate to this task.

A government's first line of defense against illness and disease is its health policy. Eastern Europe's public health systems are, in varying degree, replicas and interpretations of the Soviet public health system. Health care systems in all Warsaw Pact nations are characterized by relatively high ratios of medical personnel and hospital beds to population, and provide extensive services that are nominally free of charge. As Table 10.12 illustrates, however, there is a striking dissonance between inputs in the public health system and the resulting health of the Warsaw Pact populations. The relationship between the availability of medical personnel and the health level of the national population, in fact, appears in Table 10.11 to be broadly *negative*: countries with greater numbers of medical personnel per 10,000 population generally seem to have lower levels of adult life expectancy. This seems to be true not only among Warsaw Pact countries at any given point in time, but also within any given Warsaw Pact state during the period in question. The anomalous correlation in Table 10.12 should not necessarily be taken to mean that Eastern Europe's medical personnel have contributed to health decline within the region; it does offer evidence, however, that the Warsaw Pact's labor-extensive health care strategy, in which priority accords to the quantity of doctors fielded rather than to the quality of training or equipment for those people

TABLE 10.12
Medical and Health Resources in Eastern Europe and U.S.S.R., 1980–1983

A. *Doctors, Including Stomatologists, per 10,000 Population*

	1960	1970	1980	1983
Bulgaria	17.0	22.2	30.0	32.9
Czechoslovakia	17.5	23.1	32.4	34.8
German Democratic Republic	12.1	20.3	26.1	28.2
Hungary	15.3	22.1	28.1	30.0
Poland	12.7	19.3	22.5	23.5
Romania	13.5	14.7	17.9	19.7
Unweighted Average Eastern Europe	14.7	20.3	26.2	28.2
U.S.S.R.	20.0	27.4	37.5	40.0
Industrialized Market Economies (IME)	12.3	—	18.1	—
Ratio, Eastern Europe to U.S.S.R. (U.S.S.R. = 100)	74	73	70	70
Ratio, IME: U.S.S.R. (U.S.S.R. = 100)	62	—	48	—
Ratio, IME: Eastern Europe (Eastern Europe = 100)	84	—	69	—
Index, Eastern Europe (1960 = 100)	100	138	178	192

Note: "Industrial Market Economies" in the World Bank Classification, includes 14 Western European Countries, Canada, the United States, Australia, New Zealand, and Japan.

B. *Percentage of Public Consumption Funds Allocated to Free Public Health and Physical Education*

	1960	1965	1970	1980	1983
Bulgaria	15.6	14.1	13.4	15.0	16.7
Czechoslovakia	15.3	14.7	15.0	15.2	15.8
G.D.R.	19.0	17.7	15.3	17.9	19.0
Hungary	22.9	22.9	16.7	14.7	14.8
Poland	NA	25.1	25.3	25.7	19.3
Romania	NA	NA	NA	NA	NA
Unweighted Average		(18.9)	(17.1)	(17.7)	(17.1)
U.S.S.R.	18.4	16.5	15.6	14.6	14.2

Sources: Council of Mutual Economic Assistance Secretariat, *Statistical Yearbook 1979* (Moscow: Statistika, 1979); Soviet Ekonomicheskoi Vzaimopomoshchi, *Statisticheski Ezhegodnik Stran—1984* (Moscow: Finansi i Statistika 1984); World Bank, *World Development Report 1984* (New York: Oxford University Press, 1984).

Note: NA = not available

designated to be medical professionals, is ineffective in meeting the current health needs of the local populations.

In the command economies of the Warsaw Pact states, where prices need not respond to scarcities and where income does not necessarily provide access to goods, patterns of state expenditures do not always give a reliable measure of the quality, or even the quantity, of resources allocated by government to its subsidiary services. To the extent that recorded state expenditures reflect the actual allocation of public resources, it appears that the share of resources devoted to health care in the Warsaw Pact countries fell between 1960 and 1980, even as the overall health level of various national populations was stagnating or declining. As Table 10.12 illustrates, percentage of public consumption funds allocated to free medical care and physical education dropped, in the four Eastern European nations for which continuous data are given, from 18.2 percent in 1960 to 15.7 percent in 1980. By 1983, that fraction had risen to 16.8 percent; even so, it was lower than the figure twenty-three years earlier. Among all nations for which such data can be found, the Warsaw Pact is the only large region in which a smaller share of national resources appears to be devoted to health care in the 1980s than in the early 1960s. It is noteworthy that the two nations in which the fractional share of public consumption funds earmarked for health care dropped most sharply (Hungary and the U.S.S.R.) also suffered the sharpest reversal in adult health conditions.[17] In Eastern Europe, as in the Soviet system, the labor-extensive health care strategy promoted over the past two decades was not a focus for increased health care allocations; rather, in some significant sense, it was an alternative to them. This strategic choice is all the more consequential in a system of socialized medicine. Soviet and Eastern European medical care is, in principle, financed directly and virtually entirely by the state; thus, the quantity, quality, and composition of national health care resources are determined, in principle, not by the consumers of these services, but by their rulers.

Since the mid-1960s, Eastern Europe's social policies have failed, in broad measure, to protect adults against lifestyle-related stresses. It also appears that they have failed to protect adult populations against health stresses attendant on fluctuations in, or shocks to, the local economy. Table 10.13 highlights the problem. The early 1980s (or in the case of Poland, the late 1970s and early 1980s) was a period of economic difficulty for all Warsaw Pact states. While the interpretation of statistics concerning the volume and quantity of goods and services in centrally planned, command-oriented, economies is necessarily a tricky and ambiguous business, there is little doubt that the pace of economic growth dropped significantly during those years.[18] In at least some of those states, the actual level of aggregate production may have dropped as well. Social policy, as it is understood in the West, is supposed to provide support and protection for those elements within a society who find themselves endangered by the consequences of economic slowdowns or contracts. With the exception of the German Democratic Republic (where adult mortality in the early 1980s fell for both men and women), Eastern Europe's Warsaw Pact states evidently failed to mitigate the vulnerability of their adult populations to life-imperiling risks during a period of economic trouble. In Western Europe, social policies are in large measure independent of economic trends, or consciously designed to operate countercyclically against these trends; thus health conditions in Western Europe have since the end of the Second World War tended to improve irrespective of the current state of the local economy. However social policies may be designed in Eastern Europe, mortality rates suggest that the vulnerable and the exposed have not acquired the additional protection that would be needed simply to keep death rates stable during a period of economic turbulence. The "business cycle" may no longer affect the health of the general populace in Western countries, but adult Eastern European populations, as a whole, do not appear to enjoy that same good fortune.

Mongolia

Outer Mongolia was the first country in which a Marxist–Leninist government was brought to power with Soviet assistance. Since the

TABLE 10.13

Mortality Change for Five Eastern European Nations' Adult Populations During the Economic Slowdown of the Early 1980s
(percentage change)

Males

	30/34	35/39	40/44	45/49	50/54	55/59	60/64	65/69	70/74	75/79	80/84
Bulgaria (1980–1983)	+6	+8	+14	+8	+2	+5	+3	+4	+7	+2	−7
Czechoslovakia (1981–1983)	−5	+3	+2	+7	+5	+2	+5	+8	+1	+1	+4
Hungary (1980–1982)	+14	0	+2	+5	+4	+6	+2	+2	+2	−1	−5
Poland (1978–1980)	−4	+5	+9	+5	+8	+8	+2	+4	0	+6	+8
Romania (1980–1983)	+5	−6	+2	+3	+6	+2	0	+5	−5	−4	−8
Unweighted Average	+3	+2	+6	+6	+5	+5	+2	+5	+1	+1	−1

Females

	30/34	35/39	40/44	45/49	50/54	55/59	60/64	65/69	70/74	75/79	80/84
Bulgaria (1980–1983)	0	0	0	−7	0	−1	−2	−4	0	0	−10
Czechoslovakia (1981–1983)	0	0	+12	0	−2	0	+4	+8	+2	+2	+2
Hungary (1980–1982)	+10	+6	−4	−5	−3	0	−4	+2	−3	+1	−4
Poland (1978–1980)	0	0	+5	+6	+2	+4	+2	+3	+1	+2	+4
Romania (1980–1983)	0	−6	0	−3	−2	−3	−1	+2	−6	−4	−13
Unweighted Average	+2	0	+3	−2	−1	0	0	+2	−1	0	−4

Sources: United Nations. *Demographic Yearbook,* various years;

Statisticka Godischnik na Narodna Republika Bulgariya 1984 (Sofia: Komitet po Edinna Systema za Sotsialna Informatsiya Pri Ministerksiya S'vet. 1984);

Statisticka Rocenka Ceskoslovenskoe Socialisticke Republiky 1985 (Prague: Federalny Statisiky Urad. 1985);

Anarul Statistic al Republicii Socialiste Romania 1984 (Bucharest: Directia Centrala De Statistica. 1984);

Rocznik Statystyczny 1985 (Warsaw: Glowny Úrzad Statystyczny. 1985).

establishment of the Mongolian People's Republic in 1924, the U.S.S.R. has remained intimately involved in Mongolian affairs. The U.S.S.R. currently provides Ulan Bator with credits and subsidies which may account for as much as half of all consumption in the socialized portion of the Mongolian economy.[19] Soviet advisers and technicians have played an important role in building the sinews of government in Mongolia, and in helping to set both the priorities of government and the procedures of local administration. It is, therefore, particularly interesting to note the difficulties in obtaining general information of health conditions in Mongolia today—more than sixty years after the victory of "Mongolian Socialism."

Mongolia does not lack information on its government's efforts to improve the health of the local population, as Table 10.14 details. Yet the CMEA's Statistical Yearbook has routinely omitted Mongolia from its tables on infant mortality in the member states. (Mongolia's own *Statistical Yearbook On The People's Economy* provides no information on infant mortality, even though it has chapters devoted to both population and public health.) Equally interesting, the 1984 edition of the CMEA Statistical Yearbook gives a figure for life expectancy in Mongolia—but for the mid 1960s! In the years since 1964–1965, the period of the estimate, Mongolia has conducted two full national censuses: one in 1969, the second in 1979. Under ordinary circumstances, one would expect such exercises to provide a basis for updating life expectancy estimates.

What accounts for the paucity of data on the health of the Mongolian people? Sins of statistical omission would be consistent with the Soviet approach to dealing with bad news, and the Mongolian People's Republic is perhaps more completely under Soviet tutelage than any other state in the contemporary world. But the most uncharitable interpretation is not always the most nearly correct. It is possible that an increasingly complete registration of vital events has resulted in computations which now appear embarrassing next to the seemingly salutary numbers from earlier decades, and that Mongolian authorities are waiting for reality to catch up with official depictions of the recent past.

Between 1960 and 1970 Mongolia's recorded death rate rose sharply: from 10.5 deaths per thousand to 12.4 deaths per thousand, or by more than a sixth. The change suggests improvements in statistical coverage, not a health crisis; such increases in measured death rates have been witnessed in the demographic accounts of many less developed countries as they improved their enumerative capacities. The United Nations has offered estimates for birth rates, death rates, and expectation of life at birth for Mongolia for the period since 1950.[20] For the years 1980–1985, it gives an estimate of life expectancy of 64.6 years—almost as high as the figure Mongolia offered for itself two decades before. But there is reason

238   The Poverty of Communism

TABLE 10.14
Statistics Pertaining to Health, Mongolian People's Republic

A. Medical Personnel (Including Stomatologists) per 10,000 population

1960	1970	1980	1983
9.7	17.9	21.9	23.3

B. Percent of Public Consumption Funds Allocated to Free Medical Care and Physical Education

1960	1970	1975	1980	1983
NA	NA	25.5	18.6	19.2

C. Most Recent Official Estimate of Life Expectancy at Birth

Year	Male E°	Female E°	Total E°
1964/65	64	66	65

D. United Nations Estimates of Mongolian People's Birth Rate, Death Rate, and Expectation of Life at Birth for Comparison with CMEA Data

	Birth Rate*	Death Rate*	Total E° (years)
United Nations, c. 1970	40.4	10.3	59.5
CMEA, 1970	40.2	12.3	NA
United Nations, 1980–85	34.4	7.2	64.6
CMEA	36.2	9.8	NA

Notes: *Per 1000 population
    NA = Not available

Sources: Council for Mutual Economic Assistance Secretariat, *Statistical Yearbook, 1979,* (Moscow: Statistika, 1979).

Soviet Ekonomicheskoi Vzaimopomoshchi, *Statisticheskii Ezhegodnik Stran—1984* (Moscow: Finansi i Statistika 1984);

United Nations, *Demographic Indicators of Countries: Estimates and Projections as Assessed in 1980,* (New York: United Nations Department of International Economic and Social Affairs, 1982).

to expect this UN estimate to overstate contemporary health levels in Mongolia. Mongolia's own estimate of its current crude death rate is about a third higher than the projection the UN offers (see Table 10.13, panel D). The UN's estimate of Mongolia's crude death rate for about 1970 is much closer to Mongolia's own figure for 1983; they would be consistent with a life expectancy at birth for Mongolia in the early 1980s of about sixty, or perhaps slightly less.

In comparison with some nearby states, a life expectancy in the high fifties or low sixties would seem like a considerable achievement. The UN, for example, has placed Afghanistan's life expectancy just before the Soviet invasion at about 40 years (although those projections were based on extremely scant information). Even so, a life expectancy in the high fifties or low sixties (and the living standard which would presumably accompany such conditions of health) would hardly rank as a triumph. The UN's *Demographic Yearbook 1983* puts the 1981 life expectancy at birth in Bangladesh at 53 years. The World Bank's *World Development Report 1985* gives an estimate (however it may be derived) for India's 1983 life expectancy of 55 years; some of India's states, such as Kerala and the Punjab, may now have life expectancies in the mid- or high sixties.[11] And in China, life expectancy at birth in the early 1980s was, as best as can be told, in the mid-sixties for the nation as a whole.[22] Perhaps the most interesting comparison, however, would be with Iran. The UN *Demographic Yearbook's* life tables indicate that expectation of life at birth in Iran in the period 1973–1976 was about 57 years. Fifty years and more of socialist development in Mongolia may have done slightly more for the health of the Mongolian people than seems to have done by two decades of rule by the Shah in Iran.

Vietnam

While there is little doubt that the Socialist Republic of Vietnam is today impoverished, the limited capabilities of the Vietnamese statistical system present difficulties to any analyst who wishes to carry the discussion of poverty in contemporary Vietnam far beyond generality. Despite the ostensible importance to the process of scientific socialist planning of a statistical apparatus producing timely and reliable data, Vietnam's statistical organs are still underdeveloped. Ten years after victory in the South and thirty years after the establishment of socialist power in the North, Vietnam has yet to achieve near-complete registration of births and deaths. A recent analysis by the U.S. Bureau of the Census suggested that a tenth of all births, a third of all deaths, and over half of all infant deaths may have gone unregistered in the years immediately following Vietnam's 1979 census.[23] Under those circumstances, it should not be surprising that Vietnam, though a member of the World Health Organization, provides no information to that institution on either the incidence of infectious and communicable disease or the causes of death for the general population: there is in all likelihood no way that such things can presently be known. These limitations, of course, speak to conditions of poverty in the nation as a whole. They should also chasten us against an exacting use of other Vietnamese statistics presuming to measure social or economic results.

Hanoi's own assessment is that the national life expectancy was nearly 66 years in 1979: about 64 years for men and 68 for women. These numbers, which are reprinted without qualification in the CMEA *Statistical Yearbook*, significantly overstate Vietnam's average length of life, since they have been calculated on the assumption that the registration of deaths is essentially complete. A U.S. Bureau of the Census investigation of recent demographic trends in Vietnam uses a model which implies that life expectancy in Vietnam would have been about 58 in 1979.[24] Other organizations have made lower guesses. The World Health Organization, for example, gives a figure (derivation unexplained) of 55 years for Vietnam's overall life expectancy for the years 1980–1984;[25] the United Nations' Department of International Economic and Social Affairs gives the number 53.5 to represent life expectancy in Vietnam for 1980 to 1985.[26]

If Vietnam's life expectancy in the early 1980s were similar to the WHO and UN figures, contemporary Vietnam's overall health levels would be roughly comparable to those of Bangladesh or India. On the other hand, if the Bureau of the Census' assumptions were closer to the truth, Vietnam's life expectancy might not be far different from Mongolia's, though it would be somewhat lower than those of the Philippines or Thailand. Current figures, in short, do not afford much precision in assessing material well-being in Vietnam, for there is today a world of difference between the contemporary Bengali and Filipino standard of living. It is worth noting, however, that even on their face, Vietnam's own official life expectancy estimates would fall short of Sri Lanka's, a poor country which has been able to achieve good health for its populace largely through its social welfare policies—and at a comparatively low financial cost. Moreover, it would bring Vietnam's putative life expectancy only slightly above the level independent analysts have ascribed to contemporary China.

Cuba

When the Castro forces came to power in 1959, Cuba was perhaps the healthiest Latin nation in tropical America;[27] its statistical system was one of the Caribbean's best. In the years since the consolidation of Communist power, Cuba has gained the reputation of an exemplar of health progress. The notion that Cuba's performance has been exceptional is by no means limited to sympathizers with or publicists for Havana. Under these circumstances, it might be assumed that a solid body of statistical evidence can be found by which to document a broadbased and unambiguous improvement in health conditions in Cuba since the Castro revolution. Surprisingly, this does not seem to be the case. While Cuba does appear to have experienced advances in health since the late 1950s, its pace of progress does not seem extraordinary in comparison with those nations and areas against which it might most fairly be judged. Moreover, since the early 1970s Cuba's health statistics have been beset by peculiar and puzzling inconsistencies. While no foreign observer can pronounce on these inconsistencies with absolute confidence, the simplest explanation for these paradoxes would be that certain key health figures had been deliberately falsified.

Between 1960 and 1974, according to official Cuban life tables, life expectation at birth rose by about six years, from about 64 to 70. This was a rapid rate of improvement; on the other hand, it was not unprecedented in Latin America or the Caribbean. Life expectancy in Honduras, for example, rose by over a decade between 1961 and 1974, although from a much lower base. Among countries and territories with life expectancies closer to Cuba's own, Guyana's lifespan increased by nearly seven years in a nine year period (1950/52–1959/61); Barbados' rose by over seven years in a nine year period (1950/52–1959/61); Costa Rica's rose by over seven years in the course of a decade (1962/64–1972/74); and Puerto Rico's jumped by nearly seven years in a five year period following Operation Bootstrap (1949/51–1954/56).

The rapid increases in life expectancy in Cuba in the early 1960s do not seem to have carried over into the early 1970s. According to the official life tables, expectation of life at birth for Cuban women rose by 0.3 years between 1970 and 1974; for Cuban men it rose by only 0.1 years. By the early 1970s the pace of overall life expectancy improvement, by these official estimates, appeared to be less than a tenth of what it had been in the 1960s.

One of the principal reasons for the slow pace of overall health progress in the early 1970s, as reflected in these life expectancy estimates, was the trend in infant mortality. According to Cuba's own life tables, infant mortality did not decline in the early 1970s. To the contrary: according to these official life tables, infant mortality rose by over 11 percent between 1970 and 1974. A rise in death rates in properly constructed life tables would not be a statistical artifact, insofar as reliable life tables are expected to represent the actual level of mortality for each age group for the period in question.

In point of fact, there is reason to expect Cuba's 1970 life tables to have been fairly reliable. Registration of births and deaths seems to have been nearly universal by 1970. The indirect estimate of infant mortality in Cuba's 1970 life tables, for example, and the official infant mortality tally from the vital registration system were within 2 percent of each other. By 1974, however, the life table estimate for infant mortality was 55 percent higher than the figure from the vital registration system. Over just four years, it appeared as if the Cuban vital registration system had gone from missing less than 2 percent of the nations infant deaths, to missing over 35 percent. One percent might think that an apparent breakdown in the vital registration system would augur poorly for the government's capacity to cope with problems of infant health. During these years, however, Cuba's statistical yearbooks have steadily claimed that infant mortality fell by more than a fourth; they use the official figure from the vital registration system.

The opening of a gap between the indirect (life table) and direct (vital registration) estimates of Cuban infant mortality coincided with other changes in the processing of infant mortality statistics in the early 1970s. Responsibility for verification of the infant mortality rate from vital registration statistics had previously resided with JUCEPLAN, the economic planning organ; during 1972—the year of a big drop in registered infant mortality—responsibility was transferred to the Ministry of Health. From then on, the Ministry of Health was in the position, in effect, of producing and checking those numbers which would be used to evaluate its own effectiveness. At the same time, infant mortality data were designated as henceforth "provisional"; they could thereafter be changed long after the infancy of the cohort in question, and frequently were. Cuba's 1977 and 1982 statistical yearbooks, for example, both give figures for infant mortality in the region of Isla de Juventud for 1974, but the 1977 estimate is over half again as high as the estimate which appears in the 1982 edition.

A recent National Academy of Sciences study examined Cuba's demographic data for reliability. On the whole, the study concluded, the data were internally consistent, and probably reliable. The sole exception, the author noted, was the infant mortality rate after 1970:

> From the early 1970s on, the consistency between the indirect and the official rates disappears; indirect estimates indicate constant or even rising child mortality, while the official figures show a continued rapid decline . . . The sharp drop (in infant mortality) from the mid 1970s to 1980 is not supported by the available child survivorship data . . . in the absence of evidence that registration has deteriorated, the official sequence is accepted, with the qualification that is not independently supported and requires final confirmation from surveys in the early 1980s.[28]

Unfortunately, few of the data which might verify or correct the official infant mortality series since the early 1970s have as yet been released in the 1980s. The returns from the 1981 census, for example, have yet (1986) to be publicly disseminated. Interestingly, preliminary reports on the census did not provide standard information on the distribution of population by age and sex, but instead lumped men and women together in a new and unusual set of age categories (including a single category for all boys and girls under 16 years of age). While one may speculate on the reasons for this novel mode of demographic classification, it is worth remembering that these adjustments have had the effect of frustrating efforts of outside observers to ascertain independently the level of child mortality in Cuba between the 1970 and 1981 censuses.

Other puzzles and paradoxes have appeared in Cuba's health statistics for the period since 1970. High levels of infant mortality are typically associated with a high prevalence of infectious and parasitic disease. Cuba's infant mortality rate is said to have fallen from 38.7 per thousand in 1970 to 19.6 per thousand in 1980, or by almost half in a decade. It is said to have fallen still further since then. Yet there has been no corresponding drop in the reported incidence of infectious and parasitic disease. This may be seen in Table 10.15. Between 1970 and 1980, the reported incidence of certain diseases did decline: typhoid, tuberculosis, and tetanus fell significantly; no new cases of diphtheria were reported; and the cases of measles fell dramatically (only to rise very sharply the next year).

TABLE 10.15
Reported Incidence of Selected Infectious and Parasitic Diseases in Cuba, 1959–1983
(per 100,000)

Year	Acute Diarrhea	Acute Respiratory Infections	Chicken Pox	Diphtheria	Hepatitis	Malaria
1959	NA	NA	NA	4.7	NA	2.1
1960	NA	NA	NA	8.1	NA	19.0
1965	5,707	NA	118.6	8.2	115.8	1.7
1970	7,694	10,162	150.1	0.1	102.6	—
1975	6,874	15,520	161.7	—	217.0	0.9
1980	6,839	21,980	200.7	—	208.3	3.1
1981	7,836	27,596	425.1	—	147.2	5.9
1982	8,732	27,441	191.5	—	208.4	3.4
1983	8,527	33,001	291.1	—	101.2	3.0

Year	Measles	Polio	Syphilis	Tetanus	Tuberculosis	Typhoid
1959	2.9	1.6	0.7	NA	18.0	5.1
1960	10.3	4.3	0.7	4.1	27.6	13.0
1965	121.6	—	30.4	6.7	65.0	3.1
1970	105.2	—	7.8	2.6	30.8	5.0
1975	113.4	—	47.6	0.7	14.2	4.0
1980	39.1	—	44.7	0.3	11.6	1.0
1981	190.1	—	36.9	0.2	8.6	1.8
1982	238.8	—	38.5	0.2	8.3	1.3
1983	33.2	—	44.3	0.2	7.7	0.6

TABLE 10.15 (cont)
Index (1970 = 100)

Year	Acute Diarrhea	Acute Respiratory Infections	Chicken Pox	Diphtheria	Hepatitis	Malaria
1959	NA	NA	NA	4,700	—	124
1960	NA	NA	NA	8,100	—	1,118
1965	74	NA	79	8,200	113	100
1970	100	100	100	100	100	—
1975	89	153	108	—	212	52
1980	89	216	134	—	203	182
1981	102	272	283	—	143	347
1982	113	270	128	—	203	200
1983	111	325	194	—	99	176

Year	Measles	Polio	Syphilis	Tetanus	Tuberculosis	Typhoid
1959	3	NA	9	NA	58	102
1960	10	NA	9	158	90	260
1965	116	—	390	258	211	62
1970	100	—	100	100	100	100
1975	108	—	610	27	46	80
1980	37	—	573	12	38	20
1981	180	—	473	8	28	38
1982	227	—	494	8	27	26
1983	32	—	568	8	25	12

Notes: NA = not available
— = less than .1/per 100,000

Sources: Republic of Cuba, *Anuario Estadistico de Cuba* (Havana: Comite Estatal de Estadisticas), various issues.

On the other hand, the reported incidence of syphilis, malaria, hepatitis, chicken pox, and acute respiratory infection were substantially higher in 1980 than they had been in 1970. The reported incidence of acute diarrhea was slightly lower in 1980 than it had been in 1970, but it then rose in the early 1980s, to the highest levels yet registered. It is possible that increases in the reported incidence of certain diseases reflect improvements in diagnostics and greater outreach of medical personnel, rather than an actual increase in illness for the general population. Even accepting this as a possibility, it would be surprising to witness such a high level of poverty-related diseases in tandem with such a low level of infant mortality.

Table 10.16 sharpens the paradox. It compares the reported incidence of certain infectious and parasitic diseases in the U.S.S.R. in 1974 (the last year for which infant mortality figures have been released) and Cuba in 1982. Cuba's reported infant mortality rate in 1982 was 17.4, just over half

TABLE 10.16
Reported Incidence of Selected Communicable or Infectious Diseases: Cuba 1982 and
U.S.S.R. 1974 (or most recent previous year)

	(incidence per 100,000 population)		
Disease	Cuba, 1982	U.S.S.R., 1974	Ratio, U.S.S.R. = 100
Acute Diarrhea	8,732	(409) (1966)	NA
Acute Respiratory Infection	27,441	18,623	147
Brucellosis	0.6	5.6 (1966)	11
Chicken Pox	191.5	419.4	46
Diphtheria	—	—	NA
Hepatitis	208.4	223.6	93
Malaria	3.4	.1 (1969)	2,830
Measles	239	149	160
Meningococcol Infections	8.2	6.7	122
Mumps	261	247 (1966)	106
Polio	—	—	NA
Scarlet Fever	2.3	146.2	2
Tetanus	0.2	0.2	100
Typhoid	1.3	6.6	20

Notes: — = less than .1 per 100,000; NA = not applicable; parenthetical figures
for U.S.S.R. for acute diarrhea refers incidence of bacterial dysentery.

Sources: Republic of Cuba, *Anuario Estadistico de Cuba 1983* (Havana: Comite
Estatal de Estadisticas, 1984).

Murray Feshbach, *A Compendium of Soviet Health Statistics* (Washington: U.S. Bureau of the Census, Center for International Research, January 1985).

of the U.S.S.R.'s adjusted rate of 32.2 for 1974.[29] Yet the reported incidence of poverty-related diseases is not correspondingly lower in Cuba. To the contrary: while Cuba's reported incidence of certain diseases is lower than the U.S.S.R.'s, it is in Cuba that the prevalence of a number of major diseases appears higher, including acute respiratory infection, malaria, measles, meningococcal infections, mumps, and possibly acute diarrhea. Completeness of morbidity reporting may differ in Cuba and the U.S.S.R., even though the two countries engage in numerous exchange programs, assistance schemes, and coordination projects in the area of health, both within the confines of the CMEA and bilaterally. It would seem counterintuitive to find the greater prevalence of infection and parasitic disease in the nation with the dramatically lower infant mortality rate.

With the important, and perennial, exception of defense-related numbers, the Soviet statistical system, and the statistical systems of the Warsaw Pact states, seldom resort to the falsification of inconvenient data. While such data may be suppressed, or released in misleading comparisons, comparatively few instances of seemingly deliberate alterations have been uncovered by Western observers in the period since World War II.[30] The attitude toward numbers accorded political import may be different in Havana.

According to Cuba's own life tables, infant mortality fell about 32 percent between 1960 and 1974. Over roughly the same period, according to their life tables, infant mortality fell 40 percent in Panama, 46 percent in Puerto Rico, 47 percent in Chile, 47 percent in Barbados, and 55 percent in Costa Rica.[31] If the National Academy of Sciences' reconstructions are correct, infant mortality in Cuba fell by only 25 percent in the nearly two decades between 1960 and 1978. If those estimates are reliable, the revolutionary Cuban experience would represent not the most rapid, but instead one of the slowest measured rates of progress against infant mortality in all of Latin America and the Caribbean for that period.

Concluding Remarks

A few cautionary comments are in order after this brief review of social and economic conditions with the CMEA bloc.

First, although it is today commonplace to talk of an economic slowdown in the Soviet Union and Eastern Europe between the mid-1960s and the mid-1980s, the dimensions of this slowdown can only be tentatively assessed in the West. The slowdown itself, for reasons already discussed, is not accurately represented in the data the CMEA countries publish. All independent attempts to interpret the slowdown are based upon, and therefore limited by, these data. Adjustment factors may be applied to these data in an attempt to bring them into line with Western conceptions of national income or economic output, and such efforts will reflect the care and competence of the assessor. But it is unrealistic, and indeed unreasonable, to expect a single and reliable derivation of trends to be adduced from the CMEA data. Assessment of economic trends in the CMEA bloc is further complicated by the obvious but often neglected fact that command economies and market-oriented economies are geared to perform very different sorts of tasks. Changes in aggregate output, for example, may have very different consequences with respect to the capacity to mobilize for and prosecute a war in a market-oriented economy, on the one hand, and in a centrally planned economy on the other. Economic data from centrally planned societies, as it happens, provide comparatively little assistance to the independent observers who wish to assess the material condition of the local population. Ironically, the economic data from these Socialist countries may intrinsically be of less use in assessing the material well-being of their populations than are comparable economic data from more market-oriented societies not guided by Leninist political parties.

Second, for the period since 1960, there is little convincing evidence of exceptional improvements in health conditions in any of the CMEA countries under consideration. In both the Soviet Union and much of Eastern Europe, health progress (as measured by mortality decline) has apparently ceased for broad portions of the local population, and serious reversals in health conditions, affecting major population groups, have been recorded over the past twenty-five years. Mongolia's health situation, as best as can be determined, is not distinctly superior to that of the nearby countries with which she might most easily be compared, sixty years and more of "Mongolian Socialism" notwithstanding. The dimensions of health progress in Vietnam are uncertain, for the statistical authorities in that nation are as yet apparently unable to compile, process, and analyze timely and reliable data on basic social and demographic trends. In Cuba, measured health progress was rapid, though not unparalleled, in the 1960s, but inconsistencies and discrepancies in subsequent data have raised as yet unanswered questions about statistical claims for the 1970s and the early 1980s.

Third, data on health condition in the CMEA bloc provide an insight into the interpretation of social and economic data from Soviet ally states that is not widely appreciated by students of Communist systems. It is significant that health trends in the U.S.S.R. and Eastern Europe are today broadly inconsistent with measured trends in net material product, educational advance, housing conditions, and other indicators typically taken to signify social progress. The dissonance should encourage reflection on the reliability of these basic social and economic data, and on their meaning. Moreover, it may raise questions about the very nature of material poverty itself, as experienced by individuals in centrally planned command economies. The questions surrounding the infant mortality rate in Cuba emphasize the possibilities of "important" numbers, unrelated in the Western way of thinking to defense or security considerations, under Marxist–Leninist rule. It should be remembered that the data pertaining to poverty are unavoidably fraught with political significance under Marxist–Leninist rule.

Finally, it should be remembered that poor performance against domestic poverty may only marginally constrain a mobilized country in its attempts to project power abroad. Strategy and will, often the decisive factors in contests between nations, need not be affected by performance in meeting the physical needs of a general population, or by local and international sentiments concerning such performance. Failure to alleviate material poverty more expeditiously can to some extent constrain a command society in its efforts to mobilize economic and military might. But it will have little impact on the ability or inclination of command states or Marxist–Leninist leaders to take advantage of the mistakes, the weaknesses, the incohesion, or the irresoluteness of their chosen opponents.

Originally published in Henry S. Rowen and Charles Wolf, eds., *The Future of the Soviet Empire* (New York: St. Martin's Press, 1987). Reprinted with permission; all rights reserved.

Notes

1. Morris Bornstein, "Overview: Assessing Economic Performance," in U.S. Congress Joint Economic Committee, *East European Economies: Slow Growth in the 1980s,* (Washington: Government Printing Office, 1985).
2. Charles Wolf, Jr., personal communication, April 30, 1986.

     One should not forget that the central authorities in communist countries are themselves recipients of data that has been adjusted according to more local considerations. Jan Winiecki has commented on the rules governing what he calls "cheating" in the collection and dissemination of certain types of statistics in "Soviet–type economies":

     ". . . central planners know less about real quantities in the producer goods market, which to them is more important, because they themselves do not cheat but are exclusively cheated against. By contrast, in the consumer goods market they are nearer to time figures because they know how much they have themselves cheated and they know when they have nudged enterprises to cheat and may at least try to approximate the effects."

     (Jan Winiecki, "Are Soviet-type Economies Entering an Era of Long-Term Decline?" *Soviet Studies,* July 1986.) Winiecki warns that "the law of equal cheating" may be valid "to a very limited extent (if at all)." His observations should serve as a cautionary note against those who are inclined to make use of communist statistics without first considering the specific political conditions under which these were generated. His remarks also seem to beg the question, all to seldom considered in the West, of what the consequences of "unequal cheating" may be on the formulation and adjustment of policies in the "Soviet-type economy," and thus on the welfare of the populations in question.
3. International Monetary Fund, *International Financial Statistics,* various issues; Vienna Institute for Comparative Economic Studies, *Comecon Data 1983*

(Westport, Ct: Greenwood Press, 1984); Soviet Ekonomocheskoi Vzaimopo-moshchi, *Statisticheskii Ezhegodnik Stran-1985* (Moscow: Finansy i Statistika, 1985). Computations from IMF data deflate gross fixed capital formation by producer price index for industrial goods, and deflate net material consumption by consumer price index.

4. Oskar Morgenstern, *On the Accuracy of Economic Observations* (Princeton, NJ: Princeton University Press, 1963).
5. Dan Usher, "An Imputation to the Measure of Economic Growth for Changes in Life Expectancy," in Milton Moss, ed., *The Measurement of Economic and Social Performance* (New York: Columbia University Press, 1973).
6. See especially chapters 1 and 2.
7. Computed from United Nations, *Demographic Indicators of Countries: Estimates and Projections as Assessed in 1980* (New York: United Nations, 1982).
8. Staatlichen Zentralverwaltung fuer Statistik, *Statistiches Jahrbuch 1985* (Berlin: Staatsverlag der DDR, 1985).
9. Ranier Dinkel, "The Seeming Paradox of Increasing Mortality in a Highly Industrialized Nation: the Example of the Soviet Union," *Population Studies*, Vol. 39, 1985.
10. Shiro Horiuchi, "The Long Term Impact of War on Mortality: Old-age Mortality of the First World War Survivors in the Federal Republic of Germany," *Population Bulletin of the United Nations*, No. 15, 1983. Horiuchi's study touches upon the mortality patterns of Japanese men since World War II; though the postwar era has been a time of rapid health progress in Japan, and though the Japanese teenage boys from World War II are only now entering later middle age, Horiuchi has discerned some of the same health stress patterns for them that he detailed for an earlier generation of European men.
11. P. A. Compton, "Rising Mortality in Hungary," *Population Studies*, vol. 39, 1985.
12. United Nations, *National Accounts Statistics: Main Aggregates and Detailed Tables, 1982* (New York: United Nations, 1985).
13. Charlotte Chase, "Alcohol Consumption—An Indicator of System Malfunction in Contemporary Poland," *East European Quarterly*, volume 18, no. 4, 1985.
14. *National Accounts Statistics,* loc. cit.
15. Chase, loc. cit.
16. Compton, loc. cit.
17. The similarity of deterioration in the health of the Soviet and the Hungarian adult populations is all the more interesting in view of the other differences in their health strategies. Within the limited confines of the data set of Warsaw Pact countries, Hungary and the U.S.S.R. represent differing approaches to "health management": Hungary has the Pact's most developed pharmaceutical industry, and is a leading East bloc producer of medical equipment and instrumentation, while the Soviet Union makes comparatively little use of either of these "inputs" in its national "health production function." If such differences in strategy have an impact on health progress, they are evidently overwhelmed by the factors which have made overall health "progress" in the two countries similar.
18. See, for example, International Monetary Fund, *World Economic Outlook 1985* (Washington: International Monetary Fund, 1985), and *East European Economies: Slow Growth in the 1980s,* loc. cit. Table 10.1 gives some official data pertaining to this slowdown.

19. See, for example, Lawrence W. Theriot and JeNelle Matheson, "Soviet Economic Relations with Non-European CMEA: Cuba, Mongolia, and Vietnam," in U.S. Congress Joint Economic Committee, *Soviet Economy in a Time of Change*, (Washington: Government Printing Office, 1979).

20. For example, *Demographic Indicators of Countries*, loc. cit.

21. P. N. Mari Bhat, Samuel Preston, and Tim Dyson, *Vital Rates in India, 1961–1981* (Washington: National Academy Press, 1984).

22. Judith Banister, "An Analysis of Recent Data on the Population of China," *Population and Development Review*, volume 10, no. 2, (June 1984).

23. Judith Banister, *The Population of Vietnam* (Washington: U.S. Bureau of the Census, Series P-95, no. 77, 1985).

24. Ibid.

25. World Health Organization, *World Health Statistics Annual 1983* (Geneva: World Health Organization, 1983).

26. *Demographic Indicators of Countries*, loc. cit.

27. United Nations, *Demographic Yearbook 1967* (New York: United Nations, 1967).

28. Kenneth Hill, "An Evaluation of Cuba's Demographic Statistics, 1930–1980," in Paula E. Hollerbach and Sergio Diaz-Briquets, *Fertility Determinants in Cuba* (Washington: National Academy Press, 1983).

29. Christopher Davis and Murray Feshbach, *Rising Infant Mortality in the U.S.S.R. in the 1970s* (Washington: Department of Commerce, U.S. Bureau of the Census, September 1980). Davis and Feshbach's adjustments attempt to bring Soviet infant mortality data into line with international infant mortality data; the Soviet criteria for defining "infant mortality" differ from those accepted by the United Nations agencies and most national statistical authorities.

30. See the discussions in Vladimir G. Treml and John P. Hardt, eds., *Soviet Economic Statistics*, (Durham, N.C.: Duke University Press, 1972).

31. United Nations, *Levels and Trends of Mortality Since 1950*, (New York: United Nations, 1982).

11

Progress Against Material Poverty in Communist and Non-Communist Countries in the Postwar Era

A recent corpus of scholarly literature suggests that the process of modern economic growth in the less developed countries has brought little material gain to the disadvantaged strata of poor societies, and may actually have contributed to a decline in living standards for significant fractions of many national populations. This contention, of course, is not new, but power and urgency are lent to these studies because they harness detailed arrays of economic statistics to make their point.

The conclusions of a few of these studies may be used to represent the findings of the many. A volume prepared by the World Bank and the Institute for Development Studies comes to the estimate that over 700 million people in the non-communist world subsisted on incomes of under $25 per person per year in the mid-1970s; it also divined a tendency in non-communist countries for the income share of the poorest 40 percent of the population to shrink during the "early" stages of economic development—perhaps rapidly enough for the incomes of the poor to fall even as a nation's per capita income rose.[1] The International Labor Office, in a sweeping report on rural conditions in Asia, concludes that the incidence of poverty and landlessness has been increasing in Bangladesh, Java, the Philippines, India, Pakistan and elsewhere; the only country surveyed in which rural poverty was said to be unambiguously abating was the People's Republic of China.[2] Sylvia Ann Hewlett's investigation of Brazil's postwar "economic miracle" leads her to talk of "growing poverty" and widespread declines in living standards in coexistence with a dazzling record of aggregate economic performance.[3] And Paul Bairoch, in an attempt to recreate a comprehensive picture of economic change for the less developed countries since the turn of the century, produces numbers that indicate a negligible increase in per capita income for most of the "Third World" between 1900 and 1960; according to his charts, per capita food production may have fallen in many regions of the world over much of this period.[4]

The implications of these studies are disturbing. From the immediate humanitarian standpoint, they suggest that the current material needs of the world's politically inarticulate masses are being grossly underestimated by institutions and governments which are supposed to help them. But these studies also necessarily raise questions about the political and economic arrangements under which most of humanity is living. If the non-communist countries of the poor regions may be referred to as "capitalist," then "capitalism" would seem at best an unreliable accomplice for any poor nation attempting to make its escape from mass poverty.

As we shall see, the conceptual and statistical foundations for this growing body of documents are rather flimsy. Despite more than three decades of concerted international efforts to accelerate the pace of material progress in the less developed nations, relatively little reliable and even less comprehensive data on the social and economic conditions of the poor can be found for Africa, most of Asia, and much of Latin America. By itself, this fact speaks volumes. Such data as are available, however, paint a more interesting and less hopeless picture than the monochrome brought to mind by the notion of "immiserating" growth.

This chapter will explore the differences in patterns of poverty, not between "capitalist" and "non-capitalist" countries, but rather between communist and non-communist countries. However badly abused measures of poverty may sometimes be, they afford in principle the possibility of meaningful standardization. Comparable precision is impossible in the use of the term "capitalism."

"Capitalism" is, first and foremost, a political word, and political language depends in part on ambiguity for its impact. Marxist–Leninist parties around the world claim proprietary rights in deciding what is "capitalist," and they use it to describe their adversaries of the moment. Given the premium that Leninist doctrine places on tactical maneuver and the number of years the world's many Marxist–Leninist parties have had to select enemies, it should not be surprising that a great many things have been labelled as "capitalist" by communist spokesmen—including even the planning apparatus of the Soviet State. But it is not just Marxist–Leninists who have opted for a loose interpretation of "capitalism." Many of the nationalist (and unmistakeably anti-communist) leaders who have come to power in Asia and Africa since World War II have found it convenient to label their domestic enemies and international opponents as "capitalist," entirely irrespective of what their attitudes towards public finance or private entrepreneurship might actually be. In the nationalist lexicon, "capitalism" is a cognate of "colonialism"; it is a pejorative, and few political leaders in the new nations will allow it to be applied to themselves. Singapore may seem an exemplar of "capitalism" to its overseas admirers, but Lee Kuan Yew and his ruling People's Action Party have never accepted the intended compliment. From independence until 1976, the People's Action Party was a member of the Socialist International; though PAP has broken with the Socialist International, it still officially describes the Singapore system as "socialism that works."[5]

If "capitalism" has become a less precise term in recent decades, this is not solely the fault of politicians. With the rise of the modern state apparatus, the notion of "capitalism" has been made considerably more complex. Ever since Imperial Germany's successful experiments with protected and subsidized state-sponsored investments in the nineteenth century, modern governments have been gaining confidence in the idea that they themselves can improve upon, or even replace, the workings of markets and businessmen. In time, it has become not just accepted, but expected, that governments will protect their citizens against untoward results of "normal" market behavior and preempt market decisions in the name of the greater national good.

World War II seems to have changed irrevocably the nature of the modern state (thus "capitalism") in both rich and poor regions. In the colonies, the shift from commercial to war-winning policies brought a sudden and new importance to government efforts to mobilize and augment national resources: significant fractions of some labor force were redeployed by decree; import-replacing industries were constructed at a forced pace; market-determined prices were suspended in many areas of the economy; and, for the first time, the state targeted the accumulation of capital (principally for loan to the colonizing powers).[6] A new view of the state quickly took hold in the colonies: by 1944, the British Government paper *Planning of Social and Economic Development in the Colonial Empire* was asserting that poor regions could not make full and effective use of their national resources *without* government supervision of the economic process.[7] The nationalist leaders who came to power in Asia and Africa after the war had no problem with this idea. They demanded strong, "nation-building" governments, and were supplied by the West with the intellectual, justifications and the policy tools for the work. Raul Prebisch, Sir Andrew Cohen, and others were to make the case that poor societies could not count on "price signals" from domestic and international markets for reliable stimuli in their quest for economic development; at much the same time, new econometric techniques seemed to offer new governments practical instruments for "scientific" management of the economy, and even for "fine-tuning" economic growth.[8]

In all less developed countries today, regardless of their professed ideologies, the state routinely undertakes activities which were earlier left to markets, businessmen, and entrepreneurs. This confounds easy definitions of "capitalism," even in the most unlikely places. In laissez-faire Hong Kong, about half of the city-state's stock of housing is "publicly" owned, and central authorities control a larger fraction of GNP than in the United States.[9] South Korea directs its economy through "Five-Year Plans," and, until very recently, managed the allocation of the nation's finance capital through state agencies.[10] In Taiwan, government expenditures currently account for about a third of the nation's output (a higher fraction than in Sandinist Nicaragua in the early 1980s), and state-owned enterprises account for over two-fifths of the country's annual accumulation of capital.[11]

With the rise of the modern state apparatus, "capitalism" is becoming ever less suited to serve as a criterion for distinguishing national economies from one another. Increasingly, it is governments rather than markets which take the lead in shaping economic life, and policies of political leaders, rather than entrepreneurs which must ultimately be judged in assessments of national poverty.

Modern politics and the modern state have, however, created a class of governments which stand apart from all others. These are not ones which proclaim the virtues of "capitalism," but rather the ones which embrace the tenets of Marxism–Leninism. To no small degree, communist leaders have set the terms of discourse on poverty in the modern world. They have also set a challenge for all non-communist governments by asserting that their ambitious plans for transforming society and planning economic growth offer more to the poor than any alternative system of governance. It is both manageable and instructive to compare their progress against poverty with the progress of those non-communist nations whose social and economic systems they would see overhauled and replaced.

Over the past generation a rhetoric of commitment to improving the material condition of the world's poor has become a staple of political consumption in both rich and poor countries. In itself, this is hardly surprising: as much might have been expected at a time when literally dozens of new governments were attempting to establish and assert themselves over regions in which poor health and illiteracy prevailed, and when the conflict between Marxist–Leninist states and their "bourgeois" counterparts was finally assuming the dimensions of a global struggle for power. What is surprising is the stark contrast in the less developed countries between the nearly universal rhetoric of commitment to the poor and the prevailing lack of reliable, comprehensive, and sequential data that would be needed for any serious evaluation of either the plight of the poor or the effectiveness of interventions on their behalf.

For reasons that have yet to be explained, none of the major voices of today's "development dialogue" acknowledge the sorry state of current statistics on world poverty. Yet the problem is apparent. For many countries, numerical information concerning broad portions of the economy—much less the condition of the poor within these sectors—is simply unavailable. Those figures that can be found, moreover, are often of questionable meaning. It is not too much to say that the statistics most commonly used to map out poverty in the less developed countries are neither reliable in and of themselves, nor comparable among countries or over time.

Social and economic data for the less developed countries are compromised by three sorts of problems.

The first are conceptual. Even under the best of circumstances, it is not nearly as easy to get a clear picture of patterns of poverty as is commonly imagined. Conventional analyses of poverty focus principally on per capita income: how it differs among groups, or changes over time. But determining per capita income is not a science; it is an art, necessarily requiring judgement and assumption. For this reason it is impossible to arrive at a single, precise conclusion about either differences in per capita income or changes in it over time for any active social system.

Constructing a per capita income index is, unavoidably, an exercise in rewriting history. It involves assigning constancy to a changing array of goods and services that households and nations produce or consume, and hypothesizing about the behavior of economic actors in environments to which they were never exposed.

The difficulties of "holding prices constant" illustrate the problem. Many of the changes over time in household demand and the composition of national output are occasioned by shifts in prices. In holding prices constant, as any "deflated" index of economic activity must do, response is divorced from stimulus. This is not a trivial matter: choices based on changing scarcities are at the heart of the economic process. In redoing a price structure, one implicitly proposes an alternative course for local or international events. The results need not correspond to any recognizeable reality. Holding prices constant, for example, would make it seem that American families spent about 20 percent less on energy in 1982 (after the great run-up in energy prices) than in 1972, or that Saudi Arabia ran a sizeable balance of payments deficit with its trading partners following the OPEC boom in 1973.

The conceptual problems incorporated into per capita income numbers go beyond the indelicacy of holding fixed those quantities whose function it is to vary. There is the problem of comparing purchasing power in societies whose prices, and patterns of purchase, are significantly different. There is the problem of imputing value to government services—many of which are public precisely because it is thought they cannot be properly evaluated by the marketplace. And there is the problem of technical innovation. Many of the benefits of technical innovation accrue to those who do not pay for them. This poses a fundamental challenge to the measurement of purchasing power, for technical innovation is the basis of economic change in the modern world. It affects our lives quite literally. Advances in medicine and public health technology, for example, have altered the relationship between income and longevity: at any given level of per capita income (as conventionally measured), a society could expect to obtain substantially greater life expectancy today than in the 1930s.[12] This indisputable improvement in national well-being is only the most obvious of the sorts of changes in material conditions, brought on by technological breakthrough and innovation, that go unrecorded and unvalued in conventional tabulations of per capita income. In the less developed countries, where technical change can have a rapid and discontinuous impact on patterns of daily life and the economic routine, the biases introduced into calculations of per capita income can be especially acute.

Conceptual difficulties are compounded by technical ones. As a practical matter, there are very real limits to the abilities of governments to collect accurate information on the economies and societies under their supervision. Uncertainties in American statistics, which are widely regarded as exceptionally reliable, underscore the point; according to one set of studies by the International Monetary Fund as much as $200 billion in business activity may be missed each year by the Department of Commerce.[13] Many developed countries have been still less successful in their attempts to measure economic activity. In Italy, for example, there are indications that a rapidly growing "underground" economy may account for as much as a third of the nation's overall growth during the late 1960s and early 1970s.[14] Under such circumstances, the correspondence between official economic statistics and the actual state of economic affairs is questionable. Yet Italy's ability to collect accurate statistics is considerably greater than the great majority of nations in Asia and the Caribbean, and in all likelihood, greater than that of any single country in Latin America or Africa.

From the technical standpoint, the limits of accuracy for a nation's social and economic statistics are set by the policy concerns of its leaders, the sophistication and reach of its bureaucracies and institutions, the efficacy of its channels of social communication, the ability of the population to deal in, and with, numbers, and the complexity of the phenomena to be measured. This augurs ill for measuring poverty. Poor people tend to be socially invisible; disproportionately illiterate and frequently beyond the fringes of the data-generating enclaves in their societies, they seldom leave strong statistical trails behind them. In poor societies the institutions which gather numbers are often weak or fragile, and poor governments generally lack the ability (and sometimes even the inclination) to learn about arterial conditions in the countryside in any great detail. The People's Republic of China provides a case in point. Despite the presumable need for accurate numbers in a centrally planned economy, China's State Statistical Bureau, which fell from grace in the aftermath of the "Great Leap Forward," reportedly did its work with a core staff which at one time consisted of only 14 persons.[15] Even in 1981 it employed less than 200 technicians. How they were to provide accurate data on social and economic conditions in a country of a billion people—in which about a third of all communes reportedly could not be reached by road as recently as the early 1970s[16]—has never been explained.

As a general rule, it is easier for government to measure physical quantities than to estimate economic values. Counting heads is less complicated than calculating national income. Even so, the ability of even comparatively skilled governments from among the less developed countries to measure population, or the output of basic commodities, should not be exaggerated. The reliability of demographic data from the less developed regions is suggested by the fact that scholars and policymakers did not come to recognize that the world rate of population growth had peaked until 1977; today it is believed that the slowdown may have begun in the early 1960s.[17] As for food production, even international food trade statistics appear to be beset by wide margins of error,[18] and these are the easiest data on food to compile. To this day there are no reliable numbers for tuber and root production in the less developed countries.[19] But cassava, yams, sweet potatoes and potatoes are the principal source of calories for literally millions of people in Africa, Asia, and Latin America.

The third problem with social and economic statistics from the less developed countries is that they are often distorted for political reasons. The trouble is inherent in the very nature of the modern data-gathering process. Modern governments collect information to assist themselves in making policy. Yet as soon as statistics are put to policy use, political incentives to manipulate them arise. Clumsily politicized statistics are sometimes easy to catch: one did not need special expertise, for example, to evaluate Sukarno's claim that his government completely eliminated illiteracy in Indonesia during the course of the year 1964. A great many less ambitious adjustments, however, never come to light. The adulteration of national statistics seldom requires mass complicity.[20] In most cases, the job can be done by a single hand in a single government office. The poorer a society, the less developed its statistical services, the easier it is for government officials to change numbers without detection. Since the poor usually need others to represent them and generate little independent data on their own conditions of life, statistics about poverty are particularly vulnerable to deliberate distortions. There is, unfortunately, no reason to deliberate distortions. There is, unfortunately, no reason to expect countervailing pressures for statistical adjustments to offset each other. The more likely outcome would be for unpredictable waves of bias to pass through national accounts. There is no reason to expect these biases to be the same among countries or over time.

The problems with conventionally accepted economic statistics assert themselves in any attempt to assess poverty in the less developed countries. Per capita product and per capita income numbers are the mainstay of the literature on material progress and economic development, and are used without hesitation or qualification in both academic treatments and policy papers. Let us examine some of these for a moment. Table 11.1 presents estimates of per capita product for ten countries for 1970, based on two different approaches to the calculation. The first, in accordance with accepted practice, makes an estimate of national income in local currency, divides this by a population estimate, and converts the figure into U.S. dollars at the going exchange rate. The second attempts to

TABLE 11.1
1970 Per Capita Product of Selected Nations, Computed by Different Methods

	(As Percent of U.S. Per Capita Product)		
	Foreign Exchange	**Purchasing Power**	**Difference (%)**
Kenya	2.99	5.99	+100
India	2.07	6.00	+190
South Korea	3.86	10.0	+159
Philippines	5.39	10.2	+ 89
Colombia	7.24	16.3	+125
Malaysia	8.10	17.4	+115
Iran	8.37	18.6	+122
Hungary	21.6	41.6	+ 91
Italy	36.0	49.9	+ 39
Japan	39.8	58.2	+ 46

Source: Irving B. Kravis, et al., *International Comparisons of Real Product and Purchasing Power,* (Baltimore: Johns Hopkins University Press, 1978).

equate per capita product in different countries on the basis of purchasing power rather than exchange rates: that is, it attempts to place an equivalent value on equivalent products in different societies. Neither procedure can be expected to yield a single, unassailable set of numbers; nevertheless, the differences between these two sets are striking. In the less developed countries, "purchasing power" estimates can be twice as high as those based on exchange rates; the different methods, moreover, alter not only the valuing, but the ranking of output among countries. By the conventional approach, Kenya seems to produce 44 percent more per person than India in 1970; by the second approach, it actually seems to produce less.

The second approach may be an improvement on conventional estimates of output per person in the less developed countries, but it does not provide reliable and consistent estimates. Tables 11.2 and 11.3 emphasize this. They compare "purchasing power" estimates of output per person in the less developed countries from two different teams: one sponsored by the World Bank, and the other by the U.S. State Department. Both teams produce estimates for the ten most populous non-communist LDCs for 1977. Only three of these countries' estimates differ by less than 20 percent; four of them differ by more than 50 percent, and the estimates for Bangladesh differ by more than 100 percent. Both teams provide estimates of change in per capita product from 1950 to 1977. For those same ten countries, only four countries' postwar growth numbers differ by less than a fifth; three differ by more than half. For two dozen smaller poor nations, growth rates differed by less than a fifth in only five cases; they differed by more than half in twelve cases, and came out with opposite signs in three cases!

National income, of course, is much easier to estimate than income distribution. The problems with income distribution figures can be illustrated with some examples from developed Western nations, presented in Table 11.4 Each one of these countries is better equipped to measure the income of its households than almost any less developed society. Yet estimates of pretax earnings for the poorest 40 percent of households differ by almost a quarter in three Western nations, by nearly a third in a fourth, and by almost half in the fifth.

Despite very real advances in the statistical capabilities of most less developed countries over the past generation, the margins of error for figures most commonly used in describing national and global poverty are typically greater than the differences or changes which they presume to measure. The literature which uses these numbers without qualification cannot be expected to yield meaningful conclusions.

It is for this reason that many studies of international poverty cannot be taken seriously. The World Bank's calculation that 700 million people

TABLE 11.2
Differences in Estimated Per Capita Product After Purchasing Power Adjustments
for Various LDCs, 1977 (1980 Dollars)

Largest LDCs	Kravis Group	Block	Difference (Kravis-Block)
India	658	450	46%
Indonesia	653	807	−19%
Brazil	3,345	2,359	42%
Bangladesh	534	245	118%
Pakistan	880	472	86%
Nigeria	876	1,000	−12%
Mexico	2,618	2,309	13%
Philippines	1,396	859	63%
Thailand	1,166	833	40%
Turkey	2,294	1,442	59%

Two Dozen Poor LDCs	Kravis Group	Block	Difference
Benin	437	643	−32%
Burundi	356	315	13%
C.A.R.	443	431	3%
Chad	454	209	117%
Ethiopia	345	287	20%
Gambia	526	537	−2%
Guinea	409	425	−4%
Lesotho	364	503	−28%
Madagascar	558	750	−26%
Malawi	454	399	14%
Mali	278	208	34%
Niger	524	306	71%
Rwanda	343	410	−16%
Somalia	427	263	62%
Tanzania	548	434	26%
Togo	471	650	−18%
Uganda	546	649	−16%
Upper Volta	265	296	−10%
Zaire	350	366	−4%
Afghanistan	301	454	−33%
Bangladesh	534	245	118%
Burma	420	365	15%
Nepal	428	264	62%
Haiti	535	567	−6%

Source: Calculated from Robert Summers, Irving B. Kravis, and Alan Heston, "International Comparison of Real Product and Its Composition: 1950–77," Review of Income and Wealth, March 1980, and Herbert Block, The Planetary Product in 1980: A Creative Pause?, (Washington, D.C.: State Department, 1981).

TABLE 11.3
Differences in Estimates of Percentage Change in Per Capita Product for Various
LDCs, 1950–77

Dozen Largest LDCs	Kravis Group	Block		High/Low
India	41	53		29%
Indonesia	88	540		514%
Brazil	202	214		6%
Bangladesh	4	14		250%
Pakistan	75	66		14%
Nigeria	143	219		53%
Mexico	112	97		15%
Philippines	143	122		17%
Thailand	101	139		38%
Turkey	179	139		29%
Two Dozen Largest LDCs	**Kravis Group**	**Block**	**Difference**	**High/Low**
Benin	4	8	4	100%
Burundi	− 51	− 12	39	325%
C.A.R.	− 20	− 1	19	1,900%
Chad	− 13	− 44	− 31	238%
Ethiopia	57	89	32	50%
Gambia	40	58	18	45%
Guinea	− 1	− 10	− 9	200%
Lesotho	109	118	9	8%
Madagascar	− 7	− 8	− 1	14%
Malawi	99	107	8	8%
Mali	25	114	89	456%
Niger	58	21	− 37	176%
Rwanda	2	18	16	800%
Somalia	2	− 10	− 12	− 500%
Tanzania	81	70	− 9	16%
Uganda	5	− 3	− 8	− 60%
Upper Volta	5	36	31	620%
Zaire	16	69	53	331%
Afghanistan	8	5	− 3	60%
Bangladesh	4	14	10	250%
Burma	94	80	− 14	18%
Nepal	16	32	16	100%
Haiti	4	− 0	− 4	− 800%

Source: Calculated from Robert Summers, et al., and Herbert Block, as cited in
Table 11.2.

TABLE 11.4
Comparison of World Bank and OECD Estimates of Pretax Income Share for Bottom 40 Percent of Households of Selected Developed Nations (percentage)

	World Bank	OECD	Δ%
Canada	20.0 (1970)	15.2 (1969)	−24
U.S.A.	19.7 (1970)	13.8 (1972)	−30
Sweden	14.0 (1963)	17.4 (1972)	+24
Netherlands	13.6 (1967)	16.8 (1967)	+24
France	9.5 (1962)	14.2 (1970)	+49

Source: Donald McGranahan, *International Comparability of Statistics on Income Distribution,* (Geneva: United Nations Research Institute For Social Development, 1979).

subsist on $25 per year, for example, is based on recombinations of largely meaningless numbers. On its very face the calculation is evidently without meaning: it would have been impossible for one person, let alone for 700 million, to survive for a year solely on the equivalent in goods and services of what $25 could have bought in American society in the mid-1970s. In the same fashion, the ILO study of poverty in rural Asia multiplies questionable income distribution numbers against problematic per capita income estimates. Professor Bairoch's account of economic growth in the less developed countries is even less sensitive to the use of economic statistics: in many tables he offers indices or figures for regions encompassing areas which were producing *no economic data at all* for some of the decades his survey covers. In these works and many others, students of world poverty may be said with some justice to be dignifying assumptions and prejudices with decimal points.

The false precision of so much of the work on world poverty does not stand the world's poor in good stead. In an age of powerful state apparatuses and activist social policy, the material well-being of the poor depends in no small degree on the result of government intervention. Misleading or systematically biased data, seemingly legitimized by econometric manipulations, can only misdirect government energy and frustrate the efficient use of those limited resources devoted to the alleviation of poverty. False precision furthermore increases the likelihood of erratic swings in periodic assessments of poverty, which may themselves ultimately interfere with the ability of governments to attend to the needs of the poorest. The misuse of numbers on poverty may not only limit government performance: it may actually undermine support for the problem-solving activities of the state.

Although there is reason to worry about the quality of social and economic data for a great many nations, a concern for accuracy does not justify the rejection of *all* statistics on poverty as inadequate or misleading. Through judicious use of available information, it is possible to get a sense not only of gradations in poverty in the countries representing the bulk of the population of the less developed countries, but also some idea of the progress against poverty that has been made under both communist and non-communist regimes since the end of the Second World War. In the final analysis, the choice of criteria in measuring progress against poverty is arbitrary, for poverty is a complex phenomenon which cannot be completely described by any given set of measures. It is my own opinion, however, that we might come to a useful assessment of material poverty if we focus on five areas. These are: population, nutrition, literacy, the status of women, and material or social inequalities.

Population

Demographic figures—population totals, death rates, and birth rates—are essential in any quantitative assessment of poverty. Demographic estimates for the less developed countries are more accurate today than at any time in the past, but they are still surrounded by considerable margins of uncertainty. From the demographic standpoint, only a few countries remain terra incognita. Ethiopia, Laos, and a handful of African nations have not yet attempted a count of their people (this essay was written in 1983), but while material want may be severe in these places, they are thought to represent less than one fiftieth of the population of the less developed countries.[12] More problematic is the expanse of terra infirma in Africa, Asia, and Latin America. Underregistration and misreporting are dangers in even the most careful censuses and surveys; the United States census in 1970, for example, is thought to have missed at least five million people, over 2 percent of the American public. Only a few of the smaller and more prosperous LDCs—Taiwan, Chile, some of the Caribbean islands—match Western standards of enumeration. In the rest, population counts and vital statistics must be treated as incomplete—although in varying degree. Among the non-communist countries, there are sufficient demographic data for India, parts of East Asia, and much of Latin America to make a reconstruction of the postwar experience in which assumption is not the key variable. The same cannot yet be said for sub-Saharan Africa or most of the Middle East—a fact which may in itself tell us something about the condition of the poor in those regions.

In the communist countries of Asia and Latin America, the politics of population counts seems to have a life of its own, conditioned by Lenin's dictum that statistics in a revolutionary society are not meant to serve scholarly purposes. North Korea, for reasons best known to itself, has never officially released any census results. China's 1953 census appears to have been conducted not only to gather numbers, but to symbolize the consolidation of power on the mainland; the government's assertion that its enumeration missed only 0.02 percent of the population was a political, not a scientific, statement. China's 1982 census was explicitly linked to a campaign to limit family size to one child per couple. In Vietnam, Hanoi's 1960 census preceded the collectivization of the countryside and the escalation of the war against South Vietnam; its 1974 census took stock of manpower just before the military offensives that were to topple the Saigon regime; its 1979 census was conducted as the government was devising programs to facilitate the transfer of millions of people from the North to the South, and within the South to inhospitable "New Economic Zones."[22] Broad based incentives for misrepresentation may arise when census-taking becomes associated with the imposition of hardship in the public mind.* In Cuba, as we shall see, vital statistics may today be shaped by the regime's desire to make health levels seem high. Population numbers from these Marxist–Leninist nations can of course be used, but they should be used with care.

Since poverty is a problem that affects people, it is necessary to know where the people most likely to be affected are, and in what numbers. More than 150 governments and political entities represent the approximately three and a half billion people of the less developed regions today, but nearly half of them are thought to live in two countries, China and India (see Table 11.5). Over half a billion more live in seven other countries: Indonesia, Brazil, Mexico, Vietnam, the Philippines, Thailand, and South Korea. If we add to these nine countries seven small ones— North Korea, Taiwan, Sri Lanka, Chile, Cuba, Costa Rica, and Jamaica— we make a set accounting for two-thirds or more of the population of the less developed nations, continuing every well-established independent Marxist–Leninist government in the "Third World," affording, in many cases, relatively reliable social statistics, and offering bases for comparison among nations with dramatically different political systems. The selection is arbitrary, but we are not likely to come much closer to describing both global patterns of poverty and the performance of communist and non-communist societies in a single cut.

A first, broad, indication of postwar changes in living standards in the less developed countries comes from changes in population growth rates.

*Subsequent analyses, however, indicated a high level of accuracy for the 1982 China census. See Chapter 7.

TABLE 11.5
U.S. Census Bureau Population Estimates for Selected Communist and Non-Communist LDCs, mid-year 1980 (millions)

Country	Population
China	1,013
India	685
Indonesia	151
Brazil	122
Mexico	70
Vietnam	54
Philippines	49
Thailand	48
Korea (South)	40
North Korea	18
Taiwan	18
Sri Lanka	15
Chile	11
Cuba	10
Costa Rica	2
Jamaica	2
A. Total, 16 LDCs	2,308
B. Estimated Total, "Developing Countries"	3,342
A/B	68%

Source: U.S. Bureau of the Census, *World Population 1983* (Washington, D.C.: Department of Commerce, 1983).

As is well known by now, the less developed regions have all experienced a surge of population growth since the end of the Second World War. The well-worn phrase "population explosion" connotes the abruptness of these accelerations, and the speed with which they spread to all non-European areas of the world. The global dimensions of the change in population patterns cannot be measured with any great precision, but it is thought that rates of natural increase were lower for the less developed regions than the developed regions in the 1930s, whereas they were two or three times higher by the early 1960s.[23]

At a time when governments are increasingly held responsible for supplying services and sustenance for their subjects, "rapid" population growth has come to be labelled a social problem by a wide variety of officials and institutions. Some contemporary governments even argue that population growth intrinsically reduces the living standards of any people experiencing it.[24] This is a curious contention. Whatever population growth may mean for tomorrow—and the future implications of population change

are much less clearly understood than many contemporary analyses suggest—it incontestably reflects a recent improvement in material conditions
for the less developed countries.

While there are many uncertainties about the population patterns of the
poor regions, it can be safely stated that their rapid postwar rates of
population growth have been powered principally not by a rise in birth
rates, but by significant and widespread declines in death rates. For people
in high mortality societies, a sustained drop in death rates is a very good
thing. Death rates are high in poor societies because children and parents
perish from famines, epidemics, and scourges that do not endanger the
lives of affluent peoples. Reduced death rates are perhaps the nearest thing
to a universally desired good, and may provide the best single indicator of
improvements in a people's material condition.

Ironically, conventional economic statistics treat mortality decline as an
economic liability. As P. T. Bauer has noted, measured per capita wealth
falls with the death of a calf, but rises with the death of a child.[25]

One attempt to treat improvements in mortality as a consumer good,
relying heavily on assumptions, suggested that imputing value to increases
in longevity might almost double Chile's postwar increase in per capita
product, and more than double Sri Lanka's.[26] While these computations
are only illustrative, they indicate the sorts of differences which may exist
between conventional measures of economic progress and actual changes
in personal well-being when death rates are declining rapidly.

The clearest measure of the relationship between death and the individual is life expectancy, which is based on survival probabilities. Table 11.6
presents some estimates of life expectancy at birth from about 1950 to
around 1980 for the sixteen less developed countries we have selected. For
those countries with reasonably reliable censuses and surveys, the rise in
life expectancy over the past generation has been unambiguous; for some
of them it has been quite dramatic. None have seen their lifespans increase
by less than a decade. Most have made even more significant gains. In
Brazil, where Professor Hewlett writes of "growing poverty," life expectancy has increased by nearly twenty years since World War II. In India,
life expectancy has risen by over half since the early 1950s, and may have
nearly doubled since the decade of Independence.[27] If we remember that
the countries in Table 11.6 and 11.7 represents over two-thirds of the
population of the less developed regions, the World Health Organization's
suggestion that life expectancy may have risen "in developing regions" by
fifty percent between the 1930s and the 1960s may not sound exaggerated.[28]

To be sure: "it is not yet possible to determine levels of mortality—
much less trends—in sub–Saharan Africa with any degree of confidence,"
as a recent UN demographic study noted.[29] Figures for much of the Muslim

TABLE 11.6
Estimates of Life Expectancy for Selected Communist and Non-Communist LDCs,
c. 1950–c. 1980 (years)

	1950	1960	1970	1980
1. Cuba	59 (1953)	64	70	70 (1974)
2. Jamaica	56 (1950–52)	65	68	69
3. Costa Rica	56	62 (1962–64)	69 (1972–74)	72 (1978)
4. Chile	55 (1952–53)	57	62	67
5. Mexico	48	58	60	66
6. Brazil	48	55	57	64
7. China*	(30–35)	(30–35)	(50–55)	(60–65)
8. India	32 (1951)	41 (1961)	46 (1971)	52 (1978)
9. Taiwan	59 (1952)	65	69	71
10. Vietnam*	(38)	(42)	(45)	(52)
11. Indonesia*	(38)	(42)	47	53
12. Sri Lanka	58 (1953)	62 (1962)	66 (1971)	67 (1981)
13. Thailand*	(47)	(54)	58	61 (1975)
14. Philippines*	(46)	(53)	58	61 (1974–75)
15. North Korea*				(63)
16. South Korea*	(47)	53 (1955–60)	63	65 (1978–79)

*Parenthetical figures are estimates for first half of the decade.

Note: With exception of North Korea and Vietnam, all estimates based on or extrapolated from census and survey data. Parentheses indicate adjustment or extrapolation.

Sources:

Line 1: Column 1:   Fernando Ganzalez, Q. and Jorge Debosa, "Cuba: Evaluacion y Ajuste del Censo de 1953 y las Estadisticas de Nacimientos y Defunciones entre 1943 y 1958," *CELADE Series* C#124, June 1970;
         Columns 2–4: United Nations, *Levels and Trends of Mortality Series 1950* (New York: United Nations, 1982).

Line 2: Columns 1–3: *Levels and Trends,* loc. cit.;
         Column 4:   Intra-American Development Bank, *Economic And Social Progress In Latin America* (Washington: IABD, 1983).

Line 3: Columns 1–3: *Levels and Trends,* loc. cit.;
         Column 4:   World Health Organization, *World Health Statistics 1981* (Geneva: WHO, 1982)

Line 4: Columns 1–3: *Levels and Trends,* loc. cit.;
         Column 4:   *Economic and Social Progress,* loc. cit.

Line 5: Columns 1–3: United Nations, *Demographic Yearbook,* various editions;
         Column 4:   *Economic and Social Progress,* loc. cit.

Line 6:   Columns 1–3:   *Demographic Yearbook,* loc. cit., various editions;
           Column 4:   World Bank demographic data sheets, unpublished

Line 7:   Columns 1–3:   Based on Kenneth Hill, "China: An Evaluation of Demographic Trends 1950/82" (World Bank, unpublished paper, 1983);
           Column 4:   Based on personal communication with Judith Banister, U.S. Bureau of the Census.

Line 8:   Columns 1–3:   *Levels and Trends,* loc. cit.;
           Column 4:   Government of India, *Survey on Infant And Child Mortality, 1979: A Preliminary Report* (New Delhi: Office of Registrar General, India, 1980).

Line 9:   Columns 1–4:   *Republic of China Demographic Yearbook,* (Taipei: Executive Yuan), various volumes.

Line 10:   United Nations, *Demographic Indicators of Countries: Estimates And Projections As Assessed in 1980* (New York: United Nations, 1982).

Line 11:   Columns 1–2:   *Demographic Indicators of Countries,* loc. cit.
           Column 3–4:   World Bank demographic data sheet, unpublished

Line 12:   Columns 1–3:   *Levels and Trends,* loc. cit.;
           Column 4:   World Bank demographic data sheet, unpublished

Line 13:   Columns 1–2:   *Demographic Indicators of Countries,* loc. cit.
           Column 3–4:   U.S. Bureau of the Census, *World Population* (Washington, D.C.: Department of Commerce), various issues.

Line 14:   Columns 1–2:   *Demographic Indicators of Countries,* loc. cit.
           Columns 3–4:   U.S. Bureau of the Census, *World Population* (Washington: Department of Commerce), various issues.

Line 15:   Column 4:   *United Nations, Demographic Yearbook, 1981* (New York: United Nations, 1983).

Line 16:   Column 1:   *Demographic Indicators of Countries,* loc. cit.
           Columns 2–4:   National Bureau of Statistics, *The Life Table of Korea (1978–79)* (Seoul: Economic Planning Board, July 1982).

expanse from Casablanca to Dacca are also highly problematic. But for the regions of the poor world in which mortality estimates are more firmly rooted in the results of useable censuses and surveys, it appears that the gap in life expectancies separating those less developed countries from developed societies has been narrowing. Some of the more advanced LDCs, like Taiwan and Costa Rica, have managed to eliminate the gap more or less completely; their peoples can currently expect to live as long as citizens of Western Europe. Where gaps persist, there has been progress in closing them. Mexico's life expectancy is currently estimated to be about eight years lower than the United States', but in 1950 the difference between the two nations was about eighteen years. Indian lifespans today

TABLE 11.7
Estimates of Infant Mortality for Communist and Non-Communist LDCs, c. 1950–
c. 1980 (deaths per thousand births)

	1950		1960		1970		1980	
1. Cuba	79	(1952–54)	66		40		45	(1974)
2. Jamaica	79	(1950–52)	56		35		22	(1976)
3. Costa Rica	97		87	(1962–64)	51	(1972–74)	19	
4. Chile	120	(1952–53)	115		77		35	
5. Mexico	113		78		71		61	(1977)
6. Brazil	136		107		89		81	(1976)
7. China	(225)	(1954)	(330)		(109)		(71)	
8. India	(190)*		(157)*		133*		129*	
9. Taiwan	91		42		27		22	
10. Vietnam	(180)*		(150)*		(140)*		(106)*	
11. Indonesia	(166)*		(145)*		(112)*		(99)*	
12. Sri Lanka	82		57		51		46	
13. Thailand	(135)*		(97)*		(68)*		(59)*	
14. Philippines	(132)*		(93)*		(65)*		(59)*	
15. North Korea								
16. South Korea	(116)*		(71)*		50		36	(1978–79)

*See Sources

Note: Figures in parentheses come from adjusted estimates rather than directly
from life tables or other in-country figures.

Sources:

Line 1:   Columns 1–4:   Levels and Trends Of Mortality Since 1950 (New York:
United Nations, 1982).

Lines 2–6: Columns 1–3:   S. Baum and E. E. Arriaga, "Levels, Trends, Differentials, and Causes of Infant Mortality and Early Child-
hood Mortality in Latin America," World Health Statistics Quarterly, 1981.

Column 4:   U.S. Bureau of the Census, World Population 1979
(Washington D.C.: Department of Commerce, 1980).

Line 7:   Columns 1–3:   Kenneth Hill, "China: An Evaluation of Demographic
Trends; 1950–1982", (World Bank: unpublished paper,
June 1983).

Column 4:   World Bank, World Development Report 1983 (Washington: World Bank 1983).

Line 9:   Columns 1–4:   Republic of China, Social Welfare Indicators, 1982
(Taipei: Manpower Planning Committee, Executive
Yuan, 1982).

Line 12:   Columns 1–3:   Statistical Pocketbook of Ceylon 1974 (Colombo: Department of Census And Statistics, 1974).

Column 4:   World Population 1979, loc. cit.

Line 16:   Columns 3–4:   National Bureau of Statistics, *The Life Table of Korea 1978–79* (Second: Economic Planning Board, July 1982).
All Other Figures: United Nations Secretariat, "Infant Mortality: World Estimates and Projections, 1950–2025," *Population Bulletin of the United Nations #14, 1983.* These refer to the following years: for Column 1, 1950–1955; for Column 2, 1960–1965; for Column 3, 1970–1975; for Column 4, 1975–1980.

are on average about twenty years shorter than those in the West. The gap speaks to the severity of poverty in India today; it should not make us forget, however, that there was a gap of over thirty years between India and the West in the early 1950s.

When life expectancies in poor and rich nations converge, it often seems to be the case that life expectancies within the poor nation are converging as well: that is, that health improvements for the disadvantaged strata of society are outpacing those for the more privileged. However, data about differences in life expectancy within poor nations by income levels or education are of limited availability and accuracy at the moment. On the other hand, differences in life expectancy between cities and countryside are so common in poor societies that they may almost be treated as a rule. In many poor societies, that difference is striking: in India people can expect to live nearly a decade longer in cities than in rural areas, and in Indonesia, six years; in Brazil, lifespans are nearly thirty percent longer in the vicinity of Sao Paolo and Rio de Janeiro than in the predominantly rural Northeast.[30] Interestingly, there is no evidence that this difference is less pronounced in Communist societies: Chinese data provided to the World Bank suggest that lifespans may be more than ten years longer in Peking and Shanghai than in some of the less developed provinces,[31] and Cuba's gap between city and countryside does not seem to be noticeably lower than nearby Jamaica's. Regardless of a government's professed ideology, a poor society's cities are likely to be enclaves of life-extending comforts.[32]

With a general picture of postwar progress against mortality in the less developed countries in mind, we can try to compare the performance of communist and non-communist nations. In all Marxist–Leninist societies, as we know, "Liberation" has ushered in campaigns of disease eradication, programmatic argumentations of medical and public health services, and a radical redistribution of property in the name of the poor. Have these efforts brought communist societies superior results in health improvement?

Comparisons of performance between communist and non-communist nations in the poor world are necessarily inexact. This is not only a question of statistical inexactitudes, but of the unavoidable difficulties in measuring countries with different cultures, histories and resources against one another. Nevertheless, if we move carefully we can get some idea of how well Communist states in the poor world have fared in comparison with their neighbors.

In Latin America, it is often claimed that Cuba has made unusual progress in health during the past twenty-five years under Fidel Castro and his Communist Party of Cuba. Preliminary inspection of Cuba's health statistics would lead to a different concludion. Cuba may be the only nation in Latin America or the Caribbean whose registered rate of infant mortality did not decline during the 1960s. In fact, infant mortality in Cuba, according to official figures, actually rose by over 25 percent between 1960 and 1969. Cuba's rise in infant mortality might be a statistical artifact. On the other hand, pre–revolutionary Cuba's birth and death registration systems, while not complete, were reasonably good. Recently Cuban demographers have suggested that infant mortality may have been under-reported by 15 percent in the late 1950s;[33] this would not be enough to explain away a 25 percent rise in infant deaths. Cuba's statistics on communicable diseases, moreover, fall and rise over the 1960s in very much the same pattern as its infant mortality rates, peaking first in 1962, then again in 1969.[34]

Statistics from Cuba's Ministry of Health suggest that a dramatic decline in infant mortality took place in the 1970s. According to these numbers, the rate of infant mortality would have dropped from over 40 in 1970 to about 19 in 1980—a figure not too different from the United States' a few years earlier. Salutory though these improvements appear, there is reason to examine them carefully. Approximately ninety percent of Cuba's drop in infant mortality during the 1970s took place in two years: 1972 and 1976. These were years in which the Cuban statistical system was overhauled.[35] Since 1972, Cuba's State Statistical apparatus has been relieved of direct responsibility for collecting numbers on infant mortality; these are now simply given to it by the Ministry of Health.[36]

Independent verification of infant mortality rates could be had through "life tables," which calculate survivorship for all age groups, and thus create internal consistency. Cuba did produce a "life table" in 1974, but it is at variance with the Ministry of Health pronouncements on infant mortality. The Ministry of Health puts infant mortality in 1974 at 26; the "life table" puts it at about 45.[37] Ministry of Health statistics suggest that infant mortality fell by 25 percent between 1970 and 1974; the "life tables" indicate that it *rose* by more than 11 percent!

Compared with other nations from Latin America and the Caribbean,

Cuba's progress in health appears unexceptional, as can be seen from Tables 11.6 and 11.7. In the early 1950s, Cuba may have been the healthiest nation in the American tropics; it may have enjoyed both the highest life expectancy and the lowest infant mortality rate. Today this no longer seems so. Costa Rica now appears to lead Cuba in life expectancy, and several countries appear to have lower levels of infant mortality—including possibly Chile, where, to the surprise of many observers, the Pinochet regime not only continued, but accelerated, the reduction of infant mortality rates that had been taking place under President Allende.[38] In terms of absolute improvements in life expectancy, Cuba appears to have been outpaced by Chile and Costa Rica, and looks just to have held even with Jamaica. In all, the only country in the Western Hemisphere against which its record could be compared to unambiguous advantage would seem to be Argentina. (See Chapters 9 and 10 for more information on Cuba's health situation)

In Northeast Asia, the Korean peninsula is divided between a communist and a non-communist government. Information on mortality and health for South Korea is less comprehensive then might have been expected, but basic data can be found; by contrast, North Korea has attempted systematically to seal its people off from the rest of the world, and releases only facts and assertions which are deemed to make the Democratic People's Republic of Korea seem to excel over the Republic of Korea. According to Japanese colonial records, mortality was about the same in both North and South Korea before World War II.[39] Today the situation is unclear. According to one set of UN projections, life expectancy and infant mortality are designated to be the same in North and South Korea; according to another, whose derivation is not explained, life expectancy is now about three years higher in the South.[40] At this point, perhaps the most that can be said is that there appears no reason to presume that North Korea's performance in health improvement has been any better than South Korea's.

In Southeast Asia, there are too few hard data about current health conditions in Vietnam to assess its record in detail. One set of United Nations estimates put life expectancy in Vietnam at 48 in the late 1970s—below India. By contrast, a World Bank mission visiting Vietnam in the late 1970s put life expectancy at 62—almost thirty percent higher. That figure is almost certainly too high: even Soviet researchers give a lower number. In the cautions formulation of an official country report, Vietnam's life expectancy "would be" 59 years in 1980.[41] The conditional phraseology suggests that the authors had in fact estimated life expectancy to be below that level at some earlier date. The United Nations' Population Division's most recent projection of life expectancy for Vietnam places expectation of life at birth in Vietnam in the late 1970s in the low fifties.[42] By this conjectural estimate, health conditions in Vietnam might be slightly better than in India or Indonesia, but would not be significantly better (see Table 11.6 and 11.7). (Also, see Chapter 10.) From the limited demographic accounts of the French colonial period, it would seem that health conditions in Vietnam in the 1930s were not dramatically worse than they were in India. Indonesia would offer a comparison, but its colonial demographic data are sketchy.[43] In terms of performance over time, there is as yet little reason to believe that Vietnam has done better than either its neighbors or some other populous and poor Asian societies.

Vietnam, it is true, has attempted to raise health standards against a background of continuing war, while its neighbors have had long stretches of military calm and domestic stability in which to do their work. In the modern world, however, life expectancies have typically risen rapidly in societies that were at war, so long as civil order was maintained. Moreover, it is not clear that North Vietnam's more or less continuous engagements in military hostilities are unrelated to the inclinations of the nation's leadership.

China is not easily compared with other countries. Two comparisons which suggest themselves, however, are with Taiwan, whose government also claims authority to guide the destiny of the Chinese people, and India, the world's second most populous country. China's demographic accounts are incomplete—as late as the mid-1970s only a third of the nation's infant deaths may have been registered[44]—and adjustments must flesh out the gaps.

Life expectancy in China today appears to be significantly lower than in Taiwan, and would also seem to be much lower than in Singapore, Hong Kong, Peninsular Malaya, and other regions for which we have data on the health of overseas Chinese.[45] On the other hand, Taiwan and these other regions had enjoyed civil order for many decades, and had experienced the efforts of colonial powers to promote local material advance. They began the 1950s with lifespans in the mid-to-upper fifties—not far short of Japan's at the time. China's life expectancy was then probably almost twenty years lower. It is not reasonable to equate health problems that faced these two regimes.

Comparisons against India are not much more satisfactory. There seems to be little doubt that lives are longer today in China than in India. But this does not mean that China's record in health is self-evidently superior to India's. Three things must be remembered. First, both China and India are enormous countries characterized by sharp regional differences— which national averages conceal. Liaoning province, with its Manchurian heritage and its comparatively developed industrial base, might look very good next to India's impoverished Gangeatic state of Bihar, but it is not clear that Tibet or Anhui would come off quite so well against Kerala or the Punjab. Second, despite the turmoil and bloodshed of partition, India's transfer of power in the 1940s was comparatively orderly; by contrast, China had suffered two decades of disruption of civic life, climaxed by a devastating foreign invasion and an even more destructive civil war. Life expectancy in China in the late 1940s was unnaturally low; *any* government which could bring peace and civil order might expect to reduce the nation's mortality level substantially, regardless of its other policies. Finally, China's record looks very different for different decades. Whatever else may be said about independent India's policies, they have never led to a dramatic decline in the nation's health. This is not true in China. In the wake of the "Great Leap Forward" campaign of the late 1950s, China is believed to have experienced the worst famine of the twentieth century. The loss of life during these years will never be known precisely, but recent estimates of "excess mortality" for the period center around twenty to thirty million people.[46] China's life expectancy may have fallen into the twenties by 1960. If the poor in China have gained the most when life expectancy has been rising, they also surely suffered when it was falling. (See Chapter 7 for a more detailed examination of this phenomenon.)

In short, the record of Marxist–Leninist regimes in reducing mortality does not seem to be demonstrably superior that of non-communist governments in the less developed regions. If the Communist societies of the Warsaw pact offer the poorer Marxist–Leninist states any glimpse of the future, moreover, their prospects for health performance would not necessarily seem to improve with time. The U.S. Census Bureau believes that life expectancy in the Soviet Union may have fallen by over three years since 1964;[47] life expectancy was lower in Czechoslovakia in 1977 than in 1960, and seems to have fallen in Poland, Bulgaria and Hungary from the late 1960s through at least the late 1970s.[48] (See Chapter 10 for more information.)

We have looked at population levels and at mortality. One other type of demographic datum can inform us about living standards: this is fertility. The relationship between fertility and poverty, however, is complex. Low death rates may be desired universally, but there is no corresponding consensus about appropriate levels of directions for birth rates. Birth rates can fall with the onset of economic development or with the onset of famine; they can rise because of changes in tastes, changes in health, or changes in economic conditions. Patterns of fertility and family formation in the less developed regions are diverse. The difference between population policies in communist and non-communist nations in the less developed regions, however, are distinct, and bear directly on patterns of poverty.

In non-communist societies, experiments in "population control"—that is, in pressuring parents to have less, or more, children than they would choose of their own free will—have been brief anomalies, overwhelmingly rejected by the public.[49] In the poor world's Marxist–Leninist societies, however, "population control" policies have more frequently been undertaken in the name of the public good. These interventions have not necessarily improved either health or long term prospects for reducing poverty.

In the People's Republic of China, intense efforts have been directed at pushing birth rates down since the early 1970s. In recent years, the government has promoted the "norm" of the one-child family, and has used not only positive incentives, but financial penalities, intimidation, and, according to widespread reports, at least some coercion in its attempt to make parents accede to it.[50] According to the Chinese press, one of the immediate results of this campaign has been a rise in infanticide. Chinese parents are still said to prefer boys over girls; the "one-child norm" has made this preference a deadly matter.[51] There is some concern that the "one-child norm" also imperils the health of grown women, for women who wish to violate the state's population quotas must also avoid the services of the health care authorities.[52] To the extent that China's "population control" policies are effective, they expose many to unnecessary risk of poverty in the future. Social security arrangements in China are still largely provisional; for most Chinese the family may well remain the most reliable source of support in times of hardship or danger.[53] The Chinese government has a far from perfect record in disaster management; indeed, the government itself has been an agent of disaster on more than one occasion in the past generation. To press families to have fewer children than parents deem desirable is, among other things, to attempt to override their efforts at insuring their own futures.

Nutrition

Hunger may be acutely felt by the individual, but it is imperfectly measured by statisticians. The conventional tool for judging a nation's nutritional well-being is the "food balance sheet," which estimates average per capita availabilities. Even if such numbers could be computed accurately—and these are least accurate in precisely the societies where undernutrition is most severe—they would tell us less than we would like to know. An average tells us nothing about distribution. And even if we had precise information on the caloric intake of the poor we would still know less than we should want to, for levels of food consumption by themselves tell us nothing about individual needs, which vary not only between people, but even for the same person at different points in any given year.[54]

Despite the formidable difficulties in quantifying malnutrition, we can get some basic sense of trends in serious undernutrition over the past generation in communist and non-communist countries. In a poor country the best measure of the nutritional status of a population is its health. Table 11.6 has already presented information on changes in life expectancies for many less developed countries; in a broad sense, the revolution in life chances that it outlines can be seen as a revolution in nutritional well-being as well.

Another indicator of progress against serious hunger is the death rate of children of the ages 1 to 4. Children are especially vulnerable to nutritional setback, since they need more energy and protein for their weight than do adults, and suffer more for being denied. Death rates for the 1 to 4 year olds are thought to reflect serious hunger more accurately than infant mortality rates because children who survive their first year of life typically develop resistances to many of the specific environmental hazards which can make infant mortality rates vary between settings for equally well fed children.

For those nations with reliable data, reductions have been consequential. In Mexico, the Philippines, and Thailand, child death rates are approaching the range (2–3 per thousand) at which hunger no longer makes its measureable impact through mortality. While their child death rates remain high, India's and Indonesia's nevertheless appear to have dropped by more than half since the 1950s.[55]

If child death rates prove to be a reasonable measure of serious undernutrition, it would seem that this is an especially pressing problem in black Africa and the Muslim community that extends from North Africa through Bangladesh. In Kenya—one of the few countries below the Sahara with even one good census—child death rates are estimated to be as high as India's; over most of the rest of the continent they must be considerably higher.[56] India's child death rates also appear to be lower than those in Algeria, Egypt, or Turkey;[57] whatever the reason may be, children in those countries (and, presumably, in other Muslim countries which cannot supply data) do not seem to be as well fed as one might have expected.

There is little reliable information on child death rates for poor communist countries. Cuba offers the most, and it is inconsistent. The Ministry of Health currently claims that Cuba's child death rate in the late 1970s was 1.1 per thousand—about the same as for the United States in the early 1960s. But it also states that child mortality has dropped by 61 percent since 1960. That would place Cuba's child death rate at under 3 per thousand in 1960—a rate low enough to imply that the prerevolutionary order, rather than the Castro government, should be credited with eliminating serious undernutrition in Cuba! Better figures come from Cuba's "life tables;" these suggest that child death rates were in the range of 8–9 per thousand in the early 1950s, and around 2–3 thousand in the 1970s. This would represent meaningful nutritional progress and would indicate that serious hunger no longer troubles Cuba. Yet by these numbers Cuba's performance over the past two decades would not seem to be so different from Jamaica's or Costa Rica's, and would seem to be rather less rapid than Chile's. Whatever else one may say about Cuba's social and economic policies, they do not appear to have given Cuba a special edge over its neighbors in such measured progress against undernutrition.

China's child death rate in 1980 was placed at about 8–9 per thousand by one World Bank estimate.[58] If accurate, this would be considerably lower than India's. On the other hand, it would be much higher than Taiwan's, Singapore's, or any of the other predominantly Chinese territories in East Asia. To judge by World Bank estimates, China's child death rate would seem to be close to Brazil's, and if the comparison with Brazil is meaningful, one would expect that a stratum of Chinese society, and perhaps a number of backward regions, are vulnerable to the risk of deadly hunger. News reports from China would seem consistent with such an interpretation. Since the mid-1970s, for example, at least one province a year was reported in the Chinese press to be beset by "food shortage." A document prepared for the 1979 Plenum of the Chinese Communist Party, moreover, is reported to have asserted that 100 million Chinese had "too little to eat"[59] (although there was no public explanation of precisely what this was to mean, or how it was determined). (See Chapters 6 and 7.)

There are as yet no reliable estimates for child death rates in Vietnam: the World Bank offers one, but it does so by assigning Vietnam a life expectancy, and then estimating the child death rate which would be associated with that in a "normal" population. One indirect indication of the nutritional situation in contemporary Vietnam comes from a World Bank mission from 1979, which reported that by a number of measures, including grain and cooking oil availability, Vietnam in the late 1970s appeared to have a level of per capita consumption roughly between India's and Bangladesh's.

There are no available data on child death rates for North Korea. In South Korea, child death rates, which were estimated to be higher in the 1950s than India's are today, had been reduced sufficiently by the late 1970s to suggest that serious undernutrition was no longer a pervasive phenomenon.

Marxist–Leninist governments have attempted to attack hunger by a variety of means: social revolution, rationing, enforcement of an economic mechanism whereby food and other goods are priced by their "social value" rather than in response to scarcity. If Marxist–Leninist strategies for alleviating hunger, for all their distinctiveness, have not distinguished themselves as notably more effective than those of a diverse array of non-communist nations, it may be because the Marxist–Leninist approach has intrinsic limitations.

Some of these are not hard to identify. Whatever successes Marxist–Leninist governments have achieved in distributing food evenly among their people, they have typically found food difficult to produce. Collectivization and socialist pricing policies, among other things, seem generally to have lowered the efficiency of farm production, and seem to have actually lowered per capita food output in some cases. In China, available statistics suggest that per capita grain availability was no higher in the late 1970s than it had been in the early 1930s.[60] Per capita production of most foodstuffs appears to be lower in Cuba in the late 1970s than in 1960, and despite the Cuban economy's continuing dependence on sugar, official statistics indicate that per capita production of that commodity has been falling as well.[61] In Vietnam, to judge by its spotty numbers on population and agriculture, per capita rice production may have fallen by as much as 40 percent between the mid-1930s and the late 1970s.[62]

While Marxist–Leninist regimes have put stock in the ability of politically directed flows of food to reach the poor, they have typically neglected the marketing transportation and distribution systems which work of their own to alleviate nutritional disaster, or to prevent it from striking in the first place. In the non-communist countries, the decline of famine in the modern era has been facilitated by an increase in food output per person in the aggregate, but it owes still more to the growing effectiveness of domestic and international markets in moving food quickly and without interruptions into regions where it is needed. By contrast, communist states have placed radical limits on the functions that markets may serve in their societies; very often they have let their marketing systems fall into disrepair. In communist China, where government directives have extolled regional "foodgrain self-sufficiency" and promoted rationing at the local level, the end-use interprovince trade in foodgrains had declined by 1978 to a few hundred thousand tons a year—about a tenth of a percent of the nation's recorded grain output, and quite possibly less in absolute terms than had been traded between provinces two centuries earlier for a far smaller population.[63] As a practical matter, such a meager traffic in grain would make it impossible for *any* of China's provinces to draw significantly on external resources during ordinary harvest fluctuations, or even during periods of crop failure. Debilitation of markets meant, among other things, that poor regions were left to their own devices during times of trouble, cut off from outside assistance by an unbreachable gap in physical infrastructure. (See Chapter 6.)

Finally, there is great risk under communism that government itself will create hunger. Far-reaching and unrestricted state power and low average food availability is a combination which increases the potentiality of both periodic and systemic nutritional distress.

In the post–revolutionary order, specific strata may be made hungry for the sake of principle. The classes expropriated by Communist revolution can deliberately be turned into a band of hereditary distitutes, since it is within the powers of government to deny them work, rationed food, and other social guarantees. In the wake of North Vietnam's collectivization in the late 1950s, for example, one government survey indicated that former landlords were more likely to have "too little to eat" than any other rural group.[64]

The Marxist–Leninist approach to food policy has produced not only planned nutritional insults, but also of inadvertent ones. In China, as noted above, the political campaign in the late 1950s known as the "Great Leap Forward" seems to have resulted the virtual collapse of the economy and the breakdown of the national food system. Western demographers have recently suggested that "excess mortality" may have claimed tens of millions of people in the "Three Lean Years" that followed.[65] A greater fraction of the local populace may currently suffer in India than China from hunger-related disease but over the past generation vastly more have probably perished from *famine* in the People's Republic of China than in the Republic of India. Despite their higher current levels of health, a greater fraction of the Chinese than the Indian adult population may have suffered from serious shortages of food at some point in their lives.

Literacy

Exceptional individuals can raise themselves from poverty without learning to read or write, but for a society as a whole, the escape from material poverty is impossible when illiteracy is widespread. The spread of technical skills and the improvements in administration which are vital to material progress depend heavily upon the ability to communicate by the written word.

For all its importance to modern life, literacy is not as easily measured as might first be presumed. In some surveys, everyone who has not been to school is counted as illiterate, even though people in poor societies do learn to read and write outside the classroom. Other surveys simply ask the respondent whether he or she is literate; when illiteracy confers stigma, such questions do not lend themselves to honest answers. There are other, more fundamental problems which frustrate the measurement of literacy. Criteria for literacy may differ dramatically from one nation, region, or profession to the next, in accordance with the technical requirements of daily life. Within a few decades the quality of literacy in a society can change tremendously; such changes are seldom captured by measures of literacy, much less analyzed in detail.[66]

Sample surveys and censuses in the less developed countries use different definitions for illiteracy; nevertheless, as Table 11.8 indicates, they suggest that illiteracy rates have diminished markedly among adults in many parts of the poor world. As a practical matter, the reduction of illiteracy means teaching new generations basic skills, and creating incentives and pressures for unlettered adults to adopt a literate lifestyle. Thus, the eradication of illiteracy is necessarily an historical process.

More than any other philosophy of government, Marxism–Leninism has placed a premium upon eradicating illiteracy. Every Marxist–Leninist party that has come to power has set mass literacy as an immediate goal, and has devoted considerable effort to achieving the end. Have Marxist–Leninist regimes in the poor world been especially successful in reducing illiteracy?

Communist regimes in poor nations have not only launched ambitious anti-illiteracy drives, but have made bold claims of their results. Hanoi announced that it "basically" eliminated illiteracy in the North in 1958— four years after Dienbienphu. Castro celebrated the end of illiteracy in Cuba in 1962, at the finish of a schooling campaign that lasted only a year. North Korea claims to have totally eliminated illiteracy in the course of a few months in 1947 and 1948.

These claims are extreme, and cannot be taken seriously. The elimination of illiteracy is, as mentioned, an historical process; there are limits to the extent that the process can be accelerated. Adult illiterates, accustomed as they are to a life in which the written word plays no role, are not easily trained to read and write; when they do manage to pick up basic skills under intense drilling, they typically prove unable to retain them unless they have constant reinforcement. In the rural areas of poor nations and in the daily routines of low-productivity work, such reinforcement is hard to provide.

For the most part, a government's hopes of reducing illiteracy rest on educating the young. For communist and non-communist countries, these efforts are described by gross primary school enrollment ratios, which are presented in Table 11.9 These figures must be interpreted with care: enrollment ratios can be no more accurate than the population estimates

TABLE 11.8
Estimated Rates Of Illiteracy for Communist and Non-Communist LDCs, c. 1950–c. 1980 (percentage of population over 15)

	1950	1960	1970	1980
1. Cuba	22 (1953)	(21) (1959)	13	(10) (1979)
2. Jamaica	23 (1953)	18	4	(10)
3. Costa Rica	21	16 (1963)	12 (1973)	(10) (1978)
4. Chile	20 (1952)	16	11	(6) (1979)
5. Mexico	43	35	26	17
6. Brazil	51	40	34	25
7. China	(70–80)	(55–60)		34 (1979)
8. India	81 (1951)	76 (1961)	66 (1971)	64 (1981)
9. Taiwan	42 (1952)	27	15	10
10. Vietnam	(80 + ?)			(30 + ?)
11. Indonesia	(80 + ?)	61	43	28
12. Sri Lanka	32 (1953)	15 (1963)	22 (1971)	16 (1981)
13. Thailand	48 (1947)	32	21	(12)
14. Philippines	40 (1948)	25	17	(10)
15. North Korea	(50?)			
16. South Korea	(50?)	29	12	(6)

Note: Bold figures come from Census or sample survey results; parenthetical figures have undergone census—or survey—based adjustments; parenthetical figures with question marks are tentative estimates based on limited or partial census or survey results.

Sources:

Line 1: Columns 1–3: Carmelo Mesa-Lago, *The Economy of Socialist Cuba* (Albuquerque: University of New Mexico Press, 1981).
  Column 4: Calculated on the basis of UNESCO, *Statistical Yearbook 1982* (Paris: UNESCO, 1982).

Line 2: Columns 1–4: UNESCO, *Statistical Yearbook,* various issues

Line 3: Columns 1,3: UNESCO, *Statistical Yearbook 1976* (Paris: UNESCO, 1977)
  Column 4: Intra-American Development Bank, *Economic and Social Progress in Latin America* (Washington: Intra-American Development Bank, 1981).

Line 4: Columns 1–3: UNESCO, *Statistical Yearbook 1976*
  Column 4: *Economic and Social Progress in Latin America,* loc. cit

Line 5: Columns 1–4: UNESCO, *Statistical Yearbook,* various issues.

Line 6: Column 1,3,4: UNESCO, *Statistical Yearbook 1982*
  Column 2: *Brazil Series Estatisticas Retrospectives* (Rio de Janeiro: IBGE, 1977).

Line 7: Column 1: Estimate based upon Herbert Day Lawson, *Social Pathology In China* (Taipei: Ch'eng Wen Publishing Co., 1974).

	Column 2:	Estimate based upon World Bank, *China: Socialist Economic Development* (Washington: World Bank, 1981)
	Column 4:	UNESCO, *Statistical Yearbook 1982.*
Line 8:	Columns 1–3:	UNESCO, *Statistical Yearbook,* various issues
	Column 4:	U.S. Bureau of the Census, *World Population: 1983* (Washington: Department of Commerce, 1983).
Line 9:	Columns 1–4:	*Social Welfare Indicators Republic of China 1982* (Taipei: Executive Year, October, 1982).
Line 10:	Column 1,4:	Estimated figures refer to population age six and older based upon UNESCO, *Statistical Yearbook 1965* (Paris: UNESCO, 1965) and *UNESCO Literacy In Asia: A Continuing Challenge* (Bangladesh: UNESCO, 1978).
Line 11:	Column 1:	Estimate based on data in UNESCO, *Literacy in Asia: A Concluding Challenge.*
	Columns 2,3:	UNESCO, *Statistical Yearbook,* various issues.
	Column 4:	U.S. Bureau of the Census, *World Population: 1983.*
Line 12:	Columns 1–3:	UNESCO, *Statistical Yearbook,* various issues.
	Column 4:	U.S. Bureau of the Census, *World Population: 1983.*
Line 13:	Columns 1–3:	UNESCO, *Statistical Yearbook 1982*
	Column 4:	Estimated through cohort projection based on 1970 census data, and on primary school enrollment ratios, both taken from *Statistical Yearbook 1982.*
Line 14:	Columns 1–3:	UNESCO, *Statistical Yearbook 1982*
	Column 4:	National Census and Statistics Office, "Projections of the Illiterate by Sex and Broad Age Group in the Philippines: 1970–2000," *Philippines Journal of Statistics,* V. 28, #2, 1977.
Line 15:	Column 1:	Based on Jon Halliday, "The North Korean Model: Gaps And Problems," *World Development* Sept./Oct. 1981.
Line 16:	Column 1:	Based on Paul Kuznets, *Economic Development and Structural Change in Korea* (New Haven: Yale University Press, 1977).
	Columns 2,3:	UNESCO, *Statistical Yearbook 1976*
	Column 4:	Calculated from cohort projections from 1970 census and primary enrollment ratios, in UNESCO, *Statistical Yearbook, 1982.*

that underlie them; older people as well as children may be in school when illiteracy is declining; and the varying quality of education among nations means that similar rates of gross enrollment may hide differences in dropout rates, grade repetition, and skill retention.

Cuba's record on illiteracy is easiest to measure. The Communist Party of Cuba now claims that 44 percent of Cuba's adults were illiterate before the revolution.[67] Censuses from the early 1950s, however, recorded the

TABLE 11.9

Estimated Gross Primary School Enrollment Ratios for Communist and Non-Communist LDCs, c. 1950–c. 1980 (students enrolled as a percent of children of primary school age)

	1950	1960	1970	1980
1. Cuba	74	109	121	112 (1979)
2. Jamaica	110	92	119	99 (1979)
3. Costa Rica	78	96	110	107
4. Chile	93	109	107	117
5. Mexico	62	80	104	120
6. Brazil	68	72	84 (1971)	93 (1979)
7. China	21	58 (1958)	85	121
8. India	28	61	73	76
9. Taiwan	84	96	98	99
10. Vietnam	(12)	(46)	(110)	116
11. Indonesia	45	71	77	112
12. Sri Lanka	89	95	99	100
13. Thailand	76	83	83	96
14. Philippines	91	95	114	110
15. North Korea	(near 100?)			116 (1976)
16. South Korea	83	94	103	109

Notes: Figures for Taiwan refer to *net* primary enrollment: parenthetical figures for Vietnam refer to gross primary school enrollment rates for Republic of Vietnam (South Vietnam).

Sources:

Line 1–8:   UNESCO, *Statistical Yearbook 1982* (Paris: UNESCO, 1982) and earlier years.

Line 9:   *Taiwan Statistical Data Book 1982* (Taipei: Executive Yuan, 1982).

Lines 10–14: UNESCO, *Statistical Yearbook, 1982*, loc. cit, and earlier years.

Line 15:   Column 1: Robert Scalapino and Chong-sik Lee, *Communism In Korea* (Berkeley: University of California Press, 1973).
              Column 4: UNESCO, *Statistical Yearbook 1982*, loc. cit.

Line 16:   UNESCO, *Statistical Yearbook 1982*, loc. cit. and earlier issues.

figure as close to 23 percent. Today a wide range of institutions, including the World Bank and the CIA, put Cuba's current rate of illiteracy at 5 percent. These guesses are not based on a close reading of Cuban educational statistics. In the late 1970s, Cuba's Ministry of Education released a census which put the rate of illiteracy *for adults between 15 and 45* at 5 percent. Older people, schooled before the revolution, must have higher rates, and they comprise more than a fifth of the adult population. Cuba's actual rate of illiteracy in the late 1970s or early 1980s may therefore be closer to something like 10 percent. If it were, Cuba's progress against illiteracy would appear to be no more rapid than Costa Rica's, Chile's or Jamaica's. Intriguing inconsistencies in Cuba's educational accounts, moreover, raise the question of whether it has done even that well. In 1977, for example, Cuban officials remarked to a *New York Times* correspondent that the actual rate of rural illiteracy in Cuba was 22 percent.[68] Before recent revisions, UNESCO data indicated that Cuba did not achieve universal enrollment from children of primary school age until 1975; figures from the early 1970s suggested that in both its rates of dropouts and its distribution of students among grades, Cuba's enrollment patterns more nearly resembled Guatemala's than that of more advanced Latin American societies. (See also Chapter 9.)

For China the record is less certain. According to the State Statistical Bureau, China's gross primary enrollment ratio was about 20 percent in the early 1950s; in 1980 it was said to be over 120 percent, a level high enough to be consistent with near-universal education for grade school age children. In the intervening years, however, the expansion of educational opportunity was not steady: it was disrupted not only in the aftermath of the "Great Leap Forward," but also in the ten years of "Cultural Revolution" in the decade before Mao's death. There can be no sure figure for the extent of illiteracy today, but China's Ministry of Education has reported to UNESCO that there were about 220 million illiterates on the Mainland in 1979—by their reckoning, about a third of the adult population.[70] Yet even this figure, which is considerably higher than others that the People's Republic has to date chosen to release, may put the best face on the current illiteracy problem. If Soviet sources are to be believed, over 40 percent of the recruits in the People's Liberation Army could not read or write in the late 1970s.[71] In China, as in other poor societies, the army is an elite and overwhelmingly male institution; its literacy standards would likely be higher than those for the country as a whole.

If we can judge by the limited surveys and censuses of earlier decades, China's incidence of illiteracy may have been on the order of five-sixths of the adult population at the turn of the century, and may have been on the order of 70 or 80 percent in the 1930s.[72] Communist China would seem by such numbers to have made substantial strides in reducing illiteracy, but its record of performance would depend largely on what it was compared against. China's results look impressive next to India's. Held up to China, India cannot take refuge in its geographical diversity or its immense size to explain its seemingly slow progress in reducing illiteracy. But China does not appear to come off so well against Indonesia, another populous and geographically diverse Asian nation. The Mainland also seems to suffer in comparisons with Taiwan. Of course, comparisons, however, are complicated by historical questions. In Indonesia, the Dutch colonial educational policy, accused by its critics of keeping education from the natives, may have created a political commitment to schooling on the part of nationalist leaders, and a social hunger for it on the part of the populace, which would not otherwise have existed. Taiwan, for its part, was a Japanese colony for the first half of the century, and Japanese policy put great effort into teaching the Taiwanese to read and write. Taiwan might more properly be judged against a single advanced province in the People's Republic where Japanese colonialists had also built schools, such as Kirin (Jilin) or Liaoning in Manchuria; as of yet, such data are unavailable. (Such data have subsequently become available. See Chapter 7.)

Although North Vietnam claimed to have "basically eliminated" illiteracy by 1958, it released figures to UNESCO indicating that 35 percent of its adults were illiterate in 1960. That estimate may have been too generous: it apparently counted as literate everyone who had participated in a literacy campaign, and, according to independent reports such campaigns sometimes scarcely taught peasants to do more than recognize a few slogans.[73] Gross primary school enrollment ratios are high in "unified" Vietnam; complete enrollment of school age children may be in the offing. Near-universal literacy, however, would appear to be a remote goal. According to Vietnamese officials, about a third of South Vietnam's adults were illiterates at the time of the Liberation; enrollment ratios from the 1960s suggest more people were going to school in the South than the North.[74] It seems unlikely that Vietnam's record in eradicating illiteracy has been superior to Indonesia's, against whom its efforts might perhaps best be compared, although we would need more hard data to make a firm conclusion on this score.

Japanese colonialists also built schools in Korea; there, however, they eventually insisted that instruction in these schools be in Japanese. As elsewhere in the world, the marriage of nationalism to the cause of "own language literacy" seems to have produced a tremendous impetus for literacy in Korea, and the governments of both North and South Korea seem to have gone far towards satisfying it. Illiteracy may have been somewhat higher in the South, which was somewhat more rural, than in the North, which contained most of the peninsula's heavy industry, before partition. There are no available data on illiteracy for North Korea at this date, but for what it is worth, gross primary school enrollment ratios were recorded as slightly lower in North Korea than in South Korea in the mid 1970s.

In sum, available information does not suggest communist states in the poor world have been dramatically or consistently more successful than non-communist states in reducing illiteracy. Their failure to achieve such a distinction may speak to the nature of illiteracy itself. To eliminate illiteracy, there must be both a supply of education and a demand for it. If Communist states have pushed harder than others to provide a supply, one may wonder whether they have been as successful as less ambitious forms of government in creating an environment in which people themselves are motivated to seek and retain basic educational skills.

Status of Women

Important as it may be to the assessment of material poverty, the status of women is not easily measured in numbers. In the developed Western nations, where data on women come in relative abundance, it has proven surprisingly difficult to "quantify" the position of women in society: differentials between men and women in employment and earnings, for example, are not as readily explained as one might first suppose. In poor countries, where less reliable information is available, the problem is considerably greater. Obvious degradations of women often do not make their way into statistics. It is reported, for example, that women are bought and sold as slaves in Mauritania;[75] yet it is impossible to find hard data about this in any international compendium. While we can only begin to assess the special burdens on women in poor countries, telling hints can be taken from numbers on health, literacy, and education.

In every developed nation, women can expect to live significantly longer than men. In some poor societies, however, the treatment of women of all ages is so harsh that women's lifespans are shorter than men's.

In the non-communist world, there is a regional specificity to the societies in which women perish before men. As best can be measured, the terrain marks out a crescent on the globe, encompassing territories from Casablanca to Dacca, and sweeping into Africa. Most of these are Muslim societies: postwar censuses and surveys have indicated that men live longer than women in Morocco, Jordan, Iran, Pakistan, and Bangladesh.[76] But Islam is not the only way of life associated with high mortality differentials for women. Sri Lanka, which is predominately Buddhist, had lower life expectancy at birth for women than men until the early 1960s, as did South Africa's Indian community (which is composed of Hindus as well as Muslims); and in India the gap between male and female life expectancies appears actually to have widened since Independence.[77] While very little good data can be found on life expectancy in Africa, there are indications that women may die earlier than men in several sub–Saharan societies.[78]

Differences recorded between rates for women and men for several nations can be seen in Table 11.10 In non-communist Latin America and East Asia, the gap between women and men appears to be small, or getting smaller. By contrast, a serious gap seems to have persisted over several decades in India, and may well have widened. Limited data suggests that the illiteracy gap is unusually wide in some of the other countries in the "crescent" mentioned above; it may actually be widening in some of the nations in that region.

Differences in the incidence of illiteracy in a society depend among other factors, on schooling. Table 11.11 shows recorded differences over the postwar period for male and female gross primary school enrollment ratios. The patterns are broadly consistent with differences in illiteracy rates: differences appear to be small or diminishing in non-communist Latin America and East Asia, while they are substantial and have widened in India. Limited data suggests that the enrollment differential is high in many of the other countries in the non-communist "crescent," and may have widened in some of them.[79]

Do women appear to be less disadvantaged in poor societies guided by Marxist–Leninist directorates? Hard data from these countries are limited, but they can help us answer the question.

TABLE 11.10
Estimated Difference between Female and Male Illiteracy Rates for Communist and Non-Communist LDCs, c. 1950–c. 1980 (percentage of population over 15)

	1950	1960	1970	1980
1. Cuba	−4 (1953)			(1) (1979)
2. Jamaica	−6 (1953)	−6	−1	
3. Costa Rica	2	1	0	
4. Chile	3 (1952)	3 (1963)	2 (1973)	(1) (1979)
5. Mexico	7	10	8	4
6. Brazil	11	8	6	2
7. China				
8. India	21 (1951)	28 (1961)	29 (1971)	30 (1981)
9. Taiwan	28 (1952)	21	21	13
10. Vietnam				
11. Indonesia	(under 40?)	27	25	17
12. Sri Lanka	28 (1953)	18 (1963)	14 (1971)	8 (1981)
13. Thailand	33 (1947)	23	16	(12)
14. Philippines	8 (1948)	5	3	(2)
15. North Korea				
16. South Korea	(about 40?)	25	13	(7)

Sources: Calculated from sources in Table 11.8.

TABLE 11.11

Difference between Female and Male Gross Primary School Enrollment Ratios for Communist and Non-Communist LDCs, c. 1950–c. 1980

	1950	1960	1970	1980
1. Cuba	−4	0	0	7
2. Jamaica	−6	−1	0	−2
3. Costa Rica		2	2	1
4. Chile	8	4	−1	2
5. Brazil	0	1	0	0
6. Mexico		5	5	7
7. China				22
8. India	5	1	0	0
9. Taiwan	28	40	34	39
10. Vietnam			16 (1975)	15 (1979)
11. Indonesia		28	10	15
12. Sri Lanka		10	10	6
13. Thailand	8	9	8	5
14. Philippines	6	5	2	3
15. North Korea				4
16. South Korea		10	1	2

Sources: Calculated from sources in Table 11.9.

The overwhelming majority of women in Communist societies live in the People's Republic of China. According to its 1953 census, Mainland China had sixteen and a half million more men and women. (The 1982 count also found more men than women in each of the three provinces for which it released preliminary results.) Under Liberation, China's ratio of men to women appears to have risen; this fact, taken together with the striking "excess" of men at younger ages, suggests that life expectancy for women in communist China may not have been consistently lower for women than for men. Recently released Chinese data do not allay suspicion: they show reconstructed death rates for women to be significantly higher than for men in 1957. More recently, some estimates have suggested that female life expectancy has actually fallen in the early 1980s.[80]

There are as yet no comprehensive data on differences in illiteracy rates between men and women in revolutionary China. Figures can be found, however, on differences in primary school enrollment rates (Table 11.12). In 1980, the recorded gap was higher than for any other nation in East Asia; the difference, in fact, appeared to be only somewhat lower than in India. China's gap in enrollments suggests not only that opportunities for education are still accorded first to boys, but that a sizeable discrepancy

TABLE 11.12
Indications of Intergenerational Mobility In Brazil, India and Bangladesh

Brazil

Father's Status	Individual's Status in 1973						Total
	1	2	3	4	5	6	100%
1. upper	29.8	22.5	27.1	12.5	5.0	3.1	100%
2. upper-middle	15.2	28.7	28.7	15.5	6.1	5.8	100%
3. middle-middle	8.6	14.3	36.2	18.9	10.5	11.5	100%
4. lower-middle	3.8	8.7	21.6	46.3	14.9	4.7	100%
5. upper-lower	3.2	7.4	20.7	35.4	23.8	9.5	100%
6. lower-lower	1.0	2.5	13.1	21.1	17.4	44.9	100%
Total	3.5%	6.3%	18.4%	23.8%	16.0%	32.0%	100%

(sample size: 44,307)

Bangladesh (Char Gopalpur)

Inheritance	Present Landholdings				
	Landless	Small	Medium	Large	
Landless	13	7	2	1	23
Small	11	17	1	2	31
Medium	6	3	14	8	31
Large	3	2	3	21	29
	33	29	20	32	114

India (pooled sample, 3 villages)

Inheritance	Present Holdings				
	Landless	Small	Medium	Large	
Landless	17	9	11	2	39
Small	2	20	4	1	27
Medium	0	0	23	4	27
Large	0	0	5	21	26
	19	29	43	28	119

Sources: Brazil: Jose Pastore, *Inequality and Social Mobility in Brazil* (Madison: University of Wisconsin Press, 1981). Bangladesh and India: Mead Cain, "Risk and Insurance: Perspectives on Fertility and Inequality in Rural India and Bangladesh," (Population Council, Center for Policy Studies, Working Paper #67, April 1981).

in the incidence of illiteracy may be found on the Mainland today. (See also Chapter 7.)

In all, on the basis of available information, it is not impossible that China may be the world's second great "crescent" of comparative disadvantage for women. To the extent that communist programs have actually transformed society on the Mainland, the special disadvantages of women in modern China may have been created by its government.

Neither Vietnam nor North Korea have published data on male and female death rates, or on differentials in illiteracy. Both, however, give data on differentials in primary school enrollment ratios (Table 11.12). After China's, Vietnam's appears to be the highest in East Asia. North Korea's appears to be comparatively low, but higher than South Korea's.

In its 1974 life table, lifespans in Cuba were about three years longer for women than men. In Jamaica, Costa Rica, and Chile, the difference is similar (four to six years). Differences in male and female literacy rates and enrollment ratios are likewise not dramatic. If Cuban women enjoy a more privileged status than their Caribbean and Latin American neighbors, it is not revealed through such numbers.

It is true that Marxist–Leninist regimes presiding over poor societies have typically taken action that would alter the status of women in the societies they were to transform. Upon consolidating power, for example, all communist regimes have all enacted laws prohibiting forced marriage and bride price, establishing minimum ages for marriage, and legalizing divorce, in their early days of power. It is also true that they have characteristically made efforts to expand educational opportunities for women, and to increase the participate of women in the process of "socialist construction."

But improving the status of women has never been a goal in and of itself for these regimes. It has always been explicitly pursued as a means to an end: a way of augmenting "socialist" power, or stimulating "socialist construction." The Marxist–Leninist view of the "women's issue" has proved to be extremely flexible. Women may have been exhorted to take up "men's work" in North Vietnam during the height of the manpower shortage in the war against the South, but with "unification" they were just as vocally encouraged to return to their more traditional occupations: raising crops and children.[81] In North Korea, Kim Il-sung has pointedly emphasized that the "women's issue" is a technical—not a social— question:[82] this would seem to imply that the status of women will be tailored to suit the needs of the economy.

For better or worse, "planned socialist development" has a tendency to demand more of women than of men. Women are potential producers not only of goods, but of the work force of the future. For this reason, they necessarily figure more prominently in the most comprehensive programs to shape the emerging "socialist" society. If socialist planners take an active interest in guiding society's birth rate, they must intervene in the condition of women. Such interventions are not guaranteed to improve the health of women. They are not intended to. State policies in Marxist–Leninist societies are justified by a vision of long range social good, rather than by consideration of their specific and direct impact on actual individuals.

Socio-Economic Inequality

In poor societies, the issue of inequality may seem particularly pressing. There is, however, no single satisfactory standard for measuring "inequality": human beings and human lives differ in too many ways to expect such a thing. The most commonly used measure of "inequality" is income distribution. As a tool for describing even economic "inequality," it is at best of limited use. Few affluent societies, to say nothing of poorer ones, can measure their people's incomes with enough accuracy to permit comparisons of distribution among countries or over time. This technical detail aside, there remain real questions about what an income distribution is actually measuring, or should measure. The unit of measurement can affect the assessment: households with comparatively high aggregate incomes may be composed of poor people, and comparatively well-off single wage-earners can be ranked on paper as "poorer" than families with slightly more income but many more mouths.[83] "Snapshots" of income differences at any given point in time can take no account of the extent to which seeming "inequalities" in fact reflect the transiencies of the business cycle, the shape of a society's age pyramid, or differences in "lifetime" earning strategies (such as going to school or into debt early in life in the hope of making more money later on).[84] And income distribution figures place no premium on preserving human life: if more poor people survive, income distribution may indicate that society is becoming more "unequal"; if their chances of survival diminish, income distribution can appear to "improve."

There are other ways of thinking about inequalities. One is to consider the gap that separates the desperately poor from those who enjoy a modest but secure existence. The differences between those who can expect to live long lives and those who can expect early death, between those who have steady and adequate supplies of food and those whose lives revolve around the threat of starvation, between those who can read and write and those who cannot avail themselves of the protections that come with literacy, and between men and women in those societies where to be born female is to be promised disproportionate physical hardship, are tremendous—so great, in fact, that they cannot be conveyed by conventional economic calculations and rankings.

As we have seen, the gap in life expectancy between Western countries and those poor non-communist countries for which we could obtain data has narrowed substantially since the end of World War II. The measured incidence of illiteracy in non-communist countries has fallen markedly over the past three decades. In non-communist Latin America and East Asia, women live longer than men, and differences in measured literacy rates and gross primary schooling enrollment ratios between the sexes are either small or rapidly narrowing. Within the aforementioned "crescent of poverty," women appear to be seriously disadvantaged with respect to both health and education, but in these non-communist countries, the systematic mistreatment of women appears to relate more to tradition and locally sanctioned practice than to the needs or directives of the state.

That such basic material "inequalities" have been in unambiguous decline in so much non-communist Latin America and Asia, and that many of them may be diminishing within the "crescent of poverty" as well, does not square with the widespread perception that "inequality" is on the rise throughout most of the "Third World." The discrepancy may owe much to the fact that it is easier to take the pulse of educated elites than of poor people. In many parts of Asia, Africa, and Latin America there is reason to expect today's *elites* to feel deprived. In the years following World War II, independence and "nation-building" created extraordinary opportunities for a single generation of educated people in many poor countries.[85] These opportunities were inherently irreplicable: political stability and the growing pool of educated talent would preclude such rapid advance for successive generations of young people entering business, civil service, and politics. Throughout most of the poor world, privileged groups that set their sights on the careers of their predecessors have been disappointed.[86] Much of what one hears about "inequality" in the poor nations today may have more to do with the status anxieties of the comparatively well-to-do than with the material plight of the poor themselves. Educated elites, after all, play a major role in public discussion, while the very poor are all too often without a public voice.

One way of looking at "inequality" in the less developed countries is to consider the degree to which a person can rise or fall in society according to his own actions and efforts. This "dynamic" aspect of social inequality might to some degree be traced by measures of "intergenerational social mobility": the likelihood that people will have a different social status from their parents. There are obvious difficulties in computing such a thing, including the quantification of "social status" and the choice of points in life at which parents and children are compared. Nevertheless, a few careful studies on intergenerational social mobility in less developed countries are instructive. Results from two are presented in Table 11.12.

Brazil has the reputation of being a stratified and highly inegalitarian society. Even so, a comprehensive occupational status survey from the 1970s seems to suggest that it was possible to rise from the lowest social background to the top—and perhaps more surprisingly, to fall from the very top down towards the very bottom—in the course of a single lifetime. By several statistical measures, intergenerational social mobility appears to have been at least as great in postwar Brazil as in the developed nations of Western Europe and North America. In part, this unexpected finding is explained by Brazil's rapid growth from a comparatively low economic base: with the move from agriculture to cities and industry, "occupational status," as sociologists measure it, rises almost automatically. Holding occupational structure constant, "pure" intergenerational mobility—the likelihood of moving ahead or falling back in the crowd—appears to be about twice as great in Western societies as in Brazil as a whole. But intergenerational mobility within Brazil varies dramatically from one region to the next. In the Southeast (which includes Rio de Janeiro and Sao Paolo), intergenerational social mobility appears to match or exceed levels seen in Western nations; in the impoverished Northeast, there seems to be far less chance of escaping the social trajectory set by one's station at birth.[87]

If poor regions of the non-communist world tend to enjoy less social mobility than more prosperous regions, we might expect rural India and Bangladesh to be particularly restrictive of social movement. Data on landholdings from four villages in these two countries are inconsistent with the idea of pervasive, tradition-bound barriers against social advance. These villages are not necessarily representative of the hundreds of thousands of villages in the subcontinent, but they conform to a pattern: in each a large fraction of families which today count as "large" landowners were landless a generation ago, and considerable fractions of those who are landless today came from families which had "large" holdings in the recent past. Life in this sample of villages may be characterized by poverty, but it would not seem to be marked by the inequality that comes from inheriting a fixed economic ranking in life.

These data from Brazil and the subcontinent are not a sufficient basis for broad generalizations about social mobility in poor non-communist nations. In itself, moreover, social mobility is not proof of "equality of opportunity": the link between the two would be forged on the basis of competition and merit, neither of which can be measured by these data. Nevertheless, these data do suggest that—for whatever reasons—barriers

against rising or sinking in society may be considerably less insurmountable than is commonly presumed in two regions of the poor non-communist
world that are commonly said to suffer from particularly severe cases of
stratification and stasis.

What about inequalities in the poor Marxist–Leninist countries? Marxist–Leninist regimes justify not only specific policies, but their very system, by the quest to rid society of the exploitation and inequalities that are
said to blight life under "capitalism." Once they assume power communist
parties typically oversee the redistribution of property and the alteration
of incomes of peasants and workers; thereafter, they direct the state at
their command to engage regularly in far-reaching interventions in economic and personal life, often with the expressed purpose of reducing
"inequalities" among citizens.

Despite the enormous energies the Marxist–Leninist governments seem
to devote to activities undertaken in the name of equality, they release
little of the data which would allow outsiders to judge the results of their
exertions. Nevertheless, we can attempt an evaluation on the basis of the
limited information that is in the public domain.

As we have already seen, Marxist–Leninist regimes in the poor regions
do not appear, to date, to have enjoyed any clear superiority over non-
communist governments in dealing with the material inequalities attendant
upon disease, undernutrition, illiteracy, or physical discrimination against
women. To a greater degree than in non-communist countries, both severe
poverty and the inequalities associated with it tend in Marxist–Leninist
systems to be a consequence of direct government interventions. Since
Marxist–Leninist regimes view *all* areas of life as legitimate areas for
vigorous social experimentation, and since they do not, in principle,
evaluate these experiments on the basis of their impact on any "limited"
group of individuals, the inequalities born of extreme material hardship
need not diminish with regularity in planned socialist economies.

Under Marxist–Leninist regimes, daily life is deliberately and explicitly
politicized. As a practical matter, the politicization of daily life means that
social opportunity is politicized as well.[88] This augurs ill for "equality of
opportunity." The more that particular persons can arbitrarily decide who
will gain or lose in society, the more likely it will be that connections and
background rather than effort and achievement shall determine the distribution of social and economic rewards.

Every Communist revolution of this century has been followed by a
period of rapid upward mobility for designated "friends of the people."
The dispossession of landlords and "rich peasants," the nationalization of
industry and business, and the construction of the "socialist" *apparat*
typically presented great opportunities for advancement to those who

could avail of them. But once openings in the new order were filled, mobility seems generally to have set on a different course. Once emplaced, cadres found themselves in a position to confer benefit and opportunity upon allies, relatives, and friends; to the extent that competitive forces were restricted or discredited, arbitrary personal use of power was not constrained by independent indicators of performance. As a result, the role of merit in economic life in Marxist–Leninist countries can decline over time. Social mobility can become a less regular and less orderly process, depending increasingly on either technological breakthrough or political upheaval and party purges to force it along.

There are no reliable numbers on intergenerational social mobility for the poorer communist countries, but figures for Hungary may suggest the general nature of the problem.[89] In the 1930s, one's chances of becoming "white collar" were slim—unless one's father was a white collar worker, in which case they were quite good. In the 1940s, with the Communist Party's assumption for power this "index of inheritance" dropped precip- itously. It reached its nadir in the years immediately following the 1956 uprising. In the period of prolonged political calm under President Kadar, this "inheritance index" has begun a steady rise. If trends of the 1960s and early 1970s continue, privileged work in Hungary will in the 1980s depend *even more* on family background than it did before "Liberation."

Despite the lack of statistics by which to document it, this same pattern of social inequality is evident in the poor Marxist–Leninist nations. In North Korea, it can be seen at the pinnacle of society, where Kim Il-sung is making arrangements for his son Chong-il to succeed him.[90] In China, it pervades the very foundations of society: as Soviet commentators have wryly noted, "over half of the young people entering the labor force (today) step into the shoes of their mothers and fathers, irrespective of their education, training, propensities, or sex."[91] The costs of the events that have sometimes served to unjam social arteries in these places have often proved to be high: Chinese officials now say that the Cultural Revolution—which helped boost many millions of cadres to their present positions in party and government—"affected" 100 million people. There are indications that over one million of those "affected" may have per- ished in the process.[92]

The difficulties that established Marxist–Leninist regimes seem to have in accommodating themselves to merit-based mobility and competition does not serve the interests of the poor. Restrictions on mobility tend to trap those already poor in society's lowest slots. Barriers against mobility, moreover, tend to *preserve* poverty rather than to eradicate it. Such barriers actively endanger society's most vulnerable groups. Severe res- trictions against individual attempts to move cities, change jobs, adjust production to minimize cost, or engage in independent economic activity are all integral to "planned socialist construction." But they are also prejudicial to the welfare of the poor, for they compromise both the ability of society to respond flexibly to their needs and the ability of the poor to protect themselves against natural or politically-induced disasters.[93] Emplaced barriers that restrict survival opportunities are by no means unique to Marxist–Leninist societies, but in no other present systems do they seem to be as fully incorporated into the conception and machinery of government.

Concluding Remarks

It may be useful at this point to summarize some of the principal themes of the previous pages.

First, for all the discussion about the condition of the poor in the less developed countries, it is still quite difficult to assess their plight with any precision in most regions of the world. Lack of comprehensive information on the condition of the poor cannot hasten the reduction of material poverty, and may even seem to belie commitment to the cause alleviating material poverty. In a meaningful sense, the prospects of the poor in any society today may be judged by the volume of reliable data that is generated on them.

Second, the notion that economic change in the postwar era has not brought significant material benefit to the bulk of the populations of poor non-communist countries is contradicted by meaningful statistical evidence. In all regions in which reliable data could be found, poor non-communist countries have experienced substantial improvements in life expectancy, and substantial reductions in the incidence of measured illiteracy since the end of the Second World War. Conventional methods of measuring living standards may have led to a serious underestimate of the progress against material poverty in many non-communist countries. By the same token, progress in narrowing the most important material inequalities between privileged people and the desperately poor may be systematically understated in conventional approaches to measuring "inequality."

Third, despite the tangible evidence of substantial and by some measures rapid progress against material poverty in many poor non-communist societies over the past few decades, there is a large region in which progress against poverty may have been less rapid and less certain. This "crescent of poverty" stretches from Casablanca to Dacca, and sweeps down to encompass most of sub–Saharan Africa. Countries in the "crescent of poverty" generally seem to share three characteristics: difficulty or virtual inability to track and assess the condition of their poor people; harsh patterns of physical discrimination against women; and halting improvements in education and literacy.

Fourth, there is little reason to conclude that the performance of Marxist–Leninist regimes in attending to material poverty has been consistently or even generally superior to that of the non-communist governments in the poor world against which they might most reasonably be compared. To a noticeable degree, the policies of communist governments seem to *generate* material poverty and physical hardship. It is not impossible, for example, that government policies may have today converted Mainland China into the world's second great crescent of disadvantage for women. Though in some ways China's living standards may be considerably higher than those prevailing through the non-communist "crescent of poverty," such characteristics as lack of information on the poor and harsh discrimination against women appear to be shared—not by any reason of culture of history, but because communist China's state policies have forced an unnatural convergence in patterns of material circumstance to take place. Viewed in perspective, it may be suggested that the Marxist–Leninist regimes' contribution to the less developed countries has not been so much to abolish poverty as to *modernize* it. Traditionally, lack of individual choice attendant upon material poverty has been associated with a lack of goods. Material goods without choice is a uniquely modern formulation of poverty.

Written in 1983. A longer version of this essay appeared in Peter L. Berger, ed., *Modern Capitalism, Volume II,* (Lanham, MD: Hamilton Press, 1987). Reprinted with permission, all rights reserved.

Notes

1. Hollis Chenery et al., *Redistribution With Growth* (New York: Oxford University Press, 1974).
2. International Labor Office, *Poverty and Landlessness in Rural Asia* (Geneva: ILO, 1977).
3. Sylvia Ann Hewlett, *The Cruel Dilemmas of Development: Twentieth Century Brazil* (New York: Basic Books, 1980).
4. Paul Bairoch, *The Economic Development of the Third World Since 1900* (Berkeley: University of California Press, 1975).
5. C. V. Devan Nair, ed., *Socialism That Works . . . The Singapore Way* (Singapore: Federal Publications, 1976).
6. For a description of some of these changes, see Michael Crowder, *West Africa Under Colonial Rule* (Evanston: Northwest University Press, 1968), D.G.E. Hall, *A History of Southeast Asia* (London: Macmillan, 1964), K. Venkatagiri Gowda, *Fiscal Policy and Inflation in Postwar India, 1945–1954* (Mysore: Wesley Press, 1959).

7. Sir Frederick Pedler, "British Planning and Private Enterprise in Colonial Africa," in Peter Duignan and L. H. Gann, eds., *Colonialism in Africa, 1870–1960*, Volume 4, (New York: Cambridge University Press, 1975).
8. For a description of how these arguments affected Latin America—where poor nations had enjoyed formal independence since the nineteenth century—see Albert O. Hirschman, "Ideologies of Economic Development in Latin America," in his volume *A Bias For Hope* (New Haven: Yale University Press, 1971).
9. *Wall Street Journal*, February 22, 1982.
10. David C. Cole and Yung Chul Park, *Financial Development In Korea, 1945–1978* (Cambridge: Harvard University Press, 1983).
11. *Statistical Yearbook Of the Republic of China 1981* (Taipei: Executive Yuan, Directorate-General of Budget, Accounting and Statistics, 1981).
12. Samuel H. Preston, "The Changing Relationship of Health and Economic Development," in his *Mortality Patterns in National Populations* (New York: Academic Press, 1976).
13. Vito Tanzi, ed., *The Underground Economy in the United States and Abroad* (Lexington: D. C. Heath, 1982).
14. Antonio Martino, "Measuring Italy's Underground Economy," *Policy Review*, Spring 1981.
15. S. Ivanov, "Politics and Statistics," in the Soviet journal *Far Eastern Affairs*, 3, 1982.
16. Eduard B. Vermeer, "Social Welfare Provisions and the Limits of Inequality in Contemporary China," *Asian Survey*, September 1979.
17. On the difficulties with population numbers from less developed countries, see my articles in Nick Eberstadt, ed., *Fertility Decline in the Less Developed Countries* (New York: Praeger Publishers, 1981).
18. Leonardo Paulino and Shen Sheng Tseng, *A Comparative Study of FAO and USDA Data on Production, Area, and Trade of Major Food Staples* (Washington: International Food Policy Research Institute, 1980).
19. T. James Goering, "Tropical Root Crops and Rural Development," *World Bank Staff Working Paper* #324, April 1979.
20. An exception was Nigeria's 1964 census, in which the population of the nation was apparently *overcounted* by a substantial margin. Regional and ethnic animosities explain the anomaly: revenues and representation were to be awarded on the basis of the results, and this moved the counted public to action.
21. See U.S. Bureau of the Census, *World Population, 1983* (Washington D.C.: Department of Commerce, 1983).
22. Background on this situation may be had from P. J. Honey, "Collectivizing South Vietnamese Agriculture, *China News Analysis*, March 30, 1979.
23. Simon Kuznets, *Modern Economic Growth* (New Haven: Yale University Press, 1966).
24. See, for example, *Population and Other Problems* (Peking: Beijing Review, 1981).
25. P. T. Bauer, "The Population Explosion: Myths And Realities," in his *Equality, the Third World, and Economic Delusion* (Cambridge: Harvard University Press, 1981).
26. Dan Usher, "An Imputation to the Measure of Economic Growth for Changes in Life Expectancy," in Milton Moss, ed., *Measuring Social and Economic Performance* (New York: Columbia University Press, 1973).

27. World Bank, *Health: Sector Policy Paper* (Washington, D.C.: World Bank, 1980).
28. "Mortality Trends and Prospects," *WHO Chronicle*, 28, 1974.
29. United Nations, *Levels and Trends of Mortality Since 1950* (New York: United Nations 1982).
30. *Health: Sector Policy Paper, op. cit.*; Lee-jay Cho et al., *Population Growth of Indonesia* (Honolulu: University of Hawaii Press, 1980); Brazil, *Series Estatisticas Retrospectives 1977* (Rio de Janeiro: IBGE, 1977).
31. World Bank, *China: Socialist Economic Development* (Washington, D.C.: World Bank, 1981).
32. For an elaboration of this argument, see Michael Lipton, *Why Poor People Stay Poor: Urban Bias in World Development* (Cambridge: Harvard University Press, 1977). The gap in lifespans between urban and rural people provides one of the stronger arguments that life expectancy in sub–Saharan Africa and the Muslim expanse may still be rising, for the population of the cities is believed to be rising much more rapidly than the population of the countryside in virtually all of these countries. See United Nations, *Patterns of Urban and Rural Population Growth* (New York: United Nations, 1980).
33. Alfonso Farnos Morejon and Sonia Catasus Cervera, "La Mortalidad" in *La Poblacion de Cuba* (Havana: Centro de Estudios Demograficos, 1976).
34. Carmelo Mesa-Lago, *The Economy of Socialist Cuba; A Two-Decade Appraisal* (Albuquerque: University Of New Mexico Press, 1981).
35. Carmelo Mesa-Lago, "Cuban Statistics Revisited," *Cuban Studies/Estudios Cubanos*, (July 1979).
36. This is explained in *Anuario Estadistico de Cuba 1979* (Havana: CEE, n.d.).
37. *Levels and Trends of Mortality Since 1950, op. cit.*
38. See Ministerio de Salud, *La Salud de Chile* (Santiago: 1981). Chile's reductions in infant mortality appear to be associated closely with two social programs: subsidized supplemental child feeding and children's health centers. Both have been substantially expanded since Allende's assassination.
39. Tai Hwan Kwon et al., *The Population of Korea* (Seoul: Seoul National University, 1975).
40. United Nations, *Demographic Yearbook 1981* (New York: United Nations, 1983). Although North Korea has claimed that it brought tuberculosis, trachoma, cholera, and the other communicable diseases so often associated with poverty under control shortly after the Korean Workers Party assumed power officially in 1948, the government's own administrative concerns seem to tell another story. In 1969 the Central Disease Prevention Office was made an autonomous unit of the Ministry of Public Health, and a Hygenic Propaganda Office was established in each province. Nina Vreeland *et al., Area Handbook For North Korea* (Washington, D.C.: Government Printing Office, 1976).
41. A. S. Boronin and I. A. Ognetov, *Sotsalisticheskaya Respublik Vietnam* (Moscow: Indatel'stvo Politicheskoii Literaturi, 1981).
42. United Nations, *Demographic Indicators of Countries: Estimates and Projections as Assessed in 1980* (New York: United Nations, 1982).
43. See Widjojo Nitisastro, *Population Trends in Indonesia* (Ithaca: Cornell University Press, 1970), and Gerard Kherian, *Le Problem Demographique En Indochine* (Hanoi: Impremieres d'Extreme–Orient, 1937).
44. Judith Banister and Samual Preston, *Mortality in China, Population and Development Review*, March 1981.

45. For data on overseas Chinese communities, see *Levels and Trends Mortality,* op. cit.
46. John S. Aird, "Reconstruction of an Official Data Model of the Chinese Population" (U.S. Bureau of the Census: unpublished paper, June 15, 1980) and Kenneth Hill et al., "Famine in China, 1959–61" (World Bank, unpublished paper, 1983).
47. Stephen Rapawy and Godfrey Baldwin, "Demographic Trends in the Soviet Union, 1950–2000" in *Soviet Economy in the 1980s: Problems and Prospects* (Washington, D.C.: Government Printing Office, December 31, 1982).
48. Ansley J. Coale, "A Reassessment of World Population Trends," *Population Bulletin of the United Nations,* 14, 1982.
49. Among these, India's flirtation with involuntary sterilization during the period of "Emergency" rule in the mid–1970s figures prominently. Implications and repercussions have been analyzed in Myron Weiner, *India at the Polls* (Washington, D.C.: American Enterprise Institute, 1978), and Marika Vicziany, "Coercion in a Soft State," *Pacific Affairs,* Fall and Winter 1982.
50. See, for example, Elizabeth J. Croll, "Production vs. Reproduction a Threat to China's Development Strategy", *World Development,* June 1983.
51. According to one rural survey from 1980, only 2.2 percent of the women sampled would want a single child if it were a girl. See Croll, op. cit. see also Fan Shen, "Baby Girls on Chinese Mainland," *Issues And Studies,* April 1983. According to this article, three million baby girls may have been killed or abandoned on the Mainland in the past two years.
52. Judith Banister, U.S. Bureau of the Census, personal communication, 1983.
53. On social security arrangements in rural China, see William L. Parrish and Martin K. Whyte, *Village and Family in Contemporary China,* (Chicago: Chicago University Press, 1978), and E. B. Vermeer, "Income Differentials in Rural China," *China Quarterly,* March 1982.
54. For more details on the technical difficulties with quantifying hunger, see my article "Hunger And Ideology," *Commentary,* July 1981.
55. *Levels and Trends,* loc. cit.
56. *Levels and Trends,* op. cit. It is widely believed that per capita food consumption has declined in sub–Saharan Africa in the 1970s. It may have, but there is reason to question the data upon which such conclusions have been based. See Nick Eberstadt, "A Dissenting View of the World Food Problem," *World Bank Agriculture Discussion Paper* #73, August 1983. There is reason to believe that the incidence of serious malnutrition in the less developed countries is considerably lower than would be suggested either by the World Bank estimate that over one billion people in developing countries suffer "caloric deficits," or the World Bank's suggestion that 800 million people suffer from "absolute poverty." See Thomas T. Poleman, "Quantifying the Nutrition Situation in Developing Counties," *Food Research Institute Studies,* 1, 1981.
57. *Levels And Trends,* op. cit.
58. Kenneth Hill, "China: An Evaluation of Demographic Trends, 1950–1982" (World Bank: unpublished, 1982).
59. Cited in Nicholas R. Lardy, *Agriculture in China's Modern Economic Development* (New York: Cambridge University Press, 1983).
60. *Agriculture in China's Modern Economic Development* op. cit. Grain consumption may have been made to rise in China's cities over the past generation, but without improvements in national foodgrain availability, these gains could only

be had by making the country get by on less. Nicholas R. Lardy, "Food Consumption in the People's Republic Of China," in Randolph Barker and Radha Sinha, eds., *The Chinese Agricultural Economy* (Boulder: Westview Press, 1982). By Lardy's computations, the gap in foodgrain consumption per capita between urban and rural people widened from 9 percent in 1956–1957 to 35 percent in 1978; over the same period, average consumption in the countryside is said to have fallen by over 5 percent.

61. *The Economy of Socialist Cuba,* op. cit.
62. Calculated from *Le Problem Demographique,* op. cit., Ng Shui Meng, "The Population of Indochina: Some Preliminary Observations" (Singapore: Institute of Southeast Asian Studies, July 1974), *World Population 1983,* op. cit., and U.S. Department of Agriculture *Asia, WAS Report,* 1983. Even if one takes as too bleak Douglas Pike's assessment that the Socialist Republic of Vietnam in the early 1980s could "not even meet the 1500 calories a day considered to be subsistence level" ("Vietnam in 1981: Biting the Bullet," *Asian Survey,* January 1982), and even if one discounts for the production in colonial times which went to export markets and land taxes, it nevertheless appears that both the quality and quantities of food in the peasant diet in Vietnam has deteriorated consequentially between the 1930s and the early 1980s.
63. Nicholas R. Lardy, "Prices, Markets, and the Chinese Peasant," *Yale Economic Growth Center,* Discussion Paper #428, December 1982.
64. *Nhan Dan,* May 22, 1959; quoted in David W. P. Elliott, "Political Integration in North Vietnam: The Cooperativization Period," SEADAG Papers on Problems of Development in Southeast Asia, *Asia Society,* May 1975.
65. See note 46. China is not the only communist country in which agricultural experiments have brought on famine. The Soviet Union's experiences with collectivization in the 1930s are well known; in the Ukraine alone five million people may have perished from man–made famine. See Robert Conquest, *The Ukrainian Famine* (Cambridge: Ukrainian Research Institute, forthcoming). Vietnam may also have suffered famine with its first attempt at collectivization. See Gerard Tongas, *L'Enfer Communiste Au Nord-Vietnam* (Paris: Nouvelles Editions Debresse, 1960). Tongas, who taught school in Hanoi in the 1950s, writes that statistics were juggled to cover the actual shortfall that resulted from the new agrarian policies in 1958. He also writes that North Vietnam attempted to divert attention from its own problems by announcing an offer to donate rice to the hungry in South Vietnam!
66. Data from Singapore highlight the problem: in the early 1970s, 88 percent of the adult population was estimated to be newspaper readers, but only 74 percent were considered "literate" in government statistical accounts. For a discussion of the problems of evaluating literacy, See John Oxenham, *Literacy* (London: Routledge & Kegan Paul, 1980).
67. *New York Times,* December 18, 1977.
68. Ibid.
69. UNESCO, *Statistical Yearbook 1975* (Paris: UNESCO, 1976).
70. UNESCO, *Statistical Yearbook 1982* (Paris: UNESCO, 1982).
71. V. Semyonov, "China: Internal Political and Social Problems," *International Affairs,* 4, 1981.
72. Evelyn S. Rawski, *Education and Popular Literacy in Ch'ing China* (Ann Arbor: University of Michigan Press, 1979), and H. D. Lamson, *Social Pathology in China* (Taipei: Ch'eng-wen Publishing Co., 1974).

73. *L'Enfer Communiste Au Nord-Vietnam,* op. cit. See also his "Indoctrination Replaces Education" in P. J. Honey, ed., *North Vietnam Today* (New York: Praeger Publishers, 1962).
74. *UNESCO Statistical Yearbook,* various issues.
75. John Mercer, *Slavery for Mauritania Today* (Edinburgh: Human Rights Group, 1982).
76. *Levels and Trends,* op. cit.; *Demographic Yearbook 1981,* op. cit.; United Nations, *World Population Trends and Policies, Monitoring Report 1977* (New York: United Nations, 1979); United Nations, *World Population Trends and Policies, Monitoring Report 1979* (New York: United Nations, 1980).
77. *Levels and Trends,* op. cit., *South Africa Statistics 1980* (Pretoria: Department of Statistics, 1980); also K. Mitra, *Implications of Declining Sex Ratio in India's Population* (New Delhi: Allied Publishers, 1979).
78. *Levels and Trends,* op. cit.; *Demographic Yearbook 1981,* op. cit.
79. See back issues of UNESCO *Statistical Yearbook* for estimates of these literacy and enrollment differentials.
80. Ling Ruizhu, "A Brief Account of 30 Years' Mortality of Chinese Population," *World Health Statistics Quarterly,* 2, 1981.
81. Jayne Werner, "Women, Socialism, and the Economy of Wartime North Vietnam, 1960–1975," *Studies in Comparative Communism,* Summer/August 1981.
82. Jon Halliday, "The North Korean Enigma," *New Left Review,* May/June 1981; Mun Woong Lee, "Rural North Korea Under Communism: A Study of Socio-Cultural Change," *Rice University Studies,* Winter 1976.
83. Gautam Datta and Jacob Meerman, "Household Income or Household Income Per Capita in Welfare Comparisons," *Review of Income and Wealth,* September 1980; see also Michael W. Kusnic and Julie DaVanzo, "Who Are the Poor in Malaysia? The Sensitivity of Poverty Profiles to Definition of Income," in Yoram Ben-Porath, ed., *Income Distribution and the Family* (New York: Population Council, 1982).
84. These problems and others are taken up in Alan Blinder, *Towards an Economic Theory of Income Distribution* (Cambridge: M.I.T. Press, 1974).
85. On this score, see Clifford Geertz, "After the Revolution: The Fate of the New Nation State," in his *The Interpretation of Cultures: Selected Essays* (New York: Basic Books, 1973).
86. This is the "tunnel effect" that Albert Hirschman described in "Changing Tolerance for Inequality in Development," *Quarterly Journal Of Economics,* November 1973.
87. This discussion draws heavily on Jose Pastore, *Inequality and Social Mobility in Brazil* (Madison: University Of Wisconsin Press, 1982). Pastore notes that "circulation" mobility in Argentina has been measured as unusually low. This may be related to that nation's uncertain progress against poverty over the past two decades.

   There is little information on income distribution in Marxist–Leninist societies as a whole, and still less for the poor ones. Even if such information were readily available, it would be considerably more difficult to evaluate than comparable data from poor non-communist nations. In non-market economies, income need not measure either purchasing power or standards of living with any consistency. This point is made with some force for Soviet Central Asia in Nancy Lubin, *Labor and Nationality in Soviet Central Asia* (New York: Macmillan, 1985).

88. In non-market economies, it often seems to be the case that "politically affluent" citizens not only have greater access to goods and services, but pay less for them. In Wuhan in recent years, it is said that an ordinary person paid 1.80 RMB per 1½ kilo for fish and waited three hours in line for it. While a party member paid 0.40 RMB and would not have to wait. (Stephen N. S. Cheung, "Will China Go 'Capitalist?' " *Hobart Paper, #94*, 1982). More descriptive accounts of the economic priviledges which accompany political power in different Marxist–Leninist systems include Hedrick Smith, *The Russians* (New York: Quadrangle, 1976) and Fox Butterfield, *China: Alive in the Bitter Sea* (New York: Quadrangle, 1982).
89. Albert A. Simkus, "Historical Changes in Occupational Inheritance Under Socialism: Hungary 1930–73," in Donald J. Treiman and Robert V. Robinson, eds., *Research in Social Stratification and Mobility: A Research Annual* (Greenwich: JAI Press, 1981).
90. See for example Tai Sung An, *North Korea in Transition: From Dictatorship to Dynasty* (Westport: Greenwood Press, 1983).
91. Y. Kinovalov and S. Manazhev, "Social and Economic Contradictions in China," *Far Eastern Affairs*, 2, 1981.
92. See my "Introduction" in Iosef G. Dyadkin, *Unnatural Deaths in the USSR 1928–54* (New Brunswick: Transaction Press, 1983).
93. This may be seen, among other places, in China's rural regions. At the end of a careful article, Eduard Vermeer concludes that "the forced continuation of a premodern agrarian settlement pattern, together with a doubling of the rural population since the Second World War have driven an increasing number of the ill-favored villages to the limit of possibilities for economic survival." If his evaluation sounds alarming, it is not much different in tone or conclusion from what has appeared in the Chinese press at different intervals since 1979. E. B. Vermeer, "Income Differentials in Rural China" op. cit.

Part IV

Conclusion

12

Communism and the Plight of the Poor

For better or worse, the fate of governments and the plight of the poor are bound together today as never before. A remarkable evolution in both the conception and the machinery of government over the course of the twentieth century has seen to this. Poverty has become a matter of state, and the expeditious alleviation of material want has emerged as a basic measure of the success of contemporary regimes. The recognition that mass deprivation and pauperism can be controlled or even entirely eliminated by effective government policy has made the modern state, in a very real sense, a dependent of the poor who live under it. In part, this is a result of pragmatism. In an era of total war and state-led social campaigns, logistical exigencies virtually dictate sensitivity to poverty for any ambitious government. Mass deprivation, after all, can only place limits on the resources that statesmen may marshal for great national exertions. But it is not only crude calculation that tethers the modern state to the material condition of its people. Moral attitudes towards mass poverty have changed radically since the nineteenth century. Indeed, to an extent that would be unwise to underestimate, a government's record of performance against poverty is now taken as a reflection of its legitimacy—its right to be a government at all.

The awakening of government to mass poverty, and the systematic application of its energies to the relief of ignorance, disease, hunger and destitution may be traced to many causes and events, but perhaps the most important of these has been the birth of the Marxist–Leninist state. With the consolidation of Soviet power over the wreckage of the Russian empire at the end of the First World War, a fundamentally new form of government came into being. The new state was at once secular and messianic, and saw rising living standards for the masses as part and parcel of salvation. The nascent Soviet regime claimed special insight into the problems of poverty, inequality and injustice, promised special results in relieving these afflictions, and demanded special powers and authority so that it might make concrete its vision of an earthly paradise. The party and state that implanted themselves on Russian soil immediately undertook to transform totally both economy and society in the territories under their command, and presented the great variety of upheavals they set in motion as part of a larger effort to serve the poor and hasten material progress. The leaders of this continuing revolutionary "social experiment" insisted that they were building a system whose ability to improve life for the common people could not be equalled, and insisted that other systems of governance less effective in aiding the poor than their own had no right to survive.

Since the Russian Revolution of 1917, Marxist–Leninist states have been erected in Mongolia, Korea, China, Vietnam, Cuba and throughout Eastern Europe. All told, these states preside over about a third of the world's population. Despite the great differences in histories, cultures, and economic levels of the peoples over whom Marxist–Leninists came to rule, despite the striking differences in the struggles which brought radical leaders to power, and despite the crucial distinctions in inclination and strategy among the parties and the national figures who planned these respective marches into socialism, the campaigns for material progress and their results in these many different countries are in many ways alike. There have been recognizable rules and difficulties in this series of battles against poverty. It is possible to identify these and to speak of the plight of the poor under Marxist–Leninist rule as we have known it. These are some reflections on the evolving relationship between Marxist–Leninist governance, poverty and material progress.

Whatever the motivations of those it attracts or the intellectual merits of its nuances, Marxism–Leninism is first and last a strategic doctrine. In the cause of constructing Utopia, it is the set of guidelines for command and control. The primary and decisive consideration in Marxist–Leninist governance is, and must be, the preservation and augmentation of unchallengeable power under the Party's direction. In poor societies where Marxist–Leninists have gained control, there is an objective correlation of interests, if one can excuse the term, between the goals of the revolutionaries and the needs of the broad mass of the poor. A debilitated and illiterate populace can only serve the cause of the socialist construction imperfectly. Hunger and social isolation frustrate the full mobilization of society, and reduce the regime's freedom to maneuver both at home and overseas. The liberation of women from historical roles of subordination not only expands the labor force, but strikes at a traditional and exceedingly resistant alternative center of social authority: the family. With the dispossession of capitalists and landlords, opportunities for social advancement can be made to arise for those in poorest strata.

As revolutionary government develops into an established order, the correlation of interests changes. From the standpoint of the Party and those who direct it, social mobility should henceforth be no more rapid than development plans require or political struggles necessitate. The importance of women in the class struggle gives way to a recognition of their importance in reproducing the labor force and filling the cracks in manpower plans. The drive to eliminate illiteracy is succeeded by a concern with preventing the populace from learning certain things. Marxist–Leninist regimes, in short, have something like a "window of opportunity" in dealing with the problems of the poor; as this window closes, it becomes increasingly difficult to implement policies which stand the disadvantaged in good stead.

The Marxist–Leninist regime's preoccupation with command and control can work to the material advantage of the population in poor societies in the years immediately after a communist party comes to power. Once in charge, a Marxist–Leninist government has an interest in civil order— on its own terms, to be sure, but in civil order nonetheless. It is sometimes easy to forget what a scarce and precious resource civil order has been in many parts of the world. The sad fact of modern history is that less ambitious forms of government have been unable to maintain civil order in important regions of the poor world: the Chinese empire, the Altaic expanse of Central Asia, seemingly even in the Indo-Chinese peninsula. In the short run, the poor almost invariably profit from the restoration of civil order, even when it is imposed on the harshest terms. This fact is less of an insight into the merits of repressive government than a sad reflection on the universally precarious position of the very poor.

The politicization of everyday life is necessary and inevitable under Marxist–Leninist rule. No facet of personal life or social routine is beyond the purview of planners and the Party under Marxism–Leninism, although of course governmental capacities or tactical considerations at any given time may limit the pursuit of certain sorts of policies. In an environment shaped by a government's quest for total control over economic and social life and by its exacting plans for the future, the incidence of poverty ebbs and flows in a special tide. The politicization of life can bring immediate material advantage to targeted beneficiaries, who will gain at the expense of targeted adversaries. (These latter, incidentally, often become a distinct and even hereditary class of miserables in the new society.) There are longer-term effects upon patterns of poverty as well, and most of them are adverse. The decision to alter the flow of populations to ease pressures on the government has direct implications on the welfare of families. The occasional need, for reasons of state, to disrupt social life and throw the daily routines of great numbers of people into disarray has punitive effects upon those who are most vulnerable, both politically and economically. The absolute primacy of political power over economic power in the determination of living standards has serious implications for both the strategy through which to acquire material comforts and the actual patterns of material comfort in communist societies. None of these basic differences between the nature of poverty in communist and non-communist societies are highlighted by conventional comparisons of international statistics.

Western measures of inequality systematically underestimate even the purely economic dimensions of inequality in Marxist–Leninist states, since the premises behind them are not valid in Marxist Leninist countries. While equalitarian redistributions of assets and alterations of social entitlements have played an important role in raising a large fraction of the populace out of destitution in some Marxist–Leninist societies, redistribution of output knows both logistical and political limits; these generally become more apparent as revolutionary upheaval fades into the past. In the established Marxist–Leninist states, the overall prospects for combatting poverty now depend primarily upon the ability of the state to improve overall levels of efficiency. As of yet, Marxism–Leninism has found no permanent and regularized solution to the productivity problem. Instead, there appears to be a "Socialist" counterpart to the business cycle, which involves the successive relaxation and tightening of political control as considerations of efficiency become more or less salient. The incidence of poverty in the Marxist–Leninist nations is probably changed at least as much by these cycles as the incidence of poverty is altered by cyclical economic fluctuations in the market economies. But fluctuations in the incidence of poverty in the Marxist–Leninist societies may be even more dramatic than in the market economies, since the latter can pursue "counter-cyclical social policies" and the former cannot.

The correlations between distrust of price signals and the quest for international power is strong within the "Socialist camp." This makes not only for economic distortions, but also for a complex politics of subsidy, with implications not only for national but also for international poverty. Within the Soviet bloc the Marxist–Leninist version of the "New International Economic Order" has come into force. In this scheme, the most "politically wealthy" area transfers funds on a continuous basis to the more "politically impoverished" areas to finance their social consumption. As the subsidy grows, independently generated economic growth (or more properly, the need to generate independent growth to maintain freedom to maneuver) reduces. While it is true that certain states within the Western alliance structure derive substantial assistance for political reasons (Egypt and Israel, for example), *every* state in the alliance structure of the leading Marxist–Leninist power is deemed strategic, and all are supported in varying degrees. From the standpoint of power politics, this international redistribution of funds may be progressive; from an economic standpoint, it is typically regressive. Material standards of living are higher in most of the Warsaw Pact countries than in the U.S.S.R., and in some respects appear to be higher in Cuba as well.

If we look at statistical indicators alone, the record of the Marxist–Leninist states in reducing destitution may sometimes seem to correspond to that of the non-communist nations with whom comparisons would be appropriate; when it comes to inculcating prosperity, their performance for the most part appears poor.

Yet if the Marxist–Leninist states have an undistinguished record when it comes to bringing prosperity to their own people, they have played an important role in bringing material comfort to many countries in the "capitalist world." This dialectic of socialist competition is seldom recognized, yet it is entirely in keeping with the "challenge–response" patterns outlined by C. P. Kindleberger and economic historians before him.

In the Western world, consider only what the effects of the "oil crisis"— the contrived scarcity of international petroleum supply—had on the economies of the less developed countries over the past decade. For most, the immediate repercussions of this series of shocks were quite disturbing: balance of payments deficits, sharp increases in inflation, and slow-downs or even reversals in the pace of economic growth. Over only a very few years, however, governments, industries and people began to adjust themselves to the expectation of constantly increasing real costs of energy. Throughout the less developed world, energy-saving practices were introduced, although these were of course adopted very much more quickly in some places than in others. While some countries—particularly those in sub–Saharan Africa—still appear to be crippled by the oil shock, the surprising fact is that aggregate per capita rates of economic growth in the poor world did not drop after this "disaster." Indeed, until the financial crisis of the early 1980s, their rates of growth actually seemed to pick up. Through no kindness of its own, the OPEC cartel appears to have forced many of the policy-makers in the poor world to learn, and some economies to reform. In at least certain cases, this crisis has brought about "dynamic" changes which have improved longer-term prospects for the struggle against poverty.

If an oil shock, which causes a state on the receiving end economic inconvenience, can stimulate creative and far-reaching responses on the part of governments, how much more it must concentrate the collective mind of the state to be locked into competition with an adversary who on *principle* denies one's very right to exist! The history of the modern wars shows the extent to which managerial techniques, policy-making capacities, systems of communication and even technology, can be stimulated by life-or-death challenges. Though the need to adapt and respond is not quite as pressing in cold war as in hot war, the patterns of stimulus are not entirely different.

The postwar restoration of Western Europe, and the prolonged boom that followed it, ranks as one of the economic "miracles" of this century. The Marshall Plan and the policies which followed it were specifically conceived to "contain" Soviet expansion. The rebuilding of Japan after Hiroshima under the guidance of American architects is not only a great economic, but also an historic political accomplishment; in large part the impetus for reform and development came from the increasingly menacing political situation in China, Korea and the Soviet Far East. South Korea and Taiwan, fighting for their very survival, could not afford the luxury of kleptocracy; to meet not only the economic but also the political challenge posed by their enemies, they had to incorporate their entire populace into the process of rapid social and economic development. Even in the United States, the seeming success of the East European and Soviet health policies, and the anxiety about being "overtaken" by an antithetical political system, may have played a role in the social policies of the past two decades: whatever else may be said about it, the expansion of welfare services in the United States since the Great Society has dramatically improved health conditions and reduced the incidence of material poverty in this country. It may not be too much to suggest that communism has brought out the best in "capitalism."

To pursue this argument further, it is possible that there is a sort of process of negative selection writ national in the rise to power of Marxist–Leninist regimes. Not all attempts at communist revolution in the postwar world have been successful. In both Greece and Malaysia, for example, communist insurgencies failed to gain the support, legitimacy and power, that would be necessary to establish a new order. By contrast, the existing system could not withstand the communist challenge in Cuba and Vietnam. If we look at the record of these four states over the past generation, we might wonder whether there were not a sort of selection of the fittest at work here. If there were, then it would not be too much to say that *history* appears to be biased against the Marxist–Leninist regimes in their attempts to reduce poverty and to stimulate prosperity.

Marxist–Leninist regimes can also profit from history, or more specifically from their inability to alter it. If the efficiency problem dogs most Marxist–Leninist regimes, it has been much less oppressive a constraint in certain countries. East Germany and North Korea seem to have records for achieving economic growth and augmenting productivity that rank high in the world. Incentive structures appear to be less economically compelling in East Germany than in Hungary, or in North Korea than in post–Mao China, yet it is these others who have to grapple with the political dilemmas of insufficient improvements in total factor productivity. The enduring importance of culture and history in the struggle against poverty has not been vitiated by the first generation of Marxist–Leninist rule.

The process of modern economic growth depends not only upon the mobilization of existing resources, but also on what Theodore Shultz has termed "the ability to deal with disequilibria." This is in essence a matter of entrepreneurship, involving competence in discerning and surmounting problems of scarcity in the face of uncertainty. The Marxist–Leninist regimes are systematically handicapped on this score. Information about the ways in which scarcities may best be overcome is transmitted naturally by price signals; when the sounds these signals give off are deliberately muffled, or must be ignored for political reasons, not only immediate output but also long-term *competence* is compromised. The greater the uncertainties in the economic environment, the more serious the costs.

At the governmental level, Marxist–Leninist regimes are to some degree economic victims of their own political successes. The shift in the "correlation of forces" towards the socialist camp over the past generation has been responsible in no small degree for the increasing fluctuation in both real levels of international economic activity and nominal international prices. It is not only the monopsonistic role of Marxist–Leninist states in international markets which is an issue here; the Marxist–Leninist states have encouraged the politicization of "North–South" relations, which at times destabilized some international economic patterns. Yet market-oriented economies are very much better at responding to these fluctuations and uncertainties than are the centrally-planned systems of the Marxist–Leninist states. The great difficulties which communist nations are now having in coping with their energy problems speaks for this.

At the human level, there is little doubt that the common man is highly sensitive to the problems of dealing with disequilibrium; his well-being, and at times his very survival, depends on this. Yet the signals to which he has become sensitized are principally *political*. Though adroitness and creativity are required for response to either political or economic disequilibria, success in these two arenas goes by different rules. Politics, unlike economics, is a zero-sum game. Preoccupation with political disequilibrium, as a consequence, fosters distinct attitudes towards progress whose long-term impact may be to retard economic development. In the Soviet Union, the third generation of children is now being socialized in an environment in which the importance of successfully responding to political disequilibria is repeatedly emphasized, by both parents and experience. Leaders in the Kremlin cannot be heartened by the thought that they may actually have *succeeded* in creating the "New Soviet Man."

This discussion of patterns of poverty in the Marxist–Leninist regimes has concerned itself explicitly—some will probably say single-mindedly— with material conditions. As I hope should be clear, a review of prospects for reducing poverty and stimulating prosperity cannot be conducted through the examination of material conditions alone. The great imponderable in the escape from poverty is incentive and motivation. Yet the study of incentives and motivations is more than a perusal of a probability table: it is an inquest into the human spirit. The quest to abolish poverty in the Marxist–Leninist nations cannot be understood apart from the relation between Marxist–Leninist rule and the human spirit. But here we leave economics, and enter the realms of history, philosophy and religion.

Originally published in *Survey*, Winter 1984. Reprinted with permission; all rights reserved.

Index

314   Index

Communist state, the, 63–64
Costa Rica, 272, 290
Council for Mutual Economic Assistance (CMEA), 187, 190–91, 213, 246–47
CPSU. *See* Communist Party of the Soviet Union
Cuba, 196–205, 240–46; AIDS in 9; child mortality in, 276–77; economic difficulties of, 187–88, 278; health in, 7, 199–205, 240–41, 243, 271–72; infant mortality in, 7–8, 199, 200–202, 205, 241–43, 246, 271; life expectancy in, 199–200, 241, 290; literacy in, 196–99, 282–84; progress in, 196, 197, 200, 272; statistics of, 7–8, 197, 205, 241–43, 264, 271; vs. the U.S.S.R., 245
Cult of personality, 20, 30n.41

Davis, Christopher, 12, 52
Death rates. *See* Mortality rates
Dellenbrant, Jan Ake, 65–66
Dergue, Mengistu's, 188
Dostoevsky, Fyodor, 21
Dutton, John, 14

East Germany, 226, 310
Eastern European countries, 53, 95, 96, 98, 190, 234; economies of, 190–93; Finlandization of, 194; health in, 223–24, 226, 231; and the U.S., 193; and the U.S.S.R., 185, 189–94, 213–34; and Western Europe, 192
Economic growth, 59, 66, 309–10
Engel coefficient, 152–53, 182n.94
Ethiopia, 188
Ethnic distinctions in the U.S.S.R., 25, 35–36, 38–39, 47–49, 50. *See also* Russian elements in U.S.S.R.
European Russia, 35, 38–39, 47
Expansion and Coexistence (Ulam), 189

Fei Xiaotong, 170
Feshbach, Murray, 12, 13, 47–48, 51
Finland, 194
Finlandization of Eastern Europe, 194

Gandhi, Indira, 186
Goodman, Ann, and Geoffrey Schleifer, 47, 55, 56, 57
Gorbachev, Mikhail S., 5, 6, 90, 91, 99, 110, 112n.10
Government, 308; Marxist-Leninist, 306, 310; and poverty, 304; revolutionary, 306
Great Leap Forward (China), 125, 126, 134, 150, 179n.36, 257, 274

Health, 11, 49, 51–52, 212–13, 231, 247; in China, 129–42; in Cuba, 199–205, 240–41, 243, 271–72; in Eastern Europe, 223–24, 233–34; and lifestyle, 51; in Mongolia, 237–39; in U.S.S.R., 5, 6, 11–26, 40–41, 50–53, 213, 223, 226; in Western Europe, 223
Hill, Kenneth, 201–2, 205

Income, 252–53; distribution, 29, 30n.87; index, per capita, 255–56
India, 132–33, 140, 146, 152, 158, 273–74, 287, 288, 300n.49
Indonesia, 132–33, 140, 152, 158, 285
Inequality, 291–96, 307
Infant mortality, 7, 27n.4, 34, 40, 134; in Central Asia, 38; in China, 134–36; comparison of, 12, 13, 38; in Cuba, 7–8, 199–202, 205, 241–43, 246; in Eastern Europe, 215; reduction in, 40; in U.S., 29n.30, 35, 39; in U.S.S.R., 5–6, 7, 11, 34–40; in West Germany, 35, 39; in Western Europe, 215. *See also* Mortality
"Infant Mortality Trends in the Soviet Union" (Jones & Grupp), 34–39
Institute of Ethnography (Moscow), 36, 37
Institute for the Study of the U.S.A., 74

Japan: as a consumer society, 57; health in, 133; illiteracy in, 158; infant mortality in, 135; labor unions in, 54; life expectancy in, 134
Jones, Ellen, and Fred W. Grupp, 34–39; criticism of, 35–39

K. C. Yeh, 173, 175
Kennan, George F., 83
KGB, 74, 98
Khrushchev, Nikita, 18, 30n.35, 59, 73
Kolkhoz, 46
Kosygin, Aleksei, 74
Kozlov, Viktor, 36

Labedz, Leo, 71
Labor, 43; force in U.S.S.R., 47, 48, 50–51, 52, 55; productivity, 51; unions, 54
Lange, Oscar, 58
Lardy, Nicholas, 121–23
Li Chengrui, 126
Life expectancy, 11; 27nn.2–4, 53, 135, 179n.38, 214, 256, 266, 270, 272, 299n.32; in China, 27n.2, 130–34, 135–41; comparison of, 38–39, 53, 268–70; in Cuba, 199–200, 241; in Eastern Europe, 214, 215–17; gender-related, 240;

AUG 2 5 2005